# SAINT BERNADETTE
## SOUBIROUS

*Bernadou*

Bernadette Soubirous. This photograph was taken when Bernadette was between 16 and 18 years of age.

FRANCIS TROCHU

# SAINT BERNADETTE SOUBIROUS
## *1844-1879*

*Translated and Adapted by*
JOHN JOYCE, S.J.

*"But blessed are your eyes, because they see, and your ears, because they hear. For, amen, I say to you, many prophets and just men have desired to see the things that you see, and have not seen them, and to hear the things that you hear and have not heard them."*
—Matt. 13:16-17

TAN Books
An Imprint of Saint Benedict Press, LLC
Charlotte, North Carolina

*Die Licentio Superiorum Ordinis.*

Nihil Obstat:    Joannes M. T. Barton, S.T.D., I.S.S.
                 Censor Deputatus

Imprimatur:    E. Morrogh Bernard, Vic. Gen.
                 Westmonasterii
                 die 21a Junii, 1957

First published in France under the same title by Librairie Catholique Emmanuel Vitte, Paris, 1954.

English edition copyright © 1957 by Longmans, Green and Co., Ltd., London.

This edition is published by arrangement with Longman Group Limited, London.

ISBN: 978-0-89555-253-2

Printed and bound in the United States of America.

TAN Books
An Imprint of Saint Benedict Press, LLC
Charlotte, North Carolina
2012

# CONTENTS

## I. CHILDHOOD

## II. THE APPARITIONS

v

# LOURDES, TOWN OF DESTINY

Lourdes already existed in the earliest days of the Christian era. Originally a large village, inhabited by peaceable Bigourdans but perilously set on the threshold of the Pyrenean valleys, it knew many a foreign occupation. After Caesar's conquest of Gaul, the Roman eagles were set up there; the Pont-Vieux across the Gave dates from that time. There followed Visigoths, Saracens, Franks. . . . It is with the Saracen occupation that the story of Lourdes begins to merge into the story of Our Lady on French soil.

In 732 Charles Martel, by his victory over the Saracens, halted the advance of Islam upon Christian civilization. The enemy fled toward Spain. Nevertheless, some groups of the conquered held out in the fortresses of Aquitaine, of which one was the castle of Mirambel on the rock overhanging Lourdes. In 778, Charlemagne, wearily returning from his expedition to Spain, attacked the garrison whose commander, the implacable Mirat, had sworn by Mahomet that he would not surrender to any mortal man.

The fortress seemed absolutely impregnable; it could only be starved into surrender. The siege was desperately prolonged. Then one day an eagle, carrying a trout caught in the Gave, let it fall inside the Saracen walls. Immediately the cunning Mirat sent off the still floundering trout to the besieger, as though it were merely an unwanted addition to the plentiful rations of his soldiers. So, it seemed, the supplies of the fortress were inexhaustible! Charlemagne began to despair of victory and spoke of raising the siege.

But, so the story runs, Roracius, Bishop of Le Puy and chaplain to the Frankish army, had scented the trick. He obtained an audience with Mirat and saw for himself that the Saracens were at the end of their resources. Mirat insisted on his oath. "Brave prince," replied the bishop, "you have sworn never to yield to any mortal man. Could you not with honor make your surrender to an immortal lady? Mary, Queen of Heaven, has her throne at Le Puy, and I am her humble minister there."

Thus, freed from his oath, the Saracen chief came to terms. In token of his vassalage, he agreed to bring to the sanctuary of his Queen some handfuls of grass plucked on the bank of the Gave. Baptized under the name of "Lorus," Mirat was knighted by Charlemagne and received from him the command of the fort of Mirambel. It is from "Lorus," so the learned assert, that is derived the name of Lourdes.

But over a thousand years were to pass before the sovereignty of the Blessed Virgin was proclaimed in humility, yet with divine power, over the impregnable fortress and the old grey-roofed country town. And that is where the story of St. Bernadette Soubirous begins.

The castle fortress of Mirambel on the rock overhanging Lourdes. The castle dates back to the time of Charlemagne, in the eighth century.

# MAPS

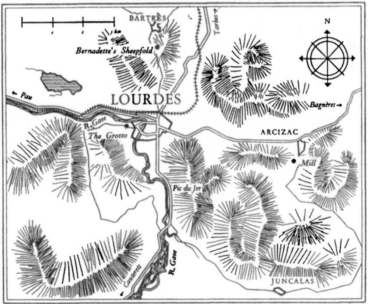

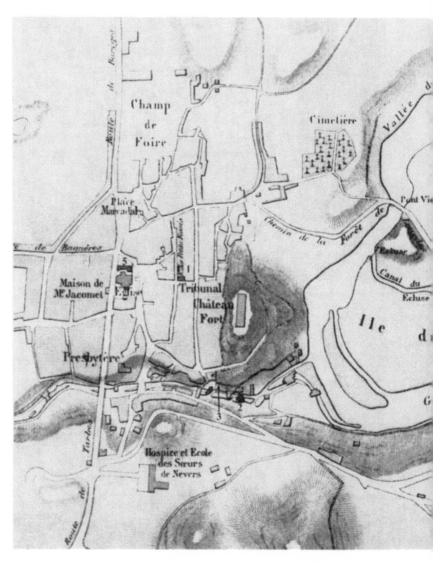

Map drawn by Henri Lasserre, contemporary historian of the Lourdes events, whose sight was restored through Lourdes water.

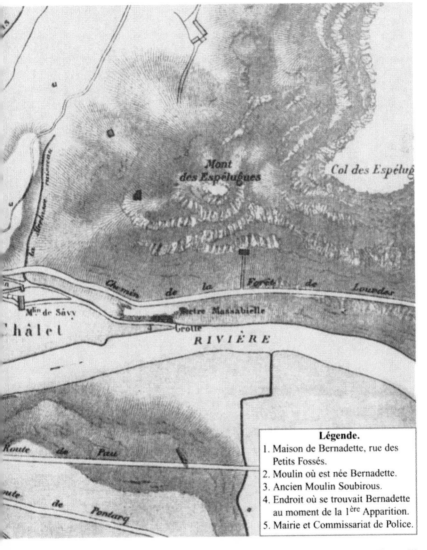

Mont
des Espélugues

Col des Espélug

M<sup>n</sup> de Sàvy

hâlet

Chemin de la Forêt de Lourdes

Porte Massabielle

Grotte

RIVIÈRE

Route de Pau

de Pontarg

*Legend:* 1. Bernadette's home at the time of the apparitions. 2. The mill where Bernadette was born. 3. The old Soubirous mill. 4. The spot where Bernadette knelt at the first apparition. 5. Town hall and police station.

# I

## CHILDHOOD

# I

## FROM MILL TO MILL

O N Tuesday, January 9th, 1844, at St Peter's Church, Lourdes, in the Bigorre, the Dean himself, Abbé Dominique Forgue, was baptising a baby girl, the first-born of François Soubirous and Louise Castérot, whose wedding had been celebrated in this same church a year ago to the day. Who would have dreamt that the very font to which this child was brought would later be preserved from destruction and be venerated on her account?

She had come into the world two days before, on the Sunday after the Epiphany, about two o'clock in the afternoon, as the bell was ringing for Vespers. She cried the whole time during her Baptism, to the sorrow and disgust of her cousin and godfather, Jean-Marie Védère, a schoolboy of eleven, whom his parents had brought from Momères, near Tarbes, together with his sister, Jeanne, aged fourteen.

During the ceremony, the Curé kept calling the child Marie-Bernarde, and this was noticed by the father. Back in the Sacristy he pointed out, on the instigation of the godmother, Aunt Bernarde Castérot, that the child had been registered the day before at the Town Hall under the Christian names, *Bernarde-Marie*. By a happy inspiration, Abbé Forgue retained the name Marie-Bernarde in the parish register, as though he had had the deliberate intention of placing the newly born, from the very start, under the protection of the Blessed Virgin. In the event, the godmother obstinately refused to give way; only in a distant future was her godchild to regain her beautiful first name of Marie. In Lourdes, although her name remained Bernarde, she would always be known by the graceful diminutive, Bernadette.

To the joyful sound of the bells—for in the Bigorre every legitimate child was entitled to a free peal of the bells—the

3

humble procession went down towards the house where she was born.

This was a mill, called Boly after an English doctor who owned it in the seventeenth century. It was not in appearance one of the smallest of the six mills which stood in echelon to the north of Lourdes along the banks of a tributary of the Gave called the Lapaca. Milling, indeed, took up a large part of the property: there was a store-room for the grain, a room to house the mill-stones and a shed for the big mill-wheel; only three rooms and the kitchen were reserved for living accommodation.

As they approached the threshold Jean-Marie Védère, who was walking beside Bernadette's father, pointed to his godchild and remarked in a disappointed tone, 'She has done nothing but cry; she will be a bad one.'

This reflection was lost in the joyful outburst of voices, for as they approached the house they began shouting their greet-ings to the young Mamma waiting inside for her Bernadette. Shedding tears of happiness this good Christian woman kissed the child's brow first, in reverence for the grace of its Baptism.

\*     \*     \*

The Lapaca quarter was cut off from the 'town', as they called it in those days, and the municipality took scarcely any interest in it. A stony track ran down beside the mills and, although there was a foot-bridge over the stream, horses and carts had to cross by a ford; and this was not without its perils during the melting of the snows.

From Boly mill little could be seen but other mills and, beyond them, towards the fields of Ribère a vista of trees and shrubs that overhung the windings of the Gave, for the Castle and its solitary rock blocked almost the whole horizon. This Lourdes castle, an outdated fortress, was, in 1844, no more than a military post and munition depot. In the evening its gigantic shadow hastened the fall of night over the valley of the Lapaca. Squatting in a semi-circle around this acropolis the town with its tangle of narrow streets, passages and blind alleys, and with its low grey houses, was not prepossessing to the eye. About the time when this story begins, a writer, Hippolyte Taine, jotted down in his travel diary these hasty notes:

Near Lourdes the hills grew bare and the landscape gloomy. Lourdes is just a cluster of dull roofs of a dismal leaden hue, huddled below the road.

Taine, in spite of his spectacles, failed apparently to see there close beside him the green foam-tipped waves of the Gave or the fresh green of the valleys, with the sparkle of clear water everywhere; and he likewise failed to see the enchanting setting of the snow-streaked Pyrenees that disappeared in the misty distance.

The population of Lourdes was about 4,000. This little town, a simple canton centre, retained, with all due deference to Argelès, the district capital, the imposing privilege of possessing, in addition to a court of the Justice of the Peace, the 'Tribunal Correctionnel' with its judges, public prosecutor, barristers, bailiffs, a police-station and naturally a constabulary complete with jail.

On days when the court was in session, the comings and goings of magistrates, suitors and witnesses added to the usual bustle, for the streets of the town were never, except during the periods of heavy snow, entirely lifeless. Morning and evening there was a ceaseless clatter of wooden shoes on the uneven pavements: great numbers of workmen going off to the marble and slate quarries that gaped on the slopes of the mountains close by; poor women on their way to the communal forest of Subercarrère, from which they would return carrying on their heads a bundle of dry wood. Then about ten o'clock, shepherds playing their pipes drove herds of pigs, sheep or goats to pasture among the rocks and waste lands on the banks of the Gave. During the fine season there were the traditional fairs, when farmworkers from the Lavedan or the Béarn, mountaineers from the high Pyrenean valleys, horse-dealers from Gascony and Languedoc and even from as far away as Aragon, made for Marcadal Square. Then, with increasing frequency and amid a tumult of shouts and bells, came the luxurious carriages and large stagecoaches loaded with tourists and bathers bound for Barèges, Luz, Cauterets and Bagnères-de-Bigorre; and they all halted at the posting-house inn. Innkeepers and shopkeepers congratulated themselves on their good luck, and even the Lapaca millers benefited by the orders for flour.

✻    ✻    ✻

At the time of Bernadette's birth François Soubirous was twice the age of his wife—a disproportion explained by the circumstances.

On June 1st, 1841, Justin Castérot, the occupant of Boly mill, was carried off by premature death at the age of forty-one. He 'left his wife in an awkward situation'. He held the mill from a certain Abadie-Boly, who lived in the village of Lézignan, some three miles from Lourdes. Whether he had made full payment for it or not remained something of a mystery. In any case the purchase was still subject to some liability. Like the rest of the local millers, the Castérots used to fatten young pigs on the bran from the grinding. Now every year the man from Lézignan had first choice of one of them as a levy. 'This,' observes Jean Barbet, a schoolmaster of Lourdes, 'was a heavy charge which took the best part of the Castérots' income.' If the annual levy of one small pig meant such a loss to them, the returns from their milling must have been meagre.

Jeanne Védère (so she affirmed) had recollections of 'a considerable property'. In reality all they had was a rather primitive mill known as a jobbing or small-sack mill, fitted with only two pairs of millstones and rudimentary cleaning apparatus. Even in Lourdes certain competitors were better equipped. And then there was the effect of wear and tear: not only had the millstones to be kept in repair, but the big wooden paddle-wheel had frequently to be reset and strengthened, for the Lapaca would be converted by the melting snow into a raging torrent which battered the wheel savagely in short bursts of fury. On the other hand, as Jean Barbet again points out, 'like all the mills built on the Lapaca, this mill also was often idle through lack of water. Expenses, increased by a fairly numerous family and possibly by a certain amount of mismanagement, rendered the Castérots' position somewhat precarious'.

That would account for the 'awkward situation' in which Justin Castérot's death had placed his widow. She was left with four daughters: Bernarde (who was to be Bernadette's godmother), aged eighteen, Louise, Basile and Lucile, who was only eleven months old; also a boy of eleven, Jean-Marie. A man was needed—a son-in-law—to take over the running of the mill.

Despite their very slender means the Castérots gave no appearance of poverty; rather they were regarded as being comfortably well off. Several suitors presented themselves, but only one of them happened to be in the trade; this was François Soubirous, a bachelor of thirty-four, whose parents, Joseph and Marie (Dassy) Soubirous, leased the neighbouring Latour mill. Already, for some months during the season when the Boly mill was humming busily throughout the day, François had given Justin Castérot a hand with his rounds or his work. 'A simple man of gentle disposition,' earnest and upright, he had always got on well with the master. He was given the preference.

It was no use the widow Castérot incessantly singing the praises of Bernarde, her eldest daughter; bashful François fixed his choice on the younger one, Louise, prettier no doubt in the flower of her seventeen years.

François was a typical Bigourdan: sturdy and rugged, with an expressionless face, angular features, eyes that were frank but veiled by the wrinkling of the eyelids, thin lips that knew neither falsehood nor complaint. Louise was 'neither big nor small, fair with blue eyes'; nor was she without charm, even on working days, with her simple foulard knotted on one side of her head; and on feast days how impressive François found her in her white nun-like 'capulet', with its folds enveloping her shoulders so gracefully!

'It is good to know,' attests Jeanne Védère of her uncle, François Soubirous, 'that this man was an excellent Catholic.' Louise also carried out faithfully her religious duties: morning and night prayers, Sunday services, Easter duties.

At the time of their engagement, some months after her father's death, the disposal of the inheritance was not yet settled. To complete the settlement it was judged necessary for François Soubirous to become one of the family. For this reason the date of the marriage was brought forward to Saturday, November 19th, 1842. However, hardly a month before this happy day, François' mother died suddenly, on October 21st, in the neighbouring mill. It looked as though they would have to do without the traditional wedding festivities altogether.

Eventually it was decided to postpone the religious ceremony. When November 19th arrived the couple presented themselves before the mayor of Lourdes for the civil formalities of marriage; after which François continued to reside at his father's mill. He could now at any rate appear before the notary with the lawful title of husband, son-in-law and brother-in-law. The settlement of the will showed him that there was not exactly a fortune in the Boly mill (which was not yet paid for), but, like Louise, he felt full of courage and was not unduly alarmed about the future.

They were married on Monday, January 9th, 1843, in the presence of a curate, Abbé Zéphirin Vergez. Nine children were to be born of their marriage.

François and Louise Soubirous were to take over the mill and pay a rent to the mother, who would continue to live there with the rest of her children. The mother would also retain some control over the household, for she was experienced, and her services were required for booking the orders and keeping accounts; neither François nor Louise had signed the marriage register for the simple reason that they could not write; they had never attended school.

*    *    *

Bernadette had come into the world during the hard Pyrenean winter. So Louise served her apprenticeship as a young mother in the chimney corner where there was a fire made of dry wood gathered on the banks of the Lapaca, which were thick with alder and willow. In the evenings, which closed in so quickly, the faint fitful gleam of a resin candle lit up mother and child.

The chubby little baby was already ten months old and beginning to find her feet when an accident occurred which was to separate her for the first time from her mother. It was in November 1844. Louise Soubirous was standing by the fireside when the stump of a resin candle, which was sputtering out there, fell on the front of her bodice and set it alight. Although the burns were not deep, the mother could not go on nursing her little one. Besides, she was expecting another child in February or March, and she was feeling very run down. Bernadette would have to have a nurse.

It happened about this time that a young couple named Basile Lagües and Marie Aravant, who lived in the village of Bartrès in a valley to the north of Lourdes, and who were good customers of the Boly mill, lost their first child. They had been married for less than a year, and the child died on November 22nd, only two weeks old. The Soubirous suggested to the broken-hearted young mother that she should take Bernadette. Marie Lagües consented, more to distract her own mind from her grief than for the sake of profit; the payment was to be five francs per month in money or in flour.

It is just under three miles by road from Lourdes to Bartrès. With the help of Aunt Bernarde, Louise Soubirous carried the little one there in her cradle. And as the child from the mill was quick to fret and knew hardly anyone but her own family, her aunt stayed with her for some days until she grew accustomed to new faces.

On February 13th of the following year a little boy was born at Boly mill, Jean Soubirous, whom his sister was never to know except in heaven: he was carried off fresh in the grace of Baptism, scarcely two months old, on the 10th of April.

At Bartrès Bernadette had found a second mother. Moreover, contrary to the prediction of her young godfather, she was turning out to be neither weepy nor 'bad', but just the opposite: winsome and all smiles. Everyone in the village began to love her.

Yet how much more fondly her own mother loved her! Louise's grief at the death of her little Jean remained acute; more and more she missed her Bernadette. At the end of ten months her kindly nurse, with tears in her eyes, brought the child back, fully weaned, to the Boly mill.

She would soon be two years old and was already stammering out quite a number of words with the variations peculiar to the Lourdes district, in the tuneful dialect of Bigorre which the Soubirous, like the Lagües, spoke among themselves. Her merry chirp mingling with the splash and rumble of the revolving mill-wheel, cheered her poor Papa (her favourite companion), white with flour in the midst of his labours. Those were peaceful days for the Boly millers, whose happiness was unclouded; days of relative prosperity when a worker reckoned himself comfortably off if he had fifteen louis laid by.

Maria Lagües had won Bernadette's heart. Out of affection for her, and for fear lest the child might forget her, she never failed, when she came to Lourdes market, to bring her some surprise gift; and her little darling knew how to find the cakes from Bartrès at the bottom of the big basket.

It had been arranged that her parents should take her to her foster-mother's house at least for Shrovetide and for the annual festival of St John the Baptist. But, for her part, Madame Lagües used to find the time of separation very long, and now and again she would come unexpectedly and claim her Bernadette. So from time to time the child returned to the village for five or six days. She used to delight in following the shepherdess through the fields. François Soubirous sadly missed his little girl's prattle and, as Jeanne Védère assures us, would frequently go and see her on the pretext of taking a sack of corn or delivering a bag of flour. After all, didn't he have regular customers in a part of the village!

\*     \*     \*

Between 1844 and 1848 business at the Boly mill seemed prosperous enough. The pleasing welcome given by Louise Soubirous and the mother-in-law retained old customers and attracted new ones. But living conditions were very cramped, as there was no accommodation beyond the three rooms which adjoined the grinding chamber. In the course of 1848, widow Castérot with her son, Jean, and her three daughters, Bernarde, Basile and Lucile—whom she would have been glad to see happily married—went off to live in a house on the Chemin de la Forêt. The following February 1st, when her godchild had just turned five, Aunt Bernarde married Jean Tarbès, a shopkeeper in the Rue du Bourg.

Until her sixth year Bernadette was strong and healthy looking. Unfortunately, she started to suffer from asthma, which was to go on troubling her to the end of her life. She was nevertheless, a lovable child with a sweet smile; but her growth was retarded. Choking fits frequently pulled her up in the midst of her games. None the less she was already making herself useful in the house, taking care of her little sister, Toinette, who was two and a half years younger than herself.

Grandmother Castérot was no longer at hand. Her departure from the mill had possibly caused the loss of some old patrons, and then, what with the continual coming and going of customers, Louise felt herself overwhelmed. The mother-in-law used to do all the 'writing'; but now the only accounts-book was the memory of the young miller's wife; and it could not hold everything. The result was that certain small accounts went unpaid. What is more—and it is a touching detail that does credit to this humble woman—she used to cancel certain debts out of charity.

'Bernadette's mother,' said a priest, M. André Labayle, 'was very kind and very charitable. She used to lend corn to the parents of Marie Cazaux—as she herself told me—and she would say to them: "You can pay me when you get some money."' Of Louise, as of her husband, M. Barbet could write: 'The Soubirous were fine people, obliging and generous, readily advancing flour to their customers in need. And they were popular with everybody.' M. Clarens, who was headmaster of the senior elementary school of Lourdes, adds that 'they were people of irreproachable integrity'.

It was the opinion of their cousin, Jeanne Védère, that their great charity, coupled with some inefficiency, would not alone have brought about their ruin. There was also at the mill a certain amount of loss which was sanctioned, one might say, by long-standing custom. Large numbers of women from Lourdes and the neighbouring villages used to bring to the mill, for grinding, just the amount of corn which they needed for the week's bread. Formerly, in the years of plenty, it had become the practice for these customers to have a snack while waiting for their flour. They would bring a bit of food with them; but while François Soubirous was busy at the grindstones, Louise, in her excessive generosity, would add to what they had brought. 'There was always bread and wine and cheese for them,' says Jeanne Védère, 'with the result that they often cost the miller more than they paid him.'

The sifters were wearing out and developing large holes, and François could not afford to get them repaired. Customers left, complaining that their flour was of coarser quality, and had more bran dust in it, than that of other millers.

The Soubirous were verging on bankruptcy. By St John's Day, 1854—Bernadette was then ten and a half years old—it was impossible for them to meet their rent. Some time previously the owner, Abadie-Boly, had decided to get rid of the mill which brought him no return, and a cousin of François, Amand Soubirous, had bought it on November 19th, 1852, with the intention of running it himself.

\* \* \*

What was to become of them? Madame Castérot decided to rent in her own name another mill named 'Maison Laborde' or 'Laborde-Lousi Mill' in order to house and provide for the entire family.

Until this time the Soubirous had enjoyed a certain standing among their equals. They were now on the way to losing it: their social decline was to get worse. The Laborde mill, which had a very small output and was eclipsed by its near neighbour, the wealthy Lacadé mill, worked only intermittently, owing to lack of customers. This was a grave threat to their daily bread. François made use of his enforced leisure by taking on odd jobs here and there.

Alas, in the course of the winter of 1854, the feast of Friday, December 8th, passed completely unnoticed by the poor Soubirous. For toilers like them, it was a working day the same as any other day. In the Laborde mill there was no time to think of the magnificent ceremonies in Rome where Pope Pius IX, beneath the resplendent dome of St Peter's, was pronouncing the great definition, 'in virtue of the authority of the Holy Apostles, Peter and Paul, and of his own', that 'the Blessed Virgin Mary was preserved from all stain of original sin from the first moment of her conception'.

At the Laborde mill there was now nothing but bitter anxiety for their daily bread. And at this critical juncture, along came another mouth to feed: little Justin Soubirous, born on February 28th, 1855.

Bernadette had turned eleven.

An epidemic of cholera swept up the valleys of Lavedan and Argelès as far as Lourdes, where it claimed its victims especially among the children. The delicate little girl was stricken by it. She recovered, God knows how; so many prayers went up from the Laborde mill to the Virgin Mary, to whom from time immemorial the people of Lourdes have had such great devotion.

Thus, from her childhood, Bernadette experienced all sorts of trials, both physical and mental, but she derived great profit from them for her soul. In watching her own dear ones suffer, and in suffering herself, she matured early, becoming detached from this 'wicked world' (1 John 2, 17) and aspiring with a yet unformed desire to higher and purer realities. By turns solemn or smiling, she seldom laughed heartily. Small in build and often racked by asthma, she took on tasks seemingly beyond her strength. See her, a devoted little mother, holding in her arms the baby Justin. The other two, Jean-Marie and Toinette, were a trifle wild, but the eldest sister knew how to scold them on occasions and make them obey her. Louise Soubirous could take on outside work without anxiety: under Bernadette's care there would be no trouble at home.

One day in July 1855, the mother had arranged with a cousin, Catherine Soubirous, and another Lourdes woman, to go and help with the harvest in a field on the Mengelattes' farm. This was to be the occasion of a delightful incident which showed Bernadette to be as downright as she was sensible.

The Mengalettes lived in Rue de Langelle, not far from the church. Between nine and ten in the morning, Bernadette appeared on their doorstep with her baby brother in her arms. Romaine, the farmer's daughter, was there and welcomed her. She was to remember this humble meeting all her life; she even noted that Bernadette, whose 'face was round and pretty, with lovely, very gentle eyes', had her usual kerchief on her head, a shawl over her shoulders, her bare feet in sabots, and her dress reaching down to the ground. She seemed tired, 'and there was every reason'. 'In she comes then,' relates Romaine Mengelatte, 'and very simply, very nicely, she says to us, "Would you kindly tell me where your field is? I must carry my little brother to my mother, for he wants to be suckled."' A neighbour, who was also off to join the harvesters, took Bernadette at once to the Mengelattes' field.

\* \* \*

On October 23rd of this year, 1855, Louise's mother, Claire Castérot, passed away. The repercussions of this bereavement were to be doubly distressing for the Soubirous, already so sorely tried. They would miss her experienced advice. She had shut her ears to the malignant gossips who always condemn the unfortunate. 'Why,' whispered the rancorous tongues, 'had they not given more attention to their business and less to regaling their customers?' Not once had she grieved her daughter and son-in-law with unjust reproaches; between son and mother-in-law there had always been peace.

As a result of this death common interests between the

Castérots and the Soubirous came to an end. From the division of the property Bernadette's parents received as their share 900 francs. Once again they had to move house. But the Soubirous couple still strove to earn their family's daily bread; anything rather than beg!

At the entrance to the village of Arcizac-ès-Angles, three miles east of Lourdes, they rented a hut. François took charge of a mill near by; Louise, undaunted, would take a job, when required, on the land. Another stream, the Magnas, a tributary of the Echez, drove the mill-wheel. Farewell to the banks of the capricious Lapaca, where they had suffered so much! On this autumn afternoon, a gleam of hope shone in the eyes of the Soubirous and their eldest daughter, as they greeted the woodland solitude where their new dwelling lay concealed.

The winter of 1855 came in with particular severity. Aunt Bernarde, who, after the death of her husband Jean Tarbès, was now married to a Lourdes farmer, Jean Nicolau, paid a visit to the hut at Arcizac. Hearing her godchild cough, she suggested taking her home with her. So Bernadette was readily handed over to her for the whole of the winter; she would not find life dull with two little cousins to entertain.

This should not have prevented the godmother from sending her regularly to the Nuns. Indeed, not very far from her house, on the hillside on the opposite bank of the Lapaca, the Sisters of Charity of Nevers, who had come to Lourdes in 1834, ran a school in a part of the town hospital. The hospital itself was also under their charge. It seems surprising that Aunt Bernarde, though able to do so, did not have her godchild educated more thoroughly.

> Bernadette [she admitted] knew the *Our Father, Hail Mary* and *I Believe,* but she seldom went to school, for her duties as nurse-maid did not allow her to go often; so she was unable to read, and her only prayer-book at Mass was a small rosary. At home, she gave no trouble to anyone. I always found her good-tempered and docile; when scolded she never answered back.

A young Lourdes girl of that time, Catherine Fourcade, had noticed that her friend, Bernadette Soubirous, was often absent from class. And Jeanne, Catherine's sister, when she was in church near this little girl—a picture of simplicity and innocence —was not surprised to see her 'turn her head like the rest of the children and have a look at what was going on around her'.

To this period, when she was staying at Aunt Bernarde's, belongs no doubt the trivial incident in which severe critics have wished to discover a trace of vanity. Uncle Jean-Marie Nicolau had given up farming and had started business as a wine-merchant. On one of his journeys, calling at Bétharram, he brought back some rings for his wife and his two sisters-in-law, Aunts Basile and Lucile, without even a thought for Bernadette. These cheap trinkets, bought at the Pilgrimage shop and bearing in an oval a tiny picture of the Madonna, were little more than pious objects. In fun, the aunts tried their rings on Bernadette; but they were too big and would not stay on her finger. She looked disappointed. 'All right! I'll get one for you,' promised Uncle Nicolau. Alas, the ring he brought back from another journey seemed too small, even for Bernadette's little finger. She managed, nevertheless, to squeeze it on. Her delight proved all too short: the finger swelled and began to hurt and a file had to be used to free it. When, towards the end of her life, Bernadette told this 'story of her youth' she concluded with a smile: 'And I never wanted a ring after that.'

At Arcizac mill the song soon died on the miller's lips. He had been let down again: the owner had exaggerated the mill's capacity and the goodwill of the business. Nevertheless, François and Louise did their best to hold on.

Mild weather had returned once more, and Bernadette wanted to see her parents again. No matter if the slices of bread and butter in the impoverished home at Arcizac were not so thick as Aunt Nicolau's! In spite of everything she was happy with Jean-Marie and Toinette, playing on the banks of the Magnas, whose crystal-clear waters were becoming turbid with the melting snows. There on those natural lawns and in among the moss-clad rocks, there bloomed so many pretty flowers! These wild flowers, simple as her own soul, would always be loved by Bernadette. Her posies and her smile brought comfort also to her parents.

A girl of Arcizac, who was one day to become the wife of Philippe Viron, a Lourdes policeman, used to call quite frequently at their mill; and she marvelled at the way 'Bernadette took care of the house and of her little brothers' in her parents' absence.

# 2

## IN THE LOURDES 'DUNGEON'

IN the course of 1856 the Soubirous, now at the end of their resources, had to leave Arcizac. They foresaw no other means of livelihood except by taking jobs in Lourdes as day-labourers. It may be imagined how humiliating and painful this decision was for them. They took lodgings in the Rue du Bourg, up against the rock of the Castle, 'in a wretched hovel by the Rives house', having arranged, explains M. Barbet, with a man called Soubies for a room to be sub-let to them. How that savours of destitution!

They found some work. From time to time a baker, M. Bertrand Maisongrosse, employed François Soubirous to transport flour and bread between Lourdes and Saint-Jean-de-Luz; M. Cazenave, the proprietor of a coach service to Bagnères-de-Bigorre, entrusted him with the care of his horses. Louise used to take work in the fields or even join the women who went gathering wood in the forest; and then she would sell her faggots in order to buy bread.

During this time Bernadette, now twelve years old, and helped by Toinette, who was ten, was kept busy at home. There were always the little brothers to take care of: Jean-Marie, a youngster of five, and Justin, who would be a year and ten months old at the end of the year. The two girls had also to keep the fire going, and warm up the soup. They used to contrive pleasant surprises for their parents. Some neighbours would be kind enough to take care of their little brothers, and the girls took advantage of this to go along the streets collecting rags, scrap iron and bones. Alexine Baron, the second-hand dealer, would exchange them for a few sous which they brought back home with delight. This was an age of scant help for the poor. For example, no Conference of St Vincent de Paul was established in Lourdes till 1874. It was a harsh age when too many of the wealthy, lacking pity because they lacked the Gospel, exploited the labour of the poor; and mothers of large families received only ten sous for a whole day's work! Although the Soubirous now managed to earn enough for their food, they were unable to pay their rent, trifling though it was. And they were too proud to beg.

One day, about All Saints' Day in 1856, they could be seen in front of the Rives house loading a hand-cart with what remained of their crockery and furniture. Their wedding wardrobe—a cherished souvenir—was to remain in pawn in the grasping hands of Soubies. Where were they off to, these poor unfortunates, dragging their cart along with their four children? Life's castaways! What bit of wreckage could they find to hold on to?

Parallel to the Rue du Bourg, which they had just left, ran the Rue des Petits-Fossés, built over the ancient moat of the castle, and at its corner stood the law-court. A little further on was the old prison. One of Louise's cousins, André Sajous, a master stone-mason, lived in this abode of grim repute, which had been bequeathed to him by an uncle. Thirty years previously the jail had been transferred for hygienic reasons from the Rue des Petits-Fossés to the Baous tower and so the uncle had come into possession of this unwanted building.

Some idea may be formed [notes Jean Barbet] of what this old house was like, built against the thick rampart wall and admitting no daylight except on the east side. There were two rooms on the first floor occupied by André Sajous; on the ground floor there was a front room which the stone-mason used as a workshop; then at the end of a passage there was a dark room opening on to a small yard facing west.

This back room, separated from the workshop by a rough partition of planks, was still known among the people of that quarter by the sinister name of the 'dungeon'.

It was to this wretched hovel, far worse than the previous one, that François Soubirous made his way one day in November with his wife and children and the remnants of his furniture. But the landlord's unvarnished description of it should be heard.

I had let another window into the wall of the 'dungeon' [states André Sajous], and put in a fireplace. The bell-ringer, the black-smith, Lafitte, and Blancard, the butcher, tried one after the other to settle in there; but they did not stick it long. In order to get some bit of profit from this unwholesome place I was reduced to sheltering penniless foreigners: Spanish navvies, for instance, who spend the winter in Lourdes, used to come and stretch themselves out there for the night on straw. At length, with no further hope of finding a tenant, and having no more convenient place at my disposal, I had dumped a heap of manure in the yard.

It was then that François Soubirous came and told my uncle that he had been put out on the street with all his family, and begged him to let the old 'dungeon' to him. . . .

When I was told by my uncle of François' request, I wasn't anxious to take him. We were poor ourselves; I had five children, and I knew that my wife, who was very kind, would give our bread to François' four children. Still we dared not refuse, and they came and took possession of the basement room."

No doubt their accommodation was not very much worse than that of other workers' families in this slum quarter. But they had known comfort and respectability at the Boly mill, and that made their present destitution all the harder and more humiliating.

Jeanne Védère, who spent a night there in March 1858, found that they had 'absolutely nothing but some necessary bits of furniture and linen'. There was a cupboard, a trunk, some chairs and three beds—one for the parents, another for the two girls and a third for the two small boys. And that left precious little space in this small hovel which measured about four yards by five.

Before moving in, the mother, assisted by Bernadette and Toinette, gave it a thorough spring-cleaning, but even then, what with the iron bars on one of the windows, the slate flag-stones and the black beams of the extra low ceiling, the room still kept the appearance of an old jail. As a further reminder one had only to try the outside door in the passage; it was a massive, grim-looking structure of stout oak planks, with the same old enormous bolt.

\*        \*        \*

Imagine having to live in this 'dark, fetid hole', where the sun never penetrated, in this atmosphere of wretchedness and demoralizing gloom! Yet they would have to put up with living here until the day when they could have their home in a mill once more; for François Soubirous never gave up hope. He continued to do odd jobs, whilst the mother went to the forest and did washing or charring in the town. Toinette, now turned ten, attended the Sisters' school fairly regularly.

As for Bernadette, she was repeatedly heard to say that books were not meant for her, that she was now over thirteen and the Sisters did not know quite in which class to put her: the most she had managed so far was to scrawl, rather badly, two or three capital letters on a slate. Then there was her asthma. But, above all, she was needed at home. She was the little victim, the little Cinderella of the 'dungeon'.

But when was she going to make her First Communion? There was already talk of Toinette's, and she would be only eleven in September. Toinette could read, and, as she enjoyed better health than her sister, could almost have been taken for the eldest of the family. Yet, how poor Bernadette would have loved to go to the catechism classes! 'Have patience, your turn will come,' her mother promised. At night, when her asthma prevented her from sleeping, she used to cry over the heart-breaking poverty of the home, over her ignorance and her frustrated longings with all the distress of a young soul in its confusion and perplexity. When morning came, once she had said her prayers, she regained her child-like gaiety. She would wash and dress her little brothers and join in their games. 'Never,' testified André Sajous, 'would you have heard them complain that they were hungry. But how often have I seen Bernadette, Jean-Marie and little Justin laugh and skip on an empty stomach!'

There were times indeed when, through unemployment, the father and mother were unable to give their children even the food they needed. Then François, leaving for his family what little food there was, would retire to bed for the day, enduring in silence the gnawing pangs of hunger. Nothing in the world would have induced him to admit this to his cousin Sajous.

The bread so hungrily devoured by the Soubirous when they had any, was merely the bread of the poor, 'milloc', made of a maize dough. But the 'milloc' used to upset Bernadette's stomach. Her mother would get her some wheat bread, a little sugar and a little wine. In later days, when she was very ill at Nevers, the infirmarian asked in the kitchen for 'more appetizing food' for her. 'Did her Mamma give her chicken every day?' was the inconsiderate reply from one of the cooks. When she was told of this remark, Bernadette, it is said, could not help answering, 'No. She did not, but anything my mother gave me, she always gave with a good heart!' There still came presents from her foster-mother: those dainties from Bartrès, which Bernadette gladly shared with her sister and her two brothers.

But the mother had stipulated that the white bread, on which Jean-Marie and Toinette used to cast envious looks, was for Bernadette alone. It was not always possible for her to carry out mother's orders. In the 'dungeon' there were no regular hours or fixed places for meals. A friend of Bernadette, Jeanne Abadie, who lived in the Rue du Bourg, often came to pay her a visit. 'How many times,' Jeanne has related, 'have I found Bernadette having her meagre bowl of soup on the window-ledge, in front of that blank wall and that dung-heap!' Now it sometimes happened that Jean-Marie and Toinette would make a sudden swoop and grab the piece of white bread lying beside the bowl. As Toinette later bore witness, Bernadette offered scarcely any resistance and never complained at all to her parents when they returned from their work.

From time to time Jean-Marie, a toddler of six, silent and self-willed, used to escape from his sister's supervision and 'go prowling'—to use Toinette's phrase. One of these escapades was to reveal to Mlle Emmanuélite Estrade, a devout Lourdes woman who was the younger sister of a chief official in the Excise, the extent to which some needy folk of the town were tormented by hunger.

One day [she relates], I was saying my prayers about two o'clock in the afternoon in front of Our Lady's altar in the parish church; I thought I was alone until I heard some chairs move. I turned round and caught sight of a child of five or six years in very poor clothes. His face was pleasing but quite emaciated, showing plainly that the child was under-nourished. I resumed my prayers, and the child continued his manoeuvres. With a very sharp

'Hush' I ordered him to keep quiet. The child tried hard, but in spite of all the precautions he took to avoid making a noise, he did not succeed. I watched him closely and noticed that he was bending down and scraping the flagstones and then putting his hand to his mouth. He was actually eating the wax which had fallen from the candles during a funeral service.

'Is that wax you're eating?' I asked him.

He nodded his head.

'You must be very hungry! . . . Wouldn't you rather eat something else?'

Several nods of the head again gave me the answer 'Yes'.

I left the church at once with the poor child, now my friend. For quite a long time at my invitation he came every day to visit us, and was like a boarder. But I could never manage to persuade him to come inside our flat. He persisted in remaining on the step of the staircase, which he used as a table.

Never could M. Estrade or his sister induce him to tell them his name or where he lived.

Louise Soubirous 'liked neatness in dress but was unable to achieve as much of it as she would have liked'. In the evening by the light of a miserable resin candle she would try, with Bernadette's help, to repair the children's clothes. They were wearing out and the mother realized with dismay that she would not be able to replace them. But she concealed her distress.

One day in that winter of 1857 Bernadette was taking a walk in Lourdes, hand in hand with her younger brother, then aged two. The child was barefoot in his little sabots. A lady passed by, accompanied by a little girl. It was Mme Irma Jacomet, the wife of the Commissioner of Police, and she was taking her Armanda for a walk. Miss Armanda, who was five and a half, was just then having her first lessons in knitting from the Sisters of the Hospice. With considerable help she had just finished her first big effort, a small pair of stockings, and had said to her mother, 'I want to give them to the poorest child we meet, even if it is a Spaniard!' (Little Miss Jacomet had not failed to notice that the navvies from Navarre and Aragon were the Commissioner's most regular customers.) Catching sight of Justin Soubirous, Mme Jacomet bent down and whispered in her daughter's ear; Armanda's chosen one had been found. 'Will you come back to our house with us?' the lady asked Bernadette.

The Jacomets lived close by the apse of the church, and the office of the Commissioner of Police was in their house. Bernadette hesitated. But it was so cold! . . . Armanda slipped the stockings on little Justin's feet and he seemed delighted with them. With a smile of happiness Bernadette thanked her benefactors politely, but without telling them who she was. And the Commissioner himself, touched by the incident, embraced his daughter for her kindness of heart.

*    *    *

Unfortunately, the Commissioner of Police was soon to be spoken of with tears in the Rue des Petits-Fossés.

On Thursday, March 27th, about noon, Sergeant d'Angla, with one of his gendarmes, called at the Soubirous' home. The father had just come in. They had followed him; he was wanted by the police. At the back of the gloomy room the four frightened children were clinging to their mother. The police had come to investigate. The previous night two sacks of flour had disappeared from the Maisongrosse bakery, and the proprietor accused his employee of stealing them. François Soubirous protested his innocence: he had never stolen anything from his master. In any case, they had only to search his one and only room.

There was certainly no trace of the two sacks in the room. The gendarmes went through into the yard. At once d'Angla stopped. What was that long, narrow beam of wood doing there, leaning against the old enclosure wall? That looked suspicious. The Police Commissioner had that very morning received an anonymous complaint about the disappearance of a similar beam. Surely they had here the 'corpus delicti'? Besides, there was a disturbing coincidence. Why had François Soubirous left his home so early on that particular night? This mysterious exit he could not deny; the police had been informed of it through a neighbour's indiscretion. He would have to account for his movements. . . .

The fact is [wrote the Examining Magistrate Rives in his official report] that he had got up about three o'clock in the morning and had set out to search for some wood at Bartrès, but on arriving opposite M. Dozous' garden he had noticed a beam propped up against the wall, and taking possession of it had returned home.

It was an object of such trifling value that no one was ever likely to claim it. François confessed to having taken it, because there was no wood at home and he knew that in taking it, he was doing nobody any wrong. But the law is the law; the larceny was proven and admitted; justice was obliged to take cognizance of it. Amid the sobbing of his wife and the cries of his children, François Soubirous was led away by the police. He appeared first before the Commissioner of Police, Jacomet, and then before the Examining Magistrate, Rives. In the evening he was locked up in the Baous prison.

The 'corpus delicti' had been deposited temporarily in the Mayor's courtyard. We shall come across this beam again at an almost tragic moment in our story.

François was to remain nine days in jail, 'remanded in custody'. The affair of this piece of wood, whose owner was never discovered, was to set in motion the whole judicial world of Lourdes. Witness the signatures affixed to the enquiries and proceedings: after the Sergeant, Adolphe d'Angla, and the Commissioner, Dominique Jacomet, follow M. Raymond Prat, Clerk of the Court; M. Clément Rives, Examining Magistrate; M. Jacques-Vital Dutour, Public Prosecutor. Bernadette herself was soon to meet all these gentlemen, one after another!

And there was poor François gnawing his fists in the cell of the Baous, thinking about the family now deprived of his earnings. In the old 'dungeon' they were exhausted with weeping, for they knew how unhappy he must be, perhaps even going out of his mind. While the mother was obliged more than ever to obtain work outside and while Toinette was at school with the Sisters, Bernadette used to take Jean-Marie and Justin to church. The church of her Baptism was quite close to the 'dungeon'. Though it was somewhat dark, Bernadette loved it, for it was easy to pray there. And the innocent child found it so pretty, with the glinting gold of the statues and altar-screen. It was before the altar of the Virgin, Comfort of the Afflicted and Help of Christians, that she used to kneel with Jean-Marie, holding Justin close to her, his little hands joined in hers.

At length, on Saturday, April 4th, the Examining Magistrate, on the Public Prosecutor's demand, withdrew the warrant of commitment. The accused was released.

There was not a word of blame from Louise as she embraced

him. Like his family and all the neighbours, she was sure
that he was perfectly innocent. And from François came no
word of bitterness against his judges or accusers. He only showed
joy at being reunited with his family. Down in the gloomy
Baous jail, far from losing the faith of his ancestors, he had felt
it grow stronger. At the close of this Saturday, by the fireside
of the 'dungeon', over which hung a crucifix and a rosary, he
was to be found again in his usual place behind the children for
the traditional night prayers which the mother used to recite
aloud, saying alternately with the family the *Pater*, *Ave* and
*Credo*. André Sajous, who was by no means emotional and
who 'used to hear them recite their prayers at night', had no
words to describe the fervour with which Bernadette and the
others besought their Father in Heaven for their 'daily bread'!

*      *      *

After so many upheavals, and amid so many trials, this family
continued to live the lessons of the Gospel: their submission
brought them peace, and love cemented their hearts. 'There
were no arguments between François and Louise,' said André
Sajous: 'Never did I hear an ill-natured word from one to the
other, nor from the children against their parents. Though they
corrected their children sternly, as the poor do, they did not
ill-treat them."

Yet their eldest daughter, who was now over thirteen years
of age. had still not been prepared for her First Communion.
Why did these good practising Catholics allow it? They did
indeed permit her from time to time to go with her younger
sister to Catechism classes. But poor Bernadette, 'unable to
read or write, a complete stranger to the French language, unable
to master her lessons, looked on herself as the most backward
of the children of her age', and in fact she used to take a seat
behind all the rest. When questioned, either in French or in
patois, she would remain silent. Besides, her small stature
caused her to be ranked among little girls two or three years
younger than herself. Bernadette made no protest; and the
priest who took the Catechism class made no further enquiries,
saying to himself that there would always be time to take this
ignorant little thing in hand later.

On the solemn feast of Corpus Christi—Sunday, June 14th—
the First Communicants went in procession through the streets.
Bernadette gazed at them with her eyes full of tears. There
must be no more delay! Her mother comforted her with the
promise that it would be soon her turn also.

# 3

## AMONG THE HILLS OF BARTRÈS

THE Lagües had kept up their friendship with the Soubirous despite their poverty, and Louise thought that her Bernadette would find it easier to attend school and Catechism at Bartrès than in Lourdes. The foster-mother readily agreed to take her in her house, this time as an extra servant, without wages, of course, just out of friendship. Outside the hours of school and Catechism, Bernadette would look after the five little Lagües: Denis, a boy of eleven; Josèphe, a small girl of nine; Jean, aged seven; Justin, four and a half; and lastly Jean-Marie, a toddler of scarcely two.

So towards the end of June 1857, the Lagües' servant, Jeanne-Marie Garros, came to Lourdes to fetch her. 'She hadn't much to pack,' said Jeanne-Marie, recounting her memories, 'and more than once during her stay at Bartrès I lent her some of my linen while she washed her own.'

Along the undulating road that rises and dips as it leads to the village, Bernadette reflected now and then that this time she was not leaving Lourdes for a short holiday, but to work. She realized that she was going to live with a 'master and mistress', who would be exacting and would no longer treat her as one of the family. But she was not depressed. Her innocent eyes lit up, for at a bend on the hill she had just caught sight above the foliage, of the massive church-tower surmounted by its slender spire. Perhaps soon in this church . . . ? Jeanne-Marie Garros felt moved and bent a little closer to catch the tender confidence.

We must now get to know this Lagües-Aravant family more intimately, and there are some well-informed witnesses, in particular M. Jean Barbet, who was schoolmaster at Bartrès during Bernadette's stay there.

'Marie Lagües,' he wrote, 'was devout, but cold and rather

parsimonious. . . . She could read a little.' This unflattering portrait of her is fortunately filled out by Abbé Zéphirin Vergez, the parish priest, although to be exact he knew her only in the last years of her life. 'She was a saintly woman, a frequent communicant, and she said her Rosary as often as three times a day. She was a Tertiary of the Order of St Francis of Assisi.' 'Her husband, Basile Lagües, who came from Poueyferré,' added Jean Barbet, 'was a worthy man, but with no education.' Marie had a younger brother, Abbé Jean-Louis Aravant, ordained priest in 1855 and appointed curate at Marsas in the district of Bagnères.

The home of the Lagües, standing at the entrance to the village near a stream, was a rustic building with the gable-end facing the street. 'It comprised at this time two large rooms separated by a passage; one served as a kitchen and contained two beds; the other was a bedroom with three beds; a third room, a very small one, was allotted to the servant. In the two large rooms one noticed especially a wide fireplace, clean beds, a few bundles of woollen and flax yarn hanging from the joists, some little statues of saints, a crucifix on the mantelpiece, and by each bed a holy water stoup, with a rosary around it and a blessed palm. There were also a few prayer books, some pictures and a few old books, remnants of a dead priest's library, which were never opened. . . .'

They worked hard in this family, for they owned a large flock of sheep, some fine cows and large scattered tracts of land. In the winter evenings the men used to shell the maize and repair the tools; the women would spin, knit or do the mending. . . . When the evening's work was over family prayers were said together in the local patois, and off they went to bed for a well-earned sleep.

It was providential that Bernadette came for a long stay with these worthy folk. The work assigned to her obliged her to spend many hours in solitude—it is then that God 'speaks to the heart'.

Marie Lagües had not failed to introduce her to the priest in charge of the parish, Abbé Ader, so that he might enrol her in the Catechism classes. M. Ader was a 'zealous, learned' priest, 'of great piety', fond of serious study and protracted meditation;

in his church and presbytery he led the life of a monk. He was little suited, it would seem, to these country folk. Moreover, his heart was divided: beyond the horizon of his parish, and set amidst different foliage, he glimpsed another steeple, plainer, more slender, above the austere enclosure of a cloister. When Bernadette arrived at Bartrès in this summer of 1857, Abbé Ader, who had only been in the parish since March 1855, was awaiting permission from Bishop Laurence of Tarbes to enter a monastery.

He used to teach Catechism on Sundays and twice during the week. In church the schoolmaster, Jean Barbet, was in charge of the boys; behind the girls knelt the schoolmistress, who lived in the village: an advantage which Bartrès possessed over many of the Pyrenean villages. The two groups of boys and girls were not large, for the population of the parish was barely 250. Jean Barbet knew everyone in this little world, and he soon noticed the small girl from Lourdes who had taken the lowest place. He found during the first weeks that she attended the Catechism class regularly 'along with the children from the village and those from the hamlets of Saux and Les Granges, chapels-of-ease of the parish'.

One day the young schoolmaster was able to form his own opinion of her mental capacity. Being over-tired, Abbé Ader had asked his friend Barbet to take his place with the children. Barbet spoke very simply, and to bring home his subject to his pupils told them some good stories. Then he called on the boys and girls to speak in their own patois, and Bernadette as well. Afterwards the schoolmaster and priest discussed together the little Soubirous girl. 'Bernadette,' stated Jean Barbet, 'has difficulty in remembering the Catechism word for word, because she cannot study it, being unable to read. But she makes every effort to master the meaning of the explanations. She is most attentive and above all very devout and very retiring.'

It was possibly during this conversation that Abbé Ader confided to him his own impressions of Bernadette. 'I assure you that many a time, on seeing her, I have thought of the children of La Salette. Assuredly if the Blessed Virgin appeared to Mélanie and Maximin, it was because they must have been good, simple and devout like her.' M. Ader, who was devoted to the Blessed Virgin, had taken a lively interest in the occurrence at

La Salette, which took place in September 1846, and he had formed his own ideal picture of the two young visionaries on the far-off mountain, Maximin Giraud and Mélanie Calvat. Happy though the comparison may be, one must not read any prophetic intuition into words inspired solely by Bernadette's tender piety and ingenuousness.

Had not domestic difficulties prevented the Lagües from keeping their promise, no doubt she would have been able to receive proper education at Bartrès. As the Feast of the Assumption drew near, the cows and ewes were left grazing up the mountain while the lambs destined for slaughter were, as usual, separated from their mothers and brought down to the farm. M. Lagües was a practical man, and seeing that the servant, Jeanne-Marie, did all the work of the house so efficiently that Bernadette had little else to do but take care of his youngest children, Justine and Jean-Marie, he decided to entrust Bernadette with the care of the lambs.

'But what about school . . . and Catechism?' protested Bernadette timidly.

'Don't worry at all,' the man replied; 'your foster-mother will arrange all that in good time.'

So now she became a shepherdess.

Up early in the morning she helped the mother to wash and dress the children, did the housework with Jeanne-Marie, and then made her way to the stable, accompanied by Pigou, one of the farm dogs. She would half-open the door and call, and the lambs would gather gaily around her. Then away they went through the dew to Puyono heath, among the rolling hills, where the grass, mixed with wild thyme and violet leaves, was luscious and tender. In a basket on her arm our shepherd-girl carried her knitting, a garment to mend and provisions for the whole day.

Around the lowly thatched shelter where the shepherdess and her flock took refuge in storms, Bernadette divided her time as her fancy dictated between work, play and saying her rosary. The latter was a cheap twopenny rosary, with black beads threaded on a string, which her mother had given her.

Her pleasures were as simple as her soul.

During Catechism classes and the Sunday services—for she was always present in the Lagües' pew for High Mass and Vespers

—her gaze must often have rested on a statue of the Madonna surrounded by a bank of flowers.

At the foot of a century-old chestnut tree Bernadette arranged some stones into a rustic altar, and placed on top of it a picture of the Blessed Virgin. Then, kneeling before it, the little shepherdess would say a decade of her rosary and then get up.

'A spotless white lamb', perhaps the last born of the flock, was her favourite. 'Why do you like that one more than the others?' asked Julie Garros, a young friend from Lourdes who had come to pay her a visit.

'Because it's the smallest,' she replied. 'I love everything that's small.' She called and it came running up to her, stretching out its neck. The shepherdess offered it a tuft of choice grass, some bread sprinkled with salt, of which it was very fond, and sent it off with a caress. But the frisky lambkin took delight in playing pranks. With its head down it would charge the heap of stones and overturn the tiny altar. The whole thing had to be put up again! Bernadette confided also to her friend from Lourdes that this little lamb which looked so innocent was up to other mischief. When, for instance, she called her flock to follow her, the little white lamb used to take the lead, butt her behind the legs and down she would come on her knees. 'That's his way of caressing you,' Julie Garros pointed out. 'No doubt,' rejoined Bernadette, 'and I reward him all the same.'

How silent it was on the slopes of this little valley almost the whole day through. Pigou seldom barked; mostly he drowsed. No other sound was heard but the whispering of the tall trees, the buzz of a bee among the flowers, the chirp of a bird, or the thin bleating of a lamb. Bernadette was accustomed to these sounds, and at times seemed no longer to hear them. Seated on the grass she would suddenly stop knitting and fall into a reverie. Her gaze was fixed away beyond Lourdes, which she could no longer see, on the Pyrenees mountains, which she caught sight of when she went up to the top of the valley, their lofty peaks sprinkled with snow; the Pic du Jer, and, rising above it, the peaks of Viscos and Gazost . . . God made all that, she said to herself. For her, God was the Creator, and also the One Who remained hidden in the Tabernacle of the church. Her eyes closed; her heart filled with a deep longing.

Bernadette was entirely ignorant of the meaning of formal

meditation. Yet her young soul, unfettered by things of earth, rose up out of itself to God, and the Spirit of God Who 'teaches His ways to the humble' (Psalm 24, 9), came down to her. He was preparing this pure soul for a unique mission.

While she was saying her beads, her thoughts would also fly to the 'dungeon' in Lourdes. Here she was out in the fresh air on these lovely hills, while her loved ones were down there in that gloomy hovel or toiling laboriously in other people's houses. . . . God grant they might prove good Christians and know how to endure.

François Soubirous was fretting at not seeing his little daughter; and as he used to do in the days when she paid short visits to Bartrès, so now he went up there as often as he could. And she always welcomed him with a cry of delight. One day, however, he found her quite sad.

'Who has been upsetting you, Bernadette?' he asked, already feeling unhappy himself.

'Just look, Papa,' she explained, 'my lambs are green on their backs.'

What simplicity! The father, who knew the answer, kept back his smile. Several lambs, in fact, had a large green spot on their curly wool; it was the mark of the dealer, who, unknown to the shepherdess, had called at the sheepfold the previous evening. However, François Soubirous declared with great seriousness, 'They are green on their backs because they have eaten too much grass."

'Could they die of it?'

'They might.'

Bernadette burst into tears. Quickly her father dried her eyes. 'Come, come, don't cry like that! The dealer painted them that way.'

Later, the companion to whom she related this story could not help saying, 'But you were very simple to believe such a thing!' And she received this touching reply: 'What else could I do? I have never told a lie, and I could not imagine that anything my father told me was not the truth.'

When, towards mid-September, the teacher re-opened her school, Bernadette set out as usual for Puyono heath, for besides taking the lambs to pasture, she now took the sheep as well, which had been brought down from the mountain at the first frosts. That same morning the eldest of the Lagües, Denis and Josèphe, were getting their school books ready in order to go and have lessons from M. Jean Barbet.

Bernadette, as M. Lagües testified, 'looked after the sheep very well'. This was the reason why he was reluctant to dispense with her services. Abbé Jean-Louis Aravant, who had come for a few days' holiday with his relations, put it strongly to his brother-in-law that he was no longer treating the little Soubirous girl sufficiently as one of the family. The reproach went home, but not for long. After the re-opening of school, he sent her there only when obliged to do so: for instance, when bad weather kept the animals in the fold. 'Did you go to school at Bartrès?' Bernadette was asked towards the end of her life by a chronicler in search of records. To which she replied, 'I scarcely ever went to the school and when I did I learnt nothing.'

She likewise admitted that from then on she went only 'very rarely' to Catechism. Although Abbé Ader had noticed her for her piety and candour, he showed little concern, it seems, at seeing her now only rarely, even on Sundays, at his Catechism classes. Perhaps he thought the little girl often went to Lourdes to visit her family. When he met her occasionally in the street, 'he never spoke to her', according to the schoolmaster's evidence. In later years Bernadette could not even recall his name—if indeed she ever knew it. Did he ever hear her Confession? One of her companions at Bartrès, Jeanne-Marie Caudeban, who was about her own age, declared, 'I never saw her at Confession'. When Bernadette herself had this last question put to her, 'Did you go to Confession to the curate at Bartrès?' all she could answer was: 'I don't remember.' Then Abbé Ader left the parish early in November and had no immediate successor.

After frankly acknowledging that in effect 'Bernadette went a few times to school and to the parish Catechism,' Mme Lagües added: 'Despite the exhaustion caused by her short and constricted breathing, she appeared lively and gay; she made no complaint about anyone or anything, obeyed everybody and never answered back impertinently. Never did she give us any trouble: she took whatever was offered her and appeared quite contented. So we were very fond of her. . . .' This foster-mother did not possess the intuition of a real mother. She had no inkling of the interior anguish of this young soul. Nor was she even aware of the wonderful spirit in which the poor little thing was enduring her severe trial.

About that time her cousin, Jeanne Védère, came from Momères and caught her by surprise in the midst of her lambs. Bernadette told her about the Abbé Aravant's intervention with her master and what little success it had had. . . . 'Why didn't you tell your father?' asked her cousin. 'Oh, no!' replied the little shepherdess. 'I think God wishes it so. When you realize that God permits a thing, you do not complain.'

Under the Bartrès roof the season of long evenings round the lamp had come. These were spent in the kitchen. While winding her foster-mother's distaff or emptying the spindles, Bernadette glanced with shy envy in the direction of Denis, the eldest of the little Lagües, who was poring over his Catechism lessons which he would have to recite next day to the teacher. The mother, who was watching them, felt a pang of remorse; after all, one had no right to neglect this child's religious instruction!

She made up her mind: as the parish priest was no longer on hand, Marie Lagües would do her best to take his place. She took her little catechumen into the large bedroom and, though patience does not seem to have been her chief virtue, she pronounced each word slowly and made Bernadette repeat it. But the poor child was so tired at the end of the day's work! Her eyes were heavy with sleep. Not only had her memory become rusty, but she did not even understand so many expressions which were too abstract for her. . . . One of M. Ader's successors, M. Vergez, collected, at a much later date, Mme Lagües' memories of these Catechism lessons. 'Bernadette's foster-mother told me frequently that she herself taught Bernadette Catechism, and that on certain days she devoted herself to it from seven to nine in the evening, without managing to get her to remember one word of the book. Bernadette often wept, grieved at giving so much trouble. . . .' 'The same word had to be repeated to her three or four times, and still she did not remember it,' adds Jeanne-Marie Garros, 'so that her foster-mother would say to her; "You will never learn anything!" And, as if in despair, she would throw down the Catechism.' Then Bernadette, in tears, would fling her arms around her neck to ask her forgiveness.

Sleep, after that, was slow in coming. Anguish gripped the poor little shepherdess. No; to instruct her in religion her foster-mother could not take the place of a priest. Even when there was a priest at Bartrès, she hardly ever went to his Catechism classes. At Lourdes they would understand better. . . . Her real father and mother would be quite willing and would, in the end, agree to everything; their little Bernadette simply must make her First Communion. They would send her to hear the parish priest or his curate every time the future communicants met. And they would take her to the dear Sisters at the Hospice, who would surely be willing to spend their time teaching her to read. . . .

Aunt Bernarde, her godmother, came to see her in December, and Bernadette confided her ardent longing to her. But her godmother knew that they were in no hurry to bring her back to the 'dungeon', where there was nothing to share but poverty. Aunt Bernarde, however, failed to persuade her to remain patient.

A woman from Lourdes, passing near the heath shortly before Christmas, came to see the shepherdess among her lambs. 'I am tired of being here,' Bernadette admitted to her. 'Let my parents know and tell them, please, to come and take me home. I want to go back to Lourdes, so that I can join a class and prepare for my First Communion.'

*　　*　　*

Was the message delivered? Undoubtedly. All the same, the parents made no move.

In the second half of January 1858, the Lagües' servant told Bernadette that she was going to the town. 'Oh,' exclaimed the child, 'beg Mamma to come and fetch me.' As Louise Soubirous remained deaf to this entreaty, her daughter, reports Jeanne-Marie Garros, 'asked the master's leave to go to Lourdes. It was a Sunday. The master gave her permission, but told her at the same time to return to Bartrès next day. Bernadette did not reappear till the Wednesday. Questioned as to the reason for this delay, she replied, 'I must go back home. The parish priest is going to have the children prepared for First Communion, and if I go back to Lourdes, I shall make mine.' She left, in fact, the next day. That was in January 1858, and probably Thursday the 28th.

This year of 1858 was, for the whole of Christendom, an outstanding year, 'a Jubilee Year', a Holy Year.

In the course of 1857, Pope Pius IX, besides making a devout pilgrimage and giving fresh proof of his tender devotion to the Blessed Virgin Mary by visiting the Holy House of Loreto, devoted several months to visiting the chief towns of his States. Now, within the pontifical domain itself, the Pope-King was distressed to discover that, 'though the world of to-day contains much good, there remain also many evil elements that are in frenzied ferment and agitation. For this reason the Shepherd of the lambs and sheep asks the Christian world for public and solemn prayers . . . in order that in every quarter of the world good may triumph over evil.'

Bernadette left Bartrès, bearing with her the affection of the whole village. She greeted everyone so politely, showed such gratitude for the least kindness, and knew so well how to say 'thank you'. One could not help smiling at her, when she herself smilingly led her bleating little battalion to pasture. The people of Bartrès were soon to learn such extraordinary things about this little shepherdess that some would like to say that they had seen them foreshadowed, within the setting of their own hills, by earlier marvels, worthy of a new 'Golden Legend'.

Bernadette was just turned fourteen when she returned to Lourdes. She still looked no more than 'ten or eleven'—she had remained so small. Her face of olive complexion was 'fresh and plump'. The striped head-scarf of foulard left visible the braids of her fine and beautiful chestnut-brown hair. Her eyes were shadowed by long eye-lashes—'eyes of velvet', they have often been called, for they were 'very soft and gentle, deep-set beneath arching eye-brows', as a woman of her time carefully described them: 'eyes which were not absolutely black, as is repeatedly stated, but a deep brown, with a tint of blue-grey which I could not define exactly'. Her mouth was rather large, and her voice stronger than would be expected from a chest so delicate. It was already noticeable how careful she was to keep her clothes very neat and clean. They were of very ordinary material and were repaired in several places.

After embracing her family Bernadette cried out joyfully:

'Now at last I shall be able to go to school and Catechism! That's why I've come back!'

Never, perhaps, had there been such utter destitution at the 'dungeon'. Nevertheless, the father and mother gave their promise. The return of their first-born put an extra burden on their poverty, but they owed this reparation to a much-neglected child. Next day, Bernadette appeared at the Hospice school. This time it was in earnest. Sharing the secret of the touching motive that brought her back among them, the Sisters lost no time in enrolling her among the future communicants, who were following the Catechism lessons given in the Hospice by the Chaplain, Abbé Bertrand-Marie Pomian, the senior curate to the parish priest, M. Peyramale.

At Bartrès there had been wide-open country, where the air was crisp and pure and the sunshine was gay on the hill-sides, white with frost or golden with heather. Yet to Berna-dette at this moment they were not so dear as the narrow Rue des Petits-Fossés, the stuffy atmosphere and the black-grimed beams of the 'dungeon'. But in this wall of gloom there would open soon a portal of light.

The mercy of heaven had resolved to manifest itself to the world once again on the soil of France. But why did it choose this little girl from the very depths of misfortune and oblivion? Why not some other young maiden from among us, noble or not, rich or poor? There were girls of distinction, of far better education, of more refined upbringing, apparently even more devout. . . . It was the simplest, the humblest one who was chosen. . . . Let us recall the words: 'At fourteen, not know-ing how to read or write, a complete stranger to the French language and ignorant of the Catechism, Bernadette looked on herself as the most worthless child of her years.'

At the appointed hour a voice of exceeding sweetness con-firmed the eternal choice: 'This one!'

# II

## THE APPARITIONS

# 4

## HEAVEN VISITS EARTH

*(First Apparition: Thursday, February 11th, 1858)*

THURSDAY, February 11th, 1858, dawned over Lourdes like other winter days: there were no cheerful gleams of sunshine, but a veil of mist shrouded the town and the mountains. Even though the fog had partly lifted, the still air was cold and damp. All the same, it was a holiday for the schoolchildren and, though François Soubirous was tired and remained in bed that morning, the young Soubirous began running about as soon as it grew a little less dark in that wretched room.

Shortly before eleven o'clock the mother was making ready to go out. She had noticed on the previous evening that they were short of firewood. 'If it's fine to-morrow,' she had announced, 'I'll go and look for some wood.' She had her hand on the latch, when, through a passage-way connecting the Rue des Petits-Fossés with the Rue du Bourg, Jeanne Abadie appeared. Jeanne, a class-mate of Toinette at the Sisters', was sturdy and forward for her twelve years; impulsive, somewhat vindictive, a leader in games, she had inherited from her parents the nickname of 'Baloum'. She brought her little brother with her.

'Where are you off to, Louise?' she asked familiarly.

'To the wood,' replied the mother.

'We'll all go!' said Jeanne 'Baloum' decisively, staring hard at Bernadette and Toinette. For these two it was an unhoped-for chance of escaping from the gloom and getting a breath of fresh air.

'Oh, yes!' they shouted, 'we'll go. Can't we, Mamma?' And the thoughtful Bernadette added: 'We must take a basket too for bones, in case we find some.'

She had a slight cold. 'Bernadette,' her mother objected, 'I would much rather you didn't go out in this nasty weather.'

'But, Mamma,' remarked the former little shepherdess, 'this sort of weather never stopped me going out at Bartrès.'

'Very well, then! Off you go with Jeanne and Toinette, but you must take the cape.'

At the 'dungeon' they always spoke of *the* cape, for in fact they had only one. 'It was not a new cape,' pointed out Toinette, 'but an old white one, very much patched, and it had been bought at a second-hand shop opposite the church. Bernadette had washed it several times. We never bought anything new, and out of doors we wore only sabots.' (And they wore the sabots without stockings. But on account of her asthma, her mother made Bernadette wear stockings all through the bad weather.)

For the event that is to follow, we must hear in turn the recollections of Toinette, Jeanne and Bernadette herself, whose memory was to preserve so accurately even the smallest details of those unforgettable hours.

'While walking along,' Toinette recalled, 'we gathered some wood and bones. Before crossing the bridge, we saw below it an old woman nicknamed "Pigouno" (Magpie), who was doing some washing. She said to us: "What are you doing here in this bitter cold?"

'"We are looking for wood."

'"You should go into M. de Laffitte's meadow: he's been felling trees. You will find some there."'

Bernadette said 'No' for they might be arrested for stealing.

However, on the assurance of 'Pigouno' that bones and dead branches could be found over there, the responsible one of the trio agreed to leave the forest track and go into the meadow.

The Laffitte property, which was reached by a foot-bridge, formed an island—a triangle of green vegetation, planted with poplar and beech, enclosed on one side by a bend in the Gave, on the other by a canal whose current worked a saw-mill and a flour-mill, called Savy. A little below the mill, the Merlasse streamlet flowed into this canal. At the extreme point of the triangle, the canal rejoined the stream that fed it, by the base of a rocky promontory, the extension of the Béout and Espélugues massif, called in the dialect 'Massabieille'—pronounced to-day 'Massabielle'—i.e. 'Masse-vieille' (Old Hump).

It was the first time Bernadette Soubirous had ever entered these parts.

On this 11th day of February, 1858, the millstones and saws on M. de Laffitte's estate were idle: the mill was under repair and so the sluice, situated almost at the canal entrance, happened to be closed and there was practically no flow of water.

'I reckon,' stated the Savy miller, 'that the space left in front of the grotto at low water was about five yards.' At the entrance lay some scattered boulders. It was a wild, chaotic site.

To the right of the large cave, some three yards above the narrow bank, there was an oval recess. From this cavity 'the stems of several shrubs and the large branches of an eglantine forced their way out; they hung down very low along the rock,' to quote 'Samson' the pigman. In spring, the wild-rose bush was ablaze with white blooms. No large trees grew at the foot of the Massabielle rocks, but opposite, on the other side of the Gave, there was a row of tall poplars.

'We arrived in front of the grotto,' continued Jeanne Abadie. 'In the canal, the water was knee-deep.' The water was exceptionally low that day, as has been remarked, for the little Merlasse stream was supplying almost the whole flow itself. 'I saw a bone on the other side of the canal, in the hollow of the rock. . . . There were also, in the same spot, some branches brought down by the water.'

*   *   *

To reach the grotto, as the canal was still too wide to jump, they had to wade across between two sand-banks. Their faggots under their arms, Toinette and Jeanne flung their sabots over to the other bank and resolutely plunged their feet into that melted snow. Bernadette was watching them. Toinette had lifted up her skirt to her knees. Though there was not likely to be any prying man in this wilderness, the modest Bernadette called out to her, 'Lower your dress!'

It was so icy cold that it brought tears to the eyes of Jeanne and Toinette. Obedient to her mother's instructions, Bernadette did not dare to follow them. Yet it was essential for her to cross over to the grotto, for she did not want Toinette to go off alone with 'Baloum'. 'Throw some biggish stones into the water,' she implored Toinette. But it was a vain request, for Toinette, sitting on the sand, had wrapped her skirt round her feet to warm them up a little. But 'Baloum', thought Bernadette, would be strong enough to carry her on her back: 'Say, Jeanne, get me across the canal.' Back came the reply, cutting and punctuated with an oath in use among the quarry-workers: 'You can do the same as me; otherwise stay where you are.' The swear-word meant nothing on a child's lips, but Bernadette seemed shocked. 'Oh! Baloum,' she replied, 'if you want to swear, go somewhere else!'

Toinette and Jeanne had already started gathering bones and dead branches. Now they were beyond the grotto, well along the bank of the Gave. They were to remain out of sight for close on a quarter of an hour.

Bernadette was all alone.

Beyond the old castle, the clock in the church tower had struck twelve: the little one could not hear it at that distance and down in those depths. Then the Angelus rang out, and the heavens above were set praying.

Leaning against a boulder, a little to the right of the large cave, Bernadette had finally decided to take off her stockings: she was anxious to rejoin her companions.

And now was to begin that series of wonders for which unwittingly the predestined child had come—on this precise spot, and no other—a place which she had had no idea of going to . . . but where she was expected! We must, however, hear the account of it from those guileless lips that could never lie:

I had hardly begun to take off my stocking when I heard the sound of wind, as in a storm. I turned towards the meadow, and I saw that the trees were not moving at all. I had half-noticed, but without paying any particular heed, that the branches and brambles were waving beside the grotto.

I went on taking my stockings off, and was putting one foot into the water, when I heard the same sound in front of me. I looked up and saw a cluster of branches and brambles underneath the topmost opening in the grotto tossing and swaying to and fro, though nothing else stirred all round.

Behind these branches and within the opening, I saw immediately afterwards a girl in white, no bigger than myself, who greeted me with a slight bow of the head; at the same time, she stretched out her arms slightly away from her body, opening her hands, as in pictures of Our Lady; over her right arm hung a rosary.

I was afraid. I stepped back. I wanted to call the two little girls; I hadn't the courage to do so. I rubbed my eyes again and again: I thought I must be mistaken.

Raising my eyes again, I saw the girl smiling at me most graciously and seeming to invite me to come nearer. But I was still afraid. It was not however a fear such as I have had at other times, for I would have stayed there for ever looking at *her*: whereas, when you are afraid, you run away quickly.

Then I thought of saying my prayers. I put my hand in my pocket. I took out the rosary I usually carry on me. I knelt down and I tried to make the sign of the Cross, but I could not lift my hand to my forehead: it fell back.

The girl meanwhile stepped to one side and turned towards me. This time, she was holding the large beads in her hand. She crossed herself as though to pray. My hand was trembling. I tried again to make the sign of the Cross, and this time I could. After that I was not afraid.

I said my Rosary. The young girl slipped the beads of hers through her fingers, but she was not moving her lips.

While I was saying the Rosary, I was watching as hard as I could. She was wearing a white dress reaching down to her feet, of which only the toes appeared. The dress was gathered very high at the neck by a hem from which hung a white cord. A white veil covered her head and came down over her shoulders and arms almost to the bottom of her dress. On each foot I saw a yellow rose. The sash of the dress was blue, and hung down below her knees. The chain of the rosary was yellow; the beads white, big and widely spaced.

The girl was alive, very young and surrounded with light.

When I had finished my Rosary, she bowed to me smilingly. She retired within the niche and disappeared all of a sudden.

When questioned later, Bernadette was to give further details about the 'young girl' who had appeared:

A 'golden cloud' preceded her, she said, then the halo; the latter remained for an instant after she had disappeared. She herself was as if penetrated with a 'soft light', which neither hurt nor dazzled the eyes.

Her face was oval in shape, and 'of an incomparable grace', her eyes were blue, her voice 'Oh, so sweet!' Her hair scarcely showed through the veil on her forehead, and was clearly visible only at the temples. (Yet, in her transports of ecstasy, Bernadette never noticed its exact shade.)

Her bare feet rested, at the threshold of the niche, on a carpet of grass and twigs, which the child sometimes called *moss*. Her hands, when she kept them joined, were pressed together along their whole length, palm to palm. Her rosary, with its white beads widely spaced, was not, strictly speaking, a 'rosary': it had only five decades, the same as Bernadette's; the Vision and the visionary kept time with each other as they slipped the beads through their fingers. While they were doing so, the 'girl' of the grotto, at her first Apparition, did not move her lips except to smile; yet Bernadette would have occasion later to explain that although during the recitation of the *Pater* and *Ave* she seemed to listen without moving her lips, when they came to the *Gloria Patri* she bowed her head and visibly recited it.

This last detail, which the little one in her ignorance could not have invented, reveals an accurate and deep theological truth. The *Gloria*, which is a hymn of praise to the Adorable Trinity, and is Heaven's Canticle, is indeed the only part of the Rosary suitable for Her, whose name Bernadette would not learn for another month. The *Pater* is the prayer of needy mortals, tempted and sinful, on their journey to the Fatherland; as for the *Ave*, the Angel's greeting, this could be used only by the visionary, as the Apparition had no need to greet her own self.

What sort of features did she have, this mysterious maiden? What material were her dress and sash made of? Of what super-terrestrial metal, of what noble alabaster or opal, was this rosary composed, that was slipped over her right wrist—her solitary piece of jewellery? Why attempt to express the inexpressible? We must rest content with the simple words used by Bernadette—always so truthful—to describe the ineffable smile, that radiance of youth, of light and of beauty. 'I cannot explain these things to you,' she declared to the Lourdes police interrogator. 'What I can assure you of is that she is real and alive, that she moves, smiles and speaks just like us.' To Abbé Pène and his sister, Jacquette, who asked: 'Don't you know any lady as beautiful as she is?' she replied briefly: 'Oh, no. I've never seen anything so beautiful.' Much later, when she was awaiting death in a corner of the Infirmary, one of the nuns,

Mother Eléonore Cassagnes, brought a small girl of five to her, little Madeleine Darfeuille, another nun's niece, who, 'in a tone of great earnestness', put her a question truly unexpected from a child of that age: '*She* was lovely?' 'Oh, yes,' exclaimed Bernadette, 'so lovely that, when you have seen her once, you would willingly die to see her again!'

* * *

The vision had lasted the space of a Rosary, said without distractions and without hurry.

Toinette and Jeanne, having finished their collecting, caught a glimpse of Bernadette towards the end of her ecstasy. As the two of them were making their way back from the banks of the Gave towards the grotto, according to Toinette's evidence, they noticed her through the bare bushes 'still on her knees, looking towards the niche'.

I called out to her: 'Bernadette!' three separate times. She made no reply and did not turn her head.

On nearing the grotto, I twice threw a small stone at her. I hit her once on the shoulder; she didn't stir. She was white, as though she were dead. I was afraid. But Jeanne said to me: 'If she were dead, she would be lying down.' I wanted to cross over. . . .

All of a sudden, Bernadette became herself once more, and looked at us. I said to her: 'What are you doing there?'—'Nothing.'—'How stupid of you to pray there!'—'Prayers are good everywhere.' Then she crossed modestly over the canal.

Bernadette confided later to her cousin, Jeanne Védère: 'I was astonished, on entering the canal, to find the water warm rather than cold.'

Bernadette [continued Toinette] put on her stockings, sitting on a rock, and did not seem to be cold. . . . Then she said to us, 'Did you see anything?'—'No. And you, what did you see?'—'Nothing, then.'

Jeanne Abadie, in a hurry to get back home, went ahead of her companions, the basket of bones on her arm, and a bundle of wood on her head. Bernadette and her young sister divided their share of the wood into two other faggots. But, like Jeanne, they did not go back by the meadow; they climbed up the steep track to the top of Massabielle.  During this ascent, Bernadette seemed endowed with a surprising strength and agility.

> I was coming after her, my faggot on my head [attested her sister], but I couldn't climb up: I dropped my faggot three times.  When Bernadette had got her faggot up onto the road, she came back to fetch mine for me.  I said to her: 'I'm stronger than you, and I can't carry mine up! '

Even before recrossing the Pont-Vieux, Bernadette began to give vent to her exuberant wonder and joy; besides, the Apparition had not enjoined secrecy.  'I've seen,' she whispered, 'a lady dressed in white, with a blue sash and a yellow rose on each foot. . . .'

When they got up to Savy mill, the two sisters sat down a moment by the side of the road.  *'Mon Dieu!'* sighed Bernadette, 'how I should love to return to the bank of Massabielle! '

Between the Pont-Vieux and the Rue des Petits-Fossés, she hardly spoke.  Toinette noticed 'that her face was different, more serious; you saw that she was thinking about something.'

On reaching home, they both put their faggots down against the passage wall, beside the door, and Bernadette stayed there, afraid, no doubt, of having to be the first to give an explanation. Toinette then went into the room alone: their father was still in bed.  The mother asked the little one if all had gone well. She was told in reply that they had collected quite a lot of wood, that Jeanne 'Baloum' had spoken of going to sell the bones and, if Mamma allowed, they would go together to Alexine Baron's. Thereupon the mother hurriedly began to tidy Toinette's unruly curls.  Toinette was itching to tell her about the incident in the grotto, and, as if clearing her throat, began 'H'm! . . . h'm . . . ! ' to draw attention.

'What are you doing that for, Toinette? ' asked Mamma. 'Are you ill? '—'No. . . . But, listen, I'll tell you something that Bernadette's told me.'

> Bernadette was in the passage at the time, and I was against the window [stated Toinette].  I told Mother everything in a low voice.  When she had heard it all she exclaimed: 'Goodness me! What's that you're telling me? '  And she called Bernadette and questioned her angrily.

Bernadette did not deny that Toinette had told the truth. . . . But what was the meaning of these childish tales? Mother seized 'the rod she used for spreading the blankets when she made the beds'. Bernadette and Toinette, without being unduly alarmed—they were used to these minor chastisements—each received some strokes with the stick. 'It's your fault, Mother hitting me!' Toinette grumbled; Bernadette 'said nothing'.

In face of this silence, the mother calmed down. 'Your eyes must have been playing you tricks,' she suggested, thus opening, without suspecting it, a long, cautious and minute enquiry; 'You must have seen some white stone.'

'No,' replied Bernadette firmly, '*she* has a lovely face.' The humble visionary did not know yet what name to give the extraordinary visitor.

'We must pray to God,' continued the mother. 'Perhaps it's the soul of one of our relations in Purgatory.' Whereas the father, more matter-of-fact, growled from his bed at his elder daughter: 'So you are starting to make trouble already!' 'He thought,' explained Toinette, 'that this vision was something evil.'

There was a previous collection of bones still in the house. Towards half-past three Jeanne 'Baloum' brought along those they had collected at Massabielle. Before nightfall, she went out with Bernadette and Toinette to sell them at the ragpicker's. 'There was six sous' worth,' stated Jeanne. 'We went and bought a pound of bread and returned to the Soubirous' to eat it. It was then that I learnt what Bernadette had seen at the grotto.'

Thus, after a vision of Paradise during the ecstasy that lasted for the duration of a Rosary, the poor little 'dungeon' girl had dropped down to earth again. To all appearance there was no change in her poverty-stricken life; but all was changed in her heart.

'That same evening,' she told the chief of the urban police some days later, 'during family prayers, I began to cry.' When the prayers were over, Louise Soubirous demanded from her daughter a promise never to return to that grotto, the memory of which was having such an effect upon her: there was enough trouble at home already!

Bernadette promised.

# 5

## FROM MASSABIELLE TO SAVY MILL

*(Second Apparition: Sunday, February 14th)*

O N the Friday morning, February 12th, Bernadette
returned quietly to the Sisters' school. Jeanne Abadie
had not been able to hold her tongue and a number of
her little friends in the Rue du Bourg and the Rue des Petits-
Fossés were already aware of the extraordinary occurrence.
Several of the schoolgirls warned Bernadette that she would do
well to mention it to one of the nuns, who was at that moment
in the playground. 'But I can't speak French,' objected Bernadette. 'You tell Sister Damien about it.' Then, each adding her
bit, the schoolgirls reported what little they knew, interrupted
now and then by the visionary who grasped several words and
made corrections: 'I didn't say that, but this. . . .' Spontaneously she revealed her care for truth and accuracy.

The child was absolutely sincere: Sister Damien did not doubt
this for a moment. However, for fear of an illusion, she deemed
it prudent to give this advice: 'My dear little Bernadette, don't
talk about it; they'll make fun of you.' Sister Damien, with her
limited discernment, judged that this backward schoolgirl, who
had entered the school but a fortnight ago, had not sufficient
standing to establish the truth of so wonderful a fact in the eyes
of companions younger than herself, several of whom were
already treating her as a liar. The chemist's little daughter,
Sophie Pailhasson, aged nine, proved the most vicious among
the opposition: she 'greeted Bernadette's story with a slap on
the face', a thoughtless act to be bitterly regretted later.

That Friday morning, on coming out from Mass, the Brothers
of Christian Instruction of Ploërmel, who conducted the communal Boys' School, got wind of the story. They were not slow
in acquiring fuller information.

*Viron*

François Soubirous, Bernadette's father, at about age 60. He was 35 at the time of his marriage. François was a simple man of gentle disposition, earnest and upright, who faithfully fulfilled his religious duties.

48-1

Louise Casterot, Bernadette's mother. Louise was 17 at the time of her marriage. Between François and Louise there were never any quarrels; perfect harmony prevailed. Louise bore nine children, five of whom died in childhood; she was quick to correct her children's slightest faults. Both parents loved their children and imparted to them their own solid faith. Louise died at age 41.

*Viron*

*Above:* Boly Mill, where Bernadette was born on January 7, 1844, the eldest of nine children, in the room on the upper floor at the extreme right. Through the yard, in front on the right, flows the stream which turned the mill to grind the flour.

*Below:* The baptismal font where Bernadette's soul was cleansed of Original Sin and where she became a child of God, two days after her birth. She was baptized "Marie Bernarde Soubirous," but was always

48-2

*von Matt*

known by the diminutive, "Bernadette." When the baptismal party returned home bringing Bernadette back to her mother, Louise kissed her child's brow, in reverence for the grace of her Baptism.

The "cachot," or "dungeon," a dark one-room former jail where the Soubirous family were living at the time of the apparitions, having come to the end of their financial resources. The crucifix and rosary show from where the family obtained their spiritual strength for daily life.   48-3

*Above:* The grotto of Massabielle in 1858, the year the Blessed Virgin Mary appeared 18 times to 14-year-old Bernadette Soubirous. In front of the grotto flows the Savy millstream just before it joins the River Gave.
*Left:* An engraving of Bernadette in ecstasy before the Blessed Virgin Mary.

This early photograph may be a picture of Bernadette herself kneeling in front of a statue in the grotto; authorities today are undecided on this point. At one apparition, Our Lady said to Bernadette, "Pray to God for sinners!" At another, Bernadette was heard to gasp and repeat: "Penance ... penance ... penance!" Our Lady also requested a chapel and processions, and she directed Bernadette to the discovery of a miraculous spring in the grotto. She finally identified herself thus: "I am the Immaculate Conception." This was only three years after Pope Pius IX had defined the dogma of her Immaculate Conception.

48-5

*Bernadou*

This is one of the earliest photographs of St. Bernadette, taken when she was about 16 years old. Everyone who questioned Bernadette about the apparitions was struck by her sincerity, straightforwardness, and truthfulness.

Viron

The Abbé Peyramale, parish priest of Lourdes at the time of the apparitions. This priest, quite a fearsome personage to Bernadette and many of the parishioners, was at first skeptical and extremely gruff with Bernadette when she came to him to report the words of the Lady in the grotto. But after not too long, the Abbé became a staunch believer. This photograph was taken much later than the time of the apparitions.

48-7

*Billard-Perin*

Two photographs of Bernadette. At the third apparition, the Blessed Virgin said to her: "I do not promise you happiness in this world, but in the next." Bernadette described Our Lady as being very young and very beautiful—"so lovely that, when you have seen her once, you would willingly die to see her again!"

*Viron*

Two more photographs of Bernadette, at about age 20 (right) and 22 (left). A priest theologian said of her: "What impressed you on seeing her was an air of candor, innocence, modesty and reserve that completely enveloped her and radiated from her through her eyes, her attitude and her bearing. It was the common opinion that she had kept her baptismal innocence . . . and had retained in all its loveliness, freshness and fragrance the lily of virginity." In the picture on the left, Bernadette is wearing the white capulet which she had worn during the apparitions. This had been purchased from a used-clothes dealer.

*Dufour*

*Above:* Bernadette praying. Bernadette performed the ordinary Catholic devotions extraordinarily well—including the Sign of the Cross, which she made slowly and reverently, with a kind of majesty. After she had entered the convent, she admonished a fellow novice: "You make the Sign of the Cross badly; you must see to that, for it is important to make it well."

*Right:* Bernadette and Mother Alexandrine Roques, superior at the Hospice of the Sisters of Nevers in Lourdes where Bernadette lived for several years as a boarding pupil before joining the Order herself.

*Billard-Perin*

*Billard-Perin*

*Above:* Bernadette and the sisters of the Hospice. One of the trials of Bernadette's life there was speaking with the continual stream of visitors who came to hear about the apparitions.

*Below:* Bernadette and the Children of Mary in Lourdes before Bernadette left for the convent in Nevers; they are forming a "chain" of unity by holding hands. When she left Lourdes, Bernadette wrote to the Abbé Peyramale, asking him not to strike her name from the roll of the Children of Mary; she remained a member all her life.

48-13

*Billard-Perin*

## MANDEMENT

### MONSEIGNEUR L'ÉVÊQUE DE TARBES

PORTANT

Jugement sur l'Apparition qui a eu lieu

À LA

### GROTTE DE LOURDES.

BERTRAND-SÉVÈRE LAURENCE, par la Miséricorde
Divine et la grâce du Saint-Siège Apostolique, Évê-
que de Tarbes, assistant au Trône Pontifical, etc.

Au clergé et aux fidèles de notre diocèse, salut et
bénédiction en Notre-Seigneur Jésus-Christ.

À toutes les époques de l'humanité, Nos Bien-Aimés
Coopérateurs et Nos Très-Chers Frères, de merveilleuses
communications se sont établies entre le Ciel et la

1                                                    41

*von Matt*

*Left:* First page of the "Decree of Monseigneur the Bishop of Tarbes Passing Judgment on the Apparition which took place at the Grotto of Lourdes." In this document the Bishop stated his judgment that Mary Immaculate had indeed appeared to Bernadette, though he also stated his humble submission to the Supreme Pontiff in this matter. Further, the Bishop authorized in his diocese the veneration of Our Lady of the Grotto of Lourdes, and he proposed to build a sanctuary there, as Our Lady had requested.

*Below:* Bernadette's copy of the *Catechism or Summary of the Christian Truths,* adopted by Msgr. Bertrand-Severe Lawrence, Bishop of Tarbes, to be the sole standard in his diocese.

*von Matt*

48-14

*Above:* Bishop Lawrence of Tarbes, in whose diocese Lourdes was situated. It was his responsibility to make a judgment on the apparitions. After an investigation of two years, he proclaimed his verdict on January 18, 1862.

A few samples of the many pictures of Bernadette which circulated widely among Lourdes pilgrims during Bernadette's lifetime. She exclaimed: "I am on sale for two sous [ten cents] at every street corner!" Then she added simply and sincerely, "It's all I am worth."

48-16

I had in my class Jean-Marie Soubirous, Bernadette's brother, [attested Brother Léobard Bourneuf]. The first Apparition occurred on a Thursday. Next morning, when Jean-Marie came into class, I said to him: 'Tell your sister, will you, I should like to see her.' And Bernadette came the same day in the afternoon. She gave me an account of what had taken place at the grotto.

It is inconceivable that no rumour of a vision should have reached the ears of the parochial clergy by early Friday morning. Be that as it may, the next day, although there were large numbers at Abbé Pomian's confessional on account of the Forty Hours, Bernadette, advised no doubt by her mother or the Sisters, appeared there also. It was towards the end of the day. She told the priest what had happened to her at Massabielle. Her confessor made no comment on the story, nor raised any objection. He merely advised this poverty-stricken little girl, who was confiding such an astounding thing to him in her patois, to mention it to the Parish Priest. Bernadette was afraid and preferred him to mention it first. So that evening the question was raised in the Presbytery.

M. Pomian stated the case impartially. M. Peyramale, a man of authority, who strongly claimed, and justly so, the right to keep his eye on everything that concerned religion in his parish, seemed surprised that this senior curate, whose 'zeal and sound understanding' he appreciated, should have paid attention to such childishness. During Sunday morning, the second and third curates were informed of everything: Abbé Serres, little inclined to the mystical, burst into laughter; Abbé Pène, a young priest of twenty-five, just recently arrived in the parish, would have liked to chance some comments but he thought it wise to hold his tongue. . . . When M. Pomian was asked to describe this child, who had told him her name was Bernadette Soubirous and that she lived in the miserable Rue des Petits-Fossés, he had to admit that he had caught only a very vague glimpse of her in the confessional and was quite incapable of recognizing her, even on the Catechism benches, where he had not yet picked her out or questioned her.

*     *     *

On that Shrove Sunday, which good parishioners—and the Soubirous were such—preferred to call Forty Hours' Sunday, a dozen or so of the Sisters' pupils on leaving church after High Mass surrounded Bernadette. Bernadette knew very well why all these young friends were crowding round her: she had confided to Toinette her longing to return to the grotto this Sunday, and Toinette had let things out. But she still remained reticent: 'I should very much like to,' she pointed out to her class-mates, 'but I daren't ask Mamma.'

Soon the whole troop were to be seen in the 'dungeon' passage. 'Mother was unwilling,' says Toinette in her account. 'She ended by saying: "Go and ask your Father." We went to the Cazenaves'. Father was in the stable.' François Soubirous, who was busy grooming the relay horses, met Bernadette's request with a categorical 'no'. 'Let the little one go,' M. Cazenave said to him quietly; 'if what she sees carries a rosary, it can't be anything evil.' The father made an evasive gesture . . . but 'silence gives consent'.

Satisfied, the group of youngsters ran off to inform the mother that the ban on going to the grotto was lifted. According to Mme Hillot, it was in the Rue des Petits-Fossés that her daughter, Marie, got the idea of taking along some Holy Water. 'What shall we do,' Toinette had said, 'if it is something evil?' And so they took a small bottle from the 'dungeon', which they went and filled at the Holy Water stoup in the church. Then they proceeded by the Rue du Baous and the Chemin de la Forêt towards Massabielle. On the way, some other schoolgirls, among them Marie Labayle and Cyprine Gesta, joined Jeanne Abadie who had fallen behind a little. 'There were about twenty of us, all poor,' Toinette humbly specified, 'and a little bigger than me.' Thus, they were walking in two separate groups, somewhat anxious as to what was going to happen but not daring to say so, curious only to discover whether or not Bernadette had told the truth. In this way was improvised the very first pilgrimage to the grotto of Massabielle.

Bernadette, who was leading, went down the zigzags of the slope at an extraordinary speed; but her companions descended slowly, clutching the bushes. 'When we reached the grotto at the bottom,' Toinette continued, 'she was already on her knees. She made us kneel down and take out our beads.'

Towards the end of the first decade of the Rosary, Bernadette exclaimed: 'Look! A bright light!' Then, after a moment's silence, she began again in a loud voice, imagining that her companions were favoured with the same vision: 'Look at her . . . She has her rosary slipped over her right arm. . . . She's looking at us.' The girls questioned one another; not one of them perceived anything.

But Bernadette was on her feet again. Bracing her small figure, she took a few paces towards the mysterious being, near enough to touch the eglantine. 'If you come from God,' she enjoined, 'then stay!' And vigorously she sprinkled the rock with Holy Water.

Not merely did *she* not go away, but by a smile affirmed that *she* 'came from God'. Reassured, Bernadette came back and knelt among her companions.

Silent, motionless, she kept her eyes fixed intently on the point where *she* appeared. Marie Hillot and her companions had just started another decade of the Rosary when a stone fell from the top of Massabielle and, before rebounding into the canal, it struck the big boulder against which Bernadette was leaning. She gave a start; then, with her hands joined on her beads, her head and shoulders stretched forwards, her whole face astonishingly pale but not livid, she remained with her eyes riveted on the niche, above the eglantine. 'She's dead!' cried several of the schoolgirls, incapable of recognizing in this suspension of the senses the marvel of ecstasy.[1]

At that moment along came Jeanne Abadie with the other group of schoolgirls. It was she who had imprudently flung the stone, which had just caused such alarm in front of the grotto, in order to show her displeasure at their not waiting for her. 'Oh! Jeanne,' shouted the others, 'you've killed Bernadette!' But Jeanne realized that Bernadette, kneeling up like that, could not be dead. 'Her face,' she reported, 'was lit up. All the girls were crying. So was I.'

They all began discussing how to help poor Bernadette. They shouted her name at her, they shook her. Bernadette remained as if unconscious, but she was still smiling. They decided to carry her away. 'We could not manage it,' continues Jeanne Abadie's account, 'the slope presented too many difficulties.' Yet there was no other way out! The canal, now in full flood, was uncrossable.

Trembling and frantic at the thought of seeing their little

[1] Cf. p. 387.

friend die, several of these schoolgirls climbed the flank of Massabielle and dashed towards Savy mill; while Jeanne, leaving Toinette beside her sister, ran without stopping the whole way to the 'dungeon' and warned the Soubirous.

It was about 12.45 p.m. Mme Nicolau was strolling with her sister, Anne-Marie, near the mill. They agreed to go down to the grotto, and they tried in their turn to get Bernadette away. But in vain. Suddenly it occurred to the miller's wife that her son, Antoine, a strapping big fellow of twenty-eight, would be able to manage it. So the two women returned to the mill, where Antoine was getting ready to go to the town to join in the Shrovetide revels.

Here, in all its frank simplicity, is his pathetic but magnificent testimony:

'Bernadette Soubirous,' they told me, 'is at the grotto' [of Massabielle]. 'We don't know what she sees. We can't drag her away. Come and help us.'

Bareheaded and without a jacket, I at once followed my mother and aunt, and went down by the wretched little path to the grotto. On arriving there, I saw three or four poor girls, Toinette Soubirous and Bernadette.

The latter was on her knees, deathly pale, her eyes wide open and fixed on the niche. She had her hands joined and her beads between her fingers. Tears were streaming from both her eyes. She was smiling and her face was lovely, lovelier than anything I've ever seen. It made me feel both happy and sad, and all day long my heart was moved at the thought of it.

I remained for a time motionless, watching her. The girls were watching her like me; my mother and aunt were also spell-bound . . .

In spite of her smile, I was grieved to see her so pale. At length I went up to her, for my mother said to me: 'Take hold of her, and we'll bring her home with us.'

I took her by the right arm. She struggled to stay. Her eyes remained fixed upwards. Not a murmur. But, after the struggles, a somewhat hurried breathing. I lifted her by one arm, then by the other; my mother took one arm. While lifting her, I wiped her eyes and put my hand in front of them to prevent her seeing. I tried also to make her bend her head; but she raised it again and re-opened her eyes, with the smile. . . .

We had great difficulty in getting her to climb the path, my mother holding one hand and I the other, both of us pulling in front, and my aunt and the girls following behind. She was trying hard to go down again, without however saying a word. It took a great effort to drag her along: strong as I am, it would have been heavy work, had I been alone.

All the way up, her face [Bernadette's] remained deathly pale, and her eyes still wide open and fixed upwards.

I was sweating when we reached the top.

We went down by the wood road as far as the mill, leading the child in the same manner, my mother and I together. Mother questioned her and so did I; she made no answer. I was sad and afraid. Her face and eyes remained the same as at the grotto. Tears trickled down continuously. I again put my hand now and then in front of her eyes and dried her tears. She never stopped smiling until she reached the mill.

As we went in, on the very threshold, she lowered her eyes and head and the colour came back to her face. We took her into the kitchen and made her sit down. The girls had come in with us. When she was seated, I said to her: 'What do you see in that hole? Do you see something not very nice?' She said: 'Oh, no! I see a very lovely lady. She has a rosary on her arm and her hands are joined.'

While saying this, Bernadette pressed the palms of her hands together.

Afterwards I went off to town and called on her godmother [Aunt Bernarde], who keeps an inn. I told her the whole affair and she said: '*Mon Dieu!* What can the little one be thinking of, going down there?'

Between the flinging of the stone by the impulsive Jeanne Abadie and the arrival at Savy mill, Bernadette was therefore transported out of herself—not in a fainting fit, seeing that she was both smiling and weeping; nor in a cataleptic trance, for, instead of being reduced to the immobility of a corpse, she walked and struggled against being dragged away from the grotto—but she was in an ecstasy. For her, time and space no longer existed: she would not have been able to say whether the vision lasted an hour or a minute; when she came out of it, gently, without shock, she was astonished to find herself in the house of the Nicolaus. Up to that moment, the Apparition had been unceasingly present to her, whether it was that the ecstasy continued in spite of the departure from the grotto, or that the Lady moved in step with Bernadette, soaring up the slope, then over the plateau of Massabielle, only to disappear on the threshold of Savy mill.

Then only did Bernadette regain contact with this poor world below: almost at once she received a very clear proof of this. Louise Soubirous appeared, housewife's rod in hand, flanked by a neighbour, Cyprine Gesta, and by Jeanne Abadie; and she was not one to trifle when her offspring went astray! The assembly she discovered on arrival increased her vexation. 'There was already a millful of people,' reported Cyprine Gesta; obviously some inquisitive folk had met the visionary and her distressed escort between Massabielle and Savy. 'We found Bernadette sitting a little way from the fire,' continued Cyprine; 'tears were falling from her eyes.'

Louise began to scold her daughter in that patois, the niceties of which a mere translation renders very imperfectly: 'You little scamp! What do you mean by making everyone run after you?' Jeanne Abadie noticed how calm Bernadette remained. 'But, Mamma,' she returned in a subdued voice, 'I never told anyone to follow me.'

The mother raised her fist. 'Louise, what are you doing?' expostulated the miller's wife. 'Why strike her? Your daughter is an angel from Heaven!'

At these words the mother sank into a chair and burst into tears.

Then she took Bernadette by the hand, and together they returned to the 'dungeon'.

Meanwhile the rumour of extraordinary happenings at Massabielle was spreading in Lourdes; especially as on that Shrove Sunday afternoon there were unusual crowds of people everywhere in the town, who had come in from the farms and villages to join the merry-making. Already, before noon, Bernadette's 'fairly numerous retinue' had been 'particularly noticed by everyone who saw these young girls, full of excitement and lively determination.' By the evening, it was a very different matter. At the inn, which was crowded with customers, Antoine Nicolau had talked: so had the schoolgirls among their families. Before night, five miles from Lourdes the Curé of Omex and his housekeeper heard the first echoes of this strange news brought by Jacquette Poueymari and Antoine Primou, who, on their way towards Savy mill, had come across Bernadette and her escort in tears. It was the same in many other villages.

# 6

## PROMISE OF HAPPINESS

### (*Third Apparition: Thursday, February 18th*)

LOUISE SOUBIROUS did not relent for long. Her sister, Basile, came to see her. 'Louise, I implore you,' she begged, 'do keep your daughter at home.' And turning to Bernadette: 'You'll be making us ill with all the trouble we have, hearing people talk about you,' added the excitable young aunt.

'Depend on it, Basile,' declared the father, 'our daughter's not going to Massabielle again.'

The affair was settled then . . . once more!

When Bernadette reappeared at school on the Monday morning, February 15th, the Sister on duty took her to the Superior of the Hospice, to whom she related her vision of the previous day. For the second time she had the painful surprise of hearing these good nuns, in whom she placed all her trust, tell her in the same pitying tone: 'Put it all out of your head, my dear; it's an illusion.' All the same, she went off at once to join in the games of her companions.

On Tuesday the 16th, shortly after noon, the maid of a certain Mme Millet, who also lived in the Rue des Petits-Fossés and in whose house Louise Soubirous sometimes went to work, came and asked her to send Bernadette to her mistress. How could she refuse Mme Millet? The latter had just confided to Mlle Peyret, daughter of the Lourdes bailiff, and employed by her as a sewing-maid: 'I'll send for Bernadette and question her to see if she is telling lies.'

'Mme Millet, formerly a servant, but now fairly well off through her marriage with her last employer', was a devout woman, but slightly common, suspicious and 'boastful' and she had been affected in her own way by the rumours about Massabielle. 'What! that poor little creature . . . !' So she wanted to know all about it.

Obligingly, Bernadette called at her house on the way back to school. Mlle Peyret, who had been engaged for four days' sewing, Monday to Thursday, had not arrived. The cross-examination over, the schoolgirl departed.

For Mlle Peyret's benefit, Mme Millet reproduced Bernadette's story to the best of her ability. But, meanwhile, the lady's suspicions were being aroused: this young Soubirous, to be sure, had not the appearance of a liar; but why not make sure, on the spot, at Massabielle itself, whether or not she was telling the truth? . . . In the evening, when Mlle Peyret had returned home, Mme Millet made her way very stealthily along the Rue des Petits-Fossés.

Bernadette was at home; so were her father and mother, who both informed Mme Millet of their firm decision: no, their daughter was never going to that grotto again! No doubt, pointed out their visitor, they would have to be very cautious and not allow Bernadette to take the road to Massabielle in broad daylight among a noisy group of youngsters. But what harm was there in her going down there before daybreak in the care of responsible people like Mme Millet or Mlle Peyret? . . . It seemed difficult to go against their wishes, and the Soubirous gave way.

On the next day but one—Thursday, February 18th—shortly after 5.30 a.m., the two women knocked on the Soubirous' door. The mother had already gone off to do a day's washing at Mlle Fanny Nicolau's. Bernadette answered from within; she was not yet up. She dressed hurriedly and appeared in the doorway. 'I caught sight of her then for the first time,' states Antoinette Peyret. The bell was ringing for the first Mass. They went straight to the church, and after hearing Mass, they went out without a word into the fog. Mme Millet had a blest candle hidden under her long cloak; Mlle Peyret carried in her pocket a sheet of white paper, and a pen and ink-pot borrowed from her father's desk. On the way, she explained to her companions that she had provided herself with these articles 'in order to get the Apparition to write down her wishes at Bernadette's request'.

I had thought [she said later] that, as a lady was appearing in a white dress, with a blue sash and a rosary, it was our President of the Children of Mary, Elisa Latapie, who had died only a few months before; we had, in fact, a medal with a blue ribbon and we used to carry our rosaries on our wrist on the day of consecration and at funerals. I was thinking that, if she needed our prayers, she would write down her request . . .

Later, another compatriot of Bernadette's, Julie Garros, asked her 'whether the clothes [of the Apparition] resembled the uniform of the Lourdes Sodality'. She answered: 'As to the dress, sash and veil, there's no resemblance at all.' But Mlle Peyret had kept to the details of clothing as given her by Mme Millet, who had very possibly confused ribbon with sash.

Then [continued Mlle Peyret], we took the Massabielle road. . . . At the beginning of the path that led to the grotto, Bernadette took the lead and, running along this slope, she disappeared like a flash of lightning. As for ourselves, we had to squat on our heels and got down there only with the greatest difficulty.

How silent it was, that morning, in this wild glen! There was Bernadette on her knees between her two companions, Mme Millet on her right and on her left Mlle Peyret, who lit the candle (the first that had ever shone in front of Massabielle) and placed it, sheltered from the breeze, against a rock.

All three had taken out their rosary beads. Bernadette, with her eyes turned towards the eglantine, had fallen into profound recollection. Suddenly she exclaimed: 'There she is!' 'Be quiet!' Mme Millet boldly ordered her, still incredulous and, no doubt, vexed at perceiving nothing. 'Let's say the Rosary,' suggested Mlle Peyret.

Bernadette agreed. There was no apparent change in her: she was gazing at the Apparition, and this time she did not seem to leave the earth in spirit; externally there was nothing in her features or in her eyes that indicated ecstasy. That morning she was to be the intermediary between two worlds and so, for the intercommunication of one to the other, she was to remain free in her movements: she would act with perfect ease and lucidity, the opposite to hallucination, with its fixed stare and automaton's actions.

As the Rosary was not being recited in common, Antoinette Peyret, her lips moving rapidly, was the first to finish the five decades. 'Go and ask the Lady what she wants,' she told the child, who had not taken her eyes off the niche above the wild-rose bush. Holding the ink-pot, pen and paper handed to her by Mlle Peyret, Bernadette rose, stepped forward and almost grazed the drooping branches of the eglantine. But suddenly she swerved and made towards the grotto. The two women guessed that she wanted to place the ink-pot on the table-shaped stone that stood almost in the centre. 'We were making ready to follow her,' related Mlle Peyret, 'and we had already taken two or three steps behind her, when, without turning round, she made a sign to us with her right hand to retire, and we drew back behind the fold of the rock to the foot of the path, where we knelt down.' From this position, as day was now breaking, they were still able to watch Bernadette.

The two women saw her stand on tip-toe, holding out pen and paper. Therefore the Lady must have graciously drawn nearer the child in order to be within easier reach. 'Bernadette stated afterwards that she had spoken to the Apparition,' attested Antoinette Peyret, 'but we did not hear her voice.' The reason was that, even in an incomplete ecstasy such as this one, Berna-dette's voice did not reach the outside: at times, merely the movement of her lips was seen; yet, 'feeling herself to be speak-ing', she imagined she was heard by those present. 'I was speaking very loud, just as now,' she explained many times to such as questioned her about her conversations with the Lady of Massabielle.

What had happened? Let us hear the visionary herself:

While I was moving forward, the Lady drew back as though retiring to her own private chamber. so that while placing my articles on a rock I saw her in front of me. . . . She made me a sign that I was to stay and the others were to retire. 'Madame,' I then said, 'would you be so kind as to write down your name?' For the first time, I heard her voice.

To Abbé Pène, the curate in Lourdes, who asked her soon afterwards whether she heard the Apparition's voice distinctly, she made this touching reply: 'Oh, yes! Most clearly. Only it seems to me the sound of her voice reaches me *here*.' While saying this, she placed her hand on her breast.

'The conversations between the Apparition and Bernadette,'

as has been explained, 'were therefore chiefly colloquies of the soul, colloquies of the heart, with an impression produced in the imagination, of the true sound and the actual tone of both voices.' But it is very difficult to explain such a mystery in human language.

The Apparition did therefore speak, and in the Lourdes dialect. Her reply was negative. At once, Bernadette went and communicated it to her two companions, for these women were thirsting to know! They got up at her approach.

'She began to laugh,' Bernadette explained, 'and said, "There is no need to write down what I have to say."'

'Go again,' begged Mme Millet, 'and ask if we may come back.' Had M. Millet's widow suddenly remembered that there was a time when she had been somewhat slandered in her district? Possibly. Such a memory was bound to disquiet her: suppose Bernadette did really see someone and hear something from the other world! . . . A weight was lifted off her mind when the child came back with the reply: 'There is nothing to prevent your coming.' The two women came up close again, and, kneeling down, resumed their *Aves*.

Standing in front of the boulder, Bernadette was listening again: for the second time the 'very gentle voice' spoke.

'Will you do me the favour of coming here for a fortnight?'

'After asking permission from my parents, I will come,' agreed Bernadette. Then to make it very clear to the little pauper girl of the Lourdes 'dungeon' that she would have to come with complete disinterestedness, without hope of any human favour or of any vain, fleeting worldly delight—but what was that for the devout child in comparison with a happiness unlimited and unending?—the Apparition added: 'I do not promise to make you happy in this world, but in the next.'

'When she had said that, she rose towards the roof, and disappeared.'

In the simplest possible manner Bernadette came back and knelt down between her companions, and all three prayed for some moments. Before getting up again, the young visionary leant towards Mlle Peyret and whispered: '*It* looked at you smiling.' 'But,' the cautious Child of Mary was to admit, 'I did not at the time believe in the reality of these visions. On our way back to Lourdes, just as we had done while going down to the grotto, we kept saying to Bernadette: "Beware! If you're telling lies, God will punish you."' It is not known whether the child protested her sincerity: probably she kept silence, still wholly absorbed by the Apparition's words and the tender promise she herself had just made, confident that the truth would one day assuredly shine forth.

What is more, unexpected as was the meeting, she kept perfectly calm when she saw her mother coming towards her along one of the streets. Louise Soubirous, while doing her washing, had told Mlle Nicolau how Bernadette was to return to Massabielle that morning in the care of absolutely reliable people. 'What's that you say, Louise?' protested the teacher. 'Why do you let the little girl go like this to the grotto? You're in for trouble with the Commissioner.'

The way Mlle Nicolau said that! Police Commissioner! Hadn't Bernadette's father appeared before him last year for a a mere nothing? And now, because she went and said her prayers in front of a lonely grotto, far from the centre of Lourdes, what fresh trouble could this dreadful M. Jacomet cause? What would François think? . . . Her heart was in her mouth. Flinging down the beater, off she ran to the Petits-Fossés: Bernadette had left there hours ago. The mother dashed off to Massabielle to find her again.

Mme Millet had no difficulty in calming her: what would the Commissioner be doing here? Nobody, on the way there or back, had bothered about Bernadette: no disorder then to fear down there, and so, no interference by the police. The little girl was not wrong in promising to return there. . . .

'For another fortnight,' explained Bernadette. 'You'll be quite willing, Mother, won't you?' She repeated the Apparition's request and what she had promised her. Mme Millet insisted: 'Louise, let the little one go. I'll go with her, and you come too. We shall pass unnoticed, for we shall go very early again to-morrow morning, and your daughter won't miss school.' Louise did not dare say no.

Mme Millet added that, if the mother had no objection to trusting her with her daughter all that day, she would see to it that she had a rest in her house, away from the noisy games of her sister and little brothers. Bernadette would take her meals at her table along with Mlle Peyret, and at night would have a good, comfortable bed. . . . Louise, now herself once more, agreed to everything.

But, while these four were busy talking, people were on their way to market. A little later, Louise, who had returned to Mlle Nicolau's, failed to notice people from the country mingled with townsfolk making their way down from Marcadal Square towards the Chemin du Bois; during that morning's marketing, the news had spread. 'The weather was glorious,' the sun having dispersed the fog quite early. Many people wanted to see the unknown grotto where such strange things were reported to be happening; someone was appearing there from Heaven or from Purgatory—they were not too sure which! . . . Before noon, the rumour ran round that the Apparition was to be repeated again for a whole fortnight starting from the next day.

The excited chatter, the unusual movement of people in the direction of Massabielle, had not escaped the gendarmes posted, as was usual every market Thursday, on Marcadal Square or along the adjoining streets. They questioned, from time to time, any passers-by who looked more ready to talk. On their return to barracks, they made a first report: at once the case seemed serious to Sergeant d'Angla, who, without delay, informed the Lieutenant of Argelès, M. Bourriot. The latter, in his turn, immediately on being warned (Saturday, February 20th), sent a despatch to M. Renault, Major of Gendarmerie at Tarbes.

# 7

## THE 'FORTNIGHT' BEGINS

*(From the Fourth to the Sixth Apparition: Friday, February 19th, Saturday 20th, Sunday 21st)*

As sure of the reality of the previous visions as of her own existence, Bernadette never doubted for an instant that the first appointment of the hallowed fortnight was fixed for the very next day after the third Apparition, namely Friday, February 19th.

This little girl of fourteen felt perfectly assured. Some of the Hospice or school sisters—incredulous at first—vainly taunted her with, 'Ask the Lady, then, to help you learn your Catechism'; the child, with her innate common sense, perceived that there was no connection whatever; she was already adopting the attitude she would most frequently maintain in face of misunderstandings, quibbles, abuse and pointless remarks: this was a polite silence, accentuated at times by a sad smile.

Regarding the events of this fortnight, the ecclesiastical Commission, charged by Bishop Laurence with a first enquiry, left only this extremely brief summary:

Bernadette was faithful to her appointment: she went most punctually to the grotto for a fortnight. She always obtained the same favours there, except on two days when the Apparition did not appear.

But from now on she was accompanied by an ever increasing crowd. When she had the happiness of seeing the Vision, she forgot everything: she no longer noticed what was taking place around her: she was entirely absorbed.

Bernadette usually saw the Vision in the opening mentioned above; sometimes in a winding passage of the grotto, farther within; always in white, with a blue sash and an enchantingly beautiful face.

Fortunately, we have other more immediate and more circumstantial evidence regarding this ever memorable fortnight.

On the morning of Friday, February 19th, along with Mme Millet, at whose house she had spent the night, Bernadette had heard the first Mass. The weather was bitterly cold, and her temporary guardian had placed a small black hood over the child's white cape. At the 'dungeon' the mother was waiting for her Bernadette to return from church, fully resolved to accompany her in future to Massabielle, as long as was necessary. Standing by the door, ready to follow them, were a few other women, among them Josèphe Ouros, wife of Baringue the shoemaker.

At daybreak they made their way into the Rue du Baous—now known as the Rue de la Grotte. As agreed, they tapped on Aunt Bernarde's window. She appeared, holding in her hand the Child of Mary's candle belonging to Aunt Lucile—for 'you certainly needed some blest object down there'.

Aunt Bernarde, who was going there for the first time, was amazed to see her godchild, nimble as a young mountain goat, 'go bounding towards the bank of the Gave down that sort of path through the undergrowth'. When they caught up with her again, she was 'kneeling on the slope of earth and sand that goes down to the canal'. They lit the candle and Bernadette held it in her left hand; with the right she was already telling her beads. At the third Hail Mary she entered into ecstasy.

As soon as the Apparition appeared [reported Josèphe Baringue], her smile became lovely and her countenance changed. She gave a greeting with her hand and head. It was a delight to see her. It was as if she had done nothing else all her life but learn how to bow.

Aunt Bernarde also noticed Bernadette's 'bows and smiles, and from time to time a very slight movement of the lips. . . . To see her face like that, brought tears to your eyes'.

There were, indeed, some touching moments during this fourth Apparition. Around Bernadette, who 'seemed to belong no more to this world', or rather, white as her candle, seemed ready to leave this world, all the women had risen to their feet. 'How lovely she is like that!' cried one of them. 'She's dying,' exclaimed another. 'Ah! poor little thing! . . . What a wretch I am!' sobbed Aunt Bernarde: while Louise Soubirous uttered a fervent entreaty to the Lord of life and death: 'My God, I implore You, don't take my child away from me!'

At the end of about half an hour, the vision ceased and Bernadette sank into her mother's arms. Not that this half-hour of bliss had exhausted her: 'she never felt any weariness after the Apparitions', but 'the impression on her eyes as she emerged from the vision was like that which is felt when one passes from bright sunshine into a dark place'; and so, during this moment of tremendous transition, she would feel blinded and would grope for someone to support her.

On the way back to the Petits-Fossés, Bernadette revealed how at a certain moment the Apparition seemed different from before. Suddenly loud yells, belched from the Gave, had rent the sacred silence of Massabielle. They 'challenged, crossed, collided with one another, like the clamour of a brawling crowd'. One voice, more furious than the rest, dominated them all and roared out: 'Get out of here! . . . Get out of here!' Bernadette guessed rightly that the threatening curse was by no means addressed merely to her humble self, but was an attack directed beyond her to the Vision of Light standing above the eglantine.

The Vision merely glanced in the direction of the rushing stream. This single look, one of sovereign authority, reduced the invisible mob to silence: the enemy of all good would not drive her from the grotto where she gave her audiences. 'HE is in a rage. So much the better!' the saintly Curé d'Ars used to say of the *grappin*. 'He lets me know himself when big sinners are coming!'

At Massabielle, the future was to prove that the Spirit of evil, in this burst of fury, had admitted his defeat; he was not to extinguish the great radiance that would issue from this dark, peaceful nook, where so many sinners would renounce sin!

In the Rue du Baous Bernadette stopped to greet her Aunt Basile, who, attracted by the sound of voices, was just opening the window: Louise Soubirous, in a hurry to get to her work, went on her way.

The child [reported the aunt] was returning accompanied by a large number of people: there were women from the town and country: they all wanted to see her and speak to her. . . . Bernadette, closely hemmed in, said to me, 'Good-bye, Auntie!' She was full of happiness. Breaking away from the women accompanying her, she came into my house. I began to scold her: 'People are talking a lot about you: all sorts of things are being said. You mustn't go there any more!' She answered: 'I'm not bothered about them. Let them talk; it doesn't worry me. . . . Would you like to go there with me to-morrow?' I felt a shudder inside me. 'I'd really like to go,' I said to her, 'but I would rather there were not so many people. Let's go there either earlier or later in the day.' It was settled we should go to the grotto at six in the morning.

Half an hour after this hurried conversation, without even a thought for a reputation that was growing—and was full of danger—the schoolgirl was on her way back to the Sisters, to learn her spelling, continue her copy-book and throw herself whole-heartedly into her recreation with the little girls in the lowest class.

*       *       *

The day before, on returning from Mass, Mlle Rosine Cazenave, a Lourdes woman of thirty-four, had 'met Mme Millet with a little girl wrapped in a black hood'. 'It's that Bernadette Soubirous,' they explained to her, 'who goes and prays at the grotto; she'll be there again to-morrow.' It was a lucky chance for Mlle Cazenave, who was suspicious and wanted to see for herself. 'I went,' she said, 'and asked one of our friends, Germaine Raval, then a girl of about twenty, and to-day a Sister of Charity, to accompany me on Saturday morning to Massabielle.'

When Basile Castérot and her niece, one pace ahead of the mother, reached the grotto, the aunt had the satisfaction of finding that 'there were few people', due no doubt to the still severe cold and the very early hour; also, a number of devout folk, anxious though they were to watch the child in ecstasy, had been unwilling to miss their Mass; whereas Bernadette, to oblige Aunt Basile, had forgone hers.

On her knees, candle in hand, she took out her beads. 'I also was holding a rosary, but I was distracted on her account,' admitted a worthy townswoman, Mme Lannes, who had come there with her maid. 'After a short while, her face became all smiles, and the women present said: "Now she sees *her*!" She was looking upwards and smiling; then she became thoughtful and seemed to be listening with great devotion and reverence. I was very close to her, and several times I heard a long breath come through her lips; it was scarcely perceptible, as though she had uttered a very low and prolonged *yes*.'

'Entirely prejudiced as I was against such things,' Rosine Cazenave confessed, 'I could not help marvelling at what I saw: the face, the smile, the graceful bows of Bernadette . . .' 'I was facing her, about two yards away,' recounted Romaine Mengelatte. 'If you had only seen her eyes! It was enough to bring you to your knees.' 'I can no longer recognize my child!' exclaimed Louise Soubirous, deeply moved and wonderstruck.

They came back to the town at a very leisurely pace. On her way up the street the miraculous child found herself the centre of even greater curiosity and attention than yesterday. As she walked along, she confided to those nearest to her that the Vision had taught her patiently, 'word by word', a prayer which was to be for herself alone and which she would have to say every day of her life. She recited it 'at all the Apparitions'. 'I say it every day,' she declared some twenty years later, 'and no one except myself knows it.'

Naturally, since this prayer was her secret, people would scheme to wrest it from her, but she would never give it away. What is to be gained then by subtle discussions about the contents of this heavenly dictation?

At Tarbes, during the course of this same morning, the Major of Gendarmerie, Renault, notified his secretary, Sergeant Bigué: 'Extraordinary things are happening at Lourdes: people are going to a grotto and being present at visions. We shall leave this afternoon.'

'We set out in fact on horseback about two o'clock,' as the

sergeant testified, 'and arrived at night, stabled our horses at the gendarmerie and dined at the hotel.'

\* \* \*

It was the First Sunday of Lent, February 21st, only ten days since the first Apparition: a Sunday destined to prove for little Bernadette most fruitful in surprises.

A cold wind was blowing that morning. When she reached the grotto, accompanied this time by her mother and her Aunt Bernarde, there was a considerable crowd gathered there: a number of housewives who were unable to leave their homes on week-days, women who worked in the fields and many men, shop-keepers, artisans, slate-workers, quarrymen and labourers, who were free from work on Sundays.

What word of command had caused this, the first of 'Lourdes crowds', to assemble here?

It was evident that the clergy, remaining aloof, had nothing whatever to do with this gathering; no more had the press: the local newspaper, an ordinary weekly called the *Lavedan*, that derived its name from the valleys of the Gave de Pau, had so far breathed not a word about the Massabielle incidents. Only the poorer folk were discussing them openly: the middle-class showed more reserve, but were nevertheless talking about them.

At St John's Club, conversation on the subject had just taken a livelier turn. Its members used to meet in a room of the Café Français near the church—and here were to be found the not-ables of the town, independent gentlemen, doctors, lawyers, magistrates, officials of all ranks.

The frequenters of St John's Club were not anti-clericals: not one of them would have passed the parish priest without greeting him or, on occasion, shaking hands with him. Moreover, no one in authority could have taken any exception to their con-victions or their conduct. At this period, the Imperial govern-ment showed itself favourable to Catholics: the Revolution had not as yet had time to 'recapture Napoleon III' on the morrow of his attempted assassination by Orsini on January 14th of this same year, 1858.

Nevertheless, in spite of its name and possibly without its members being fully conscious of the fact, there was at St John's

Club a certain Voltairianism in the air.  On the tables of the
Café Français lay the two Paris dailies, *La Presse* and *Le Siècle*,
which—to quote Montalembert—'have three times as many sub-
scribers as all the other newspapers put together and contain
almost daily attacks on religion and the clergy.'

Among the registered members of the club, the big Catholic
daily, the *Univers*, counted but one solitary subscriber, Pailhasson, the chemist.  The others no doubt considered that the
'ultramontane' journal of the fiery Louis Veuillot put the Pope
too much above the Emperor, and so they fell back upon *Le
Siècle* and *La Presse*.  Periodically these two very secular papers
would remind their readers that in those days of electric tele-
graphy and the steam-engine it was absurd simplicity, stupidity
and obscurantism to admit the possibility of apparitions and
miracles.

The previous evening, at the Lourdes club, in between two
games of cards, the more free-thinking among the groups of
friends found much amusement in the story of this young
neurotic falling into trances every morning at the foot of the
Massabielle rocks.  But the genteel laughter of these gentlemen
did not even shake the Café windows.

The movement of the crowd, on that Sunday morning, was
entirely spontaneous; no one instigated or organized it.  It was
far more than curiosity that mustered them around Massabielle
and in the meadow on the other bank of the Gave.  As a witness
wrote, 'Everyone in that crowd was convinced of the supernatural character of the grotto incidents.'  For these worthy
folk, the little Soubirous girl certainly saw someone, someone
kind and lovable, and this 'someone' was . . . ?  Already a
name of special reverence was being whispered.  Bernadette, it is
true, had always said till then that the Apparition had not yet
given her name.  Even so with a thrill of the heart they
hazarded: 'Oh!  If it were *She*. . . . !'

There was no hostility in the expectant crowd.  Yet, in the
grey light of early morning, disquieting figures were detected.
First, three gendarmes.  Several stripes sparkled on the sleeves of
the eldest: Renault the Major was there, supported by the Sergeant, Bigué, from Tarbes, and the gendarme Malé of Lourdes.
They were standing 'about fifteen paces' from Bernadette, whom
they picked out unmistakably in the flickering gleam of her

candle. They were merely doing their job, one supposed: there was nothing aggressive in their attitude: they were content to watch. Besides, what need was there to interfere? No dispute, no disorder, no incident or accident. The three gendarmes were to remain there in silence for possibly a quarter of an hour. 'When the Major has seen enough of it, he'll retire.'

It was a fashionably dressed civilian who attracted more attention than the police. Who ever expected to find Dr Dozous at the grotto? He was reputed for his learning and his philanthropy, but he was a man who scarcely ever went to church, except for funerals or official festivals. Why had he come down to Massabielle? Why had he planted himself in that select place, right beside Bernadette?

Not one of those around the child could be aware that the doctor had been priding himself at the club on possessing in Bernadette a neat case of neuropathy. He was going to surprise the young visionary in the middle of her ecstasy at Massabielle itself. No fear of error. Simply by examining her pulse he would expose both the disorder of her sense-perception and the imbalance of her wretched brain. . . . The simple-minded folk frequenting this wild nook (which was now to be so skilfully converted by the clever practitioner into a consulting room), would then have no other alternative but to go home.

But it is simplest to hear Dr Dozous give his own honest account of an experiment that upset all his calculations.

As soon as she was in front of the grotto, Bernadette knelt down, took her rosary out of her pocket and began to pray, telling her beads.

Soon her face underwent a transformation, noticed by everyone near her and showing that she was in touch with her Apparition.

While her beads were moving through her right hand, she held in the other a lighted candle which was often blown out by the very strong breeze blowing along the Gave; but she handed it each time to the person nearest her to be immediately relighted.

I myself was following most attentively all Bernadette's movements in order to study her from more than one aspect, for I wanted to check at that moment the circulation of her blood and her breathing. I took one of her arms and put my fingers on the radial artery. The pulse was calm and regular, the breathing easy: nothing in the young girl indicated any undue nervous excitement that had reacted in any peculiar way upon the whole system.

After I had let go her arm, Bernadette advanced a short distance towards the top of the grotto. Soon I saw her face, which up to now had expressed the most perfect happiness, grow sad; two tears fell from her eyes and rolled down her cheeks.

When 'the mysterious being had disappeared and Bernadette had finished her prayers,'—thus Dr Dozous described the end of the ecstasy—he could not refrain from asking her the reason for these tears after such happy smiles.

The Lady [she replied] took her eyes off me for a moment and gazed into the distance, over my head. Then, looking at me again, as I had asked her what was making her sad, she said to me: 'Pray to God for sinners.' I was quickly reassured by the expression of kindness and serenity I saw once more on her face, and she straightway disappeared.

A day was to come when the visionary of Massabielle would be 'ceaselessly preoccupied with the conversion of poor sinners'.

'Bernadette,' finally observed the doctor, 'withdrew in the simplest, most unassuming manner, paying no attention to the public ovation she received.'

# 8

## CIVIL AUTHORITY TAKES ACTION

SUNDAY morning in Lourdes was always very quiet in winter. All work was at a standstill, and practising Catholics, when the bell tolled, made their way to church for one or other of the Masses, while the indifferent had a good long sleep or went and took a seat at one of the tables in the tavern. As people came out from Mass, the gendarme on duty strolled leisurely round the Square, shaking hands good-naturedly and distributing official leaflets.

But on this Sunday, February 21st, something unusual happened. Instead of dispersing after a short chat, those of the artisans, quarrymen and slate-workers, who had been down at Massabielle before dawn, remained standing in a group. Noisily they compared impressions on the Apparition, and called out to some comrades who had not been down there. The latter, annoyed perhaps at missing the sight, shouted: 'It's all a pack of lies! . . . Ridiculous! ' They began arguing and soon became heated, one side trying to shout the other down. No blows were exchanged, but there was every likelihood of it!

It was not surprising, therefore, that about ten o'clock the Lourdes constabulary drew up almost at full strength in a corner of the Square. In his two-cornered hat and his sabre at his side, Sergeant d'Angla—aged forty-two and cutting a fine figure in his uniform—was conversing with his men. Now and then the gendarmes turned their heads as one man towards the Mairie, quite close to the church.

The reason was that Mayor Lacadé, Public Prosecutor Dutour, Major Renault, Examining Magistrate Rives and Police Commissioner Jacomet had just met in the Town Hall to exchange views on the situation. These official gentlemen had had their Sunday upset all on account of a certain little Soubirous girl, a poor child from the Rue des Petits-Fossés!

In all fairness, these men of 1858 should be judged in relation to those earliest days of the Lourdes events, days of inevitable misconstructions, gropings in the dark, and nervous tension; they should be judged at that stage and not in the light of later developments. Account must also be taken of their mentality as officials responsible for public order. They were not qualified to inquire into the Invisible: this young Soubirous girl was recounting things that stretched much too far beyond their usual horizon and would appear to them as based on illusion or even fraud. Before long, they would be dumbfounded or exasperated by what Louis Veuillot termed 'the strangeness of this conviction established among a whole people on the sole word of an ignorant, poverty-stricken little girl'. They themselves made no move . . . not yet at least.

Modelled on Imperial law, the urban regulations were explicit: no gatherings to be permitted that threatened to degenerate into brawls. Besides, by temperament, M. Anselme Lacadé, the notary, disliked 'scenes'. He was, as a Lourdais wrote, 'a practising Catholic and wholly devoted to religious interests'; but he was Mayor as well, and anxious to retain his 'sash of office'! On the other hand, the Police Commissioner and gendarmes were there to prevent or suppress any disorder or any possibility of accidents. Now all this excitement in the streets . . . and those dangerous slopes leading down to the grotto of Massabielle . . . should they delay taking action until corpses were being carried up from that valley, until supporters and opponents of these alleged Apparitions came to blows over them?

But what action were they to take? Nothing simpler! Suppress the cause; prevent this little girl from going and kneeling at Massabielle. Hypocrite or mad woman, she would be induced to contradict herself, and this would put an end to the farce.

'I'll see to it,' declared the Commissioner. 'After me,' added the Prosecutor, correcting him.

On this reply the meeting closed. As he left the Mairie, M. Dutour said a word to the caretaker of the premises; then he went straight to the Court.

\*      \*      \*

While they were discussing her at the Mairie, Bernadette, with just a kerchief round her head (for the one and only cape had not fallen to her lot that morning!) was in the benches reserved for the Sisters' pupils, attending High Mass. Her little rosary was gliding slowly through her fingers. In church, that Sunday, the Sister in charge could not help noticing her among the other children. Bernadette did not seem quite the same as a fortnight before: she was praying with more attention. 'For sinners,' she told them—as she had been urged to pray by this Apparition in which the Sisters still refused to believe.

Yesterday evening the poor little girl had had her meal at Mme Millet's for the last time. Her parents thanked the lady very much, but they no longer wished their daughter to be under her care. So Bernadette slept at the 'dungeon' and without the least sign of resentment she resumed her usual life of poverty.

As the pupils were coming out of church, the man from the Mairie asked for Bernadette Soubirous. He told her that on the way home she was to present herself at the law-court—that grim building at the corner of the Rue du Tribunal and the Rue des Petits-Fossés, which she knew only too well. Awaiting her there was the Public Prosecutor, M. Jacques-Vital Dutour.

M. Dutour was a magistrate of the old bourgeois stamp. He was still a young man, aged forty-one, having been appointed Public Prosecutor when only thirty-five. Respected father of a family and a good Catholic, he was proud of his two sisters who had become Daughters of Charity. 'With an acute mind and a sincere heart,' as Adolphe d'Angla testified, 'he was respected and loved by all.' Although he frequented the Café Français, he did not share the scepticism of certain members of the club as to beliefs and the question of miracles. But at his desk that Sunday morning, he was merely the 'public official' charged with proceeding against every infringement of the law before the Lourdes court of first instance.

In the clerk's austere office, with its imposing array of registers, the Prosecutor was sitting deep in thought beside the fire, which had just been lit. He was somewhat on edge: neither he nor his clerk of the court was accustomed to being in this place on a day of legal rest.

Ah, yes, this chit of a girl. . . . The magistrate was taking his bearings. Jacomet had just been reminding him that the humble individual in question was no other than the daughter of a man who had been held on a charge last year: the ruined miller, François Soubirous, whose tears and state of collapse came vividly before him again. He pulled out a file. Theft by pauper, piece of wood—owner unknown—taken in the open . . . against a wall . . . one winter night. . . . The case had been filed, the man being discharged without further proceedings. . . . This was a mere trifle compared with the daughter's doings: hallucination possibly; more probably fraud . . . concerted movements among the people, gatherings that were only at their first stage: but with these hot-headed Pyreneans, how far might things go? Skirmishes, pitched battles! . . . But had not the visionary some accomplices? The parents were bound to be mixed up in the business: it was a well-known trick of these paupers to make cat's-paws of their children. Visions, apparitions—an ingenious brain-wave, which had, besides, already proved profitable. Thanks to his great friend, Sergeant d'Angla, that sharp sleuth, Jacomet, was aware of everything: eager to display her generosity and to attract attention, Mme Millet had allowed herself to be taken in, and there was the young Soubirous girl installed in her house for good, like an adopted child, an heiress. . . . Here again there might possibly be an offence with aggravating circumstances: begging under false pretences, breach of trust. . . .

A clatter of wooden clogs in the passage suddenly interrupted his thoughts. Here was the accused herself! In she came, the hood of her little black cloak thrown back over her shoulders. The Public Prosecutor had not imagined her so small and frail, yet so dignified and indeed so appealing. Maybe, in a flash, there came before his mind the picture of a Daughter of Charity bending over some poor child like this one. But the magistrate steeled himself: his sole duty was to conduct an enquiry. He remained distant, and, never forgetting his position, carefully avoided using *thou* in place of *you*, when addressing this child of poor people. He might have asked Bernadette to sit down, but he did not do so, lest his authority should suffer. She had to 'answer him standing, leaning against his desk'.

That very evening, February 21st, M. Dutour drafted the minute of an official report for the Attorney General of Pau: later, in reply to certain slanderous insinuations, he drew up a brief memoir on his own attitude during the Lourdes events.

In this, once he was rid of his prejudices, he described Bernadette's entrance upon the scene:

> Bernadette was neither brought nor led before the Public Prosecutor: she came of her own free will on a mere verbal invitation. . . . No one accompanied her there.
> When she appeared, there was nothing in her attitude to indicate that she had any repugnance or fear. Her face was serene and confident, devoid of shyness or boldness. Nothing she heard seemed to cause her any trouble: what she said, she said quite simply in her patois, entirely at her ease, and required no urging.

And here is the portrait of her, left by this man of the law, who was accustomed to see appearing before him in this place the very opposite to innocence:

> Everything about Bernadette was simple, one might even say common, at first sight. There was nothing remarkable about her face, when in repose. Her dress was plain and simple with an irreproachable neatness, indicative of self-respect and dignity amid poverty; that is all. Her head-dress (a sort of madras with the patterns almost faded out from frequent washing) covered half her forehead and was bound tightly round her hair. Her neck, shoulders, waist, wrapped in folds of a material similar to her head-dress, recalled one of those busts roughed out by the sculptor's chisel. Afflicted with some complaint of the respiratory passages, the poor child wore a chest-protector so heavy and ill-fitting that she seemed to breathe with even greater difficulty.
> It is true that, when she spoke, her unaffected language and her quiet, earnest tone won one's confidence. It is equally true that, when she expressed some noble sentiment or less commonplace thought, there spread over her features a charm all the more impressive in that one could discover there nothing but the outpouring of a sincere soul.

The writer of these lines which, years later, still reveal a genuine compassion, must undoubtedly at the time have been profoundly moved, both as a man and a father. Once more he forced himself to allow none of this to appear while questioning Bernadette. She gave her surname and Christian names: she stated that she thought she was thirteen or fourteen years old, could neither read nor write and had not yet made her First Communion. Then she described the first Apparitions; while the Prosecutor, encouraging her when necessary, was rapidly taking notes. When she had finished he felt his magisterial rigour relaxing: would he really have the heart to hurt this child? He hardened his voice. Some of his insinuations would be cruel.

'Do you intend going to the grotto like this every morning?'
    'Yes sir: I've promised to go there every day for a fortnight.'
    'But the Superior of the Hospice and the Sister-in-charge, who are both very devout women, have told you to put it all out of your head; that your vision was a dream, an illusion. Why not follow their advice? You would stop all this bother about you.'
    'I feel too much joy when I go to the grotto.'
    'You could give it up . . . and, besides, you might be stopped going.'
    'I feel myself drawn by an irresistible force.'
    'Be careful! There are many people who suspect that you and your parents might be very glad to trade on people's credulity. I might even think it myself. Your family is very poor. Since your visits to the grotto, you are being supplied with nice things which you never had before and you are hoping for more. I must make it clear to you that supposing you were not sincere in your accounts of apparitions, or supposing you and your parents were to gain any profit from them, you would be liable to prosecution and a severe sentence.'
    'I'm not counting on any profit in this life.'
    'So you say. But have you not already accepted Mme Millet's hospitality? Are not your parents hoping to better their position by making use of you and your visions, though they may be nothing but dreams or, worse still, lies?'
    'Mme Millet wanted to have me at her house. She came to fetch me. I gave way to her requests in order to please her. I was not thinking of myself. I have not lied to her or to anyone else.'

These last words were spoken so spontaneously and with such candour, that the Public Prosecutor no longer doubted her sincerity. He reflected quietly for a moment. This child was not trying to deceive. She was not exploiting public credulity. And so M. Dutour failed to find in her case 'the material elements of an unlawful act'. Any Jew, any Mussulman, could pray alone wherever he pleased; why could not a little Catholic girl kneel before a lonely grotto? Even supposing that a considerable number of visitors had gone there that very morning, this grotto did not on that account constitute a 'place of worship' requiring legal authorization. In the end he imposed no restrictions on her, save in the event of further incidents.

M. Dutour testified in his memoir to the kindly conclusion of the formidable interview; referring to himself in the third person, he wrote:

> Although he had—not without serious motives—entertained some prejudices, the Public Prosecutor, after having seen and heard Bernadette on February 21st, shared the opinion of the majority regarding the child's sincerity, and, judging her to be sincere, he set no obstacle to her visiting the grotto, nor any check on her liberty: but, even though the suspicion of imposture was rejected, the Public Prosecutor had by no means heard the last of Bernadette.

The sequel showed that, though he no longer suspected her integrity, M. Dutour was not ready to give up so quickly his twofold prejudice: this young girl, he believed, was genuinely convinced that she did see something at Massabielle, whereas she saw nothing; then, say what she might, it could well be that without her realizing it she was being manipulated by others. Furthermore, the decision to allow her free access to the grotto remained subject to the approval of the municipal authorities.

This was how, after lunch, the Prosecutor explained matters briefly to Jacomet, who had come for news. Confident of succeeding better than his superior, the Commissioner prepared for action.

\* \* \*

The time has come in our story to express generous thanks to the magistrates and police. One should feel grateful to them for having been, involuntarily, the most valuable auxiliaries of Providence in furnishing human proofs of His miraculous intervention. While the clergy kept silence, these civil officials, of their own accord, appointed themselves the earliest historians of the Apparitions.

Strict investigators, harsh and humiliating on more than one occasion, they successfully forestalled the Bishop of the diocese and the priests of the parish in the essential verification of the facts. Their repeated attacks, the traps they laid for the ignorant simplicity of the little Soubirous girl, provided her with the opportunity of proving triumphantly the truth of her visions.

Their cross-examinations, their notes and reports, constitute a body of evidence of the highest importance and must be given first place by the historian of the events in Lourdes, in order to make any serious denial of the facts impossible, and to provide a solid, secure foundation for the assent of believers. Investigators of every sort ended by proving, contrary to their own wishes, that Bernadette was neither a fraud, nor an exploiter, nor an hysteric.

As early as June 15th of this year, 1858, an honest-minded scientist of Toulouse, M. Vène, inspector of the mineral waters of the Pyrenees, had almost a presentiment of this unexpected role that devolved upon magistrates and police. He wrote to Dr Dozous:

Like yourself, I cannot understand why the authorities seek to put obstacles in the way of the free publication of this fact. Possibly obstacles are necessary for its manifestation. This at least may be said: if the finger of God is there, all the efforts of mankind will prove powerless.

\*       \*       \*

On leaving the court, Bernadette returned home. Seeing that the Public Prosecutor had not forbidden her to visit the grotto, their daughter's appearance before this important person caused the parents scarcely any alarm. After a little while the child returned to church for Vespers.

Shortly afterwards, two men were also on their way there, but they stopped close by, on the square known as 'du Porche', by which the child would return. The few passers-by recognized Commissioner Jacomet, escorted by Pierre Callet, the rural constable.

Nothing can take the place of Pierre Callet's delicious evidence:

M. Jacomet sent for me. I went to his house. 'It seems to me,' he said, 'this Bernadette is in church. You must point her out to me. Come with me.' We went and posted ourselves in front of the church. M. Jacomet was not in Commissioner's uniform, but in plain clothes, without even his képi.

When the crowd had disappeared, I spotted Bernadette with some of her relations and I said to M. Jacomet: 'There she is.'—'Which one?'—'That one there.'—Then he went up to Bernadette and touched her on the arm, saying: 'Come with me.' Bernadette replied: 'Yes, sir, wherever you wish.' She knew M. Jacomet; everyone did. The relations said nothing.

The relations in question were her aunts, Bernarde and Lucile, who had met their niece on the way out. Lucile Castérot left Bernarde and went to inform François and Louise Soubirous. Meanwhile, M. Jacomet, followed by the rural constable, was taking Bernadette along to his house.

In those days [continues Callet], there was no police office. . . . We had not even passed the Mairie before people began to say: 'Poor Bernadette! They're going to put you in prison!' She answered with a laugh: 'I'm not afraid; if they put me in, they'll let me out!' The crowd followed.

The Commissioner, who was then thirty-seven, occupied the ground-floor of 'Maison Cénac' in Rue Saint-Pierre, which led into the Route de Tarbes. The first floor was occupied by M. Jean-Baptiste Estrade, a bachelor of thirty-eight, and his sister, Mlle Emmanuélite, three years younger; on the second floor lived one of the Lourdes curates, Abbé Jean-Bertrand Pène, and his sister Jacquette.

Let us hear Callet again:

On reaching the door of the house, M. Jacomet said to the child, 'Follow me.' And to those behind he said, 'There's nothing for you to see here.' He had great authority, tremendous assurance. . . . I went in with M. Jacomet and Bernadette to the first room where he had his office. M. Jacomet opened the door of another room that looked on to the yard and went in with Bernadette. When we arrived, Mme Jacomet was in the first room. She remained there; so did I. During the examination, she went and glued her ear to the door, smiling across at me. . . .

Mme Jacomet, a good-natured woman to be sure, seems to have been lacking in refinement. But her husband, who was subsequently to be so greatly vilified, gained this high praise from M. Raymond Prat, at that time clerk to the Lourdes court: 'M. Jacomet was a most intelligent man and fulfilled his duties as Commissioner extremely well.' For that alone the rural constable would have had unbounded admiration for him.

> We've never had another like him in the town [attested the worthy subordinate]. He was feared, and yet he was not a hard man, out to make charges and bring folk to court. . . . A handsome fellow, most courteous and jovial. He had a pleasing appearance, especially when in uniform and cocked hat: you would have taken him for a general. . . .
>
> In the communes his first visit was always to the parish priest, and he was always welcome. I often went there with him. Never a word against religion or the priests. Never a coarse word, or swear-word. Never did he speak of anything indecent.

M. Estrade's own estimate of his former co-tenant in no way contradicts that of Pierre Callet:

> This official had a frank, open, cheerful face, predisposing you at once in his favour. Besides, he was intelligent and educated, which added a certain distinction to his physical advantages. Everyone in Lourdes, great and small, shook hands with M. Jacomet, and the dislike of his office in no way lessened his personal popularity. As Commissioner, none knew better than he how to unearth a rogue and induce him to confess . . .

The foregoing will explain his outlook, which was that of a professional policeman who had to examine more rogues than honest men, and who suspected trickery in anyone brought before him. But, as gendarme Malé affirmed, 'M. Jacomet was well thought of by even the poorer people, before the grotto affair, for he showed himself very lenient' towards the poor.

His misfortune was to become involved in—without at first understanding them—events whose repercussions would be worldwide. The mystery was beyond his comprehension, and he could not foresee the future. He shrugged his shoulders at the accounts of Bernadette's visions: but was he the only one among his associates to ridicule them? In presence of a fairly large company, Mme Jacomet joked on the subject of this unknown lady, who was honouring Mlle Soubirous with invitations to visit her!

No doubt the Police Commissioner would have shown himself more circumspect, had he felt himself in the slightest degree at variance with the clergy and local magistrates. But he flattered himself that the Public Prosecutor and the Mayor would adopt his conclusions, and he supposed, not without likelihood, that Dean Peyramale would not be sorry to see this vision business buried once and for all. Months passed, during which the Curé of Lourdes, to use his own expression, would 'wrap himself up in the most absolute reserve and silence'; he 'knew nothing of the grotto'; he did not want to know!

> Why [the clerk Prat wondered], why did M. Jacomet expend so much energy on the affair? I believe he was acting in good faith: I never observed in him any irreligion, nor anything reprehensible in his moral conduct. Believers [in the Apparitions] saw him as an enemy, and it would have been quite easy to find two hundred women ready to throw him in the Gave.

That may be! But Jacomet, believing he was merely carrying out his duty as a policeman, was about to lose a sterling reputation. Still, history has no right unjustly to perpetuate passing grudges. Moreover, the earliest chronicler of the Apparitions went so far as to draw a disparaging portrait of the Lourdes Commissioner, into which the caricatured official has consistently refused to fit. Further, the harsh judgment passed upon him and published during his lifetime so affected him, we are told, as to shorten his days—he died at the age of fifty-two, August 5th, 1873. Let us hear Lasserre's account:

> . . . confident when dealing with shady and tricky affairs, this man became confused by straightforwardness. Truth disconcerted him and seemed to him suspect; unselfishness aroused his distrust. Eager as he was to discover duplicity and evasion everywhere, frankness made him uneasy. By reason of this monomania, holiness would no doubt have appeared to him the most monstrous of impostures and would have found him implacable. . . . He was like those birds of night that can see only in darkness, and in broad daylight dash themselves against trees and walls.

Elsewhere, referring to the Lourdes Police Commissioner and to the Public Prosecutor, the same author calls up the sombre figures of 'Herod, Caiphas, Pilate . . . undisguised enemies, dastards, weaklings, sceptics. . . .'

But let us pass on.

Here then was Bernadette, this Sunday afternoon, before the Police Commissioner. He made her sit down in front of his desk, for the session would possibly be a long one. He looked her in the eyes, and saw nothing but sincerity. Perhaps he had thought to read fear there, but no. 'I was no longer myself, I was not afraid,' Bernadette confided later to a companion. 'There was something within me that made me overcome everything.' This something, one may affirm, was that strength from on high, that *gratia status* of witnesses to the supernatural. One of his immediate neighbours, very well informed, noted that at first 'M. Jacomet, guardian of the peace, saw in the events at the grotto merely something to unsettle the faith of the credulous and used his intervention solely to forestall contingencies that were likely to disturb the peace and order of the town.'

For this reason he was only interested at this time in such external facts as came within his jurisdiction: in the presence of Bernadette he made no allusion to the poverty of her parents, nor did he attribute to them yet the base mercenary motives that had just been ascribed to them by the Public Prosecutor.

Hardly had Bernadette sat down when the door opened quietly behind her. In came Mlle Estrade. Mme Jacomet had promised to let her know if the young Soubirous girl was to be cross-examined by her husband.

> I had hardly come in [she noted later], when I felt a sudden regret: my brother was going to miss hearing Bernadette. I left the room at once in haste to call him. At that moment he was writing and obstinately refused to come. I took him by the arm, I pulled his chair away, I pushed him. He gave in at last, and we went back to the room.

While his sister stayed at the back of the room, unable to see anything of Bernadette except her back or profile, M. Jean-Baptiste Estrade made a sign to the Commissioner 'explaining his visit' and seated himself in a place from which he would be able 'to see the expression and hear the words of the young ecstatic'.

The child, whom I had before me and whom I did not know [he recorded in his manuscript account], seemed about twelve years old: in reality she was fourteen. She had a round, plump face: her expression betokened great gentleness and simplicity. Her voice, although somewhat loud, had a sympathetic quality. Seated in an easy, very natural posture, she had her hands crossed on her knees and her head bent slightly forward. Her clothes were poor but clean and neat.

When M. Estrade and his sister arrived on the scene, M. Jacomet was placing paper and pencil on his desk.

Assuming an air of kindly familiarity, he said to the child: 'Don't be afraid. I've been told about an extraordinary lady who is supposed to have appeared to you at the Massabielle grottoes. As you know, people are saying this and that; I want to hear all about it for myself.'

Although the Commissioner's notes have not been recovered, the cross-examination is easily reconstructed, thanks to the two corroborating memoirs left by M. and Mlle Estrade.

'What's your name?'—'Bernadette Soubirous.'
   'Your father's name?'—'François Soubirous.'
   'And your mother's?'—'Louise—Louise Castérot.'
   'What do you do with yourself?'—'I go to school at the Sisters'. I help my mother at home. I look after my little brother.'
   'Tell me what you saw at Massabielle.'

Then, submissively, Bernadette repeated for Commissioner Jacomet the account which the Public Prosecutor Dutour had heard a few hours earlier. However, apparently wanting fuller information, the Commissioner interrupted her more than once:

'So this lady is very beautiful?'
   'Oh, yes, sir, very beautiful!'
   'Is she as beautiful as Mme X . . . as Mme Z . . . ?'
   'Far more: there is no comparison.'
   'Is she young?'
   'Yes, very young.'
   'Can you see her feet?'

'No, not much; her dress and the roses hide them, except her toes.'

'Can you see her hair?'

'A little, beneath her veil.'

'You say it's the Blessed Virgin who appears to you?'

'I don't know if it is. She didn't tell me.'

'Have you spoken to your parents about what you've seen at Massabielle?'

'Yes, sir.'

'What did your parents say?'

'They told me at first that I had been mistaken and that I must not return to Massabielle any more.'

'Yes, Bernadette, you mustn't return there any more. They're all laughing at you. Your imagination has been playing you tricks: this lady that you thought you saw didn't really exist.'

'But, sir, I've seen her several times: I can't always be mistaken.'

After each reply, M. Jacomet did some writing. 'You see,' he said, 'I'm taking down all you say in writing. Woe betide you if you're telling lies.' 'Sir, I've told you no lies.'

With this child the Commissioner had not so far gained an inch of ground. But was there not some means of catching her out, of making her contradict herself? If she did not fall into the trap, he would increase the pressure! What is more, M. Jacomet was becoming worked up: the two witnesses of the scene were causing him some embarrassment; he refused to be beaten and humiliated by this insignificant little Lourdes girl.

'No, you're not speaking the truth' [he insisted]. 'If you don't tell me who it was who forced you to tell this story, I'll prosecute you as a liar.'

'Do as you wish, sir.'

'So much the worse! She's asking for it, she shall be punished,' declared the Commissioner, talking to himself. And solemnly he raised his paper level with his eyes, as if to indicate that it was no longer any laughing matter. Bernadette has summed up part of the scene that followed:

'After writing a few lines as I dictated them to him, he noted down some other things that were strange to me; then he told me he was going to read them over to see if he had made any mistakes, so I listened carefully. He had scarcely read a few lines when I noticed some errors and I replied quickly: "Sir, I didn't say that!" He flew into a rage, saying emphatically, "Yes"; but I kept repeating "No". These disputes went on for some minutes. Seeing that I persisted in telling him that he had made a mistake, that I had not said that, he went on a bit further. He kept starting all over again like this for an hour and a half.'

'You told me at first,' pointed out the Commissioner firmly, 'that a woman as beautiful as Mme X . . . ?'
'Not at all, sir; I said she was more beautiful than all these ladies.'
'Very well, then! . . . that she had appeared at the back of the grotto?'
'Not at all: above the bush.'
'That her hair hung down behind like a veil?'
'That's not so: I said she had a veil, it was white and very long . . . Her hair could scarcely be seen.'
'That she had a yellow rose in her sash?'
'No, sir. You've changed everything I said; she has a blue sash, and there's no rose in her sash: there's a yellow rose on each foot.'

'Bernadette's account,' stated Mlle Estrade, 'was twisted and turned every possible way by M. Jacomet. He threatened her with looks and even with his hand. The child was never flustered: her story never varied. Nothing made such an impression on me as Bernadette's attitude before the Commissioner.'
'This nonsense must cease,' he said finally. 'Are you willing to promise never to go to Massabielle again?' 'Sir, I have promised to go there every day for a fortnight.' This reply particularly nettled the Commissioner, who had just realized that this headstrong slip of a girl would defy him to the end. He lost his self-control. 'You mean to go there again?' he shouted. 'Then I'll send for the gendarmes. Get ready to go to prison.' And his hand was shaking so much, said Bernadette, 'that he couldn't find the hole in the inkwell'; whereas the accused replied calmly: 'So much the better! I shall cost my father less, and in prison you'll come and teach me my Catechism.'

Things were going badly. M. Estrade thought it opportune here to intervene. 'I went up to the child,' he noted, 'and, pretending to take her side, I invited her to retract what she'd said. She understood instinctively that I had no business to intervene in the discussion, and made no reply to me.'

All during her examination, as she herself stated, Bernadette noticed a continual murmur of voices outside. A crowd was beginning to fill the Rue Saint-Pierre in front of 'Maison Cénac'. Suddenly, while M. Estrade was addressing the child, a clatter of hobnailed boots resounded in the passage: François Soubirous appeared in the half-open door. Sensing a threat to his favourite child, the shamefaced pauper, whom the gendarmes had hauled to this very place a year ago, now dared to turn up on his own. 'I'm the father of this child,' he declared.

'Ah! It's you, Soubirous,' replied the Commissioner. 'You did well to come, because I was going to send for you. You know of the farce which your daughter has been playing these last few days. The whole thing would be just ridiculous if it weren't disturbing the peace of the town. It must stop. Your daughter is under age and you are responsible for her. . . .'

The threat was now shifting. The one-time miller saw himself brought once more before the Commissioner, accused, imprisoned again, not knowing for how long. . . . He lost heart and gave in.

'Mr Commissioner,' he replied humbly, 'I'm only too pleased to have done with it all. My wife and I are sick and tired of these goings-on and having so many people coming to our place. I will make use of your orders to keep them away.'

'Now you're talking!' concluded the Police Commissioner. He escorted father and daughter and 'let them out by the back door. And the crowd dispersed.'

'The whole affair,' he rapped out, when alone with M. and Mlle Estrade, 'is obviously the scheming of pious women.' 'To my mind,' replied M. Estrade, 'it might not be a case of deliberate fraud, but just a child's dream.' 'My dear man,' retorted the other, sure of his ground, 'you are not a policeman!'

At all events, they were entirely agreed on 'ruling out the hypothesis of the supernatural'. Whether it was a trumped-up affair or an hallucination was immaterial; in their opinion, there was nothing but what was human in these tales. One could not blame an excise-officer and a guardian of the peace for being ignorant of the findings of Mystical Theology regarding apparitions and ecstasies.

It sufficed for M. Jacomet that, as far as he was concerned, it had been a good afternoon's work. All the same, this Soubirous fellow had arrived on the scene in the nick of time to counter this headstrong daughter of his. In short, the Lourdes Commissioner, who was not without ambition (at the age of thirty-seven, it is legitimate to have higher aspirations) could now rest satisfied with the turn which events were taking.

He saw the Mayor again, and the Public Prosecutor, M. Dutour, who, after congratulating him as he deserved, admitted good-humouredly his own defeat. Yes, he had been less fortunate than the Police Commissioner: he had not, it is true, conducted an enquiry properly so called, and had lacked the support of old Soubirous. However, he judged it premature to speak of victory. The fact that Bernadette was not going to Massabielle again would not pacify popular feeling. Besides, was Jacomet so certain that the child would not be taken down there again by the battalion of fanatics, whose secret machinations in this shady affair he wished to discover at all costs?

On that memorable evening, the local authorities were relieved to learn that, before starting back for Tarbes with his secretary, Bigué, Major Renault had left this instruction for the Lourdes Sergeant:

You will send a gendarme every morning to the notorious grotto. He will report to you, and you will report to me, everything said and done there: the number of persons who meet there, and the sort of people who make up the crowd.

On their side, the Mayor and Police Commissioner told their men that they would have to 'watch young Bernadette Soubirous closely and collect all the gossip from the crowd that was pressing close on her heels'.

That night, her parents heard the muffled sobs of their poor child. They were unable to understand the reason for the anguish that gripped her.

She had borne witness before men to her gentle visitor; her

conscience had nothing to reproach her with: Bernadette was crying, not for herself, but for her father and mother, whose courage she knew and whose penury she shared. Were they going to suffer because of her? . . . A fortnight . . . She must go there twelve more days then. Certainly, she would do her best to obey her father. . . . All the same, would she have the strength to resist the attraction of Massabielle? . . . At the next break of day, the heavenly Vision without doubt would be waiting for her, and Bernadette would be faithless to her promise!

Dear Lord, what would be the outcome?

# 9

## THREE SECRETS

*(Monday, February 22nd; Tuesday, 23rd: Seventh Apparition)*

FOR Bernadette, Monday, 22nd February, was a day of confusion and sorrow. First of all she was deprived of Mass. Her parents had shown themselves inflexible: who could assure them that their daughter would not be tempted to go straight down from the church to the grotto? Without any grumbling the child picked up her school-bag (the little bag in which she carried her spelling-book and little crucifix) and went off submissively to the Hospice.

Already the policeman who had been sent on duty very early in the morning to the 'notorious grotto' had returned and, smiling all over his face, had notified his superior officer that this time at any rate there was nothing to report at Massabielle.

Poor Bernadette! In the school playground everybody knew of yesterday's adventures: she had been nearly . . . jailed! 'Serves her right, serves her right!' shouted the boldest of them in chorus. At this moment when the child of the 'dungeon' was in such great need of a little understanding and tenderness, the Sisters were frowning on her with great sternness; that one of their pupils should be summoned to court and then brought before the Commissioner of Police . . . ! That was not very flattering for their school! Besides, the Superior of the Hospice, who also kept a firm hand on the school, was standing at the entrance when this Bernadette Soubirous, whom all Lourdes was talking about, arrived. '.Have you finished your Carnival capers?' she said to her, alluding to the grotesque noises of merrymaking whose distant echoes had been annoying her during the previous week. As a former class-mate testifies, 'Bernadette made no reply and remained calm.'

When she returned from school for the frugal midday meal, she heard the prohibition repeated once again. She spoke little during the meal, then made her way back to the Hospice.  However (as she later confided to Mlle Estrade), just as she was entering the outer courtyard, 'I could not get my legs to work, except to go to Massabielle.'  This time she had good hopes of getting there unescorted; so instead of going through the town, she decided to go round by the foot of the Castle.

But at the corner of the road leading to the Hospice stood the police-station, and from one of its windows the recalcitrant schoolgirl was spotted.  There she was, going down the slope parallel to the Lapaca.  Two policeman ran after her.  'Where are you going?' they asked her.  'To the grotto,' she replied, without looking at them or slackening her pace.

These two men were obeying the instructions of the Commandant of Tarbes, who had given orders for her to be watched but not obstructed.  They were in full uniform; aiguillettes, épaulettes and yellow shoulder belt.  Had Bernadette been alone, she would not have been noticed by most people; but this unusual escort drew attention to her.  The news of it spread so quickly that, to quote Mlle Estrade, 'a fairly large number of people gathered at the junction of the forest road and the path which runs round the Castle. All had their eyes fixed on this path. . . . Many of them began to shout: 'There she is, there she is! '

Bernadette was in fact coming along [continues Mlle Estrade]. Then for the first time I saw the charming face of Mary's privileged child.  She was walking along between those two policemen, as calm, serene and natural as though she were between her father and mother.

When Bernadette drew near us I heard one of the policemen saying: 'Are they really trying to make us believe such superstitious nonsense in this nineteenth century! '

The remark fell flat: nobody seemed to understand such an eloquent harangue.  Bernadette, who was not in the least perturbed by it, had stopped opposite the group that was awaiting her.  Noticing a familiar face, she asked: 'Will you, please, fetch me the candle which is at my godmother's? '  She then went on as far as this side of the Pont-Vieux, where she stopped again and waited for the candle to be brought to her.  Aunt Lucile Castérot came running up with her sister Basile, bringing the candle with her.

On arriving in front of the grotto, Bernadette knelt down as usual, took out her rosary beads, and had the candle lighted. The two gendarmes stood on either side of her. With great fervour she recited the five decades, but she did not strain forward, as before, with her eyes fixed in ecstasy; nor was her face transformed, but it began to grow sad. . . .

While she was in prayer, Sergeant d'Angla arrived in undress uniform. Exceeding his Commandant's orders, he planted himself right in front of the kneeling child deliberately, it seemed, in order to screen the grotto from her view.—Not till twenty years later did d'Angla, then a captain of gendarmes retired, bow to the 'reality of the Lourdes miracle'.

This discourteous behaviour of a man who had no right to molest her, hurt the child. When she had finished her Rosary, Bernadette could not resist making a complaint. The Sergeant turned round. He thought that she was frightened by seeing him so close to her. 'Tapping her on the shoulder in a friendly way so as not to scare her,' as he himself has related, he whispered in her ear: 'If you were not a little idiot, you would know that the Virgin, if it is she, is not afraid of policemen, since she is guiltless. Why are you yourself afraid? Do you by any chance feel guilty of having told a lie? I am staring up there as hard as you, but I can see absolutely nothing. Come, your eyes are no different from mine.'

This time it was only too true. Grievously disappointed, Bernadette had stood up again. A number of her friends gathered round her. 'You would have seen Her,' they said to console her, 'if you had come to the grotto early in the morning as usual. But she will return to-morrow morning.' Other people shook their heads and moved off muttering: 'It's all over with the Apparitions now.' And the sceptics who had remained in the town, on being told of the discomfiture of those who had gone down there for nothing, said sneeringly: 'The "Lady" of the grotto is afraid of the police; she will not appear any more.'

Basile and Lucile took their niece homewards. 'So you did not see her?' they asked. 'No,' sobbed Bernadette, 'I don't know how I failed her.'

Her face betrayed her fatigue, and her aunts took her into Savy mill. Almost at once Louise Soubirous arrived, having been told of her daughter's flight. Some other Lourdes women then came into the Nicolaus' house with Mlle Estrade, who reports:

> Bernadette was sitting down with a woman beside her. I did not know yet that it was her mother. This poor woman was pale, and was looking at her child with eyes full of anguish. I asked her if she knew the little one.
>
> 'Eh, I am her unlucky mother.'
>
> 'Unlucky!' I replied. 'But why?'
>
> 'You can see what is happening. They are threatening to put us in prison. Some people are laughing at us, others are sorry for us. They say Bernadette is ill.'
>
> 'And what do you think?' I asked.
>
> She answered: 'The little one is not a liar; I believe she is incapable of deceiving us. Nor is she ill; when I ask her if she is unwell, she replies, "No." I had forbidden her to go to the grotto. But she went all the same. Yet she is not disobedient; but she tells me that she feels herself compelled to go by something she cannot explain. . . .'
>
> The poor woman aroused one's pity.

When they reached home, her mother and her aunts told the child emphatically that she was not to return to the grotto. Sadly the girl replied: 'That hurts me very much: I must disobey either you or this Lady. 'We said to her,' adds Aunt Basile: '"But if you are put in prison, you will certainly be obliged to disobey her." Bernadette answered: "Oh, that would be quite different. If I am unable to go there, I shall not go!"'

Why did the Vision not appear that afternoon? It would be puerile to point out that it was not her usual time. Besides, did the Lady stay so far away? Who then had recalled the child as she was entering the school, if it was not She, invisible this time, but present all the same? Consequently Bernadette, while obeying her parents in setting out for the Hospice, was going nevertheless to keep her promise to the Apparition by making her way afterwards to Massabielle. In the eyes of the world and in the eyes of Heaven she had committed no fault. On her knees in front of the grotto, and not seeing *Her* who had just drawn her there, the little Soubirous girl did not reason things out in a way which might have brought her some comfort; the Lady had asked her to come to Massabielle each day for a fortnight; but the Lady had not guaranteed to appear there every time.

By not showing herself to Bernadette, who so ardently longed to see her again, she gave a first flat contradiction to the officials and men of science who were to work implacably to discover in the events at Massabielle either the mercenary schemes of a poverty-stricken home or the hallucinations of a little girl. On this Monday afternoon, 22nd February, Bernadette was again found kneeling in the same place, with the same beads and the same candle in her hand as on the morning of the previous day: had she been afflicted with a touch of madness, she would, in spite of the gendarmes, have conjured up again the object of her fancies. However, with her usual candour she admitted seeing nothing. . . . If there had been any sacrilegious scheming among the Soubirous, Aunts Basile and Lucile were bound to be in the conspiracy. But far from whispering to their niece that she should say 'I saw', they took her away from Massabielle and suggested to her insistently that she should not go there again.

But there was a loftier motive. By inflicting such a bitter disappointment on the little chosen one, the Apparition intended both to test and to teach her. In her darkness Bernadette had to continue to believe in the light; for the loss of one meeting, she was not to lose her trust in Her who would give her the only true happiness. Assessing Heaven's wishes at their true value, she would not subordinate them to the commands or countercommands of any creature.

The last and possibly the supreme motive was that this innocent girl, who had already received a mission to 'pray for sinners', should now begin to make expiation on their behalf; that during the following night her poor crushed spirit should cry out in anguish, 'Why have you abandoned me?' to the Lady, of whom a mere glimpse used to send her into ecstasy.

Meanwhile, in the silence of the night, François and Louise Soubirous were weighing the pros and cons. It would be a waste of effort to try and keep their daughter away from the grotto as they had done that morning if a mysterious power was drawing her there. . . . By not showing herself, the Lady was surely teaching the parents a lesson rather than the child. They had been wrong to struggle against Heaven. . . . But what about the Commissioner of Police and his threats? Abbé Pomian had said, and quite properly, that nobody had the right to prevent Bernadette from going to the grotto to pray—nobody!

At length the Soubirous couple came to their final decision: seeing that their daughter, impelled by an interior summons, would have no other thought in the morning but of Massabielle, very well, they would let her go.

\*　　\*　　\*

'So much the worse for the Commissioner! . . . To the devil with the police!' When Lourdes awoke on the morning of Tuesday, 23rd February, exclamations of this sort must have been heard in many a house. And a hundred or more people set out for the bank of the Gave.

In the flickering glimmer of the lanterns the people stared hard at one another as they passed. There were exclamations of surprise. That Dr Dozous should go down there again, for his own interesting experiments, drew no comment; but the Captain from the Castle, and M. de Laffitte, the Quartermaster, and barrister Dufo, former Mayor of Lourdes, and M. Estrade of the Excise office and a writer in the newspapers! . . . For what purpose were these gentlemen going to Massabielle?

How M. Estrade, who had been the principal witness of Bernadette's appearance before the Commissioner, came to be among the unexpected pilgrims, has been told by his sister with her characteristic care for detail. On the previous day, she and some of her friends had planned to go together again to Massabielle. But this time

it was necessary to set out before daybreak: but it was not proper for ladies to venture out at such an hour on a road which we believed would be deserted; so my friends commissioned me to beg my brother to accompany us. By nature he is very obliging, but he did not seem so at all on this occasion, at least to begin with; he refused point-blank. That evening he saw Abbé Pey-ramale and spoke to him about my obsessions. 'Yes, go with these ladies, certainly,' said the priest. 'There is a great deal of talk about this affair, and I should not be at all sorry to have some responsible people go and see what happens.' My brother allowed himself to be won over, and the plan which I had made with my friends was carried through. . . .

My brother had listened to Bernadette giving her testimony, so entirely simple and truthful. He did indeed believe that Bernadette was not lying; but she might have been deceived. His comments on this subject caused us much laughter; the fact was that he had not yet seen the little girl in the presence of the Apparition.

We arrived at the grotto in no very serious frame of mind, but we found a number of people there from the town and the countryside who were on their knees praying, with their rosaries in their hands.

The comparative frivolity of these ladies was due to their escort's banter and his 'silly and vulgar pleasantries', as he himself noted. He quotes some of them: 'Has one of you at least got a candle? Have you armed yourselves with Holy Water? Have you brought your opera glasses. . . ?'

He himself was going under compulsion; he had no real interest in the matter. When he reached Massabielle he caught sight of the Captain with MM. de Laffitte, Dozous and Dufo, who were talking together 'in one of the corners of the grotto with great animation.'

I went and joined these gentlemen [writes M. Estrade]. Naturally, Bernadette's case was the topic under discussion. Some saw in it a morbid phenomenon, others a mirage effect; one spoke of occult influences, another of religious mania; no one dreamed of the possibility of heavenly intervention.

Again we wondered if in the hollow of the rock there might not be some fantastic shape, or some play of light to deceive the eye of a credulous girl. So we explored the grotto in every direction, and we were led to the conclusion that no illusion of this kind seemed possible.

We were finishing our investigations when a confused murmur warned us that the young visionary was on her way down. We passed through the crowd and went to take our stand beside Bernadette.

The child was going to see the Lady for the seventh time.

Nothing can replace the first-hand evidence of Jean-Baptiste Estrade, who had come there 'to scoff and jeer'.

Bernadette knelt down, pulled out her rosary from her pocket, and made a profound reverence. All these movements were performed without any awkwardness or self-consciousness, in exactly the same way and as naturally as if the child had gone into the parish church to perform her ordinary devotions. While slipping the first few beads through her fingers, she raised her eyes to the rock in a searching gaze that betrayed her impatient longings.

Suddenly, as though a flash of lightning had struck her, she gave a start of amazement, and seemed to be born into another life. Her eyes lighted up and sparkled; seraphic smiles played on her lips; an indefinable grace spread over her whole being. From within the narrow prison of the flesh, the visionary's soul seemed to be striving to show itself outwardly and proclaim its jubilation. Bernadette was no longer Bernadette! . . .

Spontaneously we men who were present uncovered our heads and bent our knees like the humblest woman. The time for argument was past, and we, like all those present at this heavenly scene, were gazing from the ecstatic girl to the rock, and from the rock to the ecstatic. We saw nothing, we heard nothing, needless to say; but what we could see and comprehend was that a conversation had begun between the mysterious Lady and the child whom we had before our eyes.

After the first transports caused by the Lady's arrival, the visionary took up the attitude of a listener. Her face and her gestures reproduced all the phases of a conversation. By turns laughing or serious, Bernadette showed approval with a nod of the head, or seemed herself to be asking questions. When the Lady was speaking, she thrilled with happiness; on the other hand when she herself was speaking and making her petitions, she would bow down to the ground and be moved to tears.

At certain moments it could be seen that the conversation was broken off; then the child would resume her Rosary, but with her eyes fixed on the rock; you would have said that she was afraid to lower even her eyelids for fear of losing sight of the entrancing object she was gazing at.

Usually the ecstatic ended her prayers with a profound reverence to the hidden Lady. I have moved much in society, perhaps too much, and I have encountered models of elegance and distinction; but never have I seen anyone make a bow with such grace and refinement as did Bernadette.

During the ecstasy the child also made the sign of the cross from time to time, and, as I said myself on the way back from the grotto, if the sign of the cross is made in heaven, it can only be made in that manner.

The ecstasy lasted for about an hour. Towards the end the visionary moved, still on her knees, from the spot where she was praying to right underneath the eglantine which was hanging down low from the rock. There she recollected herself as if for an act of homage, kissed the ground and returned still on her knees to the spot which she had just left. Her face lit up with a last splendour; then gradually, without any sudden jerk, but almost imperceptibly, the rapture faded and finally disappeared.

The visionary continued praying for a few moments longer, but now all we could see was the pleasant but rustic face of the Soubirous' girl. At length Bernadette stood up, went and rejoined her mother and became lost in the crowd. . . .

The Lady of the rock had veiled herself in vain; I had felt her presence and I was convinced that her motherly gaze had hovered over my head. It was a most solemn hour of my life! I was thrown almost into a delirium of madness by the thought that a cynical, sneering, self-satisfied fellow like me had been permitted to come so close to the Queen of Heaven. . . .

Most of the crowd had already left Massabielle while we re-mained motionless, bareheaded, abashed and dumbfounded. We proceeded to the ravine and made our way up it in complete silence: a great change was being wrought in us; our prejudices were collapsing. At last, giving free rein to our emotions which we had so far restrained, we exclaimed in turn: 'It's prodigious! It's sublime! It's divine!'

While returning with her mother, her aunts and some neigh-bours, Bernadette gave as usual a brief account of what had passed. The Lady had spoken to her, and in what she had told her there was something of which the child could not speak, and which would remain always for herself alone.

The Vision was to confide three secrets to her altogether. One could not say with certainty that these were revealed to her in the course of one ecstasy; more probably not. Bernadette herself wrote: 'In the space of this fortnight, she gave me three secrets.' 'I presume,' affirms her Aunt Basile Castérot, 'that among these secrets there was one which was of a sorrowful nature, for once, when I had caught her crying, I asked her the reason, and she answered "I cannot tell you."' The sorrowful secret, as well as any others, might have been communicated to her during this seventh Apparition.

However that may be, Bernadette kept these three secrets inviolate to her last breath, as she did also the prayer which had been taught her word by word at Massabielle.

Had the Lady, for example, foretold that she would not have many years to live? Bernadette made no objection to acknowledging this. A Lourdes woman asked her one day: 'Why do you not pray to the Blessed Virgin to cure you?' 'It is useless,' replied Bernadette. 'She has told me that I shall die young.'

In one of these inviolable confidences would there not have been some reference to her religious vocation? Many have thought so; and it was on this point that she was most frequently questioned.

> One day [relates Brother Léobard], I was talking to Bernadette at the Hospice. I said to her: 'Has the Lady revealed any secrets to you?'—'Yes, Brother.'—'Do they concern France?'—'No, Brother.'—Then I put two or three other questions to her which she answered in the negative. 'So these secrets are personal?' I added. 'Yes, Brother.' 'I know at least one of them: it is that you are to become a nun.' Bernadette lowered her head and made no reply.

She was to maintain this attitude of cautious reserve whenever people tried to extract a word from her on one or other of her secrets. Once, however, an exclamation escaped from her lips, but it could not be interpreted as an admission. One day at Nevers the Bishop of the diocese, Bishop Forcade, asked her unexpectedly if her vocation had not been foretold her at Massabielle. 'Ah! My Lord! . . . .' she said with a little air of mystery and shyness. That was all her reply.

\*　　\*　　\*

Visitors were already beginning to flock to the Soubirous' home. Their cousin, André Sajous, owner of the house, had the tact to realize 'that these people could not be fittingly shown into the room downstairs, either because of its utter destitution

or because of the stench from the manure heap in the yard'.
Sajous had agreed that Bernadette at least might use a room
upstairs. It was there that on the evening of this February 23rd,
Mlle Estrade found the young visionary 'near a fire half out and
with a small child on her knees. Beside her, I recognized our
"boarder", Jean-Marie, and with real joy I saw that, by this
link, I had already been for a long time closely connected with
a family beloved of God'.

But from the day of this visit, Jean-Marie Soubirous, a youngster of six years and nine months, who had formed the habit,
on the way back from school, of going to get a snack on M.
and Mlle Estrade's doorstep, did not appear any more at the
'Maison Cénac'.

# I O

## 'PENANCE!' AND THE MIRACULOUS
## SPRING

*(Wednesday, February 24th, Thursday, 25th;
the Eighth and Ninth Apparitions)*

IT was twelve days after the first Apparition that an account
of it, greatly distorted, appeared in the local Press.
M. Cazenave, printer, manager and editor-in-chief of the
*Lavedan: Literary, Agricultural, Industrial,* had not taken the
trouble either to despatch someone to the grotto or to seek accurate information, either from Nicolau the miller, or from the
Police Commissioner. The barrister Bibée, charged with enlight-
ening the public regarding the events, took his responsibilities
very lightly: he deemed it sufficient to make use of the gossip
of the 'gendarmes on duty in the streets, who themselves had
picked up their information from among the people'. Armed
with such weighty evidence, Bibée collaborated with Sergeant
d'Angla in the production of a first chronicle that was going to
serve two purposes: first, that of a report for the information of
Lieutenant Bourriot at Argelès and, through him, of Major
Renault at Tarbes; then, that of providing copy for the canton
of Lourdes' newspaper.

One may guess the astonishment of most people, and the
indignation and protests of the better informed, when they read
in the *Lavedan* among the 'Miscellaneous News':

A girl, whom all indications suggest is afflicted with catalepsy, has
for some days held the attention and excited the curiosity of the
people of Lourdes. It is a question of nothing less than an
apparition of the Blessed Virgin. The occasion was as follows:
Three young children had gone to gather branches of trees, the
remains of felling, at the entrance to the town. These girls, being

surprised by the proprietor, fled at top speed and hid themselves in one of the grottoes bordering on the forest road of Lourdes.

The heroine of this story sat on a stone and rested her head on her knees. She had been in this position some moments and seemed to be asleep when she leaped up with a start, shouting to her young companions: 'Look, look at that lady dressed in white. She has just spoken to me; it is the Mother of the Angels. She cannot do anything for me on this earth, but she has promised me a place in the Kingdom of the elect, if I come every morning for a fortnight and pray to her in this same place.' And she pointed to one of the openings in the grotto. Needless to say, the witnesses of this scene ran as fast as their legs could carry them and told their parents the poor visionary's words.

We shall not recount the thousand and one versions of the incident that have been given. We shall merely state that the girl goes every morning to pray at the entrance to the grotto, a candle in her hand, escorted by more than 500 people. . . .

We shall keep our readers well informed on this craze which daily finds fresh devotees.

The *Lavedan* was not, strictly speaking, a sectarian newspaper; it was just 'progressive' and never attacked matters of religion openly, but by innuendo, in guarded, wary whispers. On occasion it even took up their defence, and this no doubt was what it considered it was doing in attacking the incident of Massabielle. Its editor was not regarded as a malicious man; he counted among his acquaintances the second curate of the parish, Abbé Serres. But, if we are to believe Dr Dozous, who had his information from his nephew, Romain Capdevielle, a barrister, and a journalist in his spare time, Abbé Serres at first showed himself 'strongly opposed' to the events at the grotto, and 'before printing the articles in his paper, Cazenave, the printer, would have submitted them to him for revision'.

If, at the time when he was dashing off his first piece of prose, in which Bernadette was not even named, Barrister Bibée had been aware that several notables of the town had already become warm supporters of her whom he styled 'the poor visionary', he would no doubt have altered his tone. Like Commissioner Jacomet at the time of the first examination, the Lourdes barrister thought, by a single article, to strike a decisive blow at popular credulity. Contrary to his expectations he had to return to the matter in a second article and then in a third, which opened with this bold pronouncement:

' "Bernadette again! " you will say to us, dear reader. A little patience, please. We have deemed it our duty to give still more details, which we have good hopes will be the last.'

The sequel would on the contrary prove that, like the Commissioner, the Public Prosecutor, and all the investigators, illdisposed or not, the little *Lavedan* of Lourdes was playing the hand of Providence, in spite of itself. It imagined it was sounding the retreat; it was in fact sounding the attack. Its publicity, gratuitous and in bad taste, was to stir up the indifferent and to win thousands of 'fresh devotees' for this 'craze'.

Unforeseen assistance arrived in the nick of time. Until then, as far as can be conjectured, the 'Lady' had devoted herself to the interior formation of her young confidante. 'She took possession of the blest child slowly, but each day more powerfully, prepared her for her mission, and disposed the people, by the repeated marvel of that tranquil ecstasy, to receive the poor and obscure Bernadette as the messenger of her good pleasure.'

On that Wednesday, 24th February, when the eighth Apparition took place, Bernadette's public mission began.

\* \* \*

In his report to his Lieutenant on February 27th, the Lourdes Sergeant certified having found '400 to 500 people' at Massabielle on Wednesday the 24th. That morning, accompanied by the rural constable, Callet, he could not refrain from parading himself again before the crowd and then in front of Bernadette, who was already in ecstasy. The visionary 'did not make the slightest movement; she did not notice anything and certainly heard nothing'. The justifiable protests of some of the men disturbed this place of prayer for a while; then there was silence.

Everything takes place quietly; we would even say, in a spirit of profound recollection [the *Lavedan* acknowledged in its issue of the following day]. This child is for the multitude to-day the interpreter, if not perhaps the image, of a higher power.

This time, even before finishing the first decade of her Rosary, Bernadette 'strained forward with a gentle movement of her whole body, as though she had caught sight of an object which enraptured her'. Her eyes remained wide open, neither dilated nor blinking; then there came 'a lovely smile and graceful bows, which she made without lowering her eyes'.

At the end of five or six minutes she suddenly emerged from her rapture and stood up. She was weeping. 'Who has touched the briar?' she cried (that was the name she gave to the eglantine). This long thorny branch, the tip of which hung down and swept the ground, had just been shaken by a girl who had stooped down in order to gain a better view of the visionary. For Bernadette this stem, on which rested the feet with the golden roses, was a hallowed thing, and to touch it without reverence was an act of disrespect towards the heavenly visitor. Surely it was for this reason that the delightful audience had been broken off. . . ?

Then the child's heart heard another summons. She handed her candle to the nearest woman and moved forward with slow steps, her eyes searching the vault.

At the same time [continues Dominiquette Cazenave], I heard her moan faintly three or four separate times. While Bernadette was going on like this, Mme Dufo, the barrister's wife, who was near me, was overcome with grief and exclaimed: 'The poor little mite!' Bernadette's face had clouded over, like the earth when the sun is hidden; then suddenly she recovered her radiance, and was heard to utter a faint 'Ah' as though she were saying, 'Ah, what joy! There she is!' While watching all this, I was saying to myself: 'This little one is not inventing this. . . .'

She had knelt down a little way from the arch. Those who accompanied her there, saw her grow sad again. What was the Lady speaking to her about? In view of what was to follow, we must conclude that she unfolded before the eyes of her pure little confidante the hideous picture of the sins of mankind and the urgency of expiation.

With tears in her eyes Bernadette stood up again, clasping her rosary in her hands and seeming to want to address the crowd. In fact, the people nearest her could hear her voice coming from the depths of her ecstasy. With a gasp she repeated the word: 'Penance . . . penance . . . penance!'

The word spread from mouth to mouth through the crowd. Bernadette had delivered her first message.

*    *    *

As the crowd dispersed that day from Massabielle, deeply moved, they kept repeating the austere lesson that had fallen first from the Lady's lips and then been re-echoed in the three-fold cry of Bernadette. Thus had the child won over their minds and hearts to her cause.

But the next day these same spectators would fail to grasp the meaning or the importance of her actions, because they perceived only their apparent weirdness; and the young visionary was destined to lose her prestige. Nevertheless, this Thursday, February 25th, was a miraculous day, one never to be forgotten. On the previous day the Vision had indicated forcefully the great means of salvation for sinful humanity; now, stooping with compassion over their infirmities and their sufferings, she was to bestow on them for their solace a royal gift.

In this ninth Apparition the Lady manifested herself even before dawn. 'It was not yet light: we had a lantern to light us,' reported a Lourdes woman, Mlle Elfrida Lacrampe, who was greatly esteemed by M. and Mlle Estrade, and whose parents kept the Hôtel des Pyrénées. Not being acquainted with Massabielle yet, she had gone down there feeling more than sceptical, indeed hostile. 'Bernadette did not keep us waiting long.'

Walking at first with a lively step behind her godmother, she then quickened her pace, impatient, it would seem, to feast her eyes a minute earlier on the mysterious friend who was already drawing her. She overtook Aunt Bernarde and called out to the groups of people who were not quick enough for her liking in making way for her: 'Let me pass. . . ! Let me pass. . . !'
'At this moment, when nearly all the sightseers had arrived,' continues Mlle Lacrampe, 'there were, I think, about four hundred people in front of the grotto and under the rocks near the Gave.'

In front of the grotto towards the left, 'a flat stone sunk in the sand' marked the spot where the visionary usually stood: a spot soon well-known and revered by all and called 'Bernadette's Place'. As soon as she reached it, the child 'raised her dress a little, so as not to muddy it, and then knelt down'. She took out her beads and made the sign of the Cross with the Crucifix. All these details were checked by Mlle Elfrida Lacrampe carefully but grudgingly. She had been able to secure a place 'on the right, up against the rock, almost beneath the niche where the Apparition used to come'.

The child [she relates] had not recited a decade of her beads when all of a sudden she set off on her knees and began to clamber in this way up the slope that led to the interior of the grotto. She passed in front of me, a short distance away. On reaching the entrance to the vault she gently, and without pausing, pushed aside the branches that hung down from the rock. . . . From there she went on towards the back of the grotto. The crowd was pressing close behind her. . . .

When she reached the back of the grotto, Bernadette turned about and came back, still on her knees, down the same slope. I witnessed there a *tour de force*, and I ought to have marvelled more at the ease and dignity of this child's movements in such a posture and on steeply sloping ground that was very uneven and strewn with stones which jutted out sharply here and there. At the time I saw nothing in Bernadette's movements, apart from the *tour de force*, but a ridiculous wriggle, for it seemed to me purposeless.

At that moment the eye-witness, still leaning against the rock, lost sight of Bernadette, who was surrounded by the moving crowd. But Aunt Bernarde had started in pursuit of her god-child. 'Everyone was astonished,' she attests. 'Finding nothing under the rock, the child turned off towards the river.' What was happening then? Only Bernadette could explain and she has done so:

The Lady said to me: 'Go and drink at the spring and wash yourself in it.' Not seeing any spring I was going to drink from the Gave. She told me that it was not there. She pointed with her finger to [the place of] the spring. I went there. I saw merely a bit of dirty water; I put my hand in it, but I could not get hold of any. I scratched and the water came, but muddy. Three times I threw it away; the fourth time I was able to drink some.

The essence of the miracle springs to life again in those few lines. If in actual fact the never-failing spring that was going to be revealed by her timid fingers, was not actually created that very minute by a miracle of the Almighty, none the less its discovery was a divine prodigy.

'There was not at this date any visible spring in the grotto at Massabielle; nothing more than an intermittent ooze or condensation.' It was one of these patches of ooze which Bernadette had in front of her when she had advanced over the heap of gravel to 'drink at the spring and to wash in it'. But when she had scratched the sand, a hidden spring began to gush forth with a far greater abundance of water than was there before.

It should be explained that the Lourdes grotto 'forms part of one of those old water tracks or courses, long since dried up', which, in prehistoric times, wore its way through the limestone and schists of the Béout massif. Massabielle, or the 'Vieille Masse', as has already been pointed out, is an extension of this massif. Now below 'the sandy gravel' which had been carried down by the Gave in flood, and which raised the floor of the grotto by a yard and a half, there still existed some 'moraine material', that is to say, débris of rock, shingle and granitic sand brought down to this valley of the Gave by the 'great glacier of Argelès' which, in the course of a geological upheaval, came down from the present region of Gavarnie. Buried below the deep embankment there existed a spring 'of remarkable purity and clearness', the presence of which was not indicated by anything in the grotto. 'Silent and unknown it flowed away' through the subsoil 'towards the Gave'.

By a commanding gesture the Lady had guided Bernadette to a point directly above its original spout (its 'bed', as the learned call it). 'I scratched and the water came, but muddy.' That means—and one can affirm it without fear of error now that the proof of it has been definitely established—that out of the fissure in the rock from which it spurted, the spring rose, in a manner humanly inexplicable, through stones, sand and gravel, right into the little hand of the child in ecstasy. And at that moment, in the sight of all, the 'spring' of which the Vision spoke came into being.[1]

When Bernadette's face was visible again, various exclamations broke from the crowd. 'They were surprised,' declared Martin

[1] Cf. p. 388.

Tarbès, 'they could not understand what it meant.' But there
was nothing astonishing in that since no one saw the Lady
whose beneficent will was directing the actions of the visionary.
After moving this way and that, and bending down to the
ground, Bernadette reappeared, her face stained with muddy
water. Distress filled their hearts. 'Everyone began to say:
"She is out of her mind!"' Aunt Bernarde quickly wiped her
godchild's mouth and chin.

The general disappointment increased, and the cry 'She's
mad!' grew even louder when the child, still on her knees, was
seen stretching out her arm towards the top of the slope and
plucking 'three small handfuls of a little weed" and putting
them between her teeth. (This weed was, it is believed, the
*dorine*, or golden saxifrage, which thrives among the moist rocks
of these mountains.)

The reason was—though again no one among those present
could suspect it—that the Lady had just given her the order:
'Go and eat that weed which you will find there.'

At that moment one of her Catechism companions, the
little Garros girl, was close beside her. In fact, as the witness
testified,

> I saw Bernadette, on the order of the Apparition, and without
> taking her eyes off her, break off the root of the plant she was
> holding, and force herself to eat some of the leaves, chewing them
> for a time and then probably spitting them out because, as she
> told me later, this weed was tough and nasty.

'After that,' reported Aunt Bernarde, 'she came down, walking upright on her feet.' She gazed again for two or three
minutes at the Apparition which lingered in the grotto. 'I went
with her for fear she might fall.' She went down again on her
knees and returned in this manner to her usual place. M.
Estrade noted then her 'magnificent sign of the cross'.

> The ecstasy over [concludes her godmother mournfully], we took
> her back. People were jeering. We walked quickly along the
> road to escape the crowd. They were following us as though it
> were a comedy.

Instead of examining the hole in the sand where the water
was already becoming clearer and was enlarging the hole, people

thought only of getting away from Massabielle, as though ashamed of ever having come there.

M. Estrade in particular was hurrying off by his sister's side, bewildered and disgusted. He heard Mlle Lacrampe, whom he had pressed into coming to the grotto, shout to him in passing: 'You would have done better to leave me at home; I did not believe in it much before; I believe still less now. That is all you have gained!' He had noticed at the 'weird performance' at the grotto the wife of the Commissioner, Mme Jacomet, who certainly 'was not going to carry home any news favourable to the faith'.

On their return home, the brother and sister continued to exchange impressions. Was it possible, all the same, that a child so calm, so prudent, so balanced usually—and they had been convinced of this on that first occasion of the Commissioner's interrogation—that a child whom only yesterday they had marvelled at when they watched her lost in ecstasy, should suddenly, on this unhappy morning of Thursday, February 25th, give signs of fantastic eccentricity, almost of madness? . . .

It was painful [wrote M. Estrade] to rid myself of my sweet illusions. On the evening of that day of mysteries I called Bernadette to my house. I wanted to see her, to question her, to examine her closely; in a word, to assure myself of her mental state.

The little girl came in as usual with her tranquil, assured and engaging air. I got her to talk and chatter away; I tried her with verbal quibbles, surprises and contradictory accounts: nothing in the child's replies or remarks could make you suspect the existence of the slightest mental derangement.

Bernadette related how she had suited her actions and her movements to and fro to the orders of the Lady.

'But why,' asked M. Estrade, 'did the Lady oblige you to drink and wash yourself in the muddy water when you had very nice water in the Gave?' 'I have no idea.'

The scene in the grotto was not yet explained.

Since then, it has been possible to understand.

Having to crawl on her knees, drink muddy water which dirtied her face, chew a wild plant which had a repulsive taste, and to crown all, listen to the hostile shouts . . . in this way the messenger of the Apparition was beginning to put into practice her austere cry of yesterday: 'Penance, penance. . . !'

There are other practical lessons here for the direction of every soul that aspires to a higher and nobler life, but which in its flight might shatter itself against self-love, the spirit of independence or the passion for pleasure. Detachment, obedience, humility, was the refrain of this miraculous spring from its first murmurings; and it reveals to the world once more that it is by the lowliest means that God, when he pleases, achieves great things.

# II

## 'A CHAPEL!'

### (Tenth and Eleventh Apparitions:
### Saturday and Sunday, February 27th and 28th)

FRIDAY, February 26th, was to prove another penitential day for Bernadette; there was none of the hoped-for consolation.

Logically speaking, had it been a question of purely human affairs, such as a well-organized hoax or the pranks of a hallucinated girl, then it was 'good-bye' for ever to the 'Lourdes crowds' on that morning of the 26th.

Why was it that Massabielle continued to maintain its mysterious attraction? During the previous day some people had returned to the grotto and made a fresh discovery. They were 'astonished to see coming down from the spot where Bernadette had scratched the ground, a ribbon of water which they had never noticed before; the little stream was growing bigger every minute'. They brought some of this water home and resolved to go back again to Massabielle.

What is more, an important market had been held on the previous day at Tarbes, and the public squares and tavern bars echoed with talk of a topic never heard of before: apparitions and visions were as much discussed as business. Then, in the evening, a number of strangers had come in from the county town to spend the night in Lourdes; they wanted to be at the grotto early the next morning. Example is catching: Lourdes people, who had been protesting that morning that the farce had gone on long enough, were proclaiming that evening their impatience to visit the bank of the Gave again. Truly a grace was at work in their hearts.

Doctor Dozous, who was present once more, has described the scene briefly:

Bernadette, on Friday, February 26th, left her home just as day was breaking and made her way to the grottoes of Massabielle in the middle of a very large crowd. . . .
The child knelt down and prayed for a long time, telling her beads. The Lady did not appear.
Bernadette stood up sad and distressed at not being able to enjoy the sight of her heavenly visitor that day.

When she withdrew between her mother and godmother, no protest, not even a murmur, arose from the crowd: they had been edified and deeply moved at seeing her pray with such profound absorption, and each of them in his own way had been joining in her prayer.

Although, in the words of Dr Dozous, Bernadette remained 'firmly confident of the return of the Lady who had until then been so kind to her', 'she wept all the way along the road, leaning on her aunt's arm', and once she was back in the 'dungeon', her young heart overflowing with grief found relief again in tears.

\*　\*　\*

Saturday, February 27th: the air was icy cold, but the gathering at the grotto was none the smaller for that; just the reverse. People had come from almost everywhere in the neighbourhood, even from quite a distance. 'We set out from Saint-Pé an hour after midnight,' related Jeanne Laborde-Cassus. 'There were three of us; the other two, a neighbour and his wife, had never been before. Towards 3 a.m. we were in our places and we prayed to the good God.'

At almost the same moment a certain person arrived at Massabielle for the first time: it was M. Clarens, the future headmaster of the Lourdes senior primary school. Married to a Soubirous, he was related to Bernadette and lived in the neighbourhood of the Petits-Fossés; but so far he had not taken the trouble to go and see his young cousin in ecstasy. During the night of February 26th-27th, 'feeling irritated by the constant clatter of sabots in the street . . . and driven more by vexation than curiosity', he got out of bed, dressed himself and went out.

It was three o'clock in the morning! Yet, he declares, 'I arrived a little late'; over the whole sandy bank between the canal and the rocks of Massabielle stood a solid mass of people . . . and the crag which stands up over the Gave was completely covered with them. . . . It was then,' explains the pedagogue, 'that I realized that certain calculators had been mistaken when they told us that in a compact mass six persons at most are reckoned per square yard. In this case there were easily ten to twelve.' And as Jeanne Laborde-Cassus testifies, 'There were people in the meadow, even, on the other side of the Gave.'

At last [continues M. Clarens] Bernadette appeared, at half-past six. A passage had to be cleared for her as far as the grotto. . . . There was considerable commotion for a time, but as soon as the little one knelt down . . . silence fell: there was on every side a kind of profound concentration that was very pleasing.

'It was an extraordinary thing, the silence of this crowd,' says Pierre Callet, the village constable. 'It was just as though you were in church.' And Cyprine Gesta said: 'During the ecstasy there was a terrible calm over everyone; you felt frightened, but you wanted to stay longer.' However, it was rather a feeling of joy that filled some other Lourdes girls of fifteen to sixteen years of age: 'At the grotto, while Bernadette was praying, many others were praying too. When we were there we felt very happy; we should have liked to stay there for ever.'
M. Clarens was able to watch Bernadette almost the whole time during this tenth Apparition. She 'fixed her gaze on the opening in the brambles, prayed a few moments with a candle in her hand and quite still; then she turned very pale, smiled and bowed her head several times in greeting, then became sad as though about to weep, smiled again and bowed. . . . She seemed as though she no longer belonged to this world.'
Jeanne Laborde observed that she fell into ecstasy 'almost as soon as she was on her knees, and it lasted about a quarter of an hour'. The visionary 'then stood up', continued M. Clarens, 'went down on her knees a second time and in this posture climbed up through the gap made for her in the crowd towards the grotto, kissing the ground frequently on the way'.
This was the first time that Bernadette had been seen perform-

ing this act of humility and penance. At the end of the ecstasy she disclosed that she had only been obeying a fresh instruction from the Lady: 'Go and kiss the ground as a penance for sinners.'

On coming out of her rapture she made her way to the miraculous spring. There she scooped up some water in the hollow of her hand, took several drinks, washed herself a little, and plucked some blades of grass.

While on her way back towards the Pont-Vieux she said an extraordinary thing to her Aunt Bernarde, in whom she now confided most readily. The Lady had given her another commission: 'Go and tell the priests to have a chapel built here.'

By the general term 'priests' the Apparition meant the clergy together with their hierarchy; and the Bishop of Tarbes was included in this order. Bernarde Castérot took it to mean simply the clergy of Lourdes, the parish priest and his curates. Now the aunt had a holy fear of Abbé Peyramale; so she advised her godchild to go and find her confessor, Abbé Pomian. The latter, who did not wish to say anything, and who, in fact, 'said nothing', was gently tactful. He listened to Bernadette 'without letting her know what was in his mind' and sent her to the parish priest.

Bernadette, as she herself has certified, 'always carried out at once the commissions given her' by the Lady of the grotto. With a determined step the child set off for the Curé's house.

But it is time to make our acquaintance with the person she was going there to see.

Son of a doctor, who was in practice in Momères, M. Marie-Dominique Peyramale had been brought into the world there on January 9th, 1811. He was therefore just over forty-seven years old at the end of this February 1858. He had been parish priest of Lourdes since 1854.

A girl from Nantes, who visited him in May 1859, sketched his outward appearance in these few strokes: 'He is a man of big build, with a broad open forehead, a sedate and impressive bearing, and eyes full of fire. . . .' M. Estrade's description of him differs little from this, but he adds a portrait of his character: 'He was of the mountaineer type, mellowed but not altogether stripped of their characteristics. . . . His speech was short and sharp, and at first one felt no attraction towards him. . . . There were two sides to him: one very rough, the other good-natured, straightforward and upright. The second made you forget the first.'

He was an original and strong personality. Somewhat jealous of his authority, which, however, no one disputed; when he was opposed he flew into fits of temper during which he used to thunder at the top of his powerful voice. 'An impulsive, enthusiastic character, a soul deeply responsive,' was the judgment of Henri Lasserre. He had his hours of depression and melancholy. But his defects were outweighed by his virtues: disinterested zeal, child-like piety, and a heart of gold. He could not encounter distress without succouring it; and he rendered himself penniless thereby. Whatever differences of opinion there might have been from time to time between himself and his three curates, it was common knowledge that the Lourdes clergy got on famously together.

However, his lordly air intimidated the ordinary folk, and Sergeant d'Angla, who 'saw him several times during the period of the Apparitions', felt justified in saying that in the parish he 'was more respected than loved'. The most popular priest in Lourdes, according to the same gendarme, was Abbé Pomian, who was 'full of good sense and had a disposition that was fatherly yet at the same time youthful'.

Unquestionably, M. Peyramale, coming from a bourgeois family, had a partiality for the higher social circles of Lourdes. 'A man who liked good company, and who had a nimble mind that went straight to the point,' remarks Abbé Pène, his curate; and what is more, being a man of wide reading, he could hold his own in conversation with the most cultured men of his town. It is not surprising that he sought them out. And Abbé Pène continues, 'towards the very ones among them who practised their religion least he paid certain kindly attentions', instigated no doubt by a desire for their reconciliation that was very understandable. The curate seems less accurate in his views when he connects M. Peyramale's early opposition to the events at Massabielle with the secret ambition 'to win or retain the good favour of these gentlemen'. Undoubtedly his attitude had less personal motives. Be that as it may, he had forbidden his curates 'to take the least part in the happenings at the grotto, even as mere spectators'.

Thus, by virtue of his good qualities as well as by his defects, Abbé Peyramale proved to be the very man for the situation. Not only did his gruffness and scoldings act as a foil to the angelic sweetness of his young parishioner, but his cautious doubts about the Apparitions (doubts that were later to be transformed into a deep faith) served the cause of truth by obliging Bernadette to explain and defend herself.

According to a judicious remark of St Gregory the Great, 'the incredulity of St Thomas was of more advantage to our faith than the faith of the other Disciples'. Likewise one may be permitted to say that a parish priest of Lourdes, kindly disposed and easily persuaded, might have served the cause of the Apparitions less effectively than the brusque and wary Abbé Peyramale. For the latter's opposition, although more veiled than that of the police and the magistrates, succeeded in bringing out the truth more clearly.

On the very day previous to that on which Bernadette came unexpectedly to see him, the Curé of Lourdes had called at the Bishop's House in Tarbes. Till then, the Curé had had to be satisfied with keeping his Bishop informed of the events at Massabielle by regular correspondence. This he had done by means of reports, more or less accurate, but not devoid of his own irony and verve. In his few brief replies the prelate had not committed himself: he preferred an explanation by word of mouth; hence the interview suggested to M. Peyramale for Friday, February 26th.

After giving a brief summary of the facts, the parish priest explained to his Bishop his own conduct in the affair, and that of his curates: his own attitude of 'wait and see'; Abbé Pomian's calm and indulgent refusal to believe; the determined opposition of Abbé Serres; and the reactions—quite lively at times—of the young Abbé Pène. On his return he told the curates the result of the interview:

> I explained to His Lordship that some of us consider that there would be no harm in our being present at the scenes in the grotto, whilst others are of a contrary opinion. I added, 'May we go there, or ought we to remain aloof?' His Lordship, after a moment's thought, said: 'Go there.' I objected: 'If we go there,

My Lord, it will be said that we are pulling the strings behind this little girl, and making her play a farce.' 'Oh, well then,' replied the Bishop, 'don't go there.'

Soon it was no longer a secret among the diocesan clergy that the austere, judicious Bishop Laurence, having received first-hand information from the parish priest of Lourdes, was in private 'ridiculing Bernadette and her visions'. He was far from being the only one. A young priest, Abbé Antoine Dézirat, who had just been present himself that very morning at the twelfth Apparition, called at the Junior Seminary of Saint-Pé and discussed Massabielle with several of the professors. They all 'started to laugh heartily at his credulity'. While returning next day to his family at Barbazan-Debat, he had occasion to meet some other colleagues. 'I told them,' he said, 'about the event that had taken place in Lourdes; all of them received my words with a pitying smile.'

Lourdes did not possess a presbytery, strictly speaking: M. Peyramale rented the 'maison Lavigne' on the Tarbes-Argelès road. It was a square building, one storey high, and very commonplace in appearance: it was surrounded by a garden, with a courtyard in front. Resolutely Bernadette opened the gate and almost at once found herself in the presence of M. le Curé, who was braving the cold and saying his breviary in the yard.

At the sound of the gate [relates M. Estrade, who states that he secured these details first-hand from M. Peyramale], the priest raised his eyes and saw a girl coming towards him. He did not know Bernadette by sight, or at least he had merely caught a glimpse of her in the church one day. . . . The priest closed his breviary and asked the girl who she was and what she wanted.

'I am Bernadette Soubirous.'

'Ah, so it's you!' said the Curé, examining the young peasant girl superciliously. 'Queer stories are being told about you, my poor Bernadette.'

Having said that, M. Peyramale (whom Bernadette was 'following like a little lamb') went towards his house. 'Come in,' he told the child, without turning round. He led her into his parlour and when he was seated he said, 'Well, now, why do you want me?' Bernadette, who 'had placed herself in front

of him without any thought for the formalities of introduction ',
replied simply:
'Monsieur le Curé, the Lady of the grotto has ordered me
to tell the priests that she wishes to have a chapel at Massabielle.'
He replied 'in a not very agreeable tone' (as Bernadette herself remarks): 'What is this lady?'
'She is a very beautiful lady, all surrounded with light, who
appears to me at Massabielle.'
'I don't understand. How has this lady shown herself to you?'
Then 'with a ring of sincerity which compelled confidence'
Bernadette repeated to the priest the account which the Public
Prosecutor and the Commissioner had already heard. In the
words of M. Estrade, the priest had to force back the tears which
rose to his eyes. Without betraying any emotion he continued
to question Bernadette in the same tone.
'What is this lady's name?'
'I don't know.'
'You have not asked her?'
'Yes, but when I ask her, she smiles but does not reply.'
'And you assert that she has instructed you to tell me that
she wants a chapel at Massabielle?'
'Yes.'
At such a categorical assertion the excitable M. Peyramale
flared up. 'Girl,' he cried, 'you are going out of your mind!
What! A lady who goes and perches on a rock! A lady you do
not know! A lady who is perhaps as lunatic as you! This
woman comes and tells you to invite us to have a chapel built
for her at the grotto! And you accept such messages? And you
imagine we are fools enough to listen to them? Look here, girl,
you are just a little joker. . . !'
Realizing, perhaps, that he had struck too hard and gone too
fast, he stopped bellowing.
'Since you stick to this lady,' he added, as if seizing on an idea
that had just crossed his mind, 'find out first who she is; then, if
she thinks she has any right to a chapel, ask her from me to
prove it by making the rose-bush at the grotto flower
immediately.'
He had said this without due reflection, without at least considering that the spring, of which he must have heard, might
already be a sign from Heaven; without saying to himself, as he

would have done in his calmer moments, that it could only be one of two things: either there was nothing there for Bernadette to see during her astonishing ecstasy except a hole in the rock—in which case the sap would remain inactive in the old eglantine which had been stripped by the winter weather; or else the Lady of the Apparitions was a 'living' reality, as the child declared; that is to say, she was a person who was superior to our human nature, and close to the Divine; who was able to command whatever she desired, and took no orders from mortals. If the wild rose failed to flower suddenly and miraculously on a winter's day, this still would not prove that the mysterious being (on whose orders the spring at Massabielle had forced its way up through impassable obstacles) could not perform new and greater prodigies. . . . The Curé of Lourdes might have done better, while he was about it, to demand that the Lady should exhibit herself to the gaze of the crowds!

As for Bernadette she did not puzzle her young head long over the matter. 'When the squall had passed,' concludes M. Estrade, 'she got up bashfully, gave M. le Curé a look that bore no grudge, bowed and departed.'

*    *    *

On Sunday, 28th February, rain fell during the latter hours of the night. In spite of this, there was a larger gathering than usual in front of the grotto: in M. Estrade's judgment, 2,000 people, among whom were a large number of workmen and many of the sixty soldiers who formed the garrison of the Castle.

Bernadette was sighted shortly before 7 a.m. 'She arrived all neat and tidy, dressed in her modest Sunday best.' Her Aunt Lucile accompanied her, carrying the candle. The child already had her beads in her hand and 'was looking down at the valley of the Gave below with the expression of one who was in a hurry to get there.'

But her advance through the serried ranks was very slow. Fortunately, exceeding his orders, the rural constable, Callet, who had gone to meet her at the door of the 'dungeon', walked ahead of her at the approach to the grotto, giving the order: 'Stand back! . . . Bernadette is here!' Yet this did not prevent the worthy fellow from summoning down, at the top of his loud voice, some foolhardy folk who were clinging to the shrubs 'above the precipice. . . . They were,' he reported, 'like birds on the branches. . . . There was every need for the Blessed Virgin to intervene: they had been there for three or four hours in that fearful cold.'

The remarkable feature of this eleventh Apparition was to be the still greater penance done by Bernadette. Having entered into ecstasy she recited two or three decades of the Rosary. Suddenly she made an effort to move forward on her knees, but could not do so because the crowd was too densely packed around her. Two of the soldiers, however, managed to get near the child and shouting, 'Make way, make way,' they led her all the way to the spot she wanted to reach. She clambered up a distance of eight or nine yards and then came down again to her place. She went up a second time and came down again, and then a third time—as often, in fact, as the Lady ordered her to perform this penitential exercise.

'You slipped when you tried to go up on your feet, as the ground was covered in a sort of slime; it was like mud,' observes Pierre Callet. 'But I did not see Bernadette's clothes dirtied; and some others noticed, as I did, that she did not get dirtied.' However—and this detail did not escape Jacquette Pène—'while kissing the ground she dirtied her lips and hands; but this did not stop her at all.'

She had passed in front of me once, and she was about to pass me again [continues Jacquette Pène]. I said to the old country constable who was standing there: 'There is something new to-day.' The constable was already greatly moved and my remark was a sort of signal for him to give vent to his feelings: 'Oh, yes,' he exclaimed, 'it gets more and more extraordinary.' And turning to the crowd he cried in a very loud voice, 'Kiss the ground, all of you!'

The crowd obeyed him. Those who could do so went down on their knees, kissing the ground several times, just as Bernadette was doing. There were so many people that the crush prevented the majority from reaching down to the ground; but all did their best to obey. The constable set the example, and on his knees he kissed the ground over and over again. . . .

Whether from a feeling of reverence or the impossibility of

doing otherwise, the crowd made no effort to protect themselves from the rain. It is true that a few umbrellas appeared, but people soon cried out, 'Put those umbrellas down.'

Abbé Pène asked his sister Jacquette later, 'if, while performing her exercises of walking on her knees and kissing the ground, Bernadette remained all the time in ecstasy.' 'Yes,' replied the girl, 'the whole time: in the sense that she seemed absorbed and remained as though alone in the midst of this vast crowd, without any noise or incident seeming to interrupt her absorption either in her contemplation of the Lady or in the execution of her orders.'

During the moments of ecstasy which preceded her exhausting movements to and fro on her knees, Bernadette was careful not to forget the embarrassing message entrusted to her by M. Peyramale. This message met with the reception it deserved. After saying her beads, as the visionary herself has recorded, she asked the Lady once more on behalf of the Curé of Lourdes, to give her name and then prove her presence by the immediate flowering of the eglantine. 'On my return,' she adds, 'I went to the Curé's house to tell him that I had carried out his order, but that the Lady had merely smiled.'

# 12

## 'COME IN PROCESSION!'

### (Twelfth and Thirteenth Apparitions,
### Monday and Tuesday, March 1st and 2nd)

THE confusion of the Lourdes civil authorities can easily be imagined. The Mayor, the Commissioner, the Public Prosecutor, though no enemies of the supernatural, had deemed it prudent to exclude it from the Soubirous affair. On the evening of Sunday, February 21st, these gentlemen had retired to bed with satisfaction, convinced that they had finally diverted Bernadette and her accomplices (if she ever had any) from the grotto. No, the contortions at Massabielle would never occur again: gendarmes, police, rural constable, were all on the watch; their chiefs could sleep in peace.

They had a rude awakening! Still the same continual clatter of sabots hurrying towards the grotto in an ironical crescendo! . . . Whom did they think they were fooling?

However, through fear of ridicule, the Public Prosecutor, M. Dutour, declined to face this stubborn little Soubirous girl again after his failure of a week ago. He no longer felt himself equal to a direct encounter with the visionary of Massabielle. In his opinion it was for the Examining Magistrate Rives to take the matter in hand. His title would inspire awe; for, in the eyes of the poorer folk, to be summoned before an Examining Magistrate was like being brought to trial. . . . It was only a short step from there to prison. Briefly, they would rely on intimidation in this case. M. Rives, when necessary, knew how to act the bully. Last year he had dealt roughly with François Soubirous; he had no intention of being more gentle with his daughter. However, there was to be no formal summons, no publicity. The placid constable, Latapie, would bring Bernadette in.

Sceptical as to the reality of the Apparitions, M. Rives does not seem to have treated the interrogation of the visionary very seriously. He has left no note of it. His method was to be brief, sharp, threatening, derisive: the attitude of a man sure of victory. He left to others the pleasantries of the Café Français!

The constable, who had a good memory, has, in default of the magistrate, reconstructed the scene in a homely and lively style.

After High Mass the Commissioner came up to me in front of the church and said, 'Wait here with me for a while.' When it was time for the Hospice Sisters and their little pupils to come out, the Commissioner said to me: 'Do you know little Bernadette?'—'Yes.—'Go and get her as soon as she comes out.'

When she came out, close to the Sister and in file like the rest, I took her gently by the arm. 'Why are you taking her away?' asked the Sister, and began to cry. 'I have orders,' I said. Bernadette said to me: 'What do you want me for?' I answered: 'Little girl, you must come with us.' She started to laugh and said: 'Hold me tight or I shall escape.' I walked beside the little girl, and the Commissioner was behind me. People were watching in astonishment, without saying anything.

We went to the house of M. Rives, the Examining Magistrate, who was lodging with M. Claverie the notary. When we entered the magistrate said to Bernadette in patois: 'Are you there, you little rascal?'—'Yes, sir, I am here.'

'We are going to lock you up. What are you after at the grotto? Why do you make everybody run after you like this? There is somebody behind you driving you on to act like this. We are going to put you in prison.'

'I'm ready. Put me in there and make it solid and well fastened, or else I shall escape.'

These gentlemen were not laughing. The Magistrate said: 'You must give up going to the grotto.'

'I shall not deprive myself of any opportunity of going there.'

'You will be locked up.'

'If I can't go, then I shan't go.'

'I shall put you to death in prison.'

At that moment the Sister Superior of the Hospice entered. She was weeping and said: 'I implore you, gentlemen, leave the little one to us. Do not put her to death!'

Little Bernadette must have been a saint or must have been greatly inspired to keep as cool as she did. The Magistrate said to the Commissioner: 'What do you want to do about it? Let us release her: we have no bone to pick with her.'

Bernadette was sitting in front of the Magistrate; the Magistrate was at a table; M. Jacomet was walking up and down; I myself was standing near Bernadette.

Then she went away with the Sister, and on leaving she said: 'I want to go there: Thursday is the last day.'

A few moments later, MM. Rives and Jacomet had a meeting with M. Dutour. All three were soon of the same opinion: the magistrates and local police, thwarted or badly supported in their action, had failed to secure a peaceful solution: this case required the support of a higher judicial personage: the Public Prosecutor had therefore to send a detailed report to inform his chief, the Attorney General, residing at Pau.

He drew up for him, in measured terms, an account of the events from Thursday, February 11th to Monday, March 1st. He did not fail to point out how, until then, the police had had 'to restrict themselves to the duty of close observation', but that they were very much afraid 'of finding themselves compelled to intervene'. The fact was that 'Bernarde Soubirous', as the Prosecutor sometimes styled her, was 'exercising a real fascina- tion. On the following Thursday, March 4th, the final visit to the grotto was to take place.' One could foresee 'an immense throng' on that Thursday, which was market-day. What was going to happen? . . . Prudence would have counselled keeping the child away from the place of her 'prolonged ecstasies'; but to do that it would have been necessary to have recourse to extreme measures, to imprisonment. Unfortunately 'it would have been difficult to justify this measure, for it was impossible to prove the bad faith of the supposed visionary, or the material elements of an indictable act'. If only one could be assured of the co-operation of the parish clergy! 'The clergy are displaying an excessive reserve in this matter.' In any case, the Public Prosecutor would act in concert with the local authority to fore- stall any disorder. . . . Should firm measures become necessary, he would devise them with a full sense of his duty. . . .'

That midday, when Bernadette returned to her family, there was a tearful scene. 'Don't cry,' exclaimed the little girl, throwing her arms round her mother's neck. 'The Blessed Virgin will defend us.'

*     *     *

At seven o'clock the following morning the child was again at Massabielle, as resolute as the day before. This Monday, March 1st, was the twelfth day of the exciting fortnight.

This time, not only her mother was at her side, but also her father. François Soubirous had felt nervous when he learned that during her ecstasies the little one was hemmed in by an inconsiderate crowd, for ill-natured folk could easily slip in among them; so he had come to protect her.

The courage of this father and mother, who have been too much forgotten, deserves our admiration. For the past week they had felt that they were living in an atmosphere of suspicion. 'Their least movement was spied upon,' reports M. Estrade, 'the children of the family were cunningly coaxed and questioned in order to obtain from them some indiscreet disclosure. During the night mysterious people came and glued their faces to doors and windows, peeping through the chinks to see what was going on in the suspected house.' Above all, there hung over the head of a darling daughter dark threats of removal or imprisonment. . . . All the same there they both were at her side as a protest and a rampart, in front of this grotto where she was forbidden to go! One might truly say that on that morning François and Louise Soubirous had heard at the same time as their daughter the interior call of the Lady.

This was not the only new feature on this Monday, March 1st; there were others no less worthy of record.

A soutane appeared at Massabielle: a priest, Abbé Antoine Dézirat, aged twenty-seven and recently ordained. While awaiting appointment he was living with his family at Brabazan-Debat, in the canton of Tarbes. He had been visiting the former Curé of his native parish, M. Glère, who had now become Curé of Omex in the canton of Lourdes itself. 'It was then,' he related, 'that I first heard mention of the marvels of Lourdes. I was curious to see for myself. . . .'

He had set out very early in a carriage with some people from Omex, but, although it was still dark, he avoided passing through the town of Lourdes on account of the prohibition laid down by M. le Curé Peyramale. (Actually it was only the clerics of the Curé's own canton who had been forbidden to go to the grotto.) The young priest arrived at Massabielle at daybreak. He could scarcely have had any preconceived ideas about the Apparitions, but he was afraid of an illusion or 'that the devil might be there, transformed into an angel of light'. He was a highly intelligent young man, refined and pious even to scrupulosity.

A report from M. Jacomet, dated the following day, specifies that 'on Monday morning, March 1st . . . 1,300 people were counted returning to the town'; there might well have been as many more along the country roads.

'People of every sort, workmen, country-folk, townsfolk and some soldiers' . . . took up their position and waited for Bernadette. The travellers from Omex joined them. And thus Abbé Dézirat was in a position to compare Bernadette in ordinary life with Bernadette in deep ecstasy.

> She arrived after about an hour [he reports]. From the moment she appeared, I watched her closely. Her face was calm, her look unassuming, her walk most natural, neither slow nor hurried. No sign of exaltation, not a trace of disease. . . .
> The crowd on the road pressed close behind the child to get to the scene of the Apparition. Once there, I did as the rest. When we arrived in front of the grotto, someone said: 'Let the priest through.' These words, though spoken softly, were easily heard, for there was a deep silence over everything. They made way for me, and advancing a few paces I was quite close to Bernadette, a yard away, not more . . .
> Between the moment when I got near to the child and the moment when the vision began, there was scarcely time to recite a decade. . . ."

In a hurry to leave early—for the tacit disapproval of M. Peyramale made him uneasy—the priest concentrated his whole attention on the young ecstatic.

> By her posture and by the expression on her face, it was evident that her soul was enraptured. What profound peace! What serenity! What lofty contemplation! Her smile was beyond all description . . . The child's gaze, fixed on the Apparition, was no less captivating. Impossible to imagine anything so pure, so sweet, so loving. . . .

I had watched Bernadette with scrupulous care while she was making her way to the grotto. What a difference between what she was then and what she was as I saw her at the moment of the Apparition. It was like the difference between matter and spirit . . .

And the crowd?

The whole crowd felt a gentle thrill. Bernadette alone saw the Apparition, but everyone felt, as it were, conscious of its presence. Joy mingled with fear was depicted on every face. It is difficult to imagine a more religious spectacle. Oh, how good it was to be there! I felt I was on the threshold of Paradise.

Abbé Dézirat was not present at the end of the ecstasy. 'I was eager to see it,' he adds, 'and it was only by a great effort that I tore myself away from this hallowed spot.' Others were to witness an incident which was lost on the puzzled crowd, and which lent itself to fantastic interpretations.

Here again we must leave the word to M. Estrade, who was present during this twelfth Apparition.

I witnessed that day a great manifestation of religious enthusiasm. Bernadette had just returned from her place under the spur of the rock. Kneeling down again she took her beads as usual from her pocket, but as soon as she lifted her eyes again to the privileged bush, her face became sad. . . . She held up her beads with surprise as high as her little arm would allow. . . . There was a moment's pause, then suddenly back went the beads into her pocket. Instantly she displayed another pair which she waved and held up as high as the first. The look of anguish vanished from her face. She bowed, smiled once more and recommenced her prayer.

With a spontaneous movement everyone took out their rosaries and waved them. Then they shouted 'Vive Marie' and went down on their knees and prayed with tears in their eyes.

The opponents of belief [in the Apparitions] spread the rumour that Bernadette had that day blessed the rosaries.

It was a rumour without any foundation, for on the very same day the visionary explained its origin. A devout woman of Lourdes, a dressmaker by profession, Pauline Sans, too feeble to go all the way down to Massabielle, had met Bernadette on her way and begged of her as a great favour to use her beads when praying at the grotto.

I promised her to do so and I did so [Bernadette afterwards told Abbé Pène and his sister Jacquette]. Towards the end of the Apparition the Lady asked me where my own beads were. I replied that I had them in my pocket. She said to me: 'Let me see them.' I put my hand in my pocket, pulled out the beads and showed them to her, holding them up a little in the air. The Lady said to me: 'Use those,' and I did so at once.

Even after so clear an explanation, M. Pène was still nettled by the rumour which was beginning to spread around the town, and asked Bernadette: 'Is it true that this morning at the grotto you blessed their rosaries?' With her exquisite smile she replied: 'Oh, no, women do not wear the stole.' It is a touching detail that the Lady commanded Bernadette to use only her own little twopenny rosary; it was a recommendation to hold on to it for it was her treasure; and there was a lesson in humility and the love of poverty, for God abominates ostentation for ostentation's sake, even in piety.

*     *     *

At the Café Français faces were growing longer and longer. . . . Some of their cocksureness had gone; these strange happenings were haunting them. The solemn M. Dutour explained that 'it was no longer a group of people who were following Bernadette, but a mob. . . . It was a movement of minds as swift as it was prodigious. . . .' The Public Prosecutor grew excited: had religion anything to gain by this performance?

'You magistrates, why don't you act?' someone retorted. Act! It was easy to give advice. But the machinery of the law should not be set in motion except for good and sufficient reasons. Now down in the perilous depths of that valley of Massabielle there had been no quarrelling among the spectators during the last ten days, no offensive language or action against the police. Moreover, during the same period neither the child nor her family had laid themselves open to judicial proceedings. Constable Philippe Viron, who had been secretly appointed to keep a close watch on the visionary, had failed to catch her in a fault.

Some people, bribed by the police, had gone to the Soubirous to commiserate with them over their poverty and had offered them money, but these paupers had remained incorruptible. . . . If this continued, justice and the judges were going to lose all prestige while struggling in the dark against adversaries, who, by a grim irony, were protected by the law against the officers of the law.

And the originator of these incidents, which were upsetting the tranquil town of Lourdes, was a chit of a girl of fourteen, an absolute illiterate, but one who—as some members of the Club remarked—had an answer for everything.

On Thursday, March 4th, she was to pay her final visit to the Lady of the grotto, and her supporters asserted that some prodigy would take place: and, of course, there would be a huge crowd at Massabielle. But the police were going to take every precaution; on Tuesday, March 2nd, the Public Prosecutor was counting on the presence in Lourdes of M. Duboé, the Sub-Prefect of Argelès.

On this Tuesday Bernadette, encircled by an audience more densely packed even than on the previous day, had the happiness of gazing on the Lady of the Rock for the thirteenth time. Apart from its brevity, the public noticed nothing to distinguish this Apparition from the previous one. When, however, an hour later, the child was seen between her aunts Basile and Bernarde making for the presbytery, it was guessed that something new had occurred.

Undoubtedly Bernadette Soubirous felt great reverence for M. le Curé, but also great fear. 'She feared him,' Basile Castérot assures us, 'more than she did a gendarme. But she was able to overcome the terror he inspired in her when it was a matter of bringing him a message from the Lady, because she believed it to be her duty.' However, under the influence of the cold reception she had met with on the first occasion, it would seem that the girl preferred not to be alone when she called at the presbytery the second time.

'We had already been forestalled by some people who had informed the Curé about the Lady's words. We were badly received.' So said Aunt Basile.

The Curé's attack was, in fact, so prompt and disconcerting that Bernadette was dismayed and had to omit half her message.

M. Peyramale 'spoke all the more loudly that day because he was more hoarse than usual. "Ah, so you are still going to Massabielle!" he shouted. "What are you back here for?"'

'The Lady told me that she wants people to come to the grotto in procession. . . .'

'Well, once again, what is this Lady's name?'

'I don't know, M. le Curé. She does not wish to give her name.'

'Well then, since she does not wish to give her name, you are a liar! It's scandalous! Workmen are leaving their jobs to go and see a liar! The farm people are wasting their morning to go and see a liar! You know'—and here the priest had no idea how true were his words—'all over the world they will talk about you and the grotto. . . . They will know the scandals you are causing. You've acted like an animal; you've eaten grass. . . . A procession to the grotto! If the Lady wants one, it's not me she should apply to, but His Lordship the Bishop. Doesn't she know that? How do you expect us to organize a procession for this Lady, you little liar? . . . We'll go one better: we'll give you a torch all to yourself, and you can go and run your own procession. You have plenty of followers; you've no need of priests!'

The little girl answered: 'I never say anything to anyone; I do not ask them to come with me.'

'M. le Curé,' continues Basile Castérot, 'was striding up and down his room in a rage and kept on saying: "It's intolerable to have a family like this that causes such disturbance in the town! . . . What nonsense! Sheer nonsense! . . . A Lady. . . . A procession! . . ." It was terrifying to see and hear him. . . . The poor little girl, all trussed up in her cape, stood there not daring to move.'

The entrance of Abbé Pomian brought a diversion. 'See this little thing that goes to the grotto,' rapped out M. Peyramale. 'She is coming and telling us lies.'

'You come and tell lies, Bernadette?' exclaimed M. Pomian.

'No, Monsieur l'Abbé. . . .'

'M. le Curé,' concludes Aunt Basile, 'put an end to this scene by saying to us, "You can go. Send her to school. Don't let her go to that grotto. Let this be the end of it!"'

Once she was outside, Bernadette expressed a regret: after

she had spoken about this procession demanded by the Lady, she should have reminded M. le Curé that he had also been asked to build a chapel. But return to the presbytery that very day! Surely the little one did not dream of doing that! Aunt Basile did not conceal her feelings about that; she tells us: 'Very timidly Bernadette said, "The Lady wishes me to go," and I replied: "*Mon Dieu*, not again!" It made you shudder to listen to M. le Curé,' adds the aunt; 'listening to him shrivelled you up to nothing.'

Before the close of day a chance meeting got poor Bernadette out of her predicament. She met an excellent neighbour, Dominiquette Cazenave, a mature Child of Mary of thirty-six. 'I implore you,' she said to her, 'come with me to M. le Curé's. Neither my mother nor my aunts will come with me.' Dominiquette had not the heart to refuse.

I took the initiative [she reports], and I said to M. le Curé: 'The little girl who goes to the grotto needs to speak to you, and her parents are unwilling to come with her. When should I bring her?'—'Bring her this evening at seven o'clock.'—'I implore you, Monsieur le Curé, please do not frighten her.'—'No, no.'—'How sorry I am, Monsieur le Curé, that you don't yourself see this child in ecstasy!'

That evening at seven o'clock I went to the presbystery with Bernadette's arm in mine. . . . M. le Curé made us sit down.

Straightway, the visionary repeated her first message: it was a matter of a chapel, 'even if it were only a little one,' she explained, as though to avoid discouraging the builder-to-be. M. Peyramale cut her short: 'Ask the Lady her name once more, and when we know her name, we will build her a chapel. And it won't be a little one, I tell you; it will be a very big one.'

M. le Curé, for whom this late visit was an annoyance (we shall soon see why), had just uttered unsuspectingly still another prophecy. 'We left,' reports Dominiquette. 'Bernadette took my arm and said to me: "I'm quite happy now: I have carried out my commission." I urged her to ask the Lady her name, because without that the chapel would not be built. "Yes," she replied, "if I remember it."' She meant to say by these words that during her ecstasies she forgot the earth and was less sure of her memory.

The visit and the commission had been for the moment quite useless. At the time of Bernadette's second visit to the presbytery, siege was being laid to M. Peyramale. The proof of this may be seen in the report, so restrained in tone, which the Public Prosecutor was just finishing, probably at that very hour, and addressing to the Attorney General in Pau.

It is now March 2nd. The number of pilgrims following Bernarde [sic] every morning is increasing daily. On Thursday, March 4th, which is a market-day in Lourdes, the fortnight expires during which the girl promised faithfully to go regularly to the grotto. One cannot but foresee a very large gathering.

I learn from a despatch that the Sub-Prefect is coming to discuss with me what arrangements to make. Everything points to the fact that on Thursday the road to Massabielle rock will be crammed. The grotto can only be reached by steep paths down precipitous slopes: a single disorderly movement among the crowd that will be gathered on the top and along the paths and on the banks of the Gave would undoubtedly lead to grave accidents.

In the conference which they have had, the Sub-Prefect and the Public Prosecutor were in perfect agreement that at present their sole duty was one of supervision, and that it would be right (since the ecclesiastical authorities cannot remain indifferent to these demonstrations) to communicate their intentions to the representatives of this same authority in Lourdes.

They called on M. l'Abbé Peyramale and informed him that they proposed issuing orders for a small detachment of infantry, gendarmes and municipal police to take the necessary safety measures required by the configuration of the ground.

M. Peyramale expressed his gratitude; he gave his approval to the proposed measures and declared them indispensable; and as he is not by temperament disposed to suppress his thoughts and feelings, he described the visits he has had from Bernarde: 'Tell her who has sent you, as you allege, that if she wishes me to believe you, she must make the eglantine blossom; if the Blessed Virgin had wanted a procession, she should have applied not to me but to the Bishop'. Such was his response and it did not encourage the ambassadress to persist.

It is clear from this consultation that at bottom the parish priest, the Prosecutor and the Sub-Prefect were in agreement: in their opinion Bernadette, in all sincerity, was living in a world of fantasy and would have no importance at all had her innocent dreams not excited the crowds; it was impossible at the moment to stem the human flood that was bursting over Massabielle!

But they had only to wait and let it pass . . . and dry up. The young Soubirous would herself help powerfully, for in a few days the supposed Lady would cease to appear and the child would go to the grotto no more.

Everything would be back to normal.

# 13

## TWENTY THOUSAND PILGRIMS

*(Fourteenth and Fifteenth Apparitions,
Wednesday and Thursday, March 3rd and 4th)*

IN Bernadette's case one might almost say that one trouble invited another. Twice already (and precisely on days following painful incidents) the Lady had failed to come and bring her the comfort of her smile. Again, no doubt, the reason was that she wished to strengthen the humble child's soul with a view to further struggles and further victories.

On the morning of Wednesday, March 3rd, the poor little Soubirous girl felt particularly sad at heart: the memory of her last interview with the parish priest weighed more heavily on her than all else. The priest to whom the Lady had sent her as her messenger still refused to believe her, though she was sure that she was not telling a lie. Or else he boldly demanded as a condition of belief miraculous proofs which Heaven was justified in not granting him.

But this morning at Massabielle the sorrows caused by men would soon be forgotten. The breaking dawn lit up the visionary as she arrived with her mother. Together they spent a long time in prayer. But then they both got up sobbing and withdrew in a deathly silence.

Three thousand people, affirms M. Clarens, who was present, witnessed their disappointment. Many among this crowd had already heard it said by the 'enlightened sort' that Bernadette was deceived, or was inventing things, or was a victim of hallucination. Among the crowd gathered there, certain minds that had been ready to believe in her began to wonder. M. Clarens was one of them: the bitter disappointment of the visionary had not been lost on him. In his report to the Prefect of Tarbes on March 4th, he wrote:

The Vision failed the little girl, and this seemed to cause her great distress.  It is important to note this point, for it might not perhaps seem to favour the hypothesis of an hallucination.

A carter, Jean-Marie Cazenave, had also clearly noticed 'the grief of Louise Soubirous and her daughter. . . . I said to myself: if the little girl were inventing things, who is there to prevent her from saying that she saw the same vision this morning as on other days?'.

Bernadette had returned home.  A friend of her family, Anna Dupas, called, bringing two teachers who wished to make the girl's acquaintance.  'We found her,' reports Anna, 'leaning against a bed, her face buried in her hands, dejected.  She kept saying: "What have I done to her?  Perhaps she is vexed with me."'

Towards half-past eight cousin André Sajous came in.  He had been at Massabielle at 7 a.m., and on seeing the child's tears he had said: 'If you wish to come back, I shall willingly come with you.'  And now once more Bernadette heard the interior voice inviting her to the meeting for which she longed.  She would have liked to be alone down there.  'If you wish to return to the grotto,' André Sajous hinted, 'we will take the road by the foot of the Castle to avoid going through the town: then the crowd will not follow us.'

We did so [he relates].  There were some people there, but not a large number; many who had slept there, had gone. . . . We reached there about nine o'clock.

Bernadette knelt down, took out her rosary, saw the Apparition and came back happy.

People in the town were saying: 'She will never see her again.  There has been some misbehaviour at the grotto.'

In the afternoon of the day of this fourteenth Apparition there arrived from Momères an aunt and a cousin of Bernadette, Mme Védère and her daughter, Jeanne-Marie, both eager to be present on the final day of this wonderful fortnight.

I was told [related Jeanne-Marie] that Bernadette was at M. le Curé's. . . . When she returned, I said to my cousin before sitting down to table, 'I have heard that you did not see the Lady this

morning. It's possible that you will not see her to-morrow either.'
She answered me: 'But I did see her during the day.' I asked her:
'Why did you not see her this morning?' She replied that the
Lady had told her: 'You did not see me this morning because
there were some people there who wished to see what you look
like in my presence, and they are unworthy of it: they spent the
night at the grotto and they dishonoured it.'

When questioned later about her short visit to the presbytery
the visionary did not conceal the fact that she had gone at the
Lady's bidding to remind the Curé for the third time of a
matter to which she appeared to attach special importance.
'What have you come to tell me? . . . What did the Lady
say to you?' asked M. Peyramale; and this time he abandoned
his gruff tone for a more pleasant one. The child felt reassured
and explained:
'She smiled when I told her that you were asking her to work
a miracle. I told her to make the rose bush, which was near her,
bloom; she smiled once more. But she wants the chapel.'
'Have you the money to get it built?'
'No, Monsieur le Curé.'
'No more have I! Tell the Lady to give you some.'
Thereupon the child curtsied and took her leave.

\* \* \*

To-morrow was to be the great day—March 4th.
All precautions had been taken in case of disturbances . . .
During the past few hours the Lieutenant of Gendarmes, Bourriot, had come across from Argelès to Lourdes 'to study the
surroundings and details of the grotto' of which he had drawn a
plan. Similarly he had 'studied the approaches' to Bernadette's
house.
For a week now in the chief town of the county they had been
cracking jokes about the Lourdes events; now their laughter was
less hearty, for the sightseers were still flocking to Massabielle.
What was Lacadé doing then, wondered the Prefect of the
Hautes-Pyrénées. Baron Oscar Massy, who ten months earlier
had been named a Knight Commander of the Order of St Gregory
by Pope Pius IX, was a practising Catholic. So too was M. Lacadé,

who was on good terms with Abbé Peyramale and whose views he readily adopted. As regards Bernadette's visions, Constable Latapie frankly remarks, 'M. Lacadé was opposed to them, like M. le Curé.' All the same, in circumstances which were becoming increasingly complicated, the Mayor would gladly leave to the police the odious task of taking repressive measures. Willy-nilly he was now caught in the toils. At seven o'clock in the evening of that Wednesday, March 3rd, an express messenger reached him from Tarbes.

> It is important [wrote the Prefect to the Mayor of Lourdes] that arrangements be made to ensure order, and I request you to co-operate to this effect with the Public Prosecutor and the Commanding Officer of the gendarmerie.

M. Lacadé hurried off to the Prosecutor's office, while the town clerk, Joanas, went to summon the Sergeant from his barracks. In this hasty conclave, the Prosecutor, Dutour, showed himself rather pessimistic. 'If it is fine to-morrow,' declared the Lieutenant of Gendarmes, Bourriot, 'there may possibly be 25,000 people at the Lourdes market and the majority will be attracted by curiosity about the miracle.' Even if there were only 20,000 down there in the ravine of Massabielle and their Pyrenean heads were to get over-heated . . .

The Sergeant, however, made a show of serenity: he had precise instructions. Trouble-makers, if there were any, would be at once overpowered. Look! Not only would there be at the gendarmerie, in case of serious disturbance, 'a horse ready saddled and an orderly prepared at the first alarm to set out for Tarbes', but by six in the morning strong reinforcements of gendarmes would arrive from Saint-Pé, Argelès and Luz. And, to make a still greater impression on these hot-headed Pyreneans, 'read this for yourselves, gentlemen,' exclaimed d'Angla:

> Order all men to carry carbines and to have a pistol in their pocket. Arms to be loaded.
>
> Dress to be full regulation field dress, and not as for town duty.
>
> . . . Recommend great calmness to your men and keep the more excitable ones near you to restrain them. . . . It will be necessary to establish a two-way stream of traffic on the road leading to the grotto. Those going to the grotto will keep to the left; those returning will keep to the right. . . . This arrangement will have

to be maintained by troops of the line. Requisition fifteen men for this purpose.

'That will be hopelessly inadequate,' sighed the notary. Consequently five minutes later an express courier was mounting the steps of the Castle with an urgent and obsequious request for all available troops. . . .

Thus Lourdes was to awake in the morning in a state of siege.

Perhaps it was an employee at the police headquarters who spread the rumour that malicious persons had planted lethal machines in the back of the grotto, or that fanatics—or practical jokers—might be preparing illuminations there, or even a firework display. So at 11 o'clock that night the Commissioner of Police, Jacomet, the Town Clerk and Sergeant d'Angla, carried out a minute inspection of every part of the grotto, while three policemen were posted at the foot of the Massabielle rocks, where they were to remain until the demonstration was over on the following day. Nothing abnormal was discovered in the grotto: no infernal machine, no illumination lamps, no boxes of fireworks. While exploring the ground, the three investigators unearthed this paltry plunder: five 5-centime coins, one of 2-centimes, an old rosary, a posy made of two rose-buds and a few sprigs of bay. The search had proved once again that there was no trickery or conspiracy around the little visionary.

On Thursday morning at 4 a.m. there was another inspection of the grotto. This time the indefatigable Commissioner was accompanied by the Assistant, Armand Capdevielle, both wearing the official sash. This second search 'did not alter in any way the previous evening's results'.

By 5 a.m. several groups of 'pilgrims', discreetly controlled by police, were waiting in the Rue des Petits-Fossés. Towards 5.30 a.m. three bolder strangers, who said they were doctors from Bordeaux, were brought along by a Lourdes lady and knocked on the door of the 'dungeon'. Whether they came with the connivance of the Tarbes police or of their own accord, Jeanne Védère, who reports the scene, was unable to say. They said they were curious to examine Bernadette. She answered all their questions patiently. In the afternoon they came back while the little girl was out, and told her parents that they considered her 'sound in mind and body'.

At 6 a.m. Bernadette was in church, at the same time as one of her Lourdes aunts and an aunt and cousin from Momères. She was kneeling a short distance away from them on her own, and as completely immersed in prayer as if she were all alone— while on her account the whole countryside, plain and mountain, was astir.

In its issue dated Thursday, March 4th, the *Ere Impériale*, the semi-official organ of the Tarbes Prefecture of Police (a journal of fluctuating opinions) thus depicted this veritable spiritual mobilization:

> Since yesterday morning all the roads of the department have been packed with vehicles, riders on horseback and pedestrians, all heading for Lourdes. The child visionary has announced that to-day, March 4th, at an hour after midday, the supernatural being with whom she converses is to make some wonderful revelations to her.

What wonderful faith, what religious enthusiasm there was among this people on the march! 'There were more than a hundred of us came from Saint-Pé during the night . . .' And what piety! 'We prayed all the way . . . We recited the Rosary, the Litany of the Blessed Virgin and the Magnificat with all the fervour of our hearts. . . .'

The Public Prosecutor, restrained by his dignity, came down to the foot of the Castle to watch and count those who passed through the town; he reckoned about 8,000. But Sergeant d'Angla, who rode his horse back and forth ten times between Marcadal Square and the Espélugues, calculated that 'there were at least 20,000. The whole country was literally thronged with the moving mass. It was a fine sight, that multitude, especially on the far side of the Gave. . . . Even had we wished to do so, we should have been obliged to give up trying to push back that flood of spectators: a dyke, even of gendarmes, is too weak to hold such a flood as that one'. 'All the streets,' reported the *Ere Impériale*, 'all the roads, all the hillocks and the fields from which the mysterious grotto could be seen, were literally covered with people; it was like a vast sea tossing and piling up its waves'. Clusters of men and children were clinging to the aspens in the meadow. 'Around Massabielle,' said the gendarme Malé, 'there was a whole crowd of people hanging over the grotto: the fall of one of them would have dragged down another ten. I was amazed that no one was killed.'

For many of them it required almost heroic endurance: but there was no grumbling. To quote only Mlle Jeanne Adrian, a teacher from Gavarnie:

> I arrived at the grotto at eleven o'clock at night and I was able to secure a small space on the left of where the Apparition usually stood, on some very sharp stones, and I had to remain in this position until nine o'clock in the morning without being able to move my feet or legs. The small place I occupied was bounded on one side by the rock, and on the other by people who had already arrived from the outskirts of Lourdes.
>
> Well! I did not experience the least pain from being so long in this cramped position. Nor did I feel the cold which should have been unavoidable so close to the Gave. I felt a very sweet joy at the thought of seeing Bernadette, whom I had not yet seen; it thrilled me with happiness.

The time at which they expected her to arrive—about 7 a.m. —had now passed. But she was hurrying on her way. She had suddenly left the church after the People's Communion, and Jeanne Védère, who had noticed this, ran off in search of her. She caught up with her in the far corner of the Square. 'Well, fancy leaving us like that!'

Bernadette explained with a smile: 'I felt the urge to leave, and I never thought of telling you.'

Together with her mother and several relations of the family, Bernadette and Jeanne took the road below the Castle, hoping to avoid the crowd. It was filled with people, and on seeing them Jeanne exclaimed, 'We shall get separated at the grotto!' 'Don't worry,' said Bernadette, 'you will be close to me.'

From that moment, observes Jeanne, Bernadette 'remained most recollected, never herself breaking the silence'.

In anticipation of the enormous crowd, several members of the Guild of Quarrymen had widened the steep path which connected the forest road with the grotto; then, to protect the visionary herself, they had just arranged at the foot of the slope a narrow passage between stout cross-beams.

Now at last the child for whom this multitude had been waiting made her appearance, preceded by two gendarmes, who cleared a way for her. 'The day had come,' reports the teacher from Gavarnie. . . . 'All eyes turned in the one direction, all heads were uncovered. . . . Never shall I forget the wild beating of my heart at the sight of that little girl. . . .'

As soon as she arrived in front of the grotto Bernadette had called out for her cousin who had been separated from her by the milling crowd. Full of goodwill, M. Jacomet and a gendarme took Jeanne Védère inside the barricaded passage, so securing for the fifteenth Apparition a first-hand witness, meticulous and trustworthy.

'Holding a candle in one hand and her rosary in the other, Bernadette recited her beads without a pause as far as the third *Ave* of the second decade, her eyes fixed all the time on the niche and the eglantine. At that moment a marvellous change came over her face and everyone cried out: "Now she can see her!" Then they went down on their knees.'

'I experienced at that moment,' continues Jeanne Védère, 'such intense feelings of joy and happiness as I could never express: I felt the presence of a supernatural being; but, though I looked hard, I could see nothing. . . .'

In the presence of the Lady, Bernadette continued her Rosary. When she had finished it, she tried three times to lift her fingers, which held the crucifix, to her forehead, but she could not. 'But on the next attempt she made a beautiful sign of the cross such as I have never seen anyone else make. I asked her later why she had only been able to make the sign of the cross at the third attempt. She answered: "Because it was only then that the Apparition, having finished running the beads through her fingers, had herself made the sign of the cross."

'Bernadette still remained a long time in the same posture, reciting her beads. Her eyes never moved from the Lady. I did not see her lower them even once. I counted her smiles: she smiled eighteen times. . . .'

At this same hour Lourdes, now emptied of its population, resembled a dead city.

When I went out to say Mass [the Abbé Pène noted], I was struck by the solitude and silence of Marcadal Square, usually so full of life. It was deserted and reminded one of a hive which has just been abandoned by a swarm. You would have thought that it was a town from which the inhabitants had fled in panic, for everywhere there was the same silence, the same solitude. . . .

Obliged by order to keep aloof, I yielded nevertheless to an irresistible curiosity and climbed up to a chestnut grove on the high ground to the north of the Pau road.

I was there at the very time when the Lady from heaven was giving audience to Bernadette. The sky was clear, the sun was beginning to gild the mountains and the valley. . . . What thoughts, what emotions stirred my soul! I was not yet entirely ready to believe, but I should so much have liked to be allowed to study at close quarters those scenes in which lay hidden perhaps the most momentous manifestations of the Divine Will. . . !

About an hour elapsed and then I saw that multitude break up and wind its way around the scene of the Apparition and then regain the roads which had brought them to the banks of the Gave.

Jeanne Védère noted that the rosary had passed three times through Bernadette's fingers. During the recitation of this Rosary the visionary's face reflected the joys and at times the sorrows of the Vision herself; for then the Lady was expressing her pity for poor sinners.

At one moment Bernadette, followed by her cousin Jeanne, 'got up, passed over a large stone without seeing it, and went right into the grotto. . . . She remained there, her eyes fixed, just as when two people are face to face and looking at one another. . . . Meanwhile I was seized with fright [Jeanne Védère admitted] and I drew back a little, as I saw Bernadette bow gracefully and smile.' When Jeanne questioned her afterwards, she explained: 'The Apparition had come so close that you could have put out your hand and touched her.'

In the course of this ecstasy, which was probably the longest of all of them during this fortnight, Bernadette went and stood in the grotto a second time, then came back and knelt down on the stone which she used as a prie-dieu.

Like Jeanne Védère in this respect, but from different motives, M. Jacomet, note-book in hand, never took his eyes off Bernadette. 'It was a pleasure to see the Police Commissioner on his knees,' confides Jeanne-Marie Adrian frankly. 'He remained four paces away from Bernadette, and was noting down the changes which took place from time to time on the young girl's face.' Did reverence for the Apparition count for anything in this humble posture? The Commissioner had not reached that stage yet: in the circumstances no doubt it was with him a matter of discretion and even of ordinary prudence: he had to avoid making himself conspicuous by remaining standing, with his bright sash round his waist, in the middle of a kneeling crowd.

The spectacle was a novelty for him and must have moved him even though he would not admit it. In any case the impression he carried away was by no means unfavourable, as may be judged from the report which he drew up that same morning for the Prefecture, and which tallies with that of Jeanne-Marie Védère as far as the external facts are concerned. Like her he describes rapidly the end of the ecstasy. Bernadette, having returned for the second time from the inside of the grotto, 'made the sign of the cross, prayed for a short while and got up. . . . She departed without saying a word to anyone. No one questioned her . . .' The Commissioner adds—which Jeanne Védère does not—'Everyone considered it a deception; they all thought they had been fooled, and yet very strangely the crowd is besieging her house at this very moment.' That was a mystery for M. Jacomet. And here was another: 'For my part,' he writes also to the Prefect of the Hautes-Pyrénées, 'I count it a miracle that we had no regrettable accident.'

No doubt on this memorable morning the Lourdes Commissioner did not carry his personal reflections any further. At all events, after two strict investigations, he was at last convinced that at Massabielle there was not, so to speak, any accomplice in the wings, and according to all the evidence Bernadette was alone the source of this immense movement of the crowds.

But M. Jacomet ought to have reflected again that the child had nothing whatever to do with the rumours which were circulating concerning coming miracles. It was no fault of the little Soubirous girl that Abbé Peyramale had rashly presented the adversaries of the Apparitions with an easy subject for mockery, in demanding as the condition of his own belief the miraculous flowering of the eglantine. Nor was it the child's fault that the popular imagination had become over-excited and a huge crowd had come and waited at her side for an extraordinary sign from Heaven, for a vision that would be granted this time to everyone.

'We were hoping for a great miracle,' attests a Lourdes lady, who was later to become a Daughter of Charity. This striking miracle did not take place: so the 'deception' was understandable.

However, for Commissioner Jacomet that was not exactly the point. If this man, riveted to his police functions, had been capable of extricating himself from his preoccupations as an inquisitor and a servant of law and order, certain reflections would have forced themselves on his mind. It was one of two things: either Bernadette did see something or she did not. If she saw nothing, then how explain this unheard-of beauty that transfigured the rather plain, ordinary features of the daughter of the Soubirous? If she saw nothing, she none the less kept the police, gendarmes, soldiers and magistrates on the move, and fooled the public by permitting them to believe that she did see something. . . . And the public revered her. . . . And the authorities left her free; indeed they were escorting her and protecting her! . . . But suppose Bernadette did really see something? Suppose her beauty was but the reflection of a more wonderful beauty? . . .

The wonderful explanation was to be discovered by M. Jacomet only much later. If Bernadette had seen nothing, the grotto would never have become such a place of prayer where faith was fostered; and, to confine ourselves to the Apparition which has just been described, if there was nothing but the human element in this story, the crowd's disappointment noted by the Commissioner would have speedily developed into an angry rage. But this 'deception' was immediately counter-balanced, one might say, by a gentle impulse of grace that remained still tangible in numerous testimonies. A single one will suffice as a summary of them all; it is that of the gendarme, Bernard Pays:

> The gendarmes were posted at intervals along the road between the grotto and the town. I was at the Pont-Vieux. A stream of people was passing down like a procession. . . . I saw Bernadette go down. . . . It produced such an effect on me that one evening soon afterwards I too went down in undress uniform to pray at the grotto with my wife.

And how explain, except by a spontaneous impulse, that surge of enthusiasm which induced 'a whole people' to follow at the heels of the young visionary, even to the extent of 'filling the

Rue des Petits-Fossés'? 'You would think,' records the Police Commissioner, 'that no one wants to leave Lourdes without having had a close view of her.'

'Once those nearest her house had succeeded in getting in,' reported the quarryman, Martin Tarbès, 'the others wanted to do the same. I had gone in with Bernadette. We made her go up to the first floor where Sajous lived, and the people began to file into the room as though they were making an offering. I helped to form them into a queue; they went in on one side and came out on the other after touching Bernadette's hand or embracing her. This went on for quite two hours.' 'I followed her home,' exclaims Jeanne-Marie Adrian, 'and I had the joy of embracing her with all the warmth of my heart!'

They each presented their rosaries to the child, who was 'worn out by this crowd'. Jeanne Védère had three rosaries with her. 'I did the same as the others,' she recounted. '"What, you as well!" said Bernadette to me. "Well, what do you want me to do? I am not a priest!" However, after a moment's reflection she added: "Give them to me; I'll touch them with mine. . . . Take care of them, not because I have touched them, but because they have touched the beads I used during the Apparitions."'

Meanwhile, the crowds outside were clamouring for Bernadette. She 'was obliged to show herself at the window. . . . I went to see her in the evening,' relates Dominiquette Cazenave, 'and I said to her: "Aren't you very tired?" She replied, "Oh, yes, if only with all this embracing!"'

During these pious demonstrations, the gendarmes, as noted by the Sergeant, had 'mounted guard over the Soubirous' home'. This apparently was in order to prevent souvenir hunters from transferring this poor little home to their own pockets! Actually the police had orders to spy on Bernadette and all her family: for surely these paupers had staged the scenes at the grotto 'to make money'?

At the very moment when the visitors were filing past the little visionary the Police Commissioner, without waiting for the Sergeant's report, was drawing up his own to be sent in the morning to the Prefecture:

'The rumour has spread,' he wrote coldly, 'that the parents of Bernadette were charging each person who wanted to see her fifteen centimes. That is possible and, I go further, I venture to believe it. But up to the present it has been impossible for us to prove it. We are, for this purpose, keeping a continuous watch.'

No one who reads between the lines will have any doubt that the very first time that the police caught them in an offence they would deal rigorously with Bernadette and her parents. Anna Dupas certified that, while standing close by the door of Bernadette's home, she heard a gendarme ask those who came out: 'Did you give the little one any money?' All replied, 'No.' 'And I heard this several times,' she asserts, 'as I waited there some time for my turn to go in.'

The close investigation therefore proved still negative. 'I never discovered,' admits Sergeant d'Angla, 'that the Soubirous couple or Bernadette accepted any money.'

Less than a fortnight later the Prefect of the Hautes-Pyrénées, contrary to the suspicions of Commissioner Jacomet, informed the Minister of Public Worship: 'It is believed that there has been no question of fraud. Though poor, the girl has refused every offer of money that has been made to her.'

Jeanne Védère attested that her cousin went back that same day and reminded the Curé of the two messages that concerned him. 'Let your "beautiful Lady" tell us her name . . .' he replied once more. 'If I knew that it was the Blessed Virgin,' he argued with more patience than in the previous interviews, 'I would do all she desires; but once again, as I do not know, I can do nothing. . . . Did she tell you to return there?'

'No, Monsieur le Curé.'

'Has she told you that she will not come back any more?'

'She has not said so.'

'Well, if she comes back, beg her to tell you her name.'


'If she comes back!' Was it not sufficient that she had already come fifteen times? . . . Did the Curé's deliberate composure seem now more disquieting to Bernadette than his sudden bursts of anger? Possibly. She set great value on her messages; he seemed to be coldly uninterested in them. And she had *seen*, had *heard*. . . ! Oh, why could she not communicate to the priest her own earnest conviction? But no: the Curé persisted in seeing in this mysterious Lady, the vision of whom had plunged her a few hours ago into a rapture of happiness, nothing but the illusions of the poor little Soubirous girl!

On her way back to the ' dungeon' the little divinely blest child wept.

# 14

## THE LADY GIVES HER NAME

*(Sixteenth Apparition: Thursday, March 25th)*

ON the morning of Friday, March 5th, Bernadette did not feel the attraction of the grotto. And it was the same during the next twenty days: she did not return there nor did she speak of doing so. From this time onwards Abbé Peyramale stiffened in his attitude of reserve. Seeing that on the last day of the famous fortnight the Apparition had not given her name, there was, humanly speaking, nothing more to expect.

All the same, as was pointed out to the pastor, Heaven could still have its say. M. Peyramale was quite willing to admit that, if Heaven did speak, he would submit. Abbé Pène has preserved one of the cautious instructions given by the Dean of Lourdes to the priests of the canton: 'Let us take care, gentlemen, not to be seen at the grotto. . . . If the affair proves abortive, we shall incur immense ridicule for having paid attention to it, and through us religion would suffer great harm. If the thing is of God, He has no need of us to achieve a victory.' Did M. Peyramale realize how aptly he was speaking?

As for the magistrates and the police, now that the alarming demonstration of Thursday, March 4th, was over (and they were counting on it being the last), they could breathe freely again. Commissioner Jacomet, fully informed of Bernadette's movements, notified the Prefect, on March 24th, that 'since the 4th, the visionary has not appeared at the grotto.'

On the other hand she had reappeared most regularly at school, all eager to learn her Catechism in view of her First Communion. Seeing her 'still as simple and nice as before', making her way to the Hospice with her sister, Toinette, people gazed in wonder at this little girl who had received the crowds' ovations. 'She seems quite unaware of herself, not seeing any difference between herself and other children of her age . . . quite surprised at being a centre of attraction.' Full of fun, and always the life and soul of the children's games, she 'loved innocent amusement'.

However, neither the Nuns nor her parents failed to notice that a change had come over her during the course of this last amazing month. She had not been favoured in vain with heavenly visions and instructions: already people were marvelling at her sign of the cross, which summed up the whole of her theology. But having seen the Lady of Massabielle weep over sin and sinners, this little girl, though she did not know her ABC, had understood the great duty of reparation and prayer.

True to its policy of disdain and disparagement, the Lourdes weekly, in its issue of Thursday, March 4th, recounted in its own manner the event of that same day. Of course, the anonymous article in the *Lavedan* began by informing its readers that these 'few details' about Bernadette would probably be the last.

The day so longed for, so impatiently awaited, arrived at last. Four to five thousand people were assembled on the hillocks adjoining the grotto as well as on the right bank of the Gave, awaiting the finale that had been advertised: the Apparition of the Virgin—in short, a miracle.

What a deception! What a humiliation for the poor incredulous dupes! . . . The crowd dispersed in silence and deep dissatisfaction. How many then realized, but alas too late, the absurdity of their conduct, and deplored their excessive credulity! Our readers should be convinced to-day. . . .

Near the grotto is a spring whose water is said to be slightly salty. . . . From the very first day the crowd have used it, one to bathe a leg, another an arm or eyes. Some drink it in order to cure a cold, and many go a distance of more than a mile to draw water from the spring for household needs. . . .

At Tarbes the *Ere Impériale*, in its issue of March 6th, joined in the chorus, and concluded:

The child is just simply a cataleptic. . . . We should not be in this predicament if the parents of the alleged saint had followed the advice of the doctors who invited them to send the sick child to hospital. . . .

Then came the riposte. On Tuesday, March 9th, in an article by the barrister, Romain Capdevielle, the Pau journal, the *Mémorial des Pyrénées* cautiously opened its campaign in support of the events at the grotto:

How explain what has taken place? [concluded this first article]. Will science give us the key to it? Is the condition of the young Bernadette's nerves or brain a sufficient explanation of her strange visions? Or on the other hand will some further occurrence confirm the views of those who believe the event to be miraculous? This is a question which we cannot take upon ourselves to resolve.

There is one circumstance which sets a particular seal upon this child's accounts—and after all everything depends upon her accounts—and that is the apparent sincerity and good faith which all who have heard her unanimously acknowledge in her statements.

The author of the article kept himself well informed on the trend of public opinion; he followed closely in particular the activities of the police. In the issue of March 16th, he took a firm but restrained stand against the insinuations of malicious critics:

Bernadette has won the interest and admiration of all those who have come to know her in connection with this remarkable event. . . .

She is a well-behaved girl, very sincere and pious and above all very gay-spirited. She attends the school of the Nevers Sisters, whose only complaint against her is her great ignorance. Her confessor, a respected ecclesiastic of the town, gives her an excellent character.

Her parents, far from encouraging her, had forbidden her to return to the grotto. . . . What is more, she and her family, despite their poverty, show a disinterestedness that is proof against every temptation: they accept absolutely nothing from anyone . . .

Since March 4th, Bernadette has not been back to the grotto. She is in excellent health and appears indifferent not only to the admiration but also to the ridicule of which she is the object. . . .

As to the facts themselves, it needs to be repeated that the same obscurity still prevails regarding their true character.

If the sole sequel to the event had been a skirmish between journalists, the Prefect of the Hautes-Pyrénées would have been

quite content. Unfortunately for his own peace of mind, before
the middle of the month a communication reached him from
the capital over the signature of the Minister of Education and
Public Worship:

> . . . I am informed that crowds of people are going to listen to and
> admire an individual who professes to be in ecstatic communica-
> tion with the Blessed Virgin. I do not know what foundation
> there is for these rather strange rumours, but I beg you to give
> me immediate and precise information.
>
> It is important that the Prefects keep the Minister of Public
> Worship accurately informed on all religious incidents which
> concern his Ministry and call for public attention.

To this thinly disguised rebuke from M. Rouland, Baron
Massy, believing himself fully and precisely informed from the
reports of MM. Lacadé, Dutour and Jacomet, and deeming a
further enquiry altogether useless, hastened to compose a pacify-
ing reply:

> . . . I now come, sir, to what is stirring up the people. Informed
> of what was going on by the Mayor, the Police Commissioner of
> Lourdes and the Sub-Prefect, I believed that it was the duty of the
> Authorities in a case like this not to interfere so long as no dis-
> order occurred. By acting otherwise, more importance in my
> opinion would have been given to the affair than it merited. . . .
>
> To-day, sir, the whole affair is finished, and those who had
> given credence to the girl's statements realize that they had been
> the dupes of her hallucinations. . . .
>
> I am bound in justice to say this for the clergy of the diocese that
> they have given proof of considerable prudence and reserve. They
> have kept completely aloof. . . . In Lourdes people were clamour-
> ing for a procession, but the Curé refused; to-day he has every
> right to congratulate himself on his conduct.

A week went by with no further complications. . . . But what
was the meaning of this unexpected report from Commissioner
Jacomet, dated March 19th? Would they never hear the last
of this Massabielle grotto? The poor Commissioner, anticipating a bad reception, began with apologies:

> I regret having to write to you again about the visionary, but it is
> necessary to do so in order that you may be kept fully informed

of the little incidents that are occurring daily and which seem to be multiplying, just when we thought that the business was almost over.

Despite Bernadette's eclipse 'there was on Friday, March 5th, and the following days, a continuous procession to and from the grotto of women and children, who were joined by some workmen and people from the country'. Then, because of bad weather, the visits became less frequent. But as soon as the sun reappeared 'the zeal of the devotees manifested itself with renewed vigour, and in actions which leave no doubt as to their meaning'.

Thus, since Sunday, March 14th, 'the grotto has been illuminated daily; on that particular Sunday there were two candles; on Monday three candles . . .' Then there was a more serious incident: on Tuesday 16th, religious emblems had been set up at the back of the grotto. 'Surrounded by branches of laurel and box there was a bone crucifix and three pictures of the Virgin; a cluster of ten candles was burning there the whole day and night from Wednesday to Thursday.'

There is now a constant succession of visitors to the grotto [continues M. Jacomet]. Almost all of them kneel down and pray. No one leaves without drinking from the miraculous spring, or at least taking some of the water away with them. So far these pilgrimages are taking place quietly and with a definite religious devotion. No disorder whatever has been reported.

I am keeping the Mayor of Lourdes fully informed day by day of all that takes place. This magistrate thinks that for the moment there is no need for action; that the people will get tired of it and then the whole thing will come to an end.

Yesterday being Lourdes market-day the number of new visitors from other parts was very considerable. Many called at the visionary's home to see her. No one was admitted; the door was closed against everyone.

However, access to the grotto remained open to everyone. People went there to draw water, and already rumours of a cure were spreading among 'the simple and credulous'. M. Jacomet bewailed their blindness. If only the Press would do its duty! But no, the *Mémorial des Pyrénées* 'seems to be endeavouring to revive emotions that are almost extinguished and ventures to speak of miraculous cures wrought by this water!'

But while the Prefect, exasperated by the Commissioner's complaints, was beseeching the Mayor to put an end to these religious displays at the grotto, in Paris the Keeper of the Seals, the Minister of Justice, Delangle, having been put on the alert by the Minister of Public Worship, Rouland, dug his spurs into the Attorney General, Falconnet, who in his turn roused the Public Prosecutor, Dutour, out of his lethargy. . . . And so this 'Lourdes affair', which, if properly handled, should have remained a mere local incident, had overleapt the department and bounded right up into the highest Government circles!

\*    \*    \*

But in Lourdes itself Mayor, magistrates, police, gendarmes, were asking each other whether the attitude of the clergy was really all that it should be? Why, for instance, did the *Mémorial des Pyrénées*, in its issue of March 16th, lay stress on 'the excellent character' given to Bernadette by 'her confessor, a respected ecclesiastic of the town'? Besides, was not everyone in Lourdes aware that Abbé Pomian, far from forbidding his penitent to go to Massabielle, had declared that no one had any right to prevent her from doing so? And if only the Curé had not insisted so much on the child learning the name of the so-called Lady . . . ? He would have done better to shout even louder and forbid her these imaginary colloquies.

But there was a fresh development. The whisper was going round that these clerical gentlemen were changing their minds about Bernadette: her tenacity in fulfilling the mission in which she believed so earnestly was by no means likely to displease them. Lent was well advanced—Easter that year fell on April 4th. By Monday, March 15th, M. Peyramale informed his Bishop that 'what has taken place in Lourdes has, rightly or wrongly, stirred the people deeply'. Never had such large attendances been seen at the week-day instructions; so much so that the zealous pastor referred the matter to his Bishop: 'in view of the circumstances' was it advisable to open the Jubilee? What need was there for special services and sermons if sinners were being brought back to God by the events at Massabielle?

To their great joy the confessors had evidence of this as Easter drew near.

And then people began to talk about cures that had been wrought by the application of water from the grotto. A boy of fifteen (M. Peyramale told Bishop Laurence) had used this water to bathe his poor eyes, which were 'very diseased' and always covered with a bandage. 'To-day his eyes are in excellent condition: I have seen him. His mother, a tobacconist, is crying "A miracle!" In the Piqués' house a child of twelve had been ill since Christmas. The doctors had done all they could for him. . . . The child asked for some water from the grotto and to see Bernadette. . . . I went to the house with my curates and we noticed a remarkable improvement in his condition. If he is completely cured we shall then be able to say with St. Augustine: *causa finita est.*'

M. Peyramale was now undoubtedly progressing fairly fast. It would have been altogether different had he known at the time about the cure of Louis Bouriette, the quarryman. Without giving the precise date, the reliable Dr Dozous places the event on 'one day in the year 1858, a short time after the events at the grotto of Massabielle'; and since, according to him, there was still a muddy deposit at the bottom of the spring, it should be concluded that it took place possibly during the first two weeks of March. Briefly, Louis Bouriette, as a result of an explosion in a mine, had been deprived of the sight of his right eye for more than twenty years. And then his doctor, meeting him in the company of a score of other workmen, ascertained by various tests that the quarryman was no longer blind: a scar on the right eye was the only evidence of the former injury. What had cured him? All he had done was to bathe the bad eye with the water which his daughter had fetched from the spring of Massabielle.

In reading M. Peyramale's accounts the Bishop was especially struck by the good that was being done in the parish. If a breath of grace was blowing over Lourdes, if sinners for whom Bernadette had prayed and got others to pray before the grotto were being moved to repentance, was it possible that the mysterious voice that had ordered her to pray and have prayers said, was merely an illusion and a lie? Thenceforward the prelate was no longer seen to smile indulgently when the grotto was mentioned; he began to ponder, to seek enlightenment from Heaven as well as from men.

As a sound administrator and a shrewd mayor, M. Lacadé himself began to view the events from another angle. As early as March 4th he caught himself confiding this secret to the Prefect:

'This grotto is situated on the left bank of the Gave, opposite the Ribère meadows, about a mile from the town. . . . It is one of the most picturesque of places, and I conjecture that strangers will come to visit it during the season.'

The cat was let out of the bag a bit further by the remark of the Public Prosecutor Dutour:

'Many of the Lourdes people would not be at all displeased to see an increasing number of visitors pouring in, bringing more and more profit to their businesses.'

After the pilgrim, the profiteer. Without any delay the Lourdes municipality realised that it had to accept and respect and cater for both. Hence its concern for restraint during the ensuing weeks.

\*    \*    \*

As the days went by the grotto continued to lose some of its wild and chaotic appearance. M. Jacomet, unceasingly on the alert, discovered that 'its lighting is superb': at 4 p.m. on Sunday, March 21st, nineteen candles were burning there; on Tuesday, March 23rd, at 8 p.m.—the Commissioner loved exactitude —a regular procession of six hundred people attended the installation in the grotto of a bower adorned with moss and flowers, in which a plaster statue of the Virgin had been placed. This wire bower, explains Pauline Bourdeu, whose family had lent the statue, was used 'every year in the Rue du Baous for the Altar of Repose for the Blessed Sacrament on Corpus Christi'.

The Commissioner reports again to the Prefect that 'the visits to the grotto, which were formerly confined to the day-time, now threaten to extend well into the night. . . . From morning until nine and even ten o'clock at night there is a continuous coming and going of people of every age, sex and rank: we have seen several carriages from Tarbes and Pau bringing people for the sole purpose of visiting the grotto. . . .'

And the Prefect, who, twelve days earlier, had assured the Minister of Public Worship that 'the whole business was over'! A plague on the Commissioner and all his exasperating, but truthful, investigations! At any rate, according to Jacomet, 'the visionary seems to have nothing to do with this movement'.

During the night of Wednesday, March 24th, Bernadette was suddenly aroused from her first sleep: the gentle voice, which three weeks ago had spoken to her heart, made itself heard again. 'Father, Mother,' she confided to her parents, 'I must return to the grotto.' She had had some fits of coughing which, combined with attacks of asthma, had exhausted her during the past few days. No matter! The Lady of Massabielle would smile on her once more; François and Louise would not deprive their daughter of so great a happiness.

But by what presentiment had the whisper gone round Lourdes during the day of the 24th that on the morrow the little Soubirous would appear again in front of the grotto? March 25th was the Feast of the Annunciation: Lady Day. The coincidence would not have been lost on pious people, and they would have concluded that on this Feast of Our Lady there might well be some fresh occurrence down there. M. Jacomet has given evidence of this. Even before noon on the 25th he recorded for the Prefect:

'Yesterday evening the rumour spread fast in the town that the visionary would go to the grotto this morning. The visits have continued far into the night, and this morning the crowds were flocking to the grotto, which has been transformed into an altar.'

Had Bernadette heard mention, either in church or at school, that one of the great feasts of Our Lady was celebrated on that day? One could not vouch for this. In any case, considering her ignorance on religious matters, this word 'Annunciation', in its French or patois form, could have had no meaning for her.

Nevertheless, on this March 25th she fully intended to pay a visit to the grotto, where she felt she was expected—a visit like those she had paid during the incomparable fortnight. And on her way there, at about five o'clock in the morning, she sent to ask her Aunt Lucile to come with her and bring her candle.

When she got back again to her own place between the canal and the rock, the soft light was already shining above the eglantine. In fact, for this sixteenth and decisive Apparition the Lady had forestalled her little visitor. 'She was there,' related Bernadette, 'tranquil and smiling and watching the crowd just as a fond mother watches her children. When I knelt down before her, I begged her pardon for coming late. Still kindly towards me she made me a sign with her head that I had no need to apologize. Then I told her of all my love and regard for her, and how happy I was to see her again. And after pouring out my heart to her I took up my beads.'

The sky was pure and lit up with the first rays of dawn.

At that moment Bernadette, in her ecstasy, felt more eager than ever to know at last the name and rank of this mysterious being who so enraptured her.

But then the oval of light moved from above the eglantine, came nearer to the ground and stopped under the arch of the vault. Springing immediately to her feet Bernadette went up towards the Vision. This time she remained standing, holding her candle in her hand. Her parents and some friends had followed her and were surrounding her. To the left, along the rock, stood the women of Lourdes who had decorated the little altar in the grotto.

*Tête-à-tête*, if one may express it so, the child resumed her conversation with the heavenly Vision. It was so important, so necessary that She should at last give her name: the priests to whom Bernadette repeated her messages would not build a chapel and would not come to the grotto in procession except on this condition. So in a resolute tone she asked:

'Madame, will you be so kind as to tell me who you are?'

Was it going to be the same as on previous occasions? A bow and a smile! Bernadette persisted. A force within her compelled her to repeat:

'O, Madame, will you be so kind as to tell me who you are?'

Again a bow and a smile. Perhaps at that very moment in the church in Lourdes a priest was celebrating the Mass of the 'Annunciation of the Blessed Virgin' and reciting in the Gradual of the Mass: 'Grace is poured abroad on thy lips; therefore hath God blessed thee for ever.'

Did Bernadette realize that this was the unique opportunity to put her question? She was not at all disheartened. 'I do not know why,' she was to explain later, 'but I felt more courageous.

*I begged her once more to do me the favour of telling me her name.'*
At this third earnest entreaty, which moved her more than all the previous ones, precisely no doubt because the child, still confident in spite of apparent refusals, was practising the importunity commended in the Gospel, the Apparition, who, until then, had kept her hands joined, opened her arms and lowered them as on the Miraculous Medal, thus causing her rosary of alabaster and gold to slip down towards her wrist: it was her blessing on the redeemed earth. Then she joined her hands again and brought them close to her breast, as if to restrain the throbbing of her heart. Finally, raising her eyes to Heaven, in the attitude of the ancient Magnificat, she delivered her secret:
'I AM THE IMMACULATE CONCEPTION.'
Then the Apparition 'smiled again, spoke no more, and disappeared smiling'.

\*     \*     \*

According to Aunt Lucile, 'at the end of the ecstasy', Bernadette asked her to make her a present of her candle. Lucile gave it her readily. The child then added: 'Will you let me leave it in the grotto?' On a sign of approval, 'she went and placed this lighted candle' among those already burning there. About midday, as Commissioner Jacomet certified, there were sixty-five of them.
'Why did you do that?' Aunt Lucile asked her later.
'The Lady,' replied Bernadette, 'asked me if I would leave the candle to burn at the grotto; and as it was yours, I could not leave it there without your permission.'
At the foot of the path some witnesses of the scene gathered round the visionary. Mme Filias-Nicolau, a friend of the family, was the first to embrace her. 'Bernadette,' she whispered in her ear, 'do you know something?' The child began to laugh; her face was beaming with joy. The friend insisted: 'Why do you look so happy?' 'She said to me: "I am the Immaculate Conception."'
On the way home one of her school friends, Jeanne-Marie Tourré, was walking near her and heard her repeat several times these same words. 'What is that you are repeating, Bernadette?'

she asked her. 'Oh, I'm repeating the name the Lady has just told me, for fear I might forget it.'

What the words 'Immaculate Conception' meant she had no idea. But as the Apparition had begun with the words 'I am', it was obvious that she was giving her name. . . .

At last M. le Curé would be satisfied!

Bernadette had scarcely arrived back home when she spoke of calling on him. So off she went again, surrounded by a small group of women and accompanied once again by her Aunt Basile Castérot, who had already braved the stern pastor on a previous visit. Did this unexpected visit upset him? The abrupt arrival of the child, who, with her thoughts elsewhere, did not pay her respects to him, incurred his displeasure. 'We were not given a good reception,' Aunt Basile declared.

On seeing Bernadette come in, Abbé Peyramale said: 'What do you want to-day?'

But without saying 'Good day' or 'Good afternoon' she kept on repeating: 'I am the Immaculate Conception.'

'What's that you say, you conceited little thing?' he cried.

'I am the Immaculate Conception. . . .' Then she bethought herself: 'It is the Lady who has just said these words to me.'

'Fine!' replied the priest, who felt a strong emotion rising within him. Nevertheless, he went on: 'Do you know what that means?'

'No, Monsieur le Curé.'

'I see you are still being deceived. How can you say things that you don't understand?'

'All the way from the grotto I have been repeating "I am the Immaculate Conception".'

'Good. . . ! I shall consider what is to be done,' added the priest, and he dismissed the two visitors.

Such were the memories which Bernadette herself recalled in the presence of her cousin, Jeanne Védère.

During the morning M. Peyramale went out to call at Ribettes', the grocery stores. 'Listen,' he confided to the proprietress, 'listen to what Bernadette Soubirous has just told me: the Lady said to her, "I am the Immaculate Conception". I was so amazed by it that I felt myself stagger and I was on the point of falling.'

It was a far more important moment in M. Peyramale's life than he even imagined. But in everything he did he revealed himself as a man of quick, strong feelings. First of all he greeted with a rebuff this poor child whom he was undoubtedly beginning to think well of, but who had none of the social graces of the world; then, when she had delivered her message and he had understood it, he was not merely startled, but was almost overcome by an attack of vertigo: the theologian in him jumped when he grazed the supernatural.

As to the words themselves which the priest blamed the ignorant schoolgirl for repeating without understanding them (and which therefore she could not have discovered for herself), who had whispered them to her? They denoted unmistakably the Virgin Mary under the first of her privileged titles. In that case would not the Lady in the blue sash be a reality? For three weeks now, in a fit of peevishness, the Curé had been treating Bernadette as a 'liar'. But what if she were speaking the truth to-day? What if these words had actually been uttered at Massabielle? . . . 'People tell lies with words they know, not with words which they do not understand.'

That these words, 'Immaculate Conception', were no more than mere sounds in Bernadette's ears, M. Peyramale was to have as many proofs as he could desire.

He readily agreed with M. Estrade. The latter, on March 25th, had sent word to the little Soubirous girl, in the course of the day, to come to his house so that he might have a first-hand account of the sixteenth Apparition. After finishing her account, Bernadette turned to M. Estrade and his sister, Emmanuélite, and asked them in all frankness: 'What does it mean, Immaculate Conception?' And she did not even manage to pronounce the last word correctly.

Some weeks later, while she was describing her ecstasy to Mme Ribettes and her daughter, Marie-Ida, her tone of voice, her gestures and the expression on her face 'drew tears from their eyes'. Then, reports Marie-Ida, 'my mother having asked her what "*I am the Immaculate Conception*" meant, she declared that she did not understand it.'

M. Peyramale certainly did not deny that the child must really have heard the words she repeated with such touching conviction. None the less a scruple, a doubt, still haunted the pastor's mind. The spirit of darkness, according to the Saints, sometimes disguises himself as an angel of light. Do we not see in the Book of Job the preternatural realm, which is the sphere of Satan's activity, pervading the supernatural realm, which is that of God Most High? . . . Vainly did the Curé look up the mystical writers in their chapters on 'true or false revelations'; he was bewildered. Unhappily, there were soon to be some astounding happenings down at Massabielle which would give even stronger grounds for his hesitation in believing. And so on the occasion of the Easter celebrations he did not make the public statement which his parishioners seemed to be expecting. In an affair of such delicacy the parish priest of Lourdes would make no pronouncement until the Bishop of Tarbes had given his verdict.

As for Bernadette, she was relishing her peaceful contentment. It had been explained to her, and she now understood, that the Immaculate Conception was none other than the Blessed Virgin whom she loved so dearly. 'With a discretion that seemed divinely inspired,' wrote M. Estrade, 'she never during the period of the ecstasies uttered the blessed name of Her who filled her mind and heart.' From habit she still spoke of 'the Lady'; but henceforward this meant the Blessed Virgin, who had become for her Our Lady of the Rock, Our Lady of Massabielle. . . .

On that Annunciation Day the joy radiating from Bernadette as she emerged from ecstasy was reflected on the faces of the fervent devotees of the grotto. The great news spread rapidly, and in the town, in hamlets and along the country roads, people greeted each other with shouts of joy: 'What a blessing! . . . She's given her name! . . . We were sure of it, weren't we? It is the Blessed Virgin herself! . . .'

And many a priest said to himself: it is only a little more than three years ago that Our Holy Father the Pope proclaimed it an article of Faith that the Blessed Virgin Mary was from the first instant of her conception preserved and exempted from all stain of original sin. Well now, the Blessed Virgin has just signed the Bull of December 8th, 1854, in Lourdes. Better still, she has summed it all up in a more arresting manner than any churchman ever dreamed of until now: I am the Immaculate Conception.

The Feast of Easter (Sunday, April 4th) followed close. . . . Happy and proud that the Queen of Heaven was being accorded her rightful position among them [observed M. Estrade, who was the very first to benefit by this spiritual renewal], the inhabitants of Lourdes went with fervour and enthusiasm to their Easter Communion; all except a few philosophers who did not have the Faith.

Humiliated at being a contemptible minority, these free-thinkers did not dare to lift their heads. It was likewise noticed that, during these unique weeks in the history of Lourdes, the local newspaper kept a petrified silence—which was a relief for everyone. Abbé Serres, now better informed and repentant, had in the nick of time advised the barrister Bibée to hold his peace.

But in Pau, Tarbes and Lourdes even, certain officials still held out. They could not bring themselves to surrender.

# 15

## REPORT OF THE DOCTORS

*(The Last Apparition but one: Wednesday, April 7th)*

ON reading through the despatches from Lourdes the Prefect of the Hautes-Pyrénées became very uneasy. Mayor Lacadé was still displaying the most reassuring optimism. Had there been even twenty thousand sightseers crowded round the Massabielle rocks there would still have been perfect order, according to him: 'Those who go to the grotto, go there only to pray, and they leave in silence.' But the point was that Baron Massy did not want this grotto on the bank of the stream to become an unlawful place of worship!

More disturbing still were the reports from Commissioner Jacomet. According to him there had been in the little town that evening perfect peace, a death-like silence; then suddenly, during the night, an enormous throng assembled; and now police and gendarmes were on a war footing. With this 'devil of a man' the so-called 'Lourdes affair' was like a fire that the Fire Brigade Chief peremptorily declares finished, but which breaks out again worse than ever, only to be put out once more and to flare up afresh. . . . So much so that after having displayed so much zeal and shouted Victory! five or six times, the disillusioned Commissioner was driven to this conclusion: 'I do not hesitate to affirm that this affair . . . which is assuming a grave character . . . will never come to an end of itself, and to count on this would indeed be self-delusion.'

Well, if this affair could not end of itself, it was going to be helped to do so . . . and before Easter! On Thursday, March 25th, a letter from M. Lacadé crossed a despatch from Baron Massy. The Mayor suspected the Prefect of having endorsed, if not inspired, those lines in his semi-official paper, the *Ere Impériale*:

We should not be in this predicament if the parents of the alleged saint had followed the advice of the doctors who invited them to send the sick child to hospital. That is the view of all sensible people.

The hospital in question was not that of Lourdes, but the one in Tarbes, where it would be easier to isolate 'the visionary'. Accordingly, on the morning of March 25th, M. Lacadé wrote to the Prefect:

> . . . to have this young girl placed in hospital might possibly be a mistake. I should be afraid that this step might provoke the people, who carry their belief to great lengths. In my opinion recourse should not be had to this measure save in the event of disorder or danger to public security. . . .

The same evening of the 25th the Prefect replied:

> I beg of you, Mr. Mayor, to have this young girl examined by a doctor, and I leave to you the responsibility of deciding, according to the results of this examination, whether it is advisable to have her placed in hospital.

In a letter he addressed next day to the Minister of Public Worship, M. Massy wrote 'interned' instead of 'placed' in hospital. He added:

> I am not sure what the role of the civil authorities should be after that. Clearly there is no offence in the actual visits to the grotto, for up to the present everything has proceeded in a most orderly manner. I do not see therefore any other means of putting an end to these demonstrations except by the intervention of the clergy.

But might not this intervention of the clergy prove disappointing? Already, in an effort to ensure their co-operation, Baron Massy had sent for the Curé of Lourdes and a Vicar General of Tarbes—in the absence of the Bishop, who was not due back from his pastoral visitation until Sunday, 28th. The Prefect quickly discovered that the positions of the ecclesiastical and civil authorities were no longer the same. The two priests, having decided together beforehand to entrench themselves

behind a wall of reserve, did not disclose to him what was really
at the back of their minds; so much so that M. Massy, dissatis-
fied and anxious, thought he was interpreting their silence when,
a few hours after the interview, he sent this communication to
the Minister, Rouland:

> Whilst giving no credence to the alleged miracle, these gentlemen
> did not seem to me very disposed to declare their opposition
> explicitly and publicly.
> Furthermore, the attitude of the clergy is not altogether the same
> as it was at the outset, and some clerics seem ready to throw off
> the cautious reserve behind which they have sheltered until now.

Meanwhile, M. Lacadé had conferred with Doctor Jean-
Baptiste Balencie. He was the doctor to the Lourdes Hospice
and was therefore the practitioner obviously indicated for the
examination of the young Soubirous girl who was still going to
school there. He would have to decide whether or not there was
any need to send the child away. M. Lacadé did not conceal
from him that he gladly handed this task over to him. 'But,
Mr Mayor, this is a serious business! And I, too, am not at all
eager to take upon myself such a responsibility.' In that case
he would be given two colleagues to assist him, MM. Peyrus
and Lacrampe—for Dr Dozous was clearly ruled out, now that
he had become such a warm supporter of Bernadette. As for
MM. Balencie, Lacrampe and Peyrus, they were still practising
Catholics, but they had not so far paid much attention to the
events at Massabielle. None of them was acquainted with
Bernadette, none of them had been to the grotto. However, for
conscience' sake they had asked M. Romain Capdevielle 'to
inform them on what took place during the Apparitions'.

On the eve of Palm Sunday, Saturday, March 27th, the doctors
called at the Hospice. It was during school hours, and one of
the nuns, without saying a word, went to fetch Bernadette from
among her companions. The consultation commenced.

The three professional men, as is indicated by their report,
had to answer two questions: Was this child suffering from a
mental disorder? Was there any need to have her treated?
The examination therefore would be both physical and psycho-
logical.

They observed the complexion and build of the little Pyrenean. They questioned her about her health, made her take several deep breaths; with the utmost seriousness they felt her skull all over 'to try and discover, according to the theories of Gall, bumps of insanity'. They had to admit that they could find nothing abnormal there.

Here are their findings:

> Young Bernadette is of delicate constitution, with a lymphatic and nervous temperament; thirteen years old [sic], though she seems no more than eleven. Her face is pleasant; her eyes have a lively expression; her head is regular in shape, but narrow and rather on the small side.
>
> Her health, she states, is very good; she has never suffered from headaches, has experienced no nervous attacks; she eats, drinks and sleeps wonderfully well. However, young Bernadette has not such good health as one might think: she is obviously afflicted with asthma, her breathing is slightly irregular and wheezing, and at times becomes very perceptibly so.

So far the three doctors had judged correctly: she was certainly a pleasant, intelligent little girl, but poorly nourished, badly housed and she had not yet completely recovered from a previous attack of cholera. What she required was good food and a life in the open air, such as she had enjoyed on the bracing hills of Bartrès. . . . But might it not be that this frail child, who drew crowds at her heels, was mentally unbalanced? To check on this, the practitioners would get Bernadette to talk at some length.

Without even asking herself why these strangers had come to question her, she recounted her visions to them. When copying out this account in the report which they sent to the Mayor of Lourdes, they displayed a certain care for accuracy. But not sharing Maître Capdevielle's views about the incidents at the grotto, they could only explain Bernadette's ecstasies on natural grounds such as hallucination . . . exaltation. What is more, to reinforce their argument, they distorted certain pieces of information received from the Lourdes barrister—as Dr Balencie later admitted repentantly. The barrister, in portraying Bernadette's penitential fervour, had said that she 'seemed to bite the ground'. But the doctors' version of this was: 'You will see her prostrating herself with her face to the ground and biting the dust in her attacks of delirium.'

Let us hear—if it is possible to do so without laughing too much—these grave doctors who were not so simple, in their own estimation, as their colleague, Dozous (upon whom they were not sorry to fasten some blame indirectly). Let us hear them expound their conclusions to the leading magistrate of the town:

> There is nothing to prove that Bernadette has had any intention of imposing upon the public. This child is of an impressionable nature; she has possibly been the victim of an hallucination. No doubt a reflection of light from the side of the grotto caught her attention. Her imagination, influenced by a mental predisposition, gave it a form such as impresses children—the form of those statues of the Virgin seen on altars. She relates her vision to her friends; they drag her off to the grotto; the rumour spreads in the town; there are cries of 'miracle' and 'apparition of the Virgin'. Surely the young child's mind would be bound to be more and more affected by it, and her exaltation worked up to a peak. What was at first a mere hallucination gains more control over her mind, absorbs her more and more and even isolates her from the outside world at the moment of the apparition, and there results a genuine state of ecstasy, a mental lesion that places the one affected by it under the domination of the absorbing idea. Examples of this kind are cited by the authors.
>
> Consequently the undersigned consider that the girl Bernadette Soubirous may possibly have exhibited a state of ecstasy that has recurred several times; there is here a case of mental disease the effects of which explain the phenomena of the vision.

So then, the three consultants commissioned by the Mayor of Lourdes gave an explanation of the grotto events as strange as the events themselves: a 'reflection of light' on grey rocks facing north hallucinates a child in the same manner fifteen times in succession, at no matter what moment, in full daylight as well as at five o'clock on a winter's morning; and to such a degree as to plunge her into a 'genuine state of ecstasy'! If only these gentlemen had observed the facts on the spot instead of studying them in 'the authors'!

But while reading their report delivered to him on Wednesday, 31st March, M. Lacadé felt anxious to learn the final ver-

dict. He breathed a sigh of relief: it was just what he himself
had foreseen and desired. In fact, MM. Lacrampe, Peyrus and
Balencie, who but a moment before had discovered a 'mental
lesion' in the young ecstatic, were content to declare at the end
of their laborious report that she had a disease that was no
disease at all, but was mere fatigue, which was quite curable
without internment in hospital:

> Is there any necessity to treat this malady? We have little to say
> on this point. The ailment which we have found in Bernadette
> cannot in any way endanger the health of this child if it is con-
> tained within its present limits.
>
> It is quite probable on the other hand that once Bernadette is
> no longer badgered by the crowd, once they cease pestering her
> for prayers, and she resumes her normal way of life, she will stop
> dreaming about the grotto and the marvellous things she relates.

On receiving this report, Baron Massy communicated it to the
Bishop of Tarbes and to the Public Prosecutor of Lourdes.

M. Dutour, who had pondered for a long time over the
incidents at Massabielle, was going to lay before M. Falconnet,
the Attorney General, on Good Friday, April 2nd, a few considerations tinged with scepticism, with irony even, but whose
import and clear-sightedness are surprising.

> Without examining whether the report justifies placing Bernadette
> in hospital, I have doubts about the efficacy of the measure. . . .
>
> The clergy of Lourdes, the curates at all events, are encourag-
> ing the pilgrimages to the grotto; the people feel drawn there; the
> municipal authorities seem little disposed to put any obstacles in
> the way: these pilgrimages will continue whether Bernadette is
> present or not. . . .
>
> The Prefect is mistaken when he attributes the renewal of the
> movement, which had seemed bound to come to an end on March
> 4th, to the circumstance that Bernadette had begun her pilgrim-
> ages to the grotto again. Bernadette has reappeared at the grotto
> on but one single occasion, March 25th, Lady Day.
>
> It is no longer on the heels of this young girl that the crowd
> has returned there. . . . In the very subdued role she now plays,
> she herself does no more than follow an impulse.
>
> Attention is concentrated more and more on the grotto. It is
> there that the Virgin deigned to appear; it is there that she wishes

to be honoured, in a chapel that *must* be built for her; it is there that souls come to drink from an inexhaustible spring of graces, and that bodies which are a prey to sickness and sufferings, find another spring, a visible and tangible one in the waters gushing from the rock and possessing the precious virtue of relief and cure.

But how was the matter to be dealt with?    Certainly not by violence or by barricades around the grotto.    Once again, without realizing it, M. Dutour uttered a prophecy:

> It is certain that any kind of repressive measures will cause immense displeasure here.    The grotto has become for Lourdes a cherished spot on various accounts: a piety worthy in itself but indiscreet in its enthusiasm and unsound in its object, has already turned the grotto into a revered and holy shrine; credulity has converted it into a place of divine predilection and a scene of daily miracles.
>     For the poor it is the hope and pledge of abundant alms.
>     For a large number of businesses it is an opportunity for considerable profits. . . .

Who was going to fight and beat all these combined interests? The clergy alone, thought the Public Prosecutor—after the Prefect, of course!    But . . . and it was a tremendous *but*—the clergy seemed to be growing less and less reliable.    The Curé of Lourdes, otherwise so intelligent, so zealous, so benevolent, so prudent—M. Dutour began by praising him to the skies—'misled no doubt by some information which he had not checked with sufficient care, has let it be seen that he is too much impressed by facts to which he would have denied all credence had he put less trust in the discernment and character of the persons who reported them to him.    These impressions have released in his curates an incautious enthusiasm. . . .'    M. le Curé had allowed 'a sort of altar' to be erected in the grotto; he had agreed to receive *for the poor* any money deposited at the foot of this altar.    At the risk of ruffling him—'henceforth by order of the administrative Authority (which lost no time in issuing orders), this money (61 francs on March 25th, 75 francs on Maundy Thursday, April 1st) was to be given to the Welfare Fund'.

Concluding his long letter, the Public Prosecutor declared himself the enemy of half-measures and disapproved of the complete inertia of the municipality.

You will judge whether in the present state of affairs the higher interests of public order, of sound morality and even of enlightened religion do not demand the closing of the road to the grotto even though up to the present there has been no physical disturbance and no offence has been proved.

The next thing was to discover the Bishop's views. M. Massy had insisted on his taking in hand this affair which came, first and foremost, under the jurisdiction of the Diocesan Authority.

In this year of 1858, Bishop Bertrand-Sévère Laurence was sixty-seven years of age and had been bishop for thirteen years. His career had been an exceptional one. Born of humble peasant folk, he was ordained priest at the age of thirty-one. Almost at once the Bishop of Bayonne commissioned him to found, in the derelict Benedictine monastery of Saint-Pé, a Junior Seminary, of which he became the first Superior. In 1834, Bishop Double of Tarbes, whose diocese had been re-established in 1823, appointed him his Vicar General, and then entrusted him with the direction of his Senior Seminary. Bishop Laurence was admirably prepared to become the spiritual leader of his own fellow countrymen. The diocese was indebted to him for the Missionaries of Garaison and for the teaching and nursing Sisters of St Joseph of Tarbes. He was to leave behind him the reputation of a great and saintly prelate.

Absent from his episcopal town for about six weeks during February and March 1858, and overwhelmed with work on his return, he had not been in a position to form an accurate judgment on the incidents in dispute. He had scarcely any knowledge of Bernadette's visions except from the varying accounts given him by M. Peyramale. Besides, what decision could he make with regard to this child, seeing that the only document he had to depend on so far was a doctors' report? He was well aware that a Bishop does not become involved in an affair of visions, genuine or alleged, without having first appointed a commission of inquiry. For the moment this was out of the question, as the first of the Massabielle Apparitions had occurred scarcely two months before, and the last one but a fortnight ago. And what if new ones occurred? No, the time had not yet come for the Ordinary of Tarbes to take the matter in hand.

It was April 11th, Low Sunday, when Bishop Laurence replied to the Prefect. Cautiously refusing to commit himself in advance, he avoided a clash with either the opponents or the supporters; the doctors might possibly be right, but perhaps some day it would be seen that the believers had not been wrong. No angel had come down to reveal the mystery to the prelate; it was man's hour; nevertheless, Bishop Laurence conceded that the hour of the Holy Spirit might possibly come. After reassuring M. Massy on the attitude of the Lourdes clergy, whose 'readiness to second the Authority's intentions' he guaranteed, the venerable Bishop added:

> I have read the report from the doctors who examined the young girl whose doings and sayings are keeping us busy.
> The doctors rule out imposture: that is one point settled. They admit hallucination and ecstasy resulting from a cerebral lesion: that is possible, very possible; it is even very probable. I myself follow this method of reasoning in practice. I merely observe that I believe in the possibility of the supernatural, but I await further proofs before seeing it in the present case.

As to the steps to be taken in regard to the little Soubirous girl, his Lordship would make no other suggestion than this:

> The day before yesterday—April 9th—I wrote to the Curé of Lourdes that he and his curates should use every means in their power to prevent the girl from going to the grotto and thus spare us the drastic measures which the civil Authority intends taking to secure this end . . .

But what would happen should Bernadette again feel herself urged towards Massabielle by a force she could not resist? That was exactly what happened even before the Bishop had written to Abbé Peyramale.

*          *          *

Sitting on her schoolgirl's bench the little Soubirous followed the Holy Week services. On Good Friday, when kissing the feet of the Crucifix, she realized that, as down at the grotto, this was also for sinners.

Starting from no one knew where, the rumour had spread during the morning that she would go to Massabielle in the early afternoon. This false rumour drew more than 600 people to the grotto, as the Commissioner noted. 'They had scarcely arrived there when they were informed in my presence that the *little one* was not coming and that she did not know if she would come.'

On Easter Sunday, April 4th, as we have already learned from a first-hand witness, M. Estrade, the Lourdes church was full to overflowing during the hours of Mass. And that day, from 5 a.m. to 11 p.m., there was a continuous stream of the faithful going to give thanks to Our Lady of Massabielle. The Police Commissioner counted them meticulously: there were, 'in all, 3,625 visitors to the grotto'.

From morning to night next day the flow of pilgrims was even more considerable: '3,433 strangers and 2,012 Lourdes people; in all 5,445 visitors. The total of visitors for these two days is 9,070.'

What would it have been had Bernadette gone down to Massabielle? 'The visionary,' as Jacomet recorded, on Easter Tuesday, April 6th, 'has not returned to the grotto since the Feast of the Annunciation.'

Then, on the evening of this same Tuesday she felt once more in her heart the invitation of the Immaculate.

Several days previously some pious Lourdes women had put up, on a flowered velvet carpet in the very hollow of the rock where the Apparitions had taken place, a small plaster statue which would recall their memory. It was in front of this that Bernadette came and knelt about six o'clock on the Wednesday morning of Easter Week. Already, as M. Jacomet reported later, 'the grotto was surrounded by more than 1,200 people'. 'All of them,' to quote M. Lacadé, 'were praying with great earnestness,' so that 'the most perfect order prevailed throughout'.

Soon, in the hollow of the rock, there was nothing for the child's enraptured gaze but the living Virgin with her ineffable smile. This ecstasy was to last 'about three-quarters of an hour'.

Two most attentive observers remained close to Bernadette: M. Jacomet, who, with a view to a report, did not miss a single one of her actions: Dr Dozous, who followed her 'step by step, his eyes constantly fixed on her' to study her case once more at leisure.

Bernadette smiles, she bows [noted the Commissioner], then she climbs up the space that separates her from the grotto and takes up her position there, motionless, smiling and bowing at intervals.

The last phase of this seventeenth Apparition was marked by what has generally been termed 'the miracle of the candle'. Bernadette, on the testimony of Dr Dozous, 'was holding a large blest candle, alight'. Her cousin, André Sajous, informs us that it was 'a twenty-sous candle'. 'As the Apparition continued,' adds Julie Garros, who was present, 'the candle gradually slipped down so that the flame was playing on the inside of her hand.' Jean-Marie, Bernadette's little brother, remembered 'seeing this very clearly as it passed between her fingers'. A big schoolboy of thirteen, Bernard Joanas, who eventually succeeded M. Pomian as chaplain to the Hospice in Lourdes, had managed to worm his way through to within two yards of where Bernadette was kneeling. 'Her face,' he related, 'was hidden from me by the doctor's body. But I saw his hand gripping the child's arm as if to feel her pulse, and at the same moment I saw the flame of the candle passing through her fingers and licking her hand. As soon as the fact was noticed, those near her shouted in patois: "My God, she is burning herself!"' And young Joanas heard the doctor's stern command: 'Leave her alone!' 'Her hand was then left in the flame for several minutes.' 'Bernadette meanwhile made no movement.'

At last, to the great relief of the onlookers, the ecstasy ended and down fell the candle. Abbé Joanas reports: 'I can still see Dr Dozous taking the child's hand; still see him rub it with his right sleeve (there must have been a little smoke on it); still hear him exclaim in a loud voice, "There's nothing." These words were passed rapidly back to the furthest part of the crowd and caused a wave of excitement approaching delirium.'

Meanwhile the doctor carried on with his experiment.

Addressing the woman who had taken the candle [he recorded], I asked her to relight it and give it back to me. I immediately put the flame of the candle several times in succession under Bernadette's left hand, and she drew it away very quickly, saying to me, 'You are burning me.'

I report this fact just as I saw it, and as several others, who were like me close to Bernadette, observed perfectly. I report it exactly as it took place, without attempting any explanation of it.

The impressive 'miracle of the candle'—which, according to reliable witnesses, had already had at least one precedent at Massabielle—instead of being a miracle on its own, could it not be simply one of the effects of a miracle more wonderful still: the ecstasy of Bernadette in her contemplation of the Virgin Mary? As mystical writers teach, the 'absorption in God' that is produced by ecstasy, is able to effect the 'suspension of the senses, even of the external senses' to such a degree as to render them completely impassible. Is it not recounted of St Thomas Aquinas that, being enraptured for a long time in God, he failed to notice that his torch was burning his fingers?

# 16

## DEVILRY AND COUNTERFEIT

THAT pale wax candle burning itself away, at one moment
extinguished and relighted the next, aptly symbolized
Bernadette's existence from this point on. After the
vision of April 7th the crowds no longer came and gathered
round to marvel at her in the beauty of her raptures. Later
undoubtedly her name, coupled with that of Our Lady of
Lourdes, was to be carried to the very ends of the earth; yet
even then she would only be the little star that vanishes in the
blaze of the sun. For the moment, as Mary's messenger, she
had carried out the main part of her mission: through her the
priests had received the Virgin's instructions. The continuous
'procession' of pilgrimages, the unending *Aves* of the grotto,
those holy innovations born of her testimony, no longer needed
her presence. Besides, the little Soubirous girl was in a hurry
to be forgotten, to retire into the shadows, absorbed in a single
thought during that month of April 1858: her First Holy
Communion.

Meanwhile, however, a fresh storm was gathering. Here
where the predestined Woman was to set her virginal foot Satan
would strive to 'bite her heel'. Already in February, to his
furious threat, 'Get out of here, get out!' the Virgin had replied
with a gesture of disgust which had sufficed. Now, having failed
in direct attack, he would discredit Bernadette's visions.

\*　　\*　　\*

For several months in the Lourdes area there raged a regular
epidemic of visionaries, some of them obviously manipulated
by occult forces, others, the sport of their own temperament,
whose weaknesses could be exploited by Satan for his perverse
ends. There were fanatics, exhibitionists, lying maniacs,

hysterics, half-wits, with a few tricksters thrown in. And there were exhibitions of contortions, fits of hysteria, grotesque and even indecent posturings, fainting attacks. . . . To disentangle human trickery from the devil's deceits in all this, would be more than a little difficult.

In every case a point of utmost importance stands out clearly: 'The suspect apparitions never showed themselves in the niche where Bernadette customarily saw Mary Immaculate,' nor on the exact spot 'where Our Lady sometimes came to continue her conversations with the visionary'.

\*　　\*　　\*

It began innocently enough. In the vault itself at the back of the grotto, some thousands of years ago, the waters hollowed out a kind of passage or rather a 'subterranean funnel', as geologists would term it. It is reached by a hole in the rock. This natural fissure gradually tapers until it becomes quite impassable beyond nine yards and does not permit the cavity to be reached in which the eglantine had its roots. On the Saturday of Easter week, April 10th, two women of rather doubtful reputation, and a Child of Mary (whom M. Jacomet was surprised to see in such company) took it into their heads to explore the mysterious passage. They climbed up there by a ladder, and crawled along the passage one by one. The flickering gleam of a candle seemed to give life to the sharp face of the rock and the stalactites.

The first woman—the Child of Mary—descried in 'a white stone, the figure of a woman carrying a child on her left arm'. The next discerned 'on the white stone something about the size of a girl of ten'; for the last woman it was 'the figure of a little girl of four'. And all three of them exclaimed: 'O Holy Virgin, how pretty you are! . . . What beautiful hair!' Before coming down they devoutly embraced a stalactite that resembled a 'little cherub's head'.

It was only to be expected that these women would have their imitators. On Wednesday, April 14th, a servant girl noticed at the back of the cavern 'a kind of vapour like a veil, with a trailing dress below, but no human shape'. On Saturday, the 17th, between those walls that frightened her, fifteen-year-old Joséphine

Albario 'was greatly upset, trembling and weeping. She was brought down to the ground and taken back home. She was trembling so much that they had to put her to bed. She declared she had seen 'the Immaculate Conception carrying an infant in her arms and beside her a man with a long beard.'

Some days later the young Albario returned to the grotto. M. Estrade and two of his colleagues in the Excise Office discovered her kneeling 'below the Massabielle vaults'. She was seen in the posture of a *Mater Dolorosa*.

> For a moment [relates M. Estrade] I thought I saw a new and real ecstatic. Something within me however checked my admiration and seemed to warn me that this was not genuine. I was making comparisons and I recalled that in presence of Bernadette's raptures I felt myself transported, whereas in presence of Josephine's . . . I was merely surprised. On examining Bernadette's ecstasies I sensed a genuine heavenly influence in them; in watching the other girl I could see nothing but the twitchings of an over-excited nervous system. . . .

To one of her friends Joséphine Albario confided that she had 'seen the Blessed Virgin in a black mantle and black veil, and she was weeping and she told me: "It is the end of the world."' The future Daughter of Charity, Eléonore Perard, watched her young compatriot from close by: 'She was going through contortions and at times uttering cries or rather shrieks.' A well-founded misgiving happily prevented this good girl from proceeding any further down such a dubious path.

> Josephine [continues M. Estrade] did not allow public opinion to be misled over the meaning of her ecstasies. After returning two or three times to the grotto, she declared frankly that various mysterious persons were appearing to her . . . But these persons seemed to her to be of evil character.

Canon Durosse, Superior of the Junior Seminary of Saint-Pé, and as level-headed a man as ever there was, studied the cases and said of Joséphine Albario and several others like her:

> There was either delusion of the imagination or Satan's wiles: more likely a case of both.

St. Bernadette as a nun—Sister Marie Bernarde. St. Bernadette entered the convent at age 22 and lived the rest of her life—until her early death at age 35—as a Sister of Charity and Christian Instruction of Nevers. This photograph was taken at the instruction of the Bishop for circulation because so many poor likenesses of Bernadette were being circulated. It was taken indoors against a painted backdrop.

176-1

Provost

Bernadette's main tasks in the convent were prayer and suffering; she had suffered from poor health—especially asthma—all her life. To a nun who reproached her with being a lazybones who was always laid up in the infirmary, Bernadette replied, "Why, I'm doing my job! My job is to be ill."

The infirmary of the Holy Cross, where Bernadette spent so much of her time in the convent and where she grew so much in holiness; she called this room her "white chapel." The bed on the right marks the spot where Bernadette's bed stood; note the holy card pinned onto the bed curtain. Toward the end of her life Bernadette suffered intensely from tuberculosis, from an enormous tumor on her knee, and from decay of the bones.

*Above:* Aerial view of the convent of the Sisters of Charity and Christian
176-4    Instruction of Nevers.
*Below:* Cloisters of the convent.

Novitiate of the convent in Nevers. Bernadette and 44 other postulants
received the novice's veil from Bishop Forcade at the clothing ceremony
on July 29, 1866.

176-5

*Above:* A description of the apparitions, written by Bernadette herself.
*Right:* Mother Marie-Thérèse Vazou, who was Mistress of Novices when
Bernadette was a novice, and who later was superior of the community for
many years. Mother Vazou's coldness and severity toward Bernadette
caused the latter much suffering during her 11 years in the convent, but
she considered that Mother Vazou had thereby done her soul much good.

176-6

The day after Bernadette's arrival at the convent, the superiors convened all the sisters—in an assembly such as the one pictured here—to hear the story of the apparitions from Bernadette herself. After this, Bernadette was

never again allowed to speak to the other sisters about the apparitions. She humbly described herself as a broom which the Blessed Mother had used for a time, but then had quite rightly laid aside.

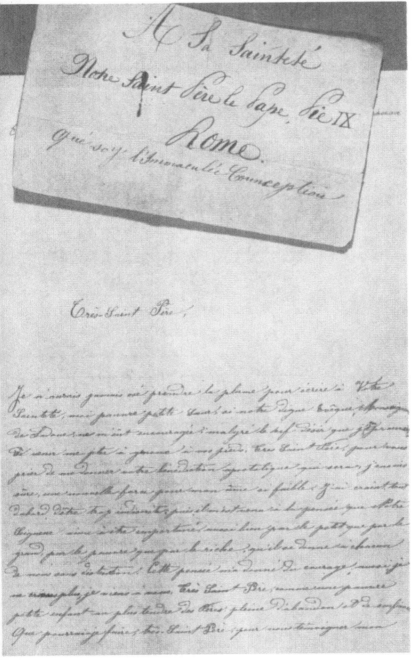

*Above:* Letter to Pope Pius IX written by Bernadette at the request of Bishop de Ladoue. At the top of the page is an address written out by someone else for Bernadette to copy.

*Left:* The gallery of the convent chapel. The gallery was near the infirmary where Bernadette spent so much of her time; when she was feeling well enough she could drag herself there to attend Mass and adore the Blessed Sacrament.

*Above:* Bishop Forcade, who helped arrange for Bernadette to enter the convent and who received her vows when she almost died at age 24. Bernadette was so weak that the bishop pronounced the formula and Bernadette simply answered, "Amen." In religious orders, novices *in articulo mortis*—"at the point of death"—are allowed to take their vows without delay; thus their souls appear before the Judgment Seat of God in the full beauty of religious profession.

*Left:* A beautiful alb made by Bernadette for Bishop Forcade. Note the date of completion embroidered near the hem.

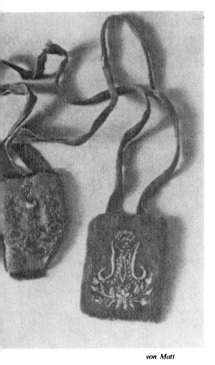

*Above and left:* Handwork done by Bernadette—sacred emblems, a scapular, and painted Hearts of Jesus.
*Below and next page:* Bernadette's little book of intimate notes which reveals the holiness of her life.

Carnet de notes intimes
de
Sainte Bernadette

176-15

B.S. 1849

Ce qui me regarde me
ne regarde... je...
... être... entièrement à Dieu
et à Dieu d'avoir
jamais à moi...

Plus je regarde mon
Dieu plus... mon
Dieu me regarde plus
je le prie plus...
il... pour...

Meanwhile, some unfortunate demented folk appeared at Massabielle. On Ascension Day, May 13th, one of them began to bawl in front of the grotto. Dressed all in white and wearing a felt hat which he had shaped into a cocked hat, he proclaimed himself 'a prophet sent from God and the Blessed Virgin' to chastise humanity. . . . Some hours later the police arrested the poor madman in a tavern where he was making a scene. About the same time another lunatic turned up. 'With a crown of laurel on his head he ordered the people who were praying at the grotto: "Recite the Rosary everybody; God is going to recite it." "Well," protested one of the Lourdes women, "the whole world must be upside down if God starts praying to the Blessed Virgin!" "Kiss the ground," commanded the lunatic, "forty times . . . forty times!" "I was laughing," observes Ursula Nicolau, the woman who had just spoken; "I had to laugh, but it also made me furious to see this devilry."'

I heard [says one of Bernadette's uncles, Dominique Vignes, who worked at the Savy saw-mill], I heard a girl of ten or eleven groaning and shouting and shrieking in front of the hollow in the rock where the caretaker's lodge now stands. The Apparition was there, according to her.

Canon Ribes, Superior of the Senior Seminary of Tarbes, having come to the grotto with a priest, who was a stranger to the diocese, saw at the entrance 'a boy of from twelve to fourteen with a lighted candle in his hand, who was aping Bernadette, slipping a rosary between his fingers, bowing to a mysterious being and advancing on his knees towards the foot of the rock. . . . His features were contracted and repulsive. My companion shouted to him: "Get out of there! You are doing the devil's work!" The visionary blew out his candle and disappeared.'

One day, just after some women had been into the upper passage, Antoine Nicolau, the Savy miller, had the silly idea of lifting up one of his little nephews in his arms to the opening of the passage. 'Now then,' said the uncle, 'look, look at that Virgin down inside there.' The child saw nothing, but being frightened he asked to be put down. When he was brought again another day, unwisely, to the same spot, he declared that he could see something. From that moment the poor child showed at certain hours signs of real diabolical possession. In order to watch him in one of his attacks, Constable Callet followed him to the mill. ' On coming near a bed he started to crawl along by the curtains, making hideous grimaces. He was grinding and gnashing his teeth and there was a wild look in his eyes.'

According to M. Estrade, ' a large number of Lourdes people were witnesses of the strange things that follow ':

A young farm-worker of ungainly appearance turned up alone on certain days at Massabielle. As soon as he drew near the grotto he was taken with a sort of seizure and started to spin round at a giddy speed. When he stopped rotating he would look up in the air and seemed to be trying to catch some chimerical being with his hands. During this last manœuvre he would rise several feet up the face of the rock and remain there contrary to all the laws of equilibrium. On returning to normal, the young villager would sink into despondency and withdraw in bewilderment. . . . When questioned he replied that he had no control of his will and that some secret power, operating from inside the rocks, compelled him to act as he did.

About this time Mlle Estrade went one afternoon to the grotto to say her Rosary. There some women called her attention to a little girl of eight or nine years of age, who was kneeling right at the back of the grotto, her eyes fixed on ' some puzzling thing which seemed to hold her features in a fixed grin. All of a sudden the young visionary fell over backwards and, like a barrel on a slope, she began to roll uncontrollably from the back of the grotto down to the edge of the Gave.' Amid loud shouts, they just managed to stop her in time.

On another occasion it was from the dizzy summit of the Massabielle rocks that a tiny girl of three or four very nearly fell headlong. Her mother was saying her prayers there, along with other women, and holding her arms round the child, who was keeping perfectly still. ' Suddenly, the little girl let out a cry of surprise, broke away from her mother and went forwards waving her hands at some invisible being. There was a general shout of panic, and the mother, like a lioness being robbed of her cubs, sprang after her child and caught her on the very brink of the precipice. One step more and both mother and child would have gone hurtling down to the bottom of the abyss.'

Antoinette Garros, then aged forty-two, who was reluctantly present at the supposed ecstasies of Mayor Lacadé's servant, Marie Courrech, had 'several times and with great effort' prevented her from throwing herself into the Gave, for she wanted to cross over the river to join the Virgin.

They had likewise to restrain Marie Pujol, a girl of about fifteen, who, 'while having some of these visions,' as Brother Léobard attests, 'was about to fling himself headlong into the torrent, where she would certainly have met her death if her companions had not stopped her.'

One afternoon, Julien Cazenave, nicknamed 'Minino', a Lourdes youth of seventeen, came down from the forest to the grotto. 'As I was saying my prayers there,' he related afterwards, 'there passed before my eyes something that had a man's face.' Returning several times to Massabielle, he caught sight of the same phantom. Seized with fear he shouted: 'Down on your knees! . . . Kiss the ground!' And he adds, 'I saw this apparition go from tree to tree in the meadow.' Some women asked him, 'What did you see?' He replied, 'The Blessed Virgin.' However, as he confessed later, 'it was certainly a man's face I saw. This face changed frequently; sometimes it had a beard.' Julien was dominated at that time by an unreasoning terror. 'I was once a witness of Minino's visions,' stated Mme Raymond Prat, the Clerk of the Court's wife; 'he was bawling and his face was so hideous that I was unable to look at it.'

This same feeling of terror is met with again in a child of eleven to twelve years old (who, like Bernadette, was in the First Communion class), Alexandre Réau, son of a Lourdes hairdresser whose house adjoined the Estrades' house. One day the mother ran to fetch Mlle Emmanuélite. The boy's eyes were starting out of his head; he had been seized by a fit of nervous trembling and could 'answer only by making desperate signs'. Mlle Estrade caressed him, reassured and calmed him. He recovered his senses and at length was able to speak. He had been for a walk with some other children along by Massabielle. He was standing in front of the grotto not thinking of anything in particular, when he saw coming towards him and seemingly issuing out of the rock 'a lady all in gold, and covered with furbelows', as he said. The lady had her hands and the lower part of her body hidden in an ash-coloured cloud like a storm cloud. 'She fixed me with her big black eyes and seemed to want to nab me. I immediately thought it was the *ugly one*'— the devil—'and I ran away.' While saying this 'the child was shaking all over and clinging desperately to his mother's skirt'.

Bernard Joanas, a thoughtful boy for his thirteen years, who had previously been present at one of Bernadette's ecstasies, was also present at one of the imitations, and having seen, as he said, the face of the genuine visionary which was 'so beautiful . . . he came away from this other spectacle with a most distressing feeling'. A certain number of schoolboys sometimes went to the Massabielle valley for their midday recreation. 'Now it happened one day,' continues Bernard Joanas, 'that one of the boys fell on his knees. By nature his face was rather ugly; now it became hideous. We all had the impression that he was seeing something peculiar. . . . Reaching the foot of the slope on the road to the Savy mill, he drew a circle on the road. "To prove that I have seen the Blessed Virgin," he challenged, "the first person to cross over this ring will be straightway struck dead." But almost at once we had proof to the contrary. A woodcutter, who had drunk more than was good for him, crossed over it and back again despite the most urgent warnings, and to finish up sat down in the middle of the circle without any harm to his life.'

To the great distress of the parents and school-teachers, there were even times when a mass frenzy seemed to take hold of the children.

Several of my pupils [states Brother Léobard] claimed to have apparitions. They often missed school. . . . Their extravagant follies took place not only at the grotto and by the brook at the bottom of the slope, but also in their homes, where they had improvised small chapels.

[Brother Cérase also states:] A crowd of small boys and girls were claiming to have seen the Blessed Virgin. I met some of them on the road to the grotto. They were holding candles in their hands and were kneeling near some pools of water . . .

Here an admission by the Brother reveals the way in which the Tempter achieved his purpose in these mimicries:

I regarded all this as sheer farce, and I came to have very grave doubts about Bernadette's visions, at which I had never been present.

Marie Portau, housekeeper at the Omex presbytery, met a swarm of these children on their way to the grotto, carrying some 'new rosaries, not yet blest: they did not want any others. They were holding them dangling, the Crucifix level with their eyes, and waving them about in front of their faces. They were tearing about in all directions, crouching down, making faces, and darting around like puppies on the hunt.'

A neighbour of the Soubirous, Jean-Pierre Gesta, surprised one of these groups at their antics in a meadow alongside the Gave. He tells how 'they were carrying on their endless tom-foolery. . . . Their eyes were wild and staring; you would have said they were the faces of madmen, although they were only children. How different was Bernadette's face!' Yet there were folk who shouted, 'They see her!' I myself answered them, and so did some others: 'It's the devil they see! Do you think the Blessed Virgin is seen like that?'

It must be said in favour of the police and gendarmes that they found these degrading demonstrations intolerable. Jean Vergez, the rural constable, states: 'Many times and in various places I've seen the visionaries, but I used to chase them away. And sometimes I have pursued them as far as the forest.' Several of them having gathered on top of Massabielle, the gendarmes drove them off with shouts of, 'Clear off, you rogues!' Com-missioner Jacomet had only to show his face and these frenzied folk took to their heels.

In Lourdes, it is true, some simpletons added to the confusion. But sensible people could only deplore the humiliating scenes that threatened to profane the grotto. The rest, confusing genuine and false visions, were the sport of their own credulity.

Time went by and the miasmas were dissipated. It will be easily understood that in the district where these sorceries raged, they have ceased to be even unpleasant memories: the families whose children had unwittingly indulged in them—as Satan's

puppets but not his accomplices—were only too anxious to
cast a thick veil of oblivion over these imitations of the
divine.

As for Bernadette, even if she was never a witness herself of
any of these 'devilries', at least some echoes reached her. She
made no protest, judging that if it pleased God, others as well as
herself could be granted the favour of contemplating the Virgin.
Actually she alone was the authentic confidante of the Immaculate; apart from her own ecstasies, everything else was lies:
above the baleful gleams of these nightmares, Bernadette shone
like a star.

# 17

## END OF THE VISIONS

*(Eighteenth and Last Apparition: Friday, July 16th)*

FULL of fun, sometimes up to mischief and always lovable, Bernadette had started to attend the Sisters' school assiduously. 'Just as before the Apparitions,' writes M. Estrade, 'she was seen going by each morning on her way to school, carrying a shabby and badly made basket, at the bottom of which, all higgledy-piggledy, lay a stocking to knit, a crust of black bread and her dog-eared spelling-book. During recreation in the Hospice playground, she joined in the games with delightful abandon, laughing, singing and skipping with her companions.'

The happy meetings at the grotto, which had so occupied her thoughts, had not, it must be admitted, favoured her progress in the art of writing or her acquaintance with the spelling-book: it was not in order to teach her to read and write that the heavenly Lady had appeared to her at Massabielle; it sufficed for the moment that the piety of the little Soubirous girl had as a result become more enlightened and more loving.

Who could unfold [asks a Religious] what the visions at the grotto had already done by way of supernatural lights implanted in this frank and simple soul? What deep wells of contemplation for her in the ineffable remembrance of half-opened Heaven? Since February 18th Bernadette had heard Mary. She did not remember every utterance, but the substance and the whole effect remained in her memory and above all in her heart.

Like a little bird that is unable to do its own pecking and has to be fed from its mother's beak, so 'the little Soubirous, being unable to read yet, had to learn her Catechism orally' laboriously, word by word. Her class-mistress, Sister Maria Géraud, did her best with her. A pious lady in the town also devoted some hours to her. The poor child had so great a desire to learn that she even agreed to study during her playtime. Her neighbour in the classroom, Julie Garros, though five years younger than Bernadette, was commissioned to go over the essential passages with her again. 'I found it a bad choice of time,' confesses Julie; 'so sometimes I would leave her and go to play with my companions. I found that she had difficulty in learning, that she was thick-headed, and I pointed this out to her.'

When class was over our little schoolgirl came home weary-headed, only to find visitors awaiting her, men and women: one would want to make the acquaintance of this privileged child of the Blessed Virgin and hear from her lips the account of the Apparitions; another would bring her some invalid that she might pray for him.

\*     \*     \*

These harmless visits troubled the suspicious police. Already, about Low Sunday, Bernadette had been summoned before the Public Prosecutor, Dutour, and then before the Commissioner Jacomet. It had had nothing to do with the grotto incidents: the Prosecutor had recovered his nerve. Scarcely any records remain of this double appearance. This time the visionary was accompanied by her mother. The interrogations were long and gruelling, and dealt chiefly with the increasing number of visits to the 'dungeon' in the Petits-Fossés.

'Some time ago,' M. Dutour wrote in a report dated Wednesday, April 14th, 'I myself questioned Bernadette and I had her questioned by the Police Commissioner with regard to the cures which she was said to have worked. She assured me that she had seen only two people and that they were still in the same condition; that she knew of no one whom she had cured by touch or prayer. . . .'

Just as on the first occasion when she appeared before him, the Prosecutor did not invite her to sit down. But, to see her mother left standing by this snob made her Pyrenean blood boil, and this led to an angry incident. Mme Dutour had to pass through the room where the interrogation had been going on for three hours: with a gesture which was no doubt intended as an apology for a husband who had forgotten his manners, she said to the poor woman and her child: 'There is a chair; you can take it.' 'No,' rejoined Bernadette sharply, 'we might dirty it.'

Was it this well-deserved snub that made him lose control of himself, or was he reflecting more bitterly than ever that this innocent-looking Lourdes girl, by setting loose the gang of hysterics and lunatics, had all the police and gendarmes harassed and exhausted? Whatever the reason, the tight-lipped magistrate began to pour out a flood of harsh words. . . . Louise Soubirous, terror-stricken by the words 'arrest', 'hospital' and 'prison', departed in tears. 'Why are you crying, Mamma?' asked Bernadette. 'We have done no wrong to anyone.'

Informed of the Prefect's intentions, M. Dutour knew, in fact, of the threat hanging over the child's head: Baron Massy had used a word for it that was full of terrifying implications: 'administrative action'. Let them once catch her playing the healer, or let her once take it into her head to appear again in the vicinity of the grotto, and the 'Administration', as the Prefect of the Hautes-Pyrénées notified the Sub-Prefect of Argelès, 'would consider what measures it would be advisable to take'; and that meant immediate internment.

Fortunately Providence was watching: the Soubirous had now a powerful protector. Abbé Peyramale had at last realized his responsibility, not only before God, but also before men, for this very humble parishioner of his, whose only wrong was that she had gone to Massabielle and had had ecstasies there. Disconcerted for the moment by the strange 'visions' of Marie Courrech and Joséphine Albario, into which he had personally conducted an enquiry, he had now recognized their dark origins; let the police attend to that—there was nothing they could do better!—but let them not lay a finger on Bernadette, so worthy, so utterly different!

To parry the blow, thought M. le Curé, would not the simplest plan be to send the child away from Lourdes for a while? Besides, she badly needed rest: she had dark rings round her eyes and was coughing; and on Tuesday, April 20th, she was clearly quite ill. M. Peyramale was anxious; he referred the matter to Bishop Laurence. The latter's advice was that the poor little girl should be sent to the thermal springs at Cauterets.

So it was that on Friday, May 6th, being now convalescent, she was taken there by a cousin, the wife of the policeman, Jean Segot, who had some of his family over there. Her cousin insisted on paying 'the small expenses; and after all it cost very little at this time of the year when the thermal establishments were almost deserted'.

Her departure from Lourdes, her arrival at Cauterets, her obscure existence among the mountains, nothing was to escape the police spies. The Prefect himself had deigned to notify the Commissioner, Cazeaux, of the new arrival.

I request you to keep a careful, though very secret, watch on the young Bernadette, her associates and her movements, and report to me all facts that seem to you likely to call for my attention.

For all his good will the Commissioner met with scant success. On Saturday, May 22nd, the eve of Pentecost, he had completed his assignment and wrote to his superior officer, the Public Prosecutor of Lourdes:

I have the honour of reporting to you that the said Bernadette Soubirous, who has been the object of my very active surveillance during her stay at Cauterets, has just left this town to-day.

This girl went regularly to bathe at the Bruzeaud Baths. It transpires from information supplied to me that several people had questioned her about the alleged vision and that she held firmly to her original statement.

Several sick people approached her, but she confined herself to telling them that if they believed in God, they would obtain their cure. She always refused any remuneration.

\*　　\*　　\*

In Lourdes her beloved grotto was mentioned in Bernadette's presence and the news was not good.

On Tuesday, May 4th, the Prefect had come to preside over the Recruitment Board. Scarcely had he arrived when he called another meeting of the Prosecutor, Mayor and Police Commissioner. He ordered the Commissioner 'to proceed to the grotto, remove all objects found there and deposit them at the Town Hall, where they would be placed at the disposal of the owners'.

Furthermore, in the council hall itself—as he informed the

Minister of Public Worship—he had taken advantage of the presence of thirty-seven representatives of the canton 'to point out to them the whole absurdity of the scenes that had been taking place at Massabielle, and the discredit they were calculated to cast upon religion'. There can be no doubt that here the Prefect's censure was directed primarily at Bernadette. In any case M. Massy, before his departure, 'instructed the Police Commissioner to make it known that any person claiming to be a visionary would be straightway arrested and taken to the Hospice at Tarbes, there to be treated as a patient at the expense of the Department'.

The meeting of the Board was not yet over by the time that M. Jacomet—always a fast worker—had emptied the grotto, and the Prefect was able to write to the Minister in complete serenity: 'There is one thing I can assure Your Excellency of: the oratory will not be restored. If any attempt is made to place fresh emblems there, I have taken measures to have them removed at once.'

So then the little improvised altar, on which Bernadette had seen the Lady look with such pleasure, had disappeared along with the little statues, flowers and votive offerings of the simple-hearted.

But what was going to be the fate of the supposed 'miraculous spring'? Now that the pilgrimage, which might have enriched the town, was no more than an idle dream, why not draw some good hard cash from a spring to which the faith of the people attributed miracles? It must possess to an unusual degree a natural curative property. Lourdes might become a celebrated spa!

At the request of M. Lacadé, a personal friend of the Prefect's, M. Latour, a chemist and member of the General Council of Trie in the district of Tarbes, had sent him an analysis of the grotto water. His report raised the wildest hopes.

The water from Massabielle, asserted the apothecary, contained some 'primary elements' in superabundance: chlorides, carbonates, silicates, iron oxides, soda-sulphates, etc. . . . 'Very light, easily digested, and imparting to the bodily system a disposition favourable to the balance of vital functioning.' This spring, concluded the chemist of Trie, 'considering the sum total and the quality of the constituent substances' could well be classed by medical science 'among the waters that form the mineral wealth of our department'.

Unfortunately for M. Latour's reputation and M. Lacadé's splendid ambitions, a number of municipal councillors were astonished that the Massabielle water, which had suddenly gushed out close by other very ordinary springs, should present so peculiar a composition. At the meeting held in the Town Hall on June 3rd, they demanded another test. M. Filhol, professor in the Faculty of Science of Toulouse, proved beyond all possible doubt that nobody would ever succeed in transforming the grotto of Massabielle into a watering place.

> This analysis [as the eminent chemist was to inform M. Lacadé on August 8th] had led me to regard the water in question as a drinking water containing the same elements as most of the spring waters met with in the mountains, and more particularly in those whose soil is rich in limestone.

So it was not a mineral spring at all. That was the final blow for the 'summary analysis' of the pharmacist from Trie.

If only M. Lacadé had had the patience to wait for M. Filhol's examination, it would have saved him from an egregious blunder. During the latter fortnight of March, the rumour had spread that, after analysing the grotto water, a pharmacist of the town, the respected M. Pailhasson, had 'declared it extremely bad'. But it had since been broadly hinted that the said M. Pailhasson was afraid of seeing those with sore eyes going to bathe them with the miraculous water instead of buying his eye-salve, and so possibly he had invented this expedient. Even so, these unfavourable rumours had discouraged the Mayor. Then had come the report from M. Latour of Trie with his 'chlorides, carbonates, silicates and iron oxides. . . .' To allow all who wanted, under pretext of piety, to drink this precious mineral water was, in the opinion of the Mayor, to squander a treasure; so on June 8th he issued a solemn municipal decree forbidding access to the grotto and the spring.

It must be said to the credit of the people of Lourdes that on four separate occasions the barrier that had been erected was pulled down and that even when it was still standing it did not prevent any who wished from drawing water from the miraculous spring.

These various events came to Bernadette's knowledge, at least in their main features, but she showed neither excitement nor apprehension: it was as if she had known them in advance. There must have been so many things she learnt in her audiences at Massabielle! When, for instance, at Lourdes in June and July of this year 1858, 'everyone was full of excitement' on learning that Professor Filhol had not failed to recognize the true purpose for which the Apparition intended the mysterious spring, the little Soubirous girl 'remained calm and kept silence'. She could not resist a smile when she heard the news that the objects of piety deposited at the Town Hall had been safely recovered by their owners and had, one by one, found their way back to Massabielle, where the prohibited oratory had been restored! Bernadette was no less overjoyed to learn that on Ascension Eve there had been a procession in honour of Mary Immaculate and by torchlight too—for the first time. On this Wednesday, May 12th, as the Commissioner recorded, 'a large body of visitors, several of them holding lighted candles in their hands, set out from the grotto in procession and walked to the entrance of the town, singing the Litany of Our Lady'.

\*     \*     \*

The First Communion had been fixed for Thursday, June 3rd, the liturgical Feast of the Blessed Sacrament. In the examination which preceded the preparatory Retreat, Bernadette appeared to have less knowledge than most of her young companions, but she was one of the most devout, and this consideration settled the matter.

'She prepared herself well, the dear child,' M. Estrade attested. This sums up the evidence of M. Peyramale himself when writing to his Bishop:

During the retreat which I gave to these children, her behaviour, her recollection, her concentration was all that could be desired. She is developing wonderfully in every way.

The ceremony took place not in the church but in the Hospice oratory—'in those days it was one of the rooms on the ground floor which served as a chapel'. With some other communi-

cants, dressed all in white like herself, with a veil on their heads
and a cape over their shoulders, Bernadette, holding a candle,
took her place on the first row of kneelers. 'She seemed,' adds
M. Peyramale, 'deeply absorbed by the sacred act she was
performing.'

> On the occasion of this delightful and holy Feast [wrote M.
> Estrade], it was hoped in Lourdes that the little visionary would
> be favoured with one of those angelic ecstasies that aroused the
> admiration of the crowds at the Massabielle rocks. There was
> nothing. Bernadette, her hands joined, advanced towards the
> altar, received her God within her virginal heart and returned to
> her place, without giving any other sign except that of an immense
> and profound happiness.
> During the visit which the child paid us [continued M. Estrade],
> my sister asked her: 'Tell me, Bernadette, which made you
> happier, receiving Our Lord or conversing with the Blessed Virgin
> at the grotto?' Bernadette hesitated a moment, and then replied:
> 'I don't know; these two things go together and can't be com-
> pared. All I know is that I was intensely happy in both cases.'

On the Feast of Corpus Christi in 1858 Lourdes received
further favours from Heaven. On that day, June 3rd, it will be
remembered, Professor Filhol of Toulouse was commissioned to
revise a pseudo-analysis; his conclusions were to remain unassail-
able. In the afternoon there took place at the grotto a sudden
cure whose supernatural character it seems impossible to deny.
Doctor Dozous, who was present, has left us a meticulous investigation of it, 'invested,' he says specifically, 'with the signatures
of more than a hundred people who were present'.

As M. Jacomet reports towards the end of April, 'twenty
workmen under the direction of Martin Tarbès, a wheelwright,
had, without any authorization, taken over the grotto and its
precincts. They raised and widened the causeway that runs
along the Gave, erected a wooden balustrade in front of the altar
and installed a long, wide iron tank, painted white, to catch the
water from the spring which was, in future, to flow down from
three separate outlets.'

On the Thursday of Corpus Christi 'six thousand strangers'
visited Massabielle, in addition to the Lourdes people, and there
was a large number of sick. M. Dozous speaks of 'three to four

hundred people afflicted with all sorts of diseases, begging from the Patroness of these places the cure of ills from which human science had been unable to deliver them'. A poor day-labourer from the Lourdes countryside came accompanied by his wife and carrying in his arms a small boy of five or six, stricken with infantile paralysis of the spine. 'The sight of this unfortunate child,' continues the doctor, 'inspired a keen interest in me. . . . "Since you have come," I remarked to the man, "to obtain from the Blessed Virgin a cure which you have asked for in vain from human science, take your child, undress him and place him under the taps of the spring." I took the child by the legs while the father held him by the shoulders, and the two of us turned his body over and over in the running water for five to six minutes. . . . The little invalid, after he had been well dried and his clothes put on, was laid on the ground. But he immediately got up by himself and made his way, walking with the greatest ease, towards his father and mother, who smothered him with vigorous hugs, shedding tears of joy.'

It was therefore a particularly propitious day for the cause of the Apparition and for the little visionary. Meanwhile, however, on the golden horizon of this Corpus Christi, a black cloud was forming. A drastic measure was being hatched. On this June 3rd, the Prefect was so exasperated that he refused to listen to reason; the Minister of Public Worship had rebuked him for his inaction—so now for it!

On the 4th, he summoned M. Jacomet to Tarbes for secret instructions. Bernadette must finally be got out of the way. There was the law of June 30th, 1838, which permitted the internment for treatment of any person suspected of mental disorder; there was the report of the three doctors which was not opposed to subjecting the Soubirous girl to this treatment; besides, it was due to her alleged visions that so many fresh visionaries of both sexes were cropping up in Lourdes . . . she was at the bottom of these disorders. . . . Next, to strike at the root of the trouble, it was imperative that henceforth the grotto be barred against all comers. The Commissioner was to pass on the Prefect's decisions to the Mayor. In view of this, M. Lacadé, who had been so vacillating until then, now felt no difficulty at all in carrying them out. This may be judged from the lines addressed to Baron Massy on June 5th by his trusty Jacomet:

> The Mayor has just summoned me to a meeting with the Public Prosecutor. He informed us that it was his intention to put an end to it all; this state of affairs could not go on any longer; if Bernadette went to the grotto this evening or to-morrow he would arrest her secretly so as to avoid provoking the people, and would take her to you at Tarbes for internment in the Tarbes hospice.
> He added that in any event he was going to Tarbes next Monday to lay before you a prohibition order for the grotto. . . . To arrest Bernadette to-day would, in my opinion, prove to be an action entirely favourable to the distressing cause against which we are contending.

Perhaps it was on leaving the clerk's office that MM. Dutour and Lacadé made their way to the presbytery: the approval of the head of the parish was essential. M. Peyramale had just posted the letter to His Lordship the Bishop in which he expressed a heartfelt eulogy of Bernadette. He let the Mayor explain to him that, considering the behaviour of certain visionaries, it was essential in the interests of religion to put an end to the regrettable scenes which were going on at the grotto of Massabielle; and consequently a municipal decree would prohibit access to it. Should any revolt take place among the already excited people, the civil authorities trusted that they could rely on the pacific intervention of the ecclesiastical authorities. . . . The Curé, taken unawares and regretting that he did not know the mind of his Bishop on this matter, promised all the same that, as far as he personally was concerned, he would willingly use his influence to calm his parishioners, should Massabielle become forbidden ground, and would recommend them to submit to the authorities; but he left all responsibility in the hands of the civil authorities, as the policing of a communal domain was quite outside his competence.

The interview having proceeded so far without any clashes or fireworks, M. Lacadé then gave some indication of the fate reserved for Bernadette. He realized at once that he would not find an ally in his friend Peyramale.

For some moments the priest remained silent. In his mind he saw again the communicant of the previous day, so calm, so recollected, all whiteness and innocence, now a lamb in the midst of the wolves. There was a story current in Lourdes that the athletic pastor had one evening, with nothing but his walking-stick, kept at bay and cowed three wolves from the mountains; he had not changed. As chaplain for three years to the civil and military Hospice of Tarbes he knew the gloomy place into which his little parishioner might vanish once she had left his fold. He stiffened, and with indignation in his voice: 'Gentlemen,' he declared, 'Bernadette is not the invalid you make out. She in no way comes under the law you invoke. She is causing no disorder; she is not a public danger. She is delicate, she is poor; but understand that she is not alone; the one who is responsible for her soul is here, on the spot! . . . Kindly tell the Prefect that his gendarmes will have to pass over my dead body before they touch a hair on the head of this child!'

It was an impassioned and moving protest that atoned for many misunderstandings and much harsh treatment. And it produced an immediate tangible result. 'The Mayor and the Prosecutor,' recorded M. Estrade, 'forwarded to Tarbes the determined threats of the Curé of Lourdes. The Prefect was frightened by them and withdrew his orders.'

This was to be the very last time that the civil authorities attacked Bernadette.

\*     \*     \*

In Lourdes, according to a custom recognized by the Sisters, the pupils of the free school, once they had made their First Communion, did not return to the school. Most of them, on leaving, took employment. There was no thought of this for Bernadette: she was too frail for regular work. But even at home she got scarcely any rest; she was besieged by visitors. Many of these intruders were astonished to see the whole Soubirous family, grown-ups and little ones, so poorly clothed and housed. But Bernadette did not appear to be humiliated in the least by their extreme poverty. She 'did not feel it hard', it has been said, 'to belong to a poor family, because this family, being profoundly Christian, was always contented with its lot'.

Nevertheless, her parents, who depended solely on their work, had never perhaps been so badly off as at this period when visitors took up the better part of their time; so much so that Bernadette for their sake sometimes felt herself obliged to accept the gift of a little bread in charity. She would smile and say: 'We have eaten our black bread; we'll now eat our white.' It was, no doubt, to ease the family finances that, at the request of Mme Grenier-Manescau, she spent some hours, from time to time, at the house of this good neighbour, who loved to entrust her children to her. This lady cherished the happiest memories of her occasional maid. 'She always showed,' she said, 'perfect obedience and very great humility.'

Towards the end of June 1858, Bernadette spent a holiday at Tarbes with an aunt, Mme Deluc. This we know from Canon Ribes, who was then Superior of the Senior Seminary, and who had occasion to ascertain for himself in an unusual way the engaging simplicity of our little Lourdes girl. We must hear his own charming account:

On Thursday, July 1st, a pious lady of the town said to me: 'Would you like to see Bernadette? She will be in the chapel during your dinner; you will be able to speak to her at the beginning of recreation.'

On leaving the refectory I went to Bernadette. She opened the door leading to the main courtyard and, noticing the seminarians on their way to the chapel through the drill-hall, she seemed amazed. She took Holy Water, made the sign of the cross very slowly, engrossed in the spectacle and following the seminarians with her gaze.

The child was taken into the porter's lodge where I questioned her about the Apparitions. I was undoubtedly very satisfied with the simplicity and straightforwardness of her replies, but still more with an incident that revealed to me fully the simplicity deep down in her soul.

It was market day, a day when many relations are wont to call and see the seminarians. The clerics went off to the parlour in groups. When Bernadette saw them arrive, she broke off her account. 'Oh! Oh!' she exclaimed and, with no further concern for her questioner, she craned her neck forward and watched them with curiosity, even coming close to the window to obtain a better view of all these young clergymen. . . .

She was more taken up with this scene, which admittedly she was seeing for the first time, than with the things she was relating to me or the role assigned her by Providence, or with all the interest that was being aroused in the Lourdes events and in her own self. You would have thought that those great events were for her a matter of little or no consequence.

Her innocence, her simplicity and this *disinterestedness* especially impressed me strongly. I said to myself as I left: 'Bernadette has no wish to deceive,' and I felt disposed to believe in the reality of the Apparitions.

At the time of her First Communion, Abbé Pomian had enrolled her as an aspirant in the Sodality of the Children of Mary, which held its meetings in the Hospice oratory. And it is perhaps to this period that belongs a recollection of her young friend, Julie Garros:

> She used to wear a small apron and always kept her hand in the pocket. I asked her what she had in this pocket . . . sweets or other things? She told me that it was her rosary. 'But why hide it like that?'—'It's sometimes good to hide one's devotions from people's eyes: they might be misunderstood and cause the Blessed Virgin to be spoken ill of.'

Bernadette had not seen the grotto again since Wednesday, April 7th; besides obeying her confessor in this, she did not feel any attraction to Massabielle; and now that the Virgin no longer invited her there, she would have scrupled to go against the Mayor's orders. A palisade of planks fenced off the grotto on all sides; at the top of the path stood a post surmounted by a notice: *It is forbidden to enter this property.* (Bernadette was never to know that this post was none other than the baulk of timber abandoned on the public road the previous year, and picked up one night by her father when there was no wood at home.) She could reasonably have had a grudge against the Prefect, Mayor and Commissioner for prohibiting all access to the grotto and the spring. But no: 'Those who have had the barricades put up will have them taken down,' she placidly confided to her cousin, Jeanne Védère. 'We must not mind what men do; God permits it; we must have patience.'

Each day, when she was not busy with her little brothers and when she had finished the house-work and done the shopping, she would retire to the modest room upstairs which cousin Sajous had offered for her use. There stood a statue of Our

Lady, which some 'young Lourdes ladies had decorated very nicely for her'. She delighted in gazing at it; then, closing her eyes, she would recapture the ineffable Vision, pour out her heart and find comfort and repose beside it.

*   *   *

On the morning of Friday, July 16th, there was unusual excitement in the streets. To begin with, it was the annual Feast of the Guild of Slateworkers. They came and heard Mass, grouped behind their banner, on which sparkled the image of their Patroness, Our Lady of Mount Carmel. Under this title Our Lady had for two hundred years had her chapel and altar in the church of St Peter in Lourdes. A large crowd escorted these fine quarrymen and received Holy Communion after them.

Then on that morning all the friends of the grotto, who had the day before been pulling long faces, broke out into 'great rejoicing', as the Curé termed it in his letter to His Lordship. On the previous Monday three Lourdes women, Cyprine Gesta, manageress of the public bakery, Anna Dupas and Joséphine Baringue, set out for Pau, where they had had to appear in the Imperial Court. Their crime? 'Spreading false news.' They were alleged to have started seditious rumours that the Emperor personally wanted the objects which had been removed from the grotto to be brought back, and that the Empress had recommended herself to Bernadette's prayers. . . . Already for this misdemeanour Cyprine Gesta, reputed to have the longest tongue of the trio, had heard herself sentenced by the local magistrate to a fine of five francs, whereas her two accomplices were acquitted. This was too light a penalty, in the opinion of Prosecutor Dutour, who had appealed against it. . . . But on Thursday evening, July 15th, the three women having been discharged, reappeared in the town, like a comic turn, to roars of laughter and loud applause. . . . It augured a lively time for the magistrate who, at that moment, had on his hands forty-two cases caught red-handed at prayer inside the barricades of Massabielle.

As I was about to set out [reports Cyprine Gesta, who was not feeling very bold at that moment], Bernadette had assured me:

'Do not be afraid; it will come to nothing.' She met me on my return and not being a great talker, for she never uses two words when one will do, she whispered in my ear with a laugh: 'I told you so!'

During the evening the little Soubirous girl was again to be seen in the church. In the morning, out of devotion to Our Lady of Mount Carmel, whose scapular she had worn since her First Communion, she had approached the Holy Table 'for the third or fourth time', observes M. Estrade. For this fresh favour she wished to renew her thanks. Now, while she was praying, the voice of the 'All-Beautiful', after more than three months' silence, made itself heard again in her heart. She made the sign of the cross, got up and went off to Lucile Castérot's, the youngest of her aunts. Quick, quick, she had to go to the grotto: she was expected there! But aunt and niece knew very well that the meeting-place was barricaded and inaccessible. They took the road by the Castle. Several women from the Lapaca district followed them.

So there was the little group in the Ribère meadow opposite Massabielle. This right bank of the Gave was almost deserted. The time was about eight o'clock; the day was closing in. From where they stood, Bernadette and her companions could make out the vault by the grotto beyond the river, but the rest was hidden by the fence of planks; the tallest shoots of the eglantine were lost in the early shadows of night. Some other women, who were praying there at this late hour, came and joined the new arrivals. Bernadette took out her beads and knelt down. They copied her.

A few Hail Marys, and then the child, with a gesture of happy surprise, unclasped her hands and stretched them out towards the wonderful Vision. 'Yes, yes, there she is!' she exclaimed in the first thrill of her ecstasy. 'She is greeting us and smiling to us over the barrier.'

'She appeared to me in the usual place, but did not say anything to me,' Bernadette declared later. 'Never had I seen her looking so beautiful.' After about a quarter of an hour, Our Lady of Lourdes ceased to show herself.

'But,' as one of her great friends asked her afterwards, 'how could you see her from the Ribère meadow? The Gave is so wide at that point and the planks of the barrier come up so high.'

'At that moment,' she replied, 'I saw neither the Gave nor the planks. It seemed to me that the distance between the Lady and myself was no greater than at other times. I saw only her.'

The eighteenth and last Apparition! On earth it was good-bye, or rather *au revoir* until the 'happiness of the next world'. Bernadette concluded with a smile of resignation: 'Since then I have not seen her any more.'

# 18

## THE CHILD WITNESS

'SHE is very intelligent,' said the Commissioner Jacomet of
Bernadette, so surprised was he to see an uneducated girl
foiling every attempt to trap her.

It is a fact worthy of admiration indeed that she did not compromise herself with any of the counterfeit visionaries, nor become involved in the heated discussions which were agitating
Lourdes, but she showed her strength of character in awaiting
with equanimity the triumph of the truth.

To such as asked her for an account of her visions she related
them as briefly as possible. If they wanted to argue with her,
she answered calmly: 'My business is not to make you believe,
but to tell you.' Her confessor ordered her not to go to Massabielle; and in this matter she fixed her boundaries for herself: she would not go beyond the Pont-Vieux. And so the
police supervision over herself and her family relaxed consider-
ably. It was owing to this that, without meeting any prying
spectators or hangers-on, a nobleman, Count de Bruissard, who
was on his summer holidays, was able to call at the home of the
Soubirous close to the church. His striking recollections of this
visit should certainly be heard:

I was at Cauterets at the time when there was so much talk of the
Lourdes Apparitions. I no more believed in them than in the
existence of God: I was a lost sheep and, what is worse, an atheist.
Having seen in the local paper that Bernadette had had an
Apparition on July 16th, and that the Virgin smiled upon her, I
resolved out of curiosity to go to Lourdes and catch the little one
red-handed in her lies.

I went to the Soubirous' home and found Bernadette on the
doorstep busy darning stockings. After long questioning about
the Apparitions I said to her: 'Lastly, how did she smile, this
beautiful Lady?' The little shepherdess stared at me with
wonder; then after a moment's silence: 'Oh, sir, you would have
to come from Heaven itself to reproduce that smile.'

'Could you not repeat it for me? I am an unbeliever and I don't believe in your Apparitions.'

The child's face clouded over. 'Then, sir, you think I am a liar?'

I felt disarmed. No, Bernadette was no liar, and I was on the point of going down on my knees to beg her pardon. Then she went on: 'As you are a sinner, I shall repeat the Blessed Virgin's smile for you.' The child got up very slowly, joined her hands and gave a heavenly smile such as I have never seen on any mortal lips. Her face lit up with a dazzling radiance of light. She smiled again with her eyes raised heavenwards. I remained motionless before her, convinced that I had seen the Virgin's smile on the face of the visionary.

Since then I have treasured this heavenly memory in the depths of my soul. I have lost my wife and my two daughters. Yet it seems to me that I am not alone in the world. I live with the Virgin's smile.

Wednesday, July 28th, 1858, as will be seen, was to remain a red-letter day in the history of Our Lady of Lourdes. About two o'clock in the afternoon a lady accompanied by three young ladies and a nun rang the bell at M. Peyramale's apartments. In the absence of the Parish Priest, one of his curates received them. The lady introduced herself as Admiral Bruat's wife, governess to the Prince Imperial. Accompanied by her daughters, Thérèse, Bertha and Marguerite, and by Sister Saint-Antonin, a nun of Bon Secours, she was on her way back from the spa of St Sauveur. All were eager to hear an account of the visions at the grotto related by the visionary herself. Bernadette was sent for and along she came. She talked to these grand ladies in her dialect, the priest acting as interpreter. 'She had something heavenly in her eyes,' observed Sister Saint-Antonin.

I begged her to go with us to the grotto [continues the nun]. 'No, no,' she replied, 'that is forbidden me; I can't.' But she added that she would take us as far as the bridge; which in fact she did. On the way she walked by my side, putting her arm in mine and taking my hand in hers.

Bernadette was scarcely back home again when she was asked to go to M. Pailhasson's. In the chemist's drawing-room there was, in the words of the Commissioner, a 'large gathering:

twelve priests, among whom should be mentioned Canon Darré, Vicar General of Auch, M. Dutirou, a professor at the Senior Seminary in the same town, M. Burosse, Superior of the Junior Seminary of Saint-Pé, Abbé Pomian and Abbé Pène, M. Peyramale's curates. . . . Each of these ecclesiastics had his eyes and ears fixed on a certain layman, Louis Veuillot, the editor-in-chief of the big Catholic daily, the *Univers,* a writer at the height of his power, whose every editorial was greeted as an event by the clergy of France. During his holiday at Bagnères-de-Bigorre, the famous journalist had come to Lourdes to satisfy a very understandable curiosity. He had read the local papers and come to the conclusion that the *Ere Impériale* and the *Lavedan* deserved a lesson—an art in which the formidable controversialist was a past master!

He had already begun his investigations. He had been seen making his way to the presbytery and then to the Hospice, where the Sisters had spoken to him about the Apparitions and Bernadette. From there, escorted by Abbé Pomian and several other priests, he had gone to say a prayer in the church, had walked up and down Marcadal Square, and finally had gone into the chemist's shop. A brilliant speaker, he was holding everyone spellbound when in they brought the little Soubirous girl.

The child showed no desire to know why all these priests happened to be gathered together around this stranger. She 'related very simply but with much assurance,' reports M. Dutirou, 'all she had seen and heard, replying with directness and unflagging patience to all the questions put to her. She left us fully convinced of her perfect sincerity.'

Then Abbé Pomian led the party to Massabielle, but he himself stopped short of the grotto 'in order to comply with the municipal prescriptions'. Louis Veuillot, deaf to the injunctions of the constable Callet, went down to the grotto with the two priests from Auch and a curé from the diocese of Tarbes.

At that time the path down to Massabielle 'no longer went dead straight but by small zigzags' down the rocky slope. 'At the grotto,' relates M. Dutirou, 'we found Mme Bruat, the Admiral's wife, and her daughters, kneeling piously on some large stones.' The ladies were holding in their hands some twigs from the eglantine which the constable had plucked for them while climbing over the palisade. As soon as M. Veuillot drew near to the women, he knelt down. 'I have not come here as a tourist,' he said. 'It is quite true that the Church has not spoken, but prayer is good anywhere.' Then he bathed his eyes with water from the spring which was escaping through an opening made at the foot of the barrier. 'I have great need for God to preserve my eyes for me,' he added.

So far there had been no unpleasant incident. But as soon as Louis Veuillot rose to his feet, Pierre Callet went and accosted him. Orders are orders, and Pierre Callet had his instructions. 'It is forbidden to enter this property'—that was the Mayor's decree. . . . 'Names and addresses, please,' shouted the constable. And he took the names of the chief offenders.

This was the supreme blunder from which there would be no recovery either for the Police Commissioner or the Mayor or the Prefect. As for Abbé Peyramale, he rubbed his hands with glee, for he at once foresaw its happy consequences.

> My Lord [he wrote to his Bishop two days later, on July 30th], you will have learned that the Vicar General of Auch and M. Veuillot went to the grotto and found themselves in good company there. You will also be aware that they were made to give their names to the police. . . .
>
> It is a very awkward business. We must admit that God seems to delight in complicating this situation; but the truth will out. The Admiral's wife will certainly tell their Majesties all that is going on. It is doubtful whether the Emperor will approve of the rigorous measures being taken against a peaceful, religious people. . . . Such a meeting in such a place is not a chance affair; it is unquestionably providential.

M. Peyramale was not mistaken; the Lourdes events were talked of, and sympathetically, in the Tuileries, and Louis Veuillot through his newspaper broadcast the facts all over France and beyond, and, wielding his nimble pen like a rapier, he engaged in a victorious polemic with the opposing press.

*          *          *

Finally on that Wednesday, July 28th, there occurred an incident that for the prospects of Bernadette and her message far surpassed in importance the visit of a Court lady and a famous journalist.

Several bishops who were travelling either to or from the spas in the Hautes-Pyrénées, naturally wished to see M. Peyramale and Bernadette on their way through Lourdes. One of them, the Bishop of Montpellier, 'departed keenly impressed by what he had just seen and heard'. It was he who, thinking to tempt the child with a 'magnificent rosary of coral beads set in gold, received the reply: "Oh, a rosary! No, thank you, My Lord, I have one."'

On Wednesday, July 21st, there was quite a gathering of bishops at Bishop's House, Tarbes. Bishop Laurence did not conceal from his venerable brethren that the events of Lourdes had been occupying his thoughts and prayers for several weeks; he had even put in writing a certain project which he would publish when the time was suitable: a commission of ecclesiastics to hold an official investigation of Bernadette's statements with a view to their acceptance or rejection.

'But now is the time!' exclaimed the Bishop of Montpellier. 'Don't hesitate any longer, My Lord. Put your signature to it and push ahead with its execution. . . . If you get into trouble for it, I'll be off to Paris to defend you.'

On July 28th the episcopal decree was signed which appointed a Commission 'charged with verifying the authenticity and nature of the events which have occurred during the past six months on the occasion of an Apparition, genuine or alleged, of the Most Blessed Virgin, in a grotto situated to the west of the town of Lourdes.'

The decree, it may be remarked, settled the fate of all the other visionaries, all the sham Bernadettes, by completely ignoring them. Nor was the Bishop of Tarbes going to allow himself to be intimidated by any barriers, material or moral, around Massabielle: he decided without even forewarning the public authorities that 'the commission would set to work immediately'. Besides, all barriers were about to be broken down. From the second week in September, by order of the Minister of the Interior, the supervision of the grotto and its surroundings ceased to be permanent and provocative. And on Saturday, October 2nd,—the eve of the Feast of Our Lady of the Rosary— the Minister of Public Worship communicated directly to Bishop Laurence the happy news that His Majesty 'desires that access to the grotto should be free, as likewise the use of the water from the spring'. Thus on Tuesday 5th, at about 3 p.m., to the beat of the drum and by the voice of the rural constable, the Mayor proclaimed to the people that 'From this day forward, access to the grotto is free.'

Loud cheers and clapping of hands drowned the last rolls of the drum. There was great rejoicing and congratulations as everyone made for the grotto. The Mayor had gone ahead of the crowd. Hailed by his townsfolk, who were delighted by his presence, he attended the destruction of the post and the notice and the barriers. All lifted their eyes to the grotto and fell on their knees and prayed and kissed the ground. 'Before nightfall all the people of Lourdes had come and drunk at the miraculous spring.'

*    *    *

On the fringe of these exciting events, like a tiny brooklet that flows scarcely visible through the grass, Bernadette's life resumed its humble course.

On Wednesday, September 8th, Our Lady's Birthday, after a Retreat given in the Hospice oratory to the Children of Mary, she became one of them. She seemed profoundly happy that day. Later, when she had left Lourdes, she sent a request to the Curé asking him as a great favour not to strike her name off the Sodality register, and in fact she remained a Child of Mary for life.

The day after her reception, the preacher of the Retreat, Father Sempé, a Missionary of Garaison, who did not yet believe in Bernadette's visions, wished to question her in the Hospice sacristy. She answered his questions 'with that simplicity which she preserved to the very end of her life'. He offered her a copper medal of Blessed Germaine Cousin and took the opportunity to give her 'a little sermon on humility'. The young shepherdess of Pibrac, he explained to Bernadette, could serve her as a model of that. 'Whether or not Our Lady had appeared to her, she must always be afraid of temptations to pride, and of being lost by yielding to them.' A very stern lecture for this little one! Even already—and one wonders what foundation there was for it on this occasion at least—already there was this obsession which was eventually to become rooted in the minds of too many of those who had authority over the visionary of Lourdes, that because this child had been privileged to see and talk to the Queen of Heaven, she was doomed to temptations of pride! The missionary of Garaison continued: 'She answered with a ring of conviction in her voice that deeply impressed me: "Thank you, Father."'

At this period it seems clear that the Soubirous were no longer living in the squalid 'dungeon'. As cousin Jeanne Védère testified: 'Shortly after the Apparitions they had rented a house near the church.'

Although it was not usual, as we have seen, for children who had made their First Communion to return to school, nevertheless when the school re-opened the Curé 'asked the Sisters to take Bernadette back as a day-girl' in the free school. Relieved at her escape from tiresome visitors—at least she hoped so—the the little Soubirous girl set herself to learning how to make upright strokes, capital letters and small letters. Then in the course of this autumn of 1858, she was once more pulled out of obscurity.

The episcopal Commission had set to work in good earnest. On Wednesday, November 17th, it sent eight of its members to Lourdes. The delegation proceeded to the grotto, led by M. Peyramale. He himself was going there for the first time, and though he tried to hide his felings he was profoundly moved. Two of his curates accompanied him, MM. Pomian and Pène. Although the clerics took a side-road in order to avoid the crowd, it was useless; they were unable to get past unnoticed. At Massabielle four hundred people gathered around the grave Commissioners.

Bernadette had been sent for from school and while waiting for her the investigators went 'to inspect the grotto itself and obtained from some old men who had always been familiar with this spot—in particular a veteran from the Espélugues farm— some precise information about the spring which is to-day so clear and copious and to the efficacy of which so many extraordinary miracles are ascribed. . . . They were unanimous in asserting that, if there had been any water there before, it was scarcely noticeable, and that there was an enormous difference between the previous state and the present one; and without any work having been done on it.'

Then along came Bernadette. 'They stepped aside to make way for her,' continued the official report.

She came into the midst of the Commission, introduced herself with a respectful modesty and yet with the utmost assurance. In the midst of this immense gathering, in the presence of venerable priests she had never seen before, but whose mission she was aware of, she behaved with as much composure and ease as if she had been alone or in the company of relations or companions.

Under the vaulted roof of the grotto the episcopal commissioners questioned Bernadette about her visions for three-quarters of an hour. Then after a three hours' break the enquiry was resumed in the sacristy of the Parish Church, 'in quiet seclusion and away from the crowd which in spite of its seemly behaviour did not favour concentration', as the Secretary to the Commission remarked in his report.

Unfortunately this official record, although drawn up during the actual session, has not preserved Bernadette's account in her original patois; it is written in French and in the third person. It is just a dry and impartial narration of the eighteen Apparitions at Massabielle. Two years later, on December 7th, 1860, the same commissioners met again and this time Bishop Laurence presided. They summoned the visionary to appear before them for 'the last time' and completed with further precise details the report of November 17th, 1858.

\*    \*    \*

Between these two interviews Bernadette had resumed her hidden life, dividing her days between school and home. Her parents had only just moved into the house near the church. With the help of the Parish Priest of Lourdes and the Bishop of Tarbes, François Soubirous had become a miller once again: he had rented the Gras mill that lay sheltered in the gully below the Castle, just above the meeting of the Gave and the Lapaca. The mill was old-fashioned, and had very few customers. Nevertheless amid the rumble of the millstones the miller recovered some of his old spirit. But how long would it last . . . ?

In this new home which reminded her of the mill where she was born, Bernadette at last had her own little room to herself.

Naturally she placed her statue of Our Lady in the place of honour. From the vicinity of the Gras mill could be seen the tall trees of La Ribère opposite the grotto, with their foliage rustling in the breezes of the valley. The visionary was nearing fifteen and she was wide awake, but the rich attire of many of the visiting ladies did not dazzle her: her simple tastes had not changed. A professor from the Junior Seminary of Auch, who saw her about that time, described 'this little country girl of frail and delicate constitution, wearing a printed calico kerchief over her head. Her features and her clear gaze were like a mirror reflecting the purity and innocence of her soul '.

On April 18th, 1859, there alighted at the Hôtel Lafitte an Englishman named Mr Standen. He had no religion and had come out of curiosity, together with some of his friends, to visit Bernadette. Mr Standen fell straightway under her spell. Here is his account:

> She was a pretty-looking child, with large dreamy eyes, and a quiet, sedate demeanour. . . . She bade us follow her into an upper room of the humble cottage attached to her father's mill. . . . As she conducted us downstairs and we passed through the room where the flour-mills were, seeing that we were eyeing them rather inquisitively, she sent her little brother, [Jean-Marie], who had been acting as our guide, to turn on the water and explained the working of them to us very intelligently herself.
>
> We certainly left her in the conviction we had been talking with a most amiable little girl, and one superior to her age and station in both manner and education.

Sometimes, at the urgent request of visitors of note, the Parish Priest sent for Bernadette to his presbytery. He had, however, 'resolved', as he confided to some colleagues, 'to let her appear as little as possible'. And when she presented herself he would say to them: 'Here is the little girl you are asking for. The Blessed Virgin has done her favours she does not deserve; many of her companions would have been more worthy.' Bernadette, with a bow but not saying a word, took the seat offered her. When asked to describe the Apparitions, she did so as if it concerned someone else rather than herself. When questioned afterwards she replied 'surprisingly to the point, and with a charming grace and simplicity'. One of her listeners acknowledged later that quite 'prejudiced as he was against the marvellous events, on which no official judgment had yet been passed, and the genuineness and character of which he had not been in a position to verify scientifically ', he was so struck by ' Bernadette's ingenuous account, by the impression of truth that emanated from her whole person ', that he went away ' hoping that the Church, when the hour came, would acknowledge the truth and supernatural character of the events whose description had affected him so greatly '.

It may be said that every fair-minded person who had the privilege of hearing Bernadette received a similar impression. M. Peyramale, though unwilling to admit it, had allowed himself to be won over like so many others; but he resisted strongly his own personal feelings. 'I am waiting,' he kept on saying, ' for episcopal authority to decide before making any pronouncement myself.' Would he really have the patience to wait?

In the month of December it looked as though he was going to give himself away in act if not in word. As the Feast of the Immaculate Conception drew near, six Children of Mary had the idea of preparing for it by a novena; and where could they do this better than at Massabielle? They assembled in the church at the first sound of the Angelus and then set out for the grotto. Once past the Baous gate they began to recite the Rosary aloud. In front of the grotto, after the Litany of Our Lady, they sang a hymn in her honour. 'But,' some friends remarked, ' are you not afraid the Commissioner may close this corner of the valley again? ' The six girls consulted the Curé and he said to them:

' Have no fear of my preventing you from singing the praises of the Blessed Virgin. Shout them at the top of your voices. Let the whole world hear you! On the eve of the Feast I'll say Mass for you.' And he did so in fact at a very early hour, and he wanted the bells pealed loudly as for the arrival of His Lordship the Bishop. The whole town was in a stir!

Once the deed was done, M. Peyramale must have wondered to himself whether he had not after all gone too far. Besides, a worrying obsession took hold of him again: undoubtedly Bernadette was no victim of hallucinations—he was absolutely certain of that; but suppose, like several others, she had been ' Satan's puppet'? He longed for the peace of certainty, for some sign, no matter what . . . ! And the saintly man reproached himself for his pretentious demands in the past; when he treated of the Apparition now, it was no longer as between equals. In humble prayer he begged a personal favour; and this favour was granted him one Sunday during Mass. He was to reveal this secret one day in the presence of the Hospice Sisters. To the youngest of them, Sister Aurélie Gouteyron, who was sharp of hearing and had a good memory, we owe the following account of what he said:

> I noticed at the altar rails someone with a bright halo round her head. I was very struck by this sight. I gave her Holy Communion without realizing who it was. But I followed her with my eyes until she was back in her place, and when she turned round to kneel down I recognized Bernadette Soubirous. From that moment my anxieties ceased and I no longer had any doubt about the Apparitions.

As sometimes on a path in the high Pyrenees a traveller on a stormy night catches a fleeting glimpse, for the space of a lightning flash, of the eternal snows on a peak that was lost to view, so in a flash of grace the Curé of Lourdes had glimpsed a reflection of the light from Massabielle on Bernadette. Yes, down at the grotto it was undoubtedly a heavenly vision that had plunged this child into ecstasy.

On the evidence of her friend, Julie Garros, Bernadette ' after her First Communion communicated regularly every month, as was the custom then. Some time later she was allowed to receive Holy Communion every fortnight, somewhat earlier than was permitted to other children.' Abbé Pomian had his reasons for granting her this privilege: to all appearances the little Soubirous girl was the most ignorant of the schoolgirls, but her confessor discerned that her visions had given her an insight into the mysteries of the Faith beyond her years, Besides, her piety, which until then had lacked personality, was showing distinctive features: at prayer the Sisters detected in her eyes a bright gleam that they did not find in those of her young companions. Bernadette's supernatural life had grown apace.

\*　　\*　　\*

At the Gras mill the practice of reciting family prayers at night was still kept up. On one occasion, reports Mother Marie-Thérèse Bordenave, Bernadette's younger brother, Jean-Marie, who was then aged eight, had lazily got into bed to say his prayers; his sister made him get up and say them with the rest in a more reverent posture. Also she could not endure in those around her anything that seemed to her an offence against God. One day her companion Jeanne Abadie who, as may be remembered, had been reprimanded by Bernadette at the time of the first Apparition for a harmless oath, came out with a bolder one in the presence of Bernadette and her sister, Toinette. 'We shan't come with you any more, Jeanne,' exclaimed Bernadette in a sharp tone. . . . 'And listen, Toinette, don't you go with Baloum any more if she starts swearing like that again.'

In the course of the year 1859, there were days and even long periods when the number of visitors she had to endure, together with her own ill-health and exhaustion, caused her to miss school. The Sisters would have liked to teach her to speak French in order to relieve them of the necessity of acting as interpreter for her, but by the end of the year their pupil was still using patois only, in giving her account of the Apparitions. She succeeded in learning to spell the words in the spelling-book, but she stumbled over every phrase. One evening, Mlle Elfrida Lacrampe took her to Massabielle, for the Curé sometimes permitted her to go there. Bernadette drank from the spring and bathed her eyes several times with the miraculous water.

'Why are you doing that, Bernadette?'

'I must bathe my eyes,' she explained, 'because I can't see with them.'

'What! You can't see with them?'

'No. . . . Because I can't learn to read.'

'Penance!' Our Lady's appeal frequently came back to her mind. At the beginning of Lent she spoke of fasting like the grown-ups until Easter. Her mother forbade her absolutely, and preferred to entrust her for some weeks to cousin Segot, who was going to visit her relations again at Cauterets. No record remains of this second stay; the complete silence on the part of the police is sufficient evidence that they had ceased spying on 'the one named Bernadette Soubirous'.

After her return to Lourdes in August, she was forced by attacks of asthma to keep to her room. One day—Saturday 13th, to be precise—several priests who could speak the Lourdes patois called at the mill to see her. Her mother showed them upstairs. It was the occasion of a charming scene.

'Well, my child,' asked one of the visitors, 'are you unwell?'
'Yes, Monsieur l'Abbé.'
'What is the matter?'
'I'm having trouble with my chest.'
'We are not tiring you?'
'Oh, no, Monsieur l'Abbé; I am able to speak to-day.'
'Don't you drink the water from the grotto?'
'Yes, Monsieur l'Abbé.'
'That water cures other sick people; why does it not cure you?'
'The Blessed Virgin perhaps wishes me to suffer.'
'Why does she wish you to suffer?'
'Oh, because I need it.'
'And why do you need it rather than the others?'
'Oh, the good God knows that.'
'Do you still go to the grotto sometimes?'
'I go there when M. le Curé allows me.'
'Why doesn't M. le Curé allow you to go there always?'
'Because everyone kept following me.'
'And yet they say that at one time you went there even though you had been forbidden.'
'Yes, Monsieur l'Abbé.'
'And how is it that you have stopped going there?'
'Oh, it is because at that time I felt a strong *urge*'—this she pronounced with great emphasis—'and I could not hold myself back. . . .'
'And now you are no longer urged?'
'No, Monsieur l'Abbé.'
'Suppose you were urged as before, what would you do?'
'No doubt I should go there as before. . . .'
'Didn't the Blessed Virgin tell you what you had to do to get to Heaven?'
'No, Monsieur l'Abbé. We already knew that very well; there was no need.'
'Did she speak to you often?'

'Yes, Monsieur l'Abbé.'

'Every time?'

'No, not every time. . . .'

We were [reports the questioner] greatly impressed by her sin-cere manner, her innocent, pleasant and gracious expression. She was most polite in her speech, repeating *Monsieur l'Abbé* in all her answers. Her modesty was no less striking. . . . She raised her eyes several times towards us, but with a perfect reserve. . . . She replied with assurance and without any embarrassment. . . . We withdrew, saying to ourselves that this was indeed a saintly child.

In September, a great joy: the birth at the Gras mill of a little brother, Bernard-Pierre Soubirous; and Bernadette was his godmother.

But in the shadow of the Castle came the October mists. The doctor prescribed another visit to the spa for the little asthmatic, for in April she had returned from there with her chest much easier. So she set out cheerfully again with her cousin Segot and her husband the policeman, who was taking his annual leave. We know something of this third visit to Cauterets, thanks to the Lyons writer, Azun de Bernétas, who was like a ferret, always hunting out material for a book. We are indebted to him for these 'jottings of a bather'.

Bernadette was again at Cauterets on All Saints' Day, and I saw her receive Holy Communion at the six o'clock Mass.

Families fought each other for her: every morning they called on her and took her either to M. le Curé's house or to someone else's, and made her repeat over and over again the story of the Apparitions.

It distressed her to see all these marks of esteem and respect, and she shunned these compulsory visits as much as she could; but they asked her relations in order to get her. . . .

People wanted to get something belonging to her, but to any who asked for a medal or other object, she would reply: 'I am not a shopkeeper.'

In the house her recreation was playing with the little boy of the family, aged two or three. . . .

Never did she speak to anyone about the Apparitions unless she was asked.

No, Bernadette was not a 'shopkeeper'. As we have already seen, she refused to accept any sort of recompense. But gifts were offered to her in all sincerity, and she had only to accept them and her parents, who were still poor and living from hand to mouth, would no longer need to work so very hard. Louise Soubirous once let slip an admission to a woman who was pitying her for the 'more than frugal meal' which Louise was putting on the table 'on which there was nothing but water': 'We should be well off if my daughter had been willing to accept the rolls of money offered her, often with insistence.' Never mind! Bernadette with wisdom beyond her years adored the designs of Providence, who makes both rich and poor.

She viewed without envy the rich things that could be hers, and she let them go without regret; she felt no bitterness against those who possessed them. As Sergeant d'Angla correctly noted, she looked upon money with no feeling of contempt or aversion, but she never accepted it. It was a disinterestedness that seemed simple to all appearances, but was in actual fact heroic. Several instances have been recorded.

A lady slipped into the pocket of Bernadette's apron one of those rolls of money mentioned by her mother. Bernadette pulled it out at once and returned it to the visitor as if the money 'might have burned her fingers'.

A gold louis sparkled in the palm of a priest's hand. Bernadette tumbled to it: 'Monsieur l'Abbé,' she said hastily, forestalling him, 'give that to the poor.'

But while the young visionary was obstinate in refusing every gift, her brother and sister were perhaps more accommodating. For instance a lady named David, from Oloron, placed a two-franc piece in Toinette's hand. 'No, no,' exclaimed Bernadette authoritatively; 'no money.'

Jean-Marie was more unlucky still. He came in one day 'triumphantly bringing home two francs'. He explained that some ladies and gentlemen whom he had taken to the grotto, and for whom he had drawn water from the miraculous spring, had rewarded him with this. But reward or not, hadn't he been given orders never to accept anything? Poor little Jean-Marie! Bernadette was 'very annoyed that he had accepted this sum', reported Mother Joséphine Forestier, 'and she gave him a box on the ear—the soundest he ever had in his life, as he related in my presence—and she ordered him to return the two francs. He obeyed and on his return, to make sure he had not hidden them, Bernadette searched him.'

'No money!' No presents in disguise either. Some wealthy people on their way to Cauterets begged M. Peyramale to use the gold refused by Bernadette to buy some white bread for her and her family. It was a useless stratagem. The first twelve-pound loaf delivered by the baker, Maisongrosse, was returned to him untouched, and the Curé sent back the money to the donors.

Some rich farmers from the Béarn asked the chaplains of Bétharram if they could 'without offending Bernadette and her family, offer them' some provisions. The Fathers, who did not suspect the lengths to which the Soubirous carried their dis-interestedness, approved of their generous scheme. But in the evening they were amazed to see these worthy people bring-ing back from Lourdes their baskets full of foodstuffs; 'to their offers the visionary's parents had given an absolute refusal'.

'A lady of high rank', affirms Dr Dozous, had conceived the idea of having Bernadette to live with her. No doubt she would have adopted her as her daughter. But her 'considerable offers' left the father and mother cold.

However, they showed themselves more compliant—for it was a question of Bernadette's health—when some acquaintances suggested taking her away for a few days either into the country around Lourdes, or to Tarbes, Pau, or Bagnères-de-Bigorre. . . . The child allowed herself to be taken, but showed no enthusiasm, for she would have to miss school and catechism.

\*      \*      \*

The Bishop used to come to Lourdes every two years for Confirmation. The last ceremony of this kind had taken place on February 10th, 1858, the very eve of the first Apparition. In 1860 Bishop Laurence had arranged his visit for February 5th, Septuagesima Sunday, and Bernadette was among those who were to be confirmed. Shortly before this she had drawn down on herself the thunderbolts of the Class Sister. The schoolmaster, Jean Barbet, has given a good description of the amusing incident:

> With regard to the Confirmation, Sister Maria Géraud told us that one day, when holding a catechism lesson, she heard some whispering and giggling going on in a corner of the room. She broke off.
>
> 'I am convinced,' she said, 'that on Confirmation day the Holy Spirit won't come down on the heads of those pupils there: they are too frivolous!' And she pointed to where Bernadette was.
>
> A little confused, Bernadette got up and said: 'Sister, I am the only one to blame.'
>
> 'What! Is it you who are upsetting the class? You who have had the privilege of seeing the Blessed Virgin!'
>
> 'Sister, you know that I have been ordered to take snuff on account of my asthma. I offered a pinch to my neighbours. They refused, and all pretended to sneeze at the same time; and that is what made them laugh. You see, Sister, they are not to blame.'

Gallantly Bernadette took the whole blame on herself. 'It may be guessed,' concludes Jean Barbet, 'that the Sister punished no one, but it took her all her time to keep a straight face.'

On Sunday, February 5th, Bernadette was confirmed. Notwithstanding the amusing threat of the Sister, the Spirit of Holiness and Fortitude, completing the grace of her Baptism, visited Bernadette's soul. Her happy dispositions so satisfied her confessor that, after her confirmation, as Julie Garros attests, she received Holy Communion every week; which for those days was an exceptional favour. She herself felt as if renewed: the Sisters noticed that during prayers in school and ceremonies in the church, Bernadette had all her attention on the altar, and the congregation no longer distracted her as formerly.

But she began to suffer more than ever from the eager attentions of her ardent admirers. For the time being her parents, whose work was being seriously interfered with by so many inconsiderate visitors, used to allow anyone who called at the mill to go up and see her. Some carried their admiration so far as to kneel down before her, as if she were a canonized saint![1] . . .

---

[1] A Jesuit recorded the following story, which he got from Abbé Peyramale himself. An American bishop came to see Bernadette and, forgetting Abbé Peyramale's recommendations, he went down on his knees before Bernadette in order to kiss her hands. The Parish Priest immediately lifted him up and, pushing Bernadette down at his feet, said: 'My Lord, bless this child.'

Then there were the journeys, and the visits she had to pay to worldly people. All these things troubled her fervent soul.

M. Peyramale heard her complaint; this innocent pious child needed a quieter and more protected environment. So 'by agreement with the Mayor of Lourdes he arranged for her to be taken as a boarder at the Hospice'. The nuns welcomed her there about mid-July, 1860—as a pupil, not as a patient.

Bernadette was then a girl of sixteen and a half.

# 19

## MISSION ACCOMPLISHED

**P**RIESTS and religious, both men and women, often say
that it was on the day of their First Communion that they
heard the call from Heaven. But this was by no means the
case with Bernadette, who made her First Communion, it may
be remembered, on the Feast of Corpus Christi, 1858. Two and
a half months previously, on Sunday, March 21st, a schoolmistress from near Lourdes communicated these curious details
to one of her family, who was a priest:

> The Mayor and several other gentlemen of Lourdes asked Berna-
> dette about the career she wished to take up. After thinking for
> a moment she replied that she wished to be a nun. 'But you may
> change your mind,' rejoined the Mayor. 'Meanwhile you should
> learn a trade.' And the child replied: 'I shall not change; but
> meanwhile I shall do whatever my Father and Mother wish.'

Bernadette's repeated denials make it certain that her vocation was not one of the three secrets which she received from
Our Lady's lips. The visionary made no mystery of the fact
that her future as a nun—without specification of place or type
or religious habit—had been revealed to her at Massabielle.
Besides, surely the contemplation of that superterrestrial beauty
would have sufficed to detach the pious child from worldly
things and make her long for the hidden life of the convent.
Surely the deepest motive for her religious vocation was wholly
contained in that sigh of hers on one Assumption evening:
'Once you have seen her, you never have any more liking for
this earth!'

That is all true; but on condition, nevertheless, that the soul,
always remaining free in its choice, does not through its own
fault make of this exceptional favour an occasion of spiritual
decline. Who indeed among the French clergy had not read the

stern pronouncement of Bishop Ginhouliac of Grenoble towards
the end of 1854, in regard to the case of Mélanie Calvat, the
visionary of La Salette? The deference she had received from
many people, including the most distinguished, had been such
as to resemble a kind of cult. As a result, she had become a
victim of self-will, and therefore, although the Community of
which she was a novice had praised her piety and her zeal in
the religious instruction of children, the Bishop had felt bound
to refuse to admit her to annual vows. Unwilling to recom-
mence her noviceship, she had left the convent. That was the
end of her peace of soul.

If Bernadette Soubirous, who was also of humble origin like
Mélanie Calvat and like her the bearer of a message from Our
Lady, was going to give way to sentimental affections and fall a
victim to inordinate flattery, forgetting her true role and failing
in her vocation, what a misfortune it would be and what a down-
fall. . . ! But unintentional blunders might compromise her
future. Abbé Peyramale, examining his conscience, thought to
himself how unwise it had been for the last two years to leave
the young visionary at the mercy, so to speak, of all comers; so
in agreement with Mother Ursule Fardes, Superior of the
Hospice, he had decided that her new boarder should not receive
visitors unless one of the nuns was present. If such a measure
failed to reduce the influx of strangers, at least (so the Curé
frankly hoped) they would be less demonstrative in their admiration and friendly attentions.

*    *    *

The Lourdes Hospice was even in those days (except for the
present mansards and chapel) the same long building that it is
to-day, with its first floor resting partially on an open colonnade.
The Sisters of Charity and Christian Instruction had received
Bernadette there with open arms: the time was past when they
had sided with the opposition; the story of the halo told by
M. Peyramale would have sufficed to dispel their last doubts.
The newcomer was treated even with honour. 'She was not,'
observed M. Estrade, 'made to follow the régime of the patients
and paupers. She was for the Sisters a sacred trust, and the
Superior of the house, prompted by this consideration, had her

installed in a very cheerful airy room of her own, and assigned a select place at the school-boarders' table.' In return, the hospitable house accepted never a penny from anyone. This religious environment, as Bernadette realized at once, suited her better than her father's mill, with the continual coming and going of busybodies and customers. It fitted in with her devout tastes and her still cherished vocation. Possibly she had in mind the idea that the nuns would keep visitors away and thus she would have all the time needed for her education.

In this Hospice school the classrooms occupied the west side: the free pupils were on the ground floor, and on the first floor were the two classes of pupils who paid fees: one class at five francs per month, the other at two francs. This last, in which the Sisters placed Bernadette, was attended by the daughters of well-to-do artisans and tradesmen.

Neither her size nor her dress distinguished the visionary of Massabielle from her companions. Even though in the five-franc class, which was pompously named 'The Boarding School', there were some wealthy girls who were forced by their mothers to wear the crinoline and dress their hair in a net, all the little Pyreneans of the two-franc class sported the local attire: a straight skirt, a pinafore and a shawl fastened with a clasp across the breast. The coloured kerchief gracefully wrapped round the head—as seen in photographs of the period—added to the innocent charm of Bernadette in her teens.

In the two-franc class an excellent nun, Sister Savignon, had some forty pupils under her. The room was lit by a wide bay window from which there was a view down to the valley of the Gave; it is easy to guess Bernadette's thoughts in her moments of distraction as her eyes fell on the swaying tops of the poplar trees of Ribère: the grotto, the Virgin and her smile. . . .

Her progress in reading, writing and arithmetic proved satisfactory. As for her writing, witness a long letter she wrote, on May 28th, 1861, to Father Gondrand, Oblate of the Bétharram residence, in which is to be found the first account of the Apparitions written in her own hand. One of her exercise-books is preserved at the Lourdes Hospice. It bears on the second page the date, February 21st, 1864. No margin: which indicates a care for economy; nor even a blot: which reveals an inborn taste for tidiness. From a considerable slant in 1861, the writing had improved somewhat and was beginning to show elegance. In this exercise-book are the usual tasks of a schoolgirl: dictation, exercises in grammar, conjugation of verbs, sentences copied out several times, grammatical analysis, easy problems. . . . After four years at the Hospice, Bernadette possessed more or less the elementary accomplishments of the girls of her age in Lourdes.

The recollections of the nuns agree in describing her as 'very submissive to her mistresses, very kind to her companions, very edifying. . . . She had a lively character, they said, and was not averse to playing pranks, even during class.'

Perhaps the best of those recorded occurred in the strawberry season. The bed where the succulent fruit was beginning to ripen extended beneath the windows of a room in which a lady from the town was giving sewing lessons to a certain number of pupils. Bernadette was one of them and she had next to her the fidgety Julie Garros. 'It was hot,' the latter related, 'and the windows were open. We were eyeing the strawberries with a certain craving.' The temptation was very strong. Without going out of the room, the children were given a short break. Julie, who, so she makes out, was merely thinking of a good trick to play, discovered an unexpected accomplice . . . in her neighbour. 'I'm going to throw my shoe into the garden,' said Bernadette in fun. 'You go and fetch it, and bring back some strawberries.' And, concludes the daring Julie, 'no sooner said than done'.

She had other escapades of that sort, and who would be surprised? There were times when she showed 'some stubbornness,' attests a Sister, 'but not enough for her companions to notice it'. One Sunday after Vespers she was told to take off her new dress; she refused. Another time she was obstinate in wanting to go down to her father's mill: she must see her little brother and godson again. But one of the Sisters reminded her that this was a chance of making a sacrifice, and Bernadette calmed down.

Did she pay the tribute of a daughter of Eve to coquetry? A little! One day Sister Victorine surprised her 'flouncing out her skirt to make it look like a crinoline', and another day 'inserting a sort of busk in her corset'. This was on the instigation of a companion. It was a fit of vanity that soon passed, leaving no trace. In short 'it was a bit of childishness'.

Of this fleeting phase of youth one only amusing memory has survived. Her cousin, Jeanne Védère, took Bernadette to Momères and arranged to have her photographed. 'But,' Jeanne pointed out to her, 'M. Duffour, the photographer, wants me to make you look beautiful and dress you in other clothes.' 'If this gentleman does not find me handsome enough,' said Bernadette, 'leave me here. I refuse to add a single pin more.'

During recreations she would have liked to join in the noisy, sometimes boisterous games of her companions, but she tired quickly. Too often her job in the playground consisted either of holding the skipping rope or of looking after the shawls and cloaks of her little friends. During short pauses her favourites would come around her so as not to leave her all alone. Those of the girls who understood would fix their gaze on her now and then, and in their eyes one could read their wonder, awe, and almost an apprehension of the divine! So she was the one who saw the Blessed Virgin! . . . It was just a momentary thought, in between a couple of races or games.

The nuns placed her in front of them during prayers and Mass and noticed nothing out of the ordinary in Bernadette's piety; and that is easily explained, for the young boarder herself did not like multiplying external signs of devotion. But there was still the lovely sign of the cross which, whether in public or when unobserved, she always made with a sort of majesty. And the Sisters knew from whom the ignorant daughter of miller Soubirous had received her lesson!

The mistresses were also edified to see her reciting her Hail Marys: spontaneously her eyes were raised upwards, far away from earth. And at night she never failed to coil her beads round her arm before going to sleep. The Sister who nursed her during her attacks of asthma saw her sometimes pressing her beads against her aching chest as she recited her Rosary.

Her confessor allowed her frequent Communion. So great was her desire for this that even after the most exhausting bouts of asthma she used to refuse the sip of herb-tea that would have broken her fast and deprived her of the Eucharist.

Usually twice a week, one of the nuns took her to Massabielle— and it was often the occasion of a joyful visit to her family, where she used to marvel at her godson's progress. Nothing could be more simple than these pilgrimages: she began by kissing the ground, drank a mouthful of the miraculous water and then, to attract the least possible attention, she would go up and kneel in the shadow of the grotto. 'Here,' as has been written, 'in deep recollection, withdrawn, often unnoticed, she would give herself up to her meditations and recite her little rosary with devotion.'

In class she occupied the first place near the door. The young visionary had no difficulty in guessing why she had been put right in front: it was to avoid disturbing anyone when she was called to the parlour. It was not long, in fact, before strangers began to call at the Hospice, asking for Bernadette. If the Superior sanctioned the interview the cloister bell gave a certain ring—as it did several times a day—and Bernadette understood. She would heave a sigh and, being dispensed from asking permission, would leave the class. At the foot of the stairs one of the nuns was waiting for her and took her to the visitors. They were all people eager to make her acquaintance and hear her speak. Obligingly, but without much apparent feeling, with no affectation of manner and without raising her voice, she would speak about the Apparition, reproducing her most impressive gestures. They used to want to take away some souvenir of Mary's privileged child, and more than once she was asked for some of her hair, but she always obstinately refused.

On the other hand she would willingly sign pictures in her still faltering handwriting, always adding the same formula: '*p. p. Bernadette*'—which obviously stood for: '*priez pour Bernadette*' (pray for Bernadette). Sometimes the schoolgirls, in a teasing mood ran after her with the refrain: '*Ha, ha, pépé Bernadette! . . . pépé Bernadette!*' She herself was amused at this, but made not the slightest change in her signature.

\*    \*    \*

After pursuing its investigations into the Lourdes events for more than two years, the episcopal Commission finally communicated to Bishop Laurence the result of its patient and thorough work. Yes, the voice of the people was here the voice of God. Those thousands of pilgrims who had come, since February 1858, and knelt at Massabielle, had not been deluding themselves: the Lady of the Grotto was indeed Our Lady.

Before officially adopting the findings of the Enquiry, Bishop Laurence insisted on presiding in person at the final session. It was held in the sacristy at Lourdes with the same Commissioners as before. In the presence of so imposing an assembly Bernadette came forward with her usual simplicity, wearing her capulet over her head and sabots on her feet. Nevertheless, at this particularly solemn moment, conscious of her mission, she spoke with an arresting authority. When she repeated: 'I am the Immaculate Conception', she lowered and joined her hands, raised her eyes and seemed enveloped in such a heavenly grace that the aged Bishop was spellbound and trembling all over. Two big tears rolled down his cheeks. And when Bernadette had left, he exclaimed, still under the stress of emotion: 'Did you see that child?'

The case having been heard, it remained only to proclaim the verdict. On Saturday, January 18th, 1862, the Feast of St Peter's Chair at Rome, Bishop Laurence signed the 'Decree passing judgment on the Apparition which took place at the Grotto of Lourdes'.

This noble document, which had been so long in the making, began by pointing out that manifestations of the supernatural, far from being the exclusive privilege of the first centuries of Christianity, had been perpetuated down the ages, as history attests, 'for the glory of religion and the edification of the faithful'. It then recounted the visions of Bernadette—'the weakest of things in the eyes of the world, a girl of fourteen, born in Lourdes, of a poor family'. Next, the Bishop proceeded to a calm discussion of the facts in the light of the suggestions made by the Commission of Enquiry and scientific authorities.

We are convinced [he continued] that the Apparition is supernatural and from God. . . . Our conviction is based on the testimony of Bernadette, and above all on the events which have occurred since and which can only be explained by divine intervention. . . . The testimony of Bernadette is of great importance in itself, but it derives entirely new force—we would say, its fulfilment—from the marvellous deeds which have been performed since the first event. If the tree is to be judged by its fruit, we can say that the Apparition described by the young girl is supernatural and divine, for the effects it has produced are supernatural and divine.

Conversions, 'marvels of grace', extraordinary, instantaneous and permanent cures 'wrought by the use of a water devoid of all natural curative property'—these were some of the 'marvellous deeds' which the Commission had been investigating. As to these cures——

> What is the power which has produced them? Is it the power of the natural organism itself? Science, consulted on this matter, has replied in the negative. These cures, then, are the work of God. But they are connected with the Apparition: she is the starting-point of them all; she has inspired the confidence of the sick. There is therefore a close link between the cures and the Apparition: the Apparition is from God because the cures bear the stamp of the divine.
>
> But what comes from God is truth. Consequently the Apparition who calls herself the Immaculate Conception, whom Bernadette has seen and heard, is none other than the Most Blessed Virgin!

Finally came the clauses for which all were waiting:

> ARTICLE 1. We judge that Mary the Immaculate, Mother of God, did truly appear to Bernadette Soubirous on the 11th February, 1858, and on subsequent days, to the number of eighteen times in all, in the grotto of Massabielle, near the town of Lourdes; that this Apparition bears every mark of truth, and that the faithful are justified in believing it as certain.
>
> We humbly submit our judgment to the judgment of the Sovereign Pontiff, who is charged with the government of the universal Church.
>
> ARTICLE 2. We authorize in our diocese the veneration of Our Lady of the Grotto of Lourdes. . . .
>
> ARTICLE 3. In order to comply with the will of the Blessed Virgin, expressed several times during the Apparitions, we propose to build a sanctuary on the site of the grotto, which has become the property of the Bishops of Tarbes. . . .

*　　*　　*

Thus Bernadette's mission as visionary, witness and messenger of Mary Immaculate seemed closed. The head of the diocese had done more than proclaim his belief in the reality of the eighteen Apparitions; what the child had requested 'from the priests' on behalf of the Lady, the Bishop of Tarbes had conceded, and was himself taking it in hand; and, now that the veneration of Our Lady of Lourdes was authorized, Christian people would be able to go in procession, singing their hymns, solemn or joyful, to the grotto of Massabielle that was for ever sanctified, and where would soon arise that 'chapel' on which the Virgin set so great a value.

# III

## IN THE CONVENT AT NEVERS

# 20

## FINDING THE WAY

How was it that Bernadette, who felt attracted to convent life and was now at liberty to follow her inclination, stayed on as a boarder in the Hospice for some years more? One reason was her ill-health. According to the Superior and Sister Victorine, she suffered all sorts of pains, rheumatism, spitting and vomiting of blood, palpitations of the heart, habitual constriction of breath, and at times such violent attacks of asthma that she had to be carried to the window to recover her breath. In her pain she used to say: 'Open my chest!'

During the first weeks of the spring of 1862 the weather was still severe. Towards the end of March Bernadette was put to bed. Dr Balencie diagnosed pneumonia, but the invalid seems to have recovered speedily enough. Easter Sunday, April 20th, was gladdened by bright sunshine, and it was thought that a stroll would do the convalescent good. Her face lit up with the happiest of smiles: they were talking of taking her to the grotto. In fact she did go down there warmly wrapped up, but on her her return she had a relapse; and the Sisters reproached themselves for having listened less to common sense than to the child's longings. On Monday in Low Week the doctor did not conceal his grave anxiety. The pupils came and prayed at the bedside of their dear companion who, they were told, was dying. Her family were summoned: 'Holy Virgin! we are going to lose our Bernadette!" exclaimed François and Louise Soubirous in tears. Abbé Pomian hurried along vested in surplice and stole. His penitent was at her last gasp; he anointed her and managed to give her Holy Communion with a tiny particle of the Host. Bernadette opened her eyes again. 'Some water from the grotto!' she implored. They managed to get a few drops of it down her throat and straightway she gave a gasp of joy: 'I'm cured . . . !' As she explained afterwards, 'I felt as if a mountain had been lifted off my chest.'

Without much hope of finding Bernadette still alive, Dr Balencie called again at the Hospice next morning. He was shown first of all into the parlour: it was in order to announce her death, he thought. But who should be there to receive him but Bernadette herself! He could scarcely believe his eyes. 'Did she take my medicine?' he asked. The invalid had not touched it.

Although Our Lady of Lourdes had cured Bernadette of her pneumonia, she had left her her asthma, her 'instrument of penance' and her cross for all the days of her life. In October she was again sent to the thermal springs of Bagnères-de-Bigorre, where the Sisters of Nevers had a residence. Among those mountains, 'at that season of the year, 1862, the temperature was extremely mild, and the encircling ring of mountain heights stood out in all their glory, lovelier than ever in that enchanting freshness and the autumn sunshine'.

When Bernadette used to be questioned by visitors to the Hospice about 'the great event of her life', the Apparitions, the visionary who was usually so sprightly would turn serious and solemn, but her replies were never hesitant or vague. However, if she were then questioned about her future, in order to avoid indiscretions she would merely indicate by a word or a gesture that she had no ideas about it. That did not prevent some ladies, nuns especially, from speaking their minds openly in her presence: this girl who had had the good fortune to see the Blessed Virgin was not made for a life in the world! Besides, how many nuns dreamed of having this pearl in their community!

'I know,' said Sister Vincent Garros, 'from what Bernadette told me herself, that some Sisters of St. Vincent de Paul came to see her in Lourdes and tried the cornette on her. Bernadette would have none of it! Likewise the Sisters of the Cross sought to attract her into their midst: they tried their long headdress on her, but she said: 'I don't want that tunnel.' A Carmelite friar from Bagnères, says Sister Aurélie Gouteyron, suggested to Bernadette one day in all simplicity: 'You ought to become a Carmelite.' 'I am very fond of Carmel,' she rejoined, 'but if I do embrace religious life, I want to join a congregation whose rule I can keep.'—'But, my child, Superiors can grant dispensations.'—'I don't want any dispensations, Father; I want to follow the rule without exceptions.'

About that time—and who would credit it?—her preference was supposed to lie in the direction of the strict Order of the Cistercians. What were the reasons for this impracticable aspiration? First and foremost probably the personality of the inspiring and attractive St Bernard, whose name she had received in Baptism together with that of the Blessed Virgin; in that case it was a matter of sentiment rather than of deliberate intention. Also she was feeling such a thirst for solitude and silence at that very time when her privacy and peace of soul were at the mercy of all comers. It may be also that she had heard the story of the reform of Cîteaux read in the refectory. In any case, her cousin Védère, who was secretly aspiring to become a Trappistine, was very surprised one day in 1861 to hear Bernadette explain to her that on donning the white and black serge habit she would have to follow the Rule of St Benedict.

In the spring of 1862 a distant relation, Madeleine Cassou, who was leaving for the Convent of Nevers together with three other girls, came to wish Bernadette good-bye. 'Bernadette,' Madeleine asked, 'aren't you going to join us soon?'—'I'm to be a nun,' she replied, 'but I don't know which Order; the Blessed Virgin has not told me. I'm waiting.' For the time being she deemed herself 'unsuited for religious life on account of her poor health' and she kept her longing 'entirely to herself'.

The Lourdes nuns were forbidden to speak to her about becoming a nun. 'I knew very well,' declared Mother Henri Fabre, 'that our Superiors were not at all eager to attract Bernadette, and were not in the least anxious to have her. The reason for their attitude, I have always thought, was that they dreaded the responsibility of accepting a subject who had been supernaturally favoured as Bernadette had been, and who would inevitably attract numerous visitors to wherever she lived.'

During her long period of suspense, Bernadette must have needed the support of a motherly heart. Unfortunately in 1862 Mother Ursule Fardes, the Superior whose devotedness she had valued, left Lourdes for Puéchabon in the Hérault. Her successor, Mother Alexandrine Roques, though very kind-hearted, was not yet sufficiently acquainted with this privileged child of Our Lady; and Bernadette, fearing that she would not be listened to if she spoke to her about her secret aspirations, did not open her heart to her till many months after her arrival.

\* \* \*

As the years went by, Bernadette, with understandable joy but without the last self-conceit, watched the chaos of Massabielle being transformed. The grotto was cleared and, as M. Peyramale wrote on January 22nd, 1862, to Bishop Laurence, 'the levelling of the ground gives it a most imposing appearance'. In February, 1861, the Bishop had acquired from the town the slopes bordering the Gave around Massabielle: it was imperative to start building the 'chapel' requested by Mary without delay. Money was lacking, it is true, but the prelate was relying on the generosity of the faithful. There was also a lack of space: an inspiration of the architect provided this.

M. Hippolyte Durand, diocesan architect of Tarbes, instead of accepting the earliest plan, which would have meant enclosing the grotto within the walls of an oratory, conceived the bold idea, which was at first considered impracticable, of erecting like a gigantic crown on the rock of the Apparition a building in harmony with the ring of graceful hills, and whose spire would raise the Cross 330 feet above the Gave. In this way the grotto would remain as it was when Bernadette's visions had hallowed it, looking out over the rippling stream, open to the azure sky, and to the stars at night.

On Tuesday, October 14th, 1862, the first blow of the pick was struck to begin preparing the foundations of the future chapel. Sixty workmen were busily employed in clearing away the earth down to the solid rock, and levelling the top of 'Masse-Vieille': for that is where the architect had decided to construct 'a rectangular plateau running from east to west'. Among the workers whom Bernadette used to greet when she came to the grotto was her father, and François Soubirous was proud to co-operate in the humblest capacity in the majestic work of Mary Immaculate.

On the afternoon of Thursday, September 17th, 1863, the Curé of Lourdes called at the Hospice with a priest and a layman. The priest was Abbé Blanc, chaplain to the De Lacour family at the Château de Montluzin, at Chasselay in the Rhône Department; the layman was M. Joseph Fabisch, Professor of Sculpture at the School of Fine Arts in Lyons. He explained to the Mother Superior that the ladies of the Château, with the sanction of the Bishop, 'desired to give a statue of the Blessed Virgin in white marble, to be set up in the place where the Apparition had stood', and that they had selected to execute this work of art the well-known sculptor of the statue of Our Lady of La Salette. But wisely the artist would only work to Bernadette's directions and guidance. According to his account:

> She came in accompanied by a nun. Her appearance in fact was not that of a girl close on twenty, but rather that of a child of twelve. . . . One's attention was attracted to her face which, without having the regularity of features looked for by the sculptor, had something most engaging, a charm that appealed to the purest and most serene faculties of the soul, an expression so sweet, so open, that it compelled respect and inspired trust.

So far, however, M. Fabisch observed only the external appearance of the visionary; her hidden mystical beauty of soul was to be revealed to him soon afterwards. He questioned her about the figure, clothing and radiant splendour of the Apparition. Finally he asked her to reproduce Her posture and gestures at the moment when She said: 'I am the Immaculate Conception.'

> The girl [he continues] stood up with great simplicity. She joined her hands and raised her eyes to Heaven. . . . But neither Angelico, nor Perugino, nor Raphael ever painted anything so appealing and at the same time so profound as the look of that young girl. . . .
> No, I shall never forget, as long as I live, that entrancing expression. I have indeed seen in Italy and elsewhere the master-pieces of the great artists, of such as have excelled in rendering the transports of Divine love and ecstasy; but in none of them have I found so much sweetness. . . .

At the end of November the Curé received a photograph from Lyons of the rough model. It was submitted to Bernadette, who demanded several extremely judicious alterations and recommended in particular 'greater fullness in the whole'.

Though I have not myself had the good fortune to see the Queen of Heaven, I consider your model already perfect [Abbé Peyramale wrote without undue flattery to the sculptor Fabisch]. As for Bernadette it is quite another matter. However delighted she may be for other reasons, I doubt whether when she sees your statue she will exclaim: It is *She!* You must not take offence: your statue will still be no less beautiful for that, and we shall have in this verdict of Bernadette's a fresh proof of the truth of the Apparition.

On Wednesday, March 30th, 1864, the artist returned to Lourdes, this time with his finished work. This statue of pure Carrara marble 'improves greatly on a close view', wrote a connoisseur who had the advantage of seeing it this way. 'At a distance the whiteness of the marble . . . gives the work an unpleasant impasto look.' But on a close view 'the face is charmingly sweet, and the posture prayerful and ecstatic, but they emphasize a certain stiffness which is aggravated by the position of the forearms and the joining of the hands a trifle low; nevertheless the dress, gathered round the neck and caught in at the waist, is a masterpiece of delicacy, and the white veil which encircles the head and almost completely enfolds the figure is so airy that it seems ready to shimmer at the least breath'.

The unveiling of the statue was fixed for the Monday in Low Week, April 4th, the day on which the Annunciation of the Blessed Virgin was to be celebrated that year. Unfortunately neither the Curé of Lourdes nor the visionary was able to be present, both being very ill and confined to bed. In the afternoon a procession of 20,000 people, with Bishop Laurence presiding, went down from the church to the grotto. The streets were magnificently decorated with garlands of ivy and box stretching from house to house, and all the walls were draped with bunting and decked with stars. When he arrived beneath the eglantine the Bishop let down the veil that covered the statue; then he blessed and incensed it. The crowd remained silent: piety alone had restrained their applause.

Then, mounting a pulpit of greenery, the preacher, M. Alix, Honorary Chaplain of Sainte-Geneviève's in Paris, spoke with infectious emotion on the text from the Song of Songs: 'Arise, said the Bridegroom to the Bride, arise, my dove in the clefts of the rock. . . . Show me thy face and let thy voice sound in my ears.'

Alone in the front of this crowd before the grotto was a man with a worried frown on his brow; it was the sculptor himself.

I must mention [he admitted later] one of the greatest griefs of my life as an artist. It is the one I suffered when I saw my statue in position lit by a reflected light from below which completely altered its expression. I realized at that moment that the polychrome sculpture of the Ancients and the Middle Ages had its justification.

As for Bernadette's verdict, it was exactly as Abbé Peyramale had forecast; the child had beheld 'what the heart of man could not comprehend' (1 Cor. 2, 19); the artist had to submit. At the end of her convalescence the girl had the consolation of returning to the grotto. Kneeling in her old place she gazed for a long time at the white image while reciting her Rosary. 'Well, what have you to say about it?' she was asked afterwards. 'Ah, it's beautiful,' she answered, 'but it isn't *Her*.' And when someone asked her later: 'Is it possible when looking at this statue to imagine the loveliness of the Lady?' she replied with vigour: 'Oh, no, it's as different as Heaven from earth!'

\*　　\*　　\*

On the morning of Friday, September 25th, 1863, an unexpected event occurred at the Hospice. Bernadette, still on holiday from school, was busy peeling vegetables. Suddenly there was a ring at the front door. A Sister soon appeared and whispered from the kitchen door: 'It's His Lordship the Bishop of Nevers! Quick, Bernadette, go and ring the bell to announce His Lordship.' Bernadette ran and pulled hard and conscientiously on the rope. '*Prou, prou, prou*' (that will do), said the Bishop in patois, mimicking the sound, and smiling at Mother Alexandrine, who was accompanying him. And Bernadette, reassured, laughed 'with all her heart' on her way back to the kitchen.

He was a prelate with a noble profile and majestic bearing and his look betokened a kindly nature. Straightforward and ener-

getic, 'he was a character'. He was, to say the truth, rather
mercurial, and 'at times', writes his biographer, 'he was lacking
in patience. . . . With no affectations and without any stiffness,
he had a genuine affability. . . . In ordinary private conversation he was exceptionally jovial and merry. He was fond of
joking and might even be accused of sometimes carrying it a bit
too far'. A man of prayer, he displayed great regularity in his
devotional practices and led an extremely austere life.

At that time the Sisters of Nevers were only a diocesan Congregation. Bishop Forcade was their Superior, and a very active
one too. He was eager to secure new recruits for them, and it
was partly for this reason that he had come to Lourdes. Even
as he entered the Hospice he gave his reason for coming: 'You
must show me Bernadette.' However, to avoid giving her the
idea that she was somebody of importance, because a Bishop
took the trouble to come and see her, he would meet her as if by
chance during his visit to the convent. In fact he inspected
several rooms in a cursory way until he reached the kitchen.
The Superior knocked on the door and the Sister cook hurried
to open it. Sitting in the chimney corner was the girl who a
moment ago had been pulling the bell so conscientiously. She
was frail and puny in appearance, poorly clad, and wore on her
head a kerchief with the corners knotted at the side. Seated on
a block of wood, she went on scraping a carrot; and Mother
Alexandrine whispered in the Bishop's ear: 'There you are!'
As the prelate turned to leave after saying a few words of
encouragement to the cook, Bernadette got up and, kneeling
close to the Sister, kissed the Bishop's ring.

Understandably, Bishop Forcade was not satisfied with such a
pointless interview. After lunch, during which she had been
sent to assist His Lordship's valet at table, the humble vegetable
peeler was called to the parlour, where she was left alone with
the Bishop of Nevers. He wished first of all to hear the visionary
give him an account of the Apparitions and then he talked to
her. 'She surprises me,' he wrote, 'by the ease with which she
understands and answers me. She expresses herself in French
correctly, clearly and precisely without having to search for a
word. She is imperturbable and nothing ruffles her. You
would think that her replies, which are always satisfying, came
spontaneously to her lips, almost without her knowing it, and

as if by inspiration.' The Bishop did his best to hide his astonishment.

'And now, my dear child,' he asked her, 'what are you going to be?'

After a moment's hesitation Bernadette replied: 'Oh, nothing.'

'What, nothing? But you simply must do something in this life.'

'Well, I am here with the dear Sisters.'

'Quite so, but you can only stay here for a time.'

'I should like to stay here always.'

'That is easier said than done.'

'Why?'

'Because you are not a Sister, and it is absolutely essential for you to be one in order to join the Community. As it is, you are nothing and at this rate you will never last long anywhere.'

This was the first time that the precariousness of her position had been pointed out to the young boarder. She seemed wrapped in thought and was at a loss for an answer. The Bishop resumed after a moment's silence: 'See, you are no longer a child. Perhaps you will be very glad to get suitably settled in the world with a little place of your own?' The reply came sharply: 'No! Certainly not that!'

'In that case why don't you become a Sister? Have you never thought of it?'

'It is impossible, my Lord. You are well aware how poor I am; I shall never have the necessary dowry.'

'But, my child, poor girls are sometimes accepted as nuns without a dowry when they have a real vocation.'

'But, my Lord, the young ladies whom you take without dowry are clever and capable ones who will compensate you well for it. . . . As for me, I know nothing and I am good for nothing.'

'What! Good for nothing!' exclaimed the prelate. 'Just now in the kitchen I noticed that there is something you are good at. In religion they would be able to make good use of you; besides, in the noviciate they would complete your education.'

Bernadette's smile had returned.

'Come now,' concluded His Lordship, 'think it over, consult your confessor and above all beg the Blessed Virgin, who condescended to appear to you, to obtain for you from her Divine

Son the light and grace you need. Then if your heart says yes,
ask Mother Superior to tell either Mother General or myself, and
leave the rest to me.'

'In that case, my Lord, I'll think it over, but I've not yet made
up my mind.'

From Lourdes Bishop Forcade went on to Toulouse, where he
saw the Superior General, Mother Louise Ferrand. "Well, do
you really want Bernadette?" said the Bishop in the course of a
private interview.

'My Lord,' she objected, 'Bernadette hasn't the necessary health;
she will be in and out of the infirmary all the time. . . . Besides,
there is not very much that she can do.' [On this last point,
observes Mother Bordenave, the Superior General was mistaken,
for Bernadette was very deft-handed: she could do delicate
embroidery and, what is more, she nursed the sick efficiently and
devotedly.]

'She will always be able,' retorted the prelate, ' to scrape carrots,'
as I saw her doing at Lourdes. . . . You are aware that many a
convent is hankering after her.'

'Oh, well,' concluded the Superior General, 'we'll take her if
she asks.'

At the Lourdes Hospice they spoke no more of the visit of the
Bishop of Nevers. Besides, they prudently desired to leave
Bernadette's soul free and open to the action of God's grace.
But she suffered in her loneliness. If only Mother Ursule Fardes
were there, thought Bernadette, she would have found guidance
and comfort in her company. When writing to her she could
only speak in vague terms about her distress, as her letters were
read by the new Superior.

I am taking this opportunity of talking to you [she confided to
her on May 2nd, 1864]. It gives me the greatest happiness, believe
me, my dear Mother. And it would be greater still if God would
grant me the favour of seeing you for a moment. My poor heart
would have many things to tell you.

Bernadette, it is true, had found a confidante for a short while
in the kindly Mother Bernard Berganot, Superior of the Lectoure
house, who sometimes visited the Lourdes Hospice. This nun

understood the young boarder who sometimes called her 'Aunt' and treated her familiarly.

> I often think of you, dear Mother [she wrote to her two years later], and I love to recall the day when we were in the wood-shed and you spoke to me about my vocation. How often have I recalled that little chat! I can still see you sitting on one step of the staircase and me on the other.

Unfortunately, Bernadette was never to meet this revered friend again, for Mother Bernard was sent as Superior to the Boarding School at Sens—such a long way off! So whom could she confide in now? Meanwhile, being free from external pressure, she never ceased praying and thinking things over. Her thoughts turned more and more to the Congregation of Nevers, which had helped her in the formation of her mind and heart. Bernadette's attitude towards the Sisters of Nevers was 'that deep and almost inborn feeling which comes naturally to us with regard to persons and things that we have always known and always loved. . . . All this assuredly would not have sufficed to settle a vocation; but as often happens in God's works Bernadette's choice was shaped by a whole series of providential coincidences and signs.'

At length, on Assumption Day, she approached Mother Alexandrine of her own accord. 'My dear Mother,' she said, 'I have made up my mind to become a nun, and if your Reverend Mother General is willing to accept me I shall be glad to join your Congregation.' What were Mother Alexandrine's reactions at this moment? Did she, like a mother, clasp this little one in her arms? We do not know. But from then on she always admitted Bernadette to the Community exercises as if she were already one of the family of Saint-Gildard. Having noticed in her 'a real taste and a remarkable aptitude for delicate needlework and embroidery', she directed her in the making of 'a very beautiful alb which even our cleverest Sisters admired'. Discovering also that 'Bernadette would have made an excellent nurse, for not only had she the kindness of heart needed for that work, but also orderliness and remarkable skill', Mother Alexandrine took her into the sick wards where a poor woman covered in sores—a cancer case—became her favourite.

But why could not the dear Mother stop the crowds of inquisitive folk who, often with M. Peyramale's consent, used to call at the Hospice? ' Some were waiting at the gate even before the Community got up in the mornings.' On feast days especially, ' the Sisters had to steal Bernadette away in order to give her something to eat . . . and she belonged to the strangers until evening '. Mother Superior had no idea how much Bernadette was suffering except from what she read in her humble letters. With laments, Bernadette unburdened herself to a young priest, Abbé Bonin, who had won her confidence.

I am for ever going up and down the stairs. . . . For some time now I have not been able to do any school work. I do nothing but receive pilgrims from morning till night. . . . I'm tired out with seeing so many people. Pray for me that God may take me or arrange for me to be admitted quickly among his spouses. That is my great desire, though I am most unworthy.

Bernadette had taken some time to decide on Nevers. When Mother Joséphine Imbert, who had just replaced Mother Louise Ferrand as Superior General, was informed by the Lourdes Superior of the aspirant's ailments, she, also, seemed in no hurry to accept her. The Bishop of Nevers grew uneasy and towards the end of 1864 he saw Mother Imbert and asked for information on Bernadette's case. ' We will accept her,' was the reply, ' as soon as her health is restored.'

Poor Bernadette! That winter of 1864-5 and the following spring were scarcely in her favour. At the slightest ' cold snap ', as she said, she dreaded a fresh attack. Fortunately, a fine summer and a mild autumn brought her some relief and strength. So much so that the Superior of the Hospice no longer refused, as she had done so far, to take her to several houses of the Sisters of Nevers, where they eagerly desired to see her.

At Pau, wearing her graceful Pyrenean costume, she was recognized by a passer-by just as Mother Alexandrine was taking her in to meet the community. In the twinkling of an eye, as the Superior related, the convent ' was besieged by a multitude of people. . . . We had to call in the police. The courtyard was crowded with mothers who wanted Bernadette to touch their children. With the help of the policemen some order was restored among these women, and Bernadette went round touching the children. . . . On leaving Pau, Bernadette had to be taken to Oloron to satisfy the Sisters there.'

At the boarding school of Sainte-Angèle in Oloron the pupils were all assembled in the study hall and Bernadette was asked to say a word to them about her visions. Standing up at the teacher's desk she began with the sign of the cross. 'Always make it like this,' she advised them; 'that is how the Blessed Virgin made it at the first Apparition.' She gave a brief summary of this Apparition. Then, taking her rosary, she recited it aloud with a fervour that impressed both pupils and mistresses. Several of the girls acknowledged afterwards that they had learned that day to love the Blessed Virgin.

On October 3rd the Védère family obtained permission to take Bernadette to Momères for three days. This was the native parish of M. Peyramale, and he turned up there opportunely. His brother was a doctor in practice there. The Curé of Lourdes allowed Jeanne to keep Bernadette there 'for more than a month if she wished'. So Bernadette had a holiday right to the end of November on the restful banks of the Adour. On October 3rd she had reached Momères about nine in the evening. 'By the following morning,' reported Jeanne Védère, 'everybody in the parish, in the neighbouring villages and as far as Tarbes, knew that Bernadette was at our house. During these seven weeks, she spent her time in prayer and reading (but she preferred meditation to reading), in work and in receiving visits and paying them, when I told her to.' She used to go and watch Jeanne teaching her class, 'for she was very fond of children and so were they of her'.

On her return to Lourdes she was attacked by fits of breathlessness, perhaps due to the change of air, but she was not unduly alarmed. 'That everlasting cough, which tires me out, seems to have disappeared,' she confided to Mother Augustine Ceyrac, who had had some beneficial medicine sent to her. 'I have spent a peaceful winter,' she wrote later to Mother Ursule Fardes. Lastly, on April 21st, 1866, a Vicar General of Tarbes gave the reassuring news that 'Bernadette is in good health, still as simple and humble as ever'.

In these circumstances the Superior of the Hospice had admitted her as a postulant at the end of 1865, along with another girl, Léontine Mouret.

By this time Bernadette had moved up into the top class, which was the smallest in numbers, but the most expensive and was given the special name of the 'Boarding School'. This was, it may be remembered, the five-francs per month class, and was attended by the young ladies of the wealthier families in Lourdes. The elder daughter of Soubirous the miller was not overawed by them; she was indeed glad to see more of certain companions, who were also aspiring to religious life, in particular the chaplain's niece, Léontine Pomian, who would one day follow her to Saint-Gildard.

If at this time her progress in spelling was not very noticeable, her writing promised to become elegant; her compositions, studded with short, set phrases, expressive and sometimes ornate, began to take on a personal note. For intelligence Bernadette could be ranked among the good pupils. Otherwise, perhaps, the Sisters would not have put her in charge of the little girls in the lowest class to teach them the alphabet and spelling. We may presume that the temporary mistress was able to control her little folk. 'My little dears,' she said to them once, 'you have been very good, and I am going to reward you. We'll say a Hail Mary together.'

*     *     *

At last the hour of Providence was about to strike. In this year of 1866, shortly after Easter, on the advice of Mother Alexandrine, Bernadette applied direct to the Novice Mistress at Nevers, Mother Marie-Thérèse Vauzou—who was for the moment taking the place of the Mother General—and placed before her her great desire of dedicating herself to God among the Sisters of Nevers. Her letter enchanted Mother Marie-Thérèse, who read it to her assembled novices. 'You realize,' she added, 'what a grace and what a favour it is for us to receive Mary's privileged child, and how grateful we should be for this. As for myself, it will be one of the greatest blessings of my life to behold the eyes that have seen the Blessed Virgin.'

The encouraging, affectionate and maternal reply of Mother Vauzou had on Bernadette the effect of a message from on high; it filled her heart with that supernatural joy which, amid the most excruciating trials, was to be her light and her strength.

It was as though she had had a revelation that the cloister—a garden enclosed and centred round the Cross—reserved for her nevertheless a foretaste of the happiness promised her at Massabielle.

My dear Mother [she wrote on April 28th to Mother Ursule Fardes], I thank you for the fervent prayers you have had the kindness to address to Our Lord for me. I believe they have already been answered, for I feel myself more eager than ever to quit the world, and I am now completely determined. I propose to leave soon. Oh, my dear Mother, how I am longing to see the glorious day when I shall have the happiness of entering the noviciate, for it must be a real Heaven on earth.

A profound joy was in store for her before her departure for Nevers. The crypt, which was to form the base of the future chapel, was now finished. On Whitsun Eve—Saturday, May 19th, 1866—Bishop Laurence consecrated its five altars and said Mass there. The solemn opening of the graceful sanctuary was arranged for two days later. The dawn of that Whit Monday was full of promise: crowds set out from great distances. About April 15th, a railway had been opened between Lourdes and Bordeaux; a special train arrived from there overloaded and had had 'to leave thousands of people behind on the stations'.

But would the approaches to Massabielle be able to hold such a multitude with safety? M. Peyramale had seen to that. 'In order to give the pilgrims easier access,' as someone wrote, 'the masses of rock have been removed, the ground has been levelled and drained, and a long wide granite ramp has been built to form a barrier against the overflow of the river.' On the site of the Savy canal, now diverted, a proper embankment ran along the Gave and extended as a promenade well beyond the grotto. The latter, happily left as the Creator fashioned it, in its 'rustic and religious beauty', was protected by an iron grille, and there was a wooden candlestick with several branches to hold the candles. The miraculous spring flowed into a small marble monument bearing the inscription engraved in red: '*Allez boire à la fontaine et vous y laver.*' (Go and drink at the spring and wash yourself in it.)

Bernadette, to tell the truth, was somewhat lost among all these transformations. To a priest, who was anxious to know

the exact spot occupied by her during the first Apparition she
had to reply: 'It is all so changed that I hardly know where
I am now; I was about there.'

The preacher for the day, Father Duboé, a missionary of
Garaison, has left an enthusiastic account of the ceremony:

> On entering the town you at once got a holiday feeling. Triumphal arches opened on to broad avenues, the houses disappeared under garlands and banners, and everywhere the eye read Mary's praises. The town was a mass of flowers.
>
> The procession formed up in the parish church. Through the serried lines of pilgrims and the magnificent decorations of the streets, an almost endless procession wound its way towards the grotto, to the singing of the choirs. On arriving we climbed the slope of Massabielle. . . .

Bernadette, in good health this time, was walking among the
Children of Mary. This most wonderful festival was the crowning
of her mission. This triumph of Our Lady of Lourdes rested
on her own testimony, on the little Soubirous girl! It would
have been enough to turn the head of a conceited youngster.
But, forgetful of herself, the unique visionary was thinking
solely of the Apparition's glory, and was lost in her radiance.
And so along she went, paying no heed to the crowds, wholly
absorbed in her own interior happiness.

The people of Lourdes pointed her out as she passed. In her
Child of Mary costume, relates Jeanne Védère, 'she was pretty
as an angel'. Everybody was admiring her in her white dress
and white veil that recalled the statue in the grotto. 'Oh, what
a pretty saint! . . . the pretty maid! . . . How happy she is!'
voices shouted from the crowd. She was not listening. Several
times spectators ran from their places and gathered round her.
'They nearly stifled her; they went so far as to snip pieces from
her veil. The nuns had to close in around her, or her clothes
would have been torn off her. She hid herself among her companions',
and, having no other words to express in French her
astonishment at seeing herself singled out in public so blatantly,
she said: 'Oh, how idiotic they are!'

An altar was erected between the grotto and the Gave, and
Bishop Laurence celebrated there. From the place to which she
had been assigned Bernadette could take in at one glance both

the altar and the Virgin of the rock. 'At the Elevation,' related Father Duboé, 'the silence of the crowd was profound; only the ripple of the Gave could be heard. It was the great moment of that great day; a moment similar to those of the Apparitions. Mary's Son was coming down on the very spot where His Mother had come. He was coming down, attracted by her. It was for Him that the Blessed Virgin had asked from men a temple. He was going to take possession of it, make His abode there, and He was bearing His own witness to the Immaculate Conception.' At this Mass Bernadette received Holy Communion.

Meanwhile, clouds had piled up and a storm was threatening. Father Duboé, who had prepared a very long discourse, delivered only the first few sentences, and then contented himself with leading the multitude assembled on both banks of the Gave in shouts of 'Hurrah for Our Lady of Lourdes! . . . Hurrah for Pius IX, the Pope of the Immaculate Conception! . . . Hurrah for our Bishop. . . ! Hurrah for the Curé of Lourdes. . . !' A worldly crowd would have cheered Bernadette as well; indeed the preacher had thought several times of mentioning her in his discourse, but he did not; and she tasted the joy of believing herself forgotten.

The storm did not break over Lourdes, and everybody confidently prepared the illuminations for the night. In the evening 'the crowd flocked to the Hospice. The front gate of the courtyard being closed they climbed the walls to get a view of Bernadette.' Some show of defence had to be organized: a few soldiers who were patients in the hospital donned their uniforms. In order to satisfy everyone Mother Ursule Court, the Superior of Bagnères, made Bernadette walk up and down under the balcony. Sick of it all she said jokingly to Mother Ursule: 'Why, you are putting me on show like a strange animal! '

\* \* \*

The departure for Nevers was fixed for one of the first days in July.

How were her father and mother going to be able to resign themselves to losing their daughter? Bernadette would be the sixth child they had lost since their marriage. At the Boly mill they had seen the death of two of their boys, quite young, both named John.  At the miserable Baudéan mill they had lost a third little boy, also with the Christian name of John.  At the more profitable Lacadé mill, which Bishop Laurence's generosity allowed them to occupy as tenants, came two more heavy sorrows: on February 1st, 1865, at the age of ten, little Justin died in his mother's arms; finally, at the beginning of this year, 1866, there came into the world, unfortunately in most difficult circumstances, a ninth Soubirous child, a little girl, who lived just long enough to receive Baptism. . . .

Ever since then a dreadful threat had hung over the home: the mother felt that her own end was drawing near.  And it was in such circumstances that she had to consent to losing Bernadette, her comfort and her pride.  Even so, neither she nor her husband would refuse to give her to God.

On the other hand the father of Léontine Mouret, the postulant who was also preparing to leave for Nevers, did not display as much Christian spirit as the Soubirous parents.  On May 26th Bernadette wrote him a very charming letter urging him to allow his daughter to enter Saint-Gildard at the same time as herself:

. . . Knowing the keen desire your daughter has had for such a long time of entering the convent, I am writing to beg you to give the consent that will bring her happiness.

I realize that it is a great sacrifice for a father and mother to see themselves separated from a darling daughter, but be generous to God who never allows Himself to be outdone in generosity. . . . One day you will be very glad that you gave Him your child, whom you cannot place in better hands than those of Our Lord.

You would make greater sacrifices to entrust her to a man who might possibly be a stranger to you, and might make her unhappy; and yet you would refuse her to the King of Heaven and earth!  Oh, no, sir!  In the first place you are too good and religious-minded to act like that; and I think on the contrary that you ought to be grateful to Our Lord, for it is a very great favour He is doing you as well as your daughter, who understands this very well.

I implore you therefore to decide as soon as possible, for if you are willing to allow her to leave with me, it will be soon.  We shall do the journey more pleasantly together and on arrival at Nevers we shall settle down more quickly.

This letter so impressed M. Mouret that he made no further opposition to Léontine's departure.

It was to be definitely Wednesday, July 4th, 1866. On the eve of departure she went down to the grotto with several of the nuns. She went inside the grille and knelt down. Deep in prayer, her eyes fixed on the statue of the Immaculate, she broke into sobs. 'O Mother, Mother, how can I leave you?' Then she got up and pressed her lips tightly against the rock below the eglantine.

'We must be going,' said the Superior to her gently.

'Oh, just a little longer,' she begged. 'It's for the last time!'

She hastily dried her eyes, casting one long look at the white statue. Then without looking back she retraced her steps to the town.

'Bernadette,' remarked Mother Alexandrine, 'why are you so upset? Surely you know that the Blessed Virgin is everywhere, and that she will be your Mother everywhere?'

'Oh, yes, I know that,' she answered, 'but the grotto was Heaven for me.'

She spent the last evening with her family at the Lacadé mill. But for her dear ones it was all too short, this late visit which stirred up so many fond memories. Early the next day, July 4th, they were seen going up to the Hospice for their last farewells: the mother on father's arm, Toinette a girl of twenty, Jean-Marie a big boy of fifteen, and Bernard-Pierre who was not yet seven; also her aunts Bernarde, Basile and Lucile. While embracing Bernadette they all began to cry, little Bernard-Pierre crying at seeing the others cry. She who was leaving was the only one with dry eyes. Yet at the grotto on the previous day she had begun to suffer cruelly for her sacrifice; nevertheless she would have liked to give a little comfort to those she was about to leave: 'You are very kind to weep for me,' said she, braving her own grief and forcing a smile, 'but I can't stay here for ever.'

For the journey she wore a light blue dress with dark blue stripes. It was a present from a benefactress, and Mother Alexandrine had the greatest difficulty in getting her to accept it. Some of her friends, among them the devout Ida Ribettes, escorted her from the Hospice to the station. Four others took the train for Nevers with her: Mother Alexandrine, the Lourdes Superior, Mother Ursule, the Bagnères Superior, Léontine

Mouret and another postulant, Marie Lerotis. Sister Victorine, who was greatly attached to Bernadette, her aunt and godmother Bernarde Nicolau-Castérot and her sister Toinette accompanied her on the train as far as Tarbes station.

For the visionary of Massabielle it was the final good-bye. She was to say: 'I've left Lourdes for ever.'

Her age at the time was twenty-two years and three months.

# 21

## JOYS AND SORROWS OF A POSTULANT

THE journey from Lourdes to Nevers was made with two
stops: at Bordeaux and Périgueux, where Mothers Alexandrine and Ursule were glad to see their Congregation's
establishments and secretly proud to introduce Bernadette to
them.

The travellers reached Bordeaux on July 4th, about six in the
evening, and stayed there two days. In this large town the
Congregation possessed six houses, all of them flourishing. They
took a carriage to go from one to the other. It was as though
the unsophisticated Bernadette had discovered life. The Imperial Institute for the Deaf and Dumb, conducted since its
foundation by the Sisters of Nevers, overawed her with its
majestic façade: 'It looks more like a palace than a religious
house,' she wrote. 'It is not like that of Lourdes. . . .'

Our Pyreneans visited some old churches, the Botanical
Gardens, the harbour. . . . The big ships filled Bernadette with
wonder, yet not as much as something else quite new to her in
which with her usual simplicity she found great delight . . .
'Guess what!' she wrote to the Lourdes Sisters. 'Some fish,
red, black, white, grey! That's what I found most beautiful—
to see those little creatures swimming about in front of a crowd
of little urchins who had their eyes glued to them.'

At the Mission Orphanage, for lack of time, all she did was
to pass along the rows of young boarders, examining them one
by one. 'I was so impressed,' stated one of them forty-three
years later, 'that even to-day I can still feel that look fastened on
me.' At Périgueux, which they reached on Friday evening about
six o'clock, their first visit was to the hospital in the heart of
the town, run by the Sisters of Nevers. Then, in the chapel of
St Ursula's Boarding School close by, she venerated the miraculous statue of Our Lady of Great Power; afterwards in the

249

school-salon mistresses and pupils listened in a tense silence
while the visionary of Lourdes replied to the questions of Mother
Xavier, their Superior.

Next day, Saturday, July 7th, the two Superiors and the three
postulants resumed their journey and reached Nevers at 10.30
p.m. The Community carriage was waiting for them. Tired
by the long journey, Bernadette noticed only a few belated
passers-by and then the dark foliage of a park. The carriage
passed through a gateway surmounted by a cross. A door
opened, casting a beam of light, and in the parlour several nuns
were waiting up. The Superior General, Mother Joséphine
Imbert, who was recovering from a serious illness, was not
present. The arrivals were quickly given supper. Then the
Superiors of Lourdes and Bagnères went up to their own rooms,
while the postulants followed a Sister through spacious cloisters
wrapped in silence to the largest of the dormitories, that of
Sainte-Marie. At the far end was a statue of Our Lady with a
night-light flickering in front of it, and there was the bed
allotted to Bernadette Soubirous. She tip-toed towards it between
the four rows of beds screened off by long white curtains.

\*       \*       \*

On entering the Congregation of the Sisters of Charity and
Christian Instruction of Nevers, the visionary of Lourdes was
not entering a world entirely unexplored. Since her childhood
she had known these nuns in the black habit with its numerous
pleats, and the white oval cap ending in two lappets which fell
down over the breast. Several of them, first at the day school and
then at the Boarding School, had prepared her and fitted her
out with clothes for her First Communion. They had taught
her the little she knew, had safeguarded her from contact with
the world, guided her by advice and example. More than once
she had heard from their lips the story of their Congregation.

This had been in existence for close on two centuries. It had
begun in the reign of Louis XIV in the small town of Saint-
Saulge. A young Benedictine monk of twenty-seven, Dom de
Laveyne, finding the work of his parish too much for him single-
handed, had appealed for help. Two young ladies offered themselves, and he set them to work visiting the sick and the poor in

their homes and in hospitals and teaching the children their catechism. The number of helpers rapidly increased and the Bishop eventually established them as a Religious Congregation with its headquarters at Nevers. When Dom de Laveyne died in 1719 in the odour of sanctity, there were already forty houses of the Congregation in various places in France.

The French Revolution scattered the nuns to the four winds; but when the storm was over they returned and began to rebuild. Towards the middle of the nineteenth century novices were joining them in great numbers, and in 1856 a new Mother-House was opened in Nevers. It stands spacious and sturdy, with its fine façade and two wings, on the top of a hill to the west of the town on the site of a former Priory of Saint-Gildard, from which the present convent takes its name.

*　　*　　*

It was therefore to an almost new convent that Bernadette came on Saturday, July 7th, 1866. And she took her place, it may be said, in a fully prosperous Congregation. The previous year, in addition to a very large number of professed, Saint-Gildard counted (in the noviciate as well as those who were temporarily dispersed in other houses), 132 novices and 30 postulants. Twenty-two new ones had arrived during the recent month of May alone.

The arrival of the visionary of Lourdes was an event particularly welcome to all. Contemporary documents give abundant evidence of this.

The *Livre des Entrées*, not usually effusive, reads:

'Mademoiselle Bernadette Soubirous, postulant from Lourdes, aged 22, entered July 8th, 1866. Admitted free; the Superior has paid in 60 francs for her clothes, and we have provided 135 francs and some articles of her trousseau valued at 22 francs 50. We are glad that the Blessed Virgin has deigned to entrust her to us.'

The *Annals of the Noviciate* could be expected to display more enthusiasm; there is in fact an almost lyrical touch:

'At last our prayers are answered! Bernadette is in the noviciate. How our hearts, so pious and devoted to Mary, longed to have among us this privileged one from the grotto of Lourdes! The noviciate has so great a love for its august Mother! It will also have great love for her who, more blessed than her new companions, has already on earth had a foretaste of Heaven.'

In this fine and good community it assuredly never entered anyone's head that Bernadette might not be loved by all, or that her entrance might prove anything but a very special blessing.

But something else was engaging the thoughts of the Superior General and her counsellors. To be sure, there was no prejudice in their minds against this child who had come and placed herself so simply in their keeping; no going back on her admission 'under the title of poverty'. They were faced with an exceptional case: they would henceforward have the task of moulding to their religious life, according to their Rules and Constitutions and in the shadow of their cloister, a girl of twenty-two, who had become famous throughout the whole world, who had been visited down in Lourdes, revered, venerated and proclaimed a Saint by multitudes. . . . So far she had appeared immune from empty vainglory, but suppose that a breath of fame, swelled by the Tempter's secret whispers, should reach her in the 'garden enclosed' of Saint-Gildard? Suppose she felt too confined between these walls, unknown to the crowds outside?

Thanks be to God, the Superiors of Nevers had learned from the spiritual writers how to deal with souls favoured with 'divine manifestations'. In his *Ascent of Mount Carmel* St John of the Cross disapproves of 'imprudent directors . . . who indulge in long discussions' with such women concerning their revelations or visions. 'In that way,' adds the holy Doctor, 'they give them to understand that they are highly esteemed, and they behave accordingly. . . . What happens to the humility of these souls, once they imagine that God sets special value on them? In such cases these souls, delivered over to their own imaginations, are no longer inspired by faith.' If such were to happen to Bernadette! What a calamity!

To prevent this happening she would, without being aware of it, be protected against herself, by having no distinction made between the visionary of Lourdes and her future companions. And if there was to be any difference, it would be rather (in accordance with sound logic) that more would be demanded from this privileged child of the Virgin. Consequently neither the novices nor the professed must show her any inconsiderate admiration or even any curiosity about the Apparitions. Bernadette would speak of them once and for all to the whole community; after that, silence.  Some well-intentioned people were likely to call at the convent to see her; in fact her accounts of the Apparitions might do some good; but what was imperative above all was to safeguard not only the vocation and formation of the young postulant, but the peace and quiet necessary for religious life in the house.  Therefore, so far as concerned Bernadette, the Superior General would reserve to herself permission to go to the parlour.  If necessary the matter would be referred to the Bishop.  This last measure was moreover prescribed by the Bishop himself:

> From the first day [he wrote] that Providence placed Bernadette under my authority and deigned to appoint me her guardian, I took the firm resolution to withdraw her absolutely from public curiosity.  The Reverend Mother General shared my views in this matter completely.

Such precautions might possibly shock the tender-hearted, but not the experienced, nor the psychologists.

Still more so than before her departure from Lourdes, Bernadette gauged the full extent of her sacrifice on the night of her arrival: that grotto which held ineffable memories for her and which she would see no more; her mother, whose eyes she would not close—for at the moment of farewell she had glimpsed death on her poor worn face—her father worn out with work, whom she knew so well how to cheer up; the little sister and little brothers whose future she would have liked to guide. . . . In her white bed at the end of the large dormitory the newcomer slept little and wept much.  Next day she wept again.

One can imagine how eager the novices were to make her acquaintance.  ' To our great surprise,' said Sister Lucie Cloris, ' she was no different from the other postulants except perhaps for a greater shyness.'  In the course of the afternoon, however, she had to make an appearance—and before what an assembly! In the majestic hall of the Noviciate all the members of the community were assembled; professed, novices and postulants, with Mother General presiding; and they had invited the Sisters from convents in the town, for not a single one of them would have liked to miss the unique opportunity of hearing the ' little confidante of the Immaculate '.

They all felt a thrill when the little Lourdes girl appeared in her plain blue dress, with the Pyrenean foulard round her head. 'All ears were alert,' said the *Annals of the Noviciate*, 'and hearts were stirred.' This very silence, the emotion that she sensed, and the leading role that was thrust upon her, did not fail to move her too: 'the ordeal was too much for her modesty'. Her account of the Apparitions was more summary than ever; and her features betrayed the fatiguing effects of the journey. 'Several times the Lourdes Superior was obliged to help her and encourage her.' The Novice Mistress, Mother Marie-Thérèse Vauzou, had to do likewise. 'It was only by dint of questions, which she answered very briefly,' reports a novice of the time, 'that we were able to get a short summary of the facts we knew already.' Nevertheless it was an extremely impressive scene.

The Superior of the Lourdes Hospice provoked a slight incident that caused everyone to smile. Speaking of the miraculous spring, Bernadette admitted that she had made several half-hearted attempts to 'drink at the spring and wash in it'. Thereupon Mother Alexandrine Roques thought fit to whisper in the Superior General's ear: 'You can judge from that her lack of mortification.' Bernadette, who had keen hearing, understood and replied with affectionate familiarity to her former Lourdes Superior: 'Well, the water was so dirty!'

The visionary had to reproduce the words and gestures of the Lady at the time when she gave her name. A transformation came over the humble girl. Her drawn features were lit up with a divine smile as she unclasped her hands, pressed them against her heart and repeated the immortal words: 'I am the Immaculate Conception.' There was a prolonged silence among the assembled Sisters.

\*    \*    \*

Once the audience had dispersed, Saint-Gildard resumed its normal life. There were merely three more postulants or, as was said familiarly among the Sisters, three more 'little bonnets', for Bernadette and her two companions retained the 'livery of the world', but wore as a distinctive mark the black tulle headband of monastic simplicity, but trimmed with a double frill over the forehead and loosely hanging strings.

That Sunday evening Bernadette was taken along to one of the novices, a compatriot of hers, Sister Emilienne Duboé, aged twenty-five, and due to leave soon for another house. For a week Emilienne was to be her young friend's angel guardian: she would take her to visit Mother General's house and give her detailed information about the rule and the exercises of the noviciate. Bernadette was most attentive and proved by her questions how eager she was to learn her new duties. And even with this companion she began the apostolate of edification that was to continue right to her death. She had noticed that on entering the chapel or starting her prayers Sister Duboé signed herself hurriedly: 'You make the sign of the cross badly,' she was not afraid to tell her; 'you must see to that, for it is important to make it well.'

During this first week there were some tears: homesickness and, above all, a longing for the grotto. 'Shall I ever be able to get used to doing without it?' she would sigh. 'Well,' Sister Emilienne would reply sweetly, 'have a good cry; it's the sign of a good vocation.' She tried her best to hide her grief, but in vain; her red eyes betrayed her. To distract her thoughts a little, Mother General took her with her in her carriage to visit a convent at Varennes-lès-Nevers which was both an orphanage and a house of retirement for aged Sisters, and introduced her to the small community.

The tears did not last. During this week of trial Bernadette had remained faithful to prayer; resolved never to seek human consolations, she had made the Stations of the Cross several times in her free moments. Twelve days after entering the convent we find her full of happiness at having made the offering of herself. On July 20th she, who could not tell a lie, wrote to her parents: 'I am well settled and perfectly happy, and I beg you not to be anxious about me. Help me just to thank God for the favour He has done me in calling me to Himself.' And to the nuns at Lourdes, referring to her departure:

I assure you that it would be a much more bitter sacrifice now if I had to leave our dear noviciate. You feel that it is God's own house. You are obliged to love it in spite of yourself. Everything inclines you that way, and especially the instructions of our dear Mistress. Every word that comes from her lips goes straight to the heart.

And so I never cease addressing my feeble prayers to Our Lord to thank Him for so many graces with which He continues to overwhelm me every day. I beg you, my very dear Sisters, to be so kind as to offer some prayers for this intention of mine, and especially when you go to my dear grotto. That is where you will find me, in spirit, clinging to the foot of that rock I love so much. I ask you to remember me very specially to that good Mother. On my side I do not forget you before Our Lady of the Waters, who is at the bottom of the garden in a sort of grotto. That was where I went to unburden my heart during the first few days, and since then our dear Mistress has kindly allowed us to go there every evening. . . .

During a stroll through the extensive gardens of the enclosure Bernadette had made a discovery: with a cry of joy she saw at the foot of a rugged path in a secluded corner, that statue of Our Lady which would always remind her, by its delightful smile and the gesture of its outstretched hands, of the Lady of the grotto.

The postulant was unaware that at the very moment when she was feeling such a need of 'unburdening her heart', strangers were calling at the front door and asking for Bernadette of Lourdes. In the *Community Journal* there is this revealing line: 'They are coming in crowds and asking to see her; our Mother replies in the negative.' Yet it seemed impossible not to make some exceptions. How refuse, for instance, to comply with requests from Bishops? On Thursday, July 19th, the Bishop of Autun celebrated the Community Mass. Next came the Bishop of Nevers and brought with him the Pope's confessor, Archbishop de Mérode, who had come to take the waters at Pougues, not far from Nevers. As the *Community Journal* recorded: 'Their Lordships asked to see Bernadette. The pious child came into the salon with charming simplicity and modesty. The venerable prelates appeared satisfied, and we ourselves could not be more grateful for this visit.'

Bernadette's postulancy had begun almost six months before, and had continued rather informally at the Lourdes Hospice. The major Superiors had the right to insist on its extension, but they did not do so. Their decision was given a special entry in the *Community Journal*, and with a touch of tenderness: 'Our little Bernadette has been admitted to the taking of the habit.'

The ceremony was fixed for Sunday, July 29th, the Feast of St Martha, patroness of the Congregation. Bernadette prepared for it in a most edifying manner.

We were in Retreat together [relates Sister Emilienne Duboé], she to prepare for her clothing, and I for my religious profession. I was struck above all by her recollectedness. Her demeanour in chapel was most impressive: the sight of Bernadette at prayer had an indescribable effect on me.

But while keeping her heart raised to heaven, Bernadette, who hated ostentation, kept her feet on the ground. 'She did the same as everyone, but better than everyone,' observed one of her companions at the clothing. During the Retreat there was a rehearsal for the taking of the habit. The future novices came up two by two, Bernadette being beside Emilie Marcillac. One of the couple in front of them was walking along with her eyes so cast down that her neighbour was obliged to guide her. 'Why,' remarked Bernadette afterwards, 'why shut your eyes when they should be kept open?'

On Sunday morning, July 29th, the forty-five postulants due to be clothed made their entrance into the chapel arranged according to size. Bernadette, maidenly, almost a child to look at, in her white dress and white veil, was walking at the head. After the address given by Bishop Forcade himself, Bernadette Soubirous received from her Bishop the novice's veil and her name in religion; then followed the Mass in honour of St Martha, sung by Archbishop de Mérode, who had come on purpose from Pougues-les-Eaux.

Sister Marie-Bernard: to Saint-Gildard the name seemed strange at first, whereas Bernadette was only happily resuming her baptismal name. She had not asked for it; the Novice Mistress decided on it quite independently of her. 'It is only right,' Mother Vauzou explained afterwards to the other novices, 'that I should give her the name of the Blessed Virgin whose privileged child she is; at the same time I wanted her to keep her patron's name, of which Bernadette is a diminutive.'

On this day of profound happiness Sister Marie-Bernard confided to a companion at the clothing: 'I have come here to hide myself.'

# 22

## FIRST THREE MONTHS OF NOVICIATE

A FORTNIGHT after her clothing, what did her closest associates think of Sister Marie-Bernard? The secretary in charge of the *Annals of the Noviciate*, who was evidently the most esteemed stylist among these many cultured and refined young women, and who, no doubt, was allowed full liberty by Mother Mistress to record her own impressions on behalf of all, wrote of Sister Marie-Bernard about this time:

> She is very much as repute portrayed her to us, humble in her supernatural triumph, simple and unassuming, even though everything so far has conspired to exalt her and advertise her; always smiling and delightfully happy, although a continuous debility has for a long time been undermining her frail and delicate constitution. That is indeed the hallmark of sanctity: constant suffering side by side with heavenly joys. And who more than she has been favoured with those ineffable consolations?

Mother Marie-Thérèse must have smiled at these words of admiration: really it was rather premature to be canonizing a raw novice, who, in spite of a flattering reputation, would doubtless need training like the rest.

Mother Marie-Thérèse Vauzou had been born in 1825. Her father and grandfather were both lawyers. She began her education with the Sisters of Charity of Nevers at Meyssac, and from there moved to their Boarding School at Brive. Quite early in life she showed a liking for authority.

> Of a lively, intense and impulsive disposition [it has been said of her], it would be rash to say that she was one of those children on whom the yoke of discipline did not weigh heavily, and who did not throw it off now and then: her intelligence and her determination gave her even before her First Communion a

258

certain dominance over her companions, and even at that age she liked to try them out to see if she could be sure of their submission.

On leaving school at seventeen she was at first attracted by the world, but her thoughts soon turned to the life of a nun. She became a postulant at Saint-Gildard on September 17th, 1844, the year of Bernadette's birth, taking the name of Sister Marie-Thérèse. Professed on June 11th, 1846, she was sent to teach in the Training College conducted by the Sisters of Nevers in Montpellier: there she trained numbers of young school-teachers in learning and piety. On September 21st, 1853, at the age of twenty-eight, she was entrusted with the delicate task of founding a combined boarding and day school at Blaye in the diocese of Bordeaux, and she made a success of it in spite of the competition of two lay institutions. Three years later she was recalled to Montpellier to direct the Training College, and meanwhile, in 1860, she established a boarding school in the town of Moulins. On July 26th, 1861, she returned as Mistress of Novices to the Mother House of Saint-Gildard, where she was one day to exercise supreme command. She had therefore been there five years when Bernadette Soubirous came under her charge.

In order to understand the attitude which she came to adopt towards the visionary of Lourdes, it is imperative to have recourse to the testimonies of her two successive secretaries, Mother Marie-Joséphine Forestier and Mother Marie-Thérèse Bordenave, who, after being closely associated with her while she was Mother General, were to succeed her in that high office. But some evidence given by ordinary nuns, who did their noviciate under her, should not be passed over in silence. One of these, Mother Julienne Capmartin, has left a good summary of their various recollections:

Mother Marie-Thérèse Vauzou was admirably gifted for the guidance of souls: she had all the gifts of mind and heart. Her exterior was somewhat cold, and there was a touch of imperiousness about her; but that did not prevent her from being very kind and very motherly. . . .

She was most eager for you to open your heart to her with absolute trust. 'Keep nothing secret from me,' she used to say, 'nothing except what concerns Confession. When I summon you for an interview my whole desire is to give you a chance to tell me whether you are unhappy, whether you have any worries, what your relations are with your companions, whether there are any among them whom you seek out with too particular an attachment. Be entirely open; that is the way to be always happy.'

Let us now hear what her two revered secretaries say about her. 'Twenty years Mistress of Novices, eighteen years Superior General, she enjoyed incomparable prestige in the Congregation,' says Mother Bordenave. 'Highly intelligent, she combined a talent for practical affairs with a most intense interior life.' But she showed herself more a woman of action than of contemplation. She possessed, says Mother Forestier, 'a vivid faith, sincere piety, zeal for souls, a heart of gold. Beneath her cold exterior there was a strong desire to give and receive much affection.'

These testimonies are on the whole flattering. Even so, do they not leave one to surmise that in Mother Marie-Thérèse virtue did not attain the perfection that constitutes sanctity? She gave, but could not forgo receiving. And as she was of a 'highly impressionable temperament' any opposition or disappointment was apt to upset her judgment and rob her 'heart of gold' of its magnanimity, and for a while, or sometimes permanently, there would be a sharp drop in her love and esteem for the subordinate who had offended or disappointed her. She restrained herself, it is true, and seldom launched out into denunciations; her disapproval took the form of a deliberate coldness and silence. She was unquestionably well endowed with a quality valuable in a superior: 'There was something magnetic in her,' according to Mother Bordenave. But there was alongside this a quality that repelled: she was, says the same witness, 'one of those people towards whom one cannot remain indifferent; one must either fear her or love her. . . . Her general bearing is such as to give either pain or pleasure.' And for proof, Mother Forestier cites an instance: 'Mother Henri Fabre, who had replaced Mother Vauzou as Mistress of Novices, a saintly nun, of quiet disposition, tactful and most kind, confided to me that she suffered much, and especially for a period of three years, from the coldness of our Mother, who used to imagine things that did not exist.'

*      *      *

What was to be the lot of 'our little Bernadette'? Filial affection or reverential awe. . . ? The first contacts were, as we have seen, full of promise. If the young Lourdes girl still appeared rather reserved towards Mother Mistress, the latter readily made allowances for this: it was initial shyness, and many postulants were like that. But during prayers in the chapel or the exercises of the noviciate Sister Marie-Bernard's behaviour was beyond reproach.

Moreover, Mother Marie-Thérèse heard what her other daughters thought about Bernadette. They were edified by the piety and enchanted by the simplicity of their new companion. Her sign of the cross, made slowly with her hand carried well out to the tip of each shoulder, 'undoubtedly as she had seen the Blessed Virgin make it', had been a revelation to all of them. Her neighbours watched her stealthily during the recital of the Rosary. 'You would have thought that she still saw the Blessed Virgin as at Lourdes,' said Sister Anastasie Carrière. And Sister Emilie Marcillac, who came on her one day in the noviciate sitting on a stool near the statue of Our Lady and meditating, saw in her eyes 'a light reflected as it were from heaven'.

Her happy disposition, too, was greatly appreciated by the Mistress of Novices: Sister Marie-Bernard showed herself 'very gay at recreation'. The first time she saw games arranged among the novices, she even asked whether they did skipping, and offered to hold the rope!

No doubt, when glancing through the young aspirant's humble correspondence, the Mother deplored the mistakes in spelling. Fortunately, the writing was becoming quite elegant, and with the help of some lessons, spelling would gradually be mastered. Progress in arithmetic still left much to be desired. . . . At Nevers the Constitutions make no distinction of grades among the nuns except that of employment; there are neither Choir nor Lay Sisters. However, the novices are divided according to ability into several classes; naturally, Sister Marie-Bernard was placed among the most backward. But this by no means prevented Mother Marie-Thérèse from setting her up as a model for the whole noviciate—in her absence, of course—and saying: 'I am always afraid she will be stolen from us!' In short, she showed a genuine affection for her.

The first weeks went by without any notable incidents for the new novice. She felt overwhelmed with delight in this noviciate, and she wrote to the Bishop of Tarbes:

> . . . happy and peaceful in the pious and holy haven to which God has brought me and where I taste the sweetest peace and pure joy, I never forget the debt of deep regard and hearty gratitude which I owe Your Lordship. . . .

At this time of the year some of the newly professed, and even some of the novices, were sent to one of the other houses, while those who were kept back had light domestic tasks assigned to them. Sister Marie-Bernard was to be partly assistant sacristan and partly assistant infirmarian. She would most certainly put all her heart into it; but even so it was not without a deep sigh that she said good-bye to her companions. 'How happy I should be if I could also go and work,' she confided to Sister Duboé, a compatriot of hers, 'but I am obliged to stay here and do nothing.' She was well aware that it was her weak health that prevented her, for in addition to her asthma, which attacked her in the stress of excitement or fatigue, she 'suffered pains in her head and stomach every day', as she herself confessed. Yet she followed the exercises of the noviciate with regularity and still had her bed in the large dormitory.

A minor incident during this month of August, 1866, witnessed by Sister Carrière—one of her patients in the infirmary whom she had nursed one day with 'much kindness and willingness'—shows us Sister Marie-Bernard subjected without exemption to the same discipline as her companions. On one occasion, 'having been detained by her duties in the infirmary she arrived late for a noviciate function. She knelt and kissed the ground very humbly. Then the Mother Mistress gave her a sharp reprimand. Thereupon Sister Marie-Bernard went up to her and gave her the reason for being late; then she went to her place looking perfectly undisturbed as though nothing disagreeable had happened.' In fact she had no reason to be surprised, still less upset: the lesson in humility which she had just received would be given to any novice in like circumstances. It was the rule. And the Mistress was only doing her duty.

So for the present, Mother Vauzou, as she had resolved, was treating the visionary of Lourdes no differently from the rest of her novices. But she did not know the future: whether she liked it or not, Sister Marie-Bernard was not going to be for her an ordinary novice like the rest and was not going to lend herself to the ordinary training in the same way as the rest.

To begin with, only a few weeks after her arrival she was partially removed for some months from the immediate influence of Mother Marie-Thérèse. Poor little sub-assistant infirmarian! Fits of coughing had brought on a haemorrhage. One day early in September the infirmarian, Sister Martha, warned her that for some weeks, instead of nursing others, she would have to submit to being nursed herself. She was given a place in St Joseph's ward: one of the white beds standing in a row along the length of this spacious room with its two large windows which made it light and airy.

It was edifying to see her joining at a distance in the activities of her companions in the noviceship. At daybreak she buried herself in deep meditation, for there was prayer in common in the chapel at that time, and then Mass. . . .

Her Mother Mistress came every day to see her, continued to instruct her in spirituality, and was anxious above all to know her state of soul. The novice gave an account of her performance of her spiritual duties and, when her sufferings were mentioned, answered meekly: 'It's all good for Heaven.' But she opened her heart no more than this.

Yet, according to the Superior of the Lourdes Hospice, Bernadette Soubirous was by nature affectionate and confiding. Was it possible, perhaps, that she might be inclined to confide in this or that companion in preference to others? Might she, consciously or otherwise, tend to 'a too particular attachment'? On this point she would soon receive a lesson, at least an indirect one.

Sister Emilie Marcillac, the assistant infirmarian, needing some help, secured the services of Léontine Mouret, the novice from Lourdes who had entered at the same time as Bernadette. She knew that this would please both of them. But one day, relates Sister Emilie, 'our Mother Mistress asked me the reason for this choice and forbade me to take Bernadette's friend in future. Next day Bernadette asked me if her Lourdes companion was ill. I said to her: "No, but Mother has forbidden me to have her again." "Ah, I understand," she replied; but she did not complain.'

Towards the end of September she was able to give her family reassuring news: 'What shall I tell you about myself?' she wrote on the 30th to her brother, Jean-Marie, a big boy turned fifteen.

My health is somewhat better, but I am still obliged to take precautions against the cold, which is my great enemy. Don't worry. I am warm in the infirmary and the dear Sister Infirmarian gives me every attention, and all the Sisters are full of kindness towards me. I am quite bewildered by it.

The last lines of her letter show that the novice of Nevers was still, though so far away, the elder sister, the little mother, watchful and firm. She gave her young brother, who was rather weak-willed and irresolute, this manly advice:

Above all, I urge you not to neglect your religious duties. Do not forget that where there's a will there's a way.

She said she was 'somewhat better'; would that be simply to reassure her family? Actually she was losing strength every day. About the middle of October Mother Marie-Thérèse asked the Community to redouble their prayers. And—what had never been done for any other nun before—the novices went in groups to pray for her in the Community chapel or in St Joseph's chapel in the garden or before the statue of Our Lady of the noviciate. And in front of the smiling statue with the outstretched arms 'a quantity of candles burned continually for several days'.

Alas, as everyone felt, Mother Marie-Thérèse had said only too truly: 'We are not worthy to have her!' All that remained now was to beg for Sister Marie-Bernard the grace of a holy death. On Thursday, October 25th, the young invalid in the next bed was moved elsewhere to spare her so painful a sight. Dated this same day, these broken-hearted lines are to be read in the *Community Journal*:

Our good little Sister Marie-Bernard is seriously ill: she has been given the Sacrament of Extreme Unction.

On the urgent advice of the Marist, Father Douce, the chaplain to the Mother House, who had just given her the last rites, and

who was her ordinary confessor, the novice had expressed her
desire to take her vows before she died. The Superior General
was also considering it. Sister Marie-Bernard had been scarcely
three months in the noviciate, but she was the visionary of
Lourdes! Mother Joséphine Imbert held a meeting of her
counsellors without delay and all agreed that Mary's privileged
child ought to belong to the Congregation. It only remained
to obtain the Bishop's consent. He came himself in haste with
his Vicar General, and not only did he authorize the religious
profession of Sister Marie-Bernard *in articulo mortis* (at the
point of death), but he reserved to himself as a favour the right
of presiding at her vows.

The doctor had said that she would not last the night. It was
then about 7 p.m. The Bishop, followed by the Superior General,
her Assistants and the Mistress of Novices, made his way
hurriedly to the dying girl. She was 'fully conscious'.

I found her [he related] gasping for breath and almost with a
death rattle in her throat; she had just brought up a basinful of
blood which was still there by the bed. I went up to her.
'You are going to die, my dear child, and I'm told that you
wish to make your profession. Here I am to receive it.'
Then in her dying voice she said: 'I shan't be able to pronounce
the formula . . . not the strength . . .'
'That's no difficulty. I'm going to pronounce it for you. You
only have to answer "Amen".'

And the prelate recited softly:

I, Sister Marie-Bernard, wishing to consecrate myself to the
service of God and works of charity, in the Congregation of the
Sisters of Charity and of Christian Instruction established in the
diocese of Nevers, vow poverty, chastity and obedience in the
manner explained in the Rules of the same Congregation,
approved by the Sovereign Pontiff. I beg Our Lord Jesus Christ,
by the intercession of the Most Blessed Virgin my good Mother, to
grant me grace faithfully to fulfil these promises.

Sister Marie-Bernard, who had listened to the pronouncing of
her vows 'with an angelic fervour', put all her heart into her
*Amen*. The Superior immediately spread a nun's veil over her
forehead, and Mother Marie-Thérèse slipped a vow-crucifix

between her clasped hands and arranged the rosary and Rule
Book on her bed.

I spoke some words of encouragement to her [concluded the
Bishop]. I gave her my blessing and begged her not to forget me
in Heaven and withdrew quite moved, convinced that I should not
see her alive again.

This pathetic scene was to be followed by an incident which
it is the historian's duty to present in its true light. After the
departure of the Bishop and his Vicar General, the Superior
General and the Mistress of Novices remained of course in the
infirmary. 'Scarcely had I gone,' the Bishop reports, 'when
the dying nun regained her speech. . . . As was learnt later by
experience, Sister Marie-Bernard used to recover all of a sudden
from these terrible crises. Just when one was expecting her to
breathe her last, she would surprise you by suddenly recovering. . . .'

What enlightenment did she receive during this consecration,
which was thought to be her last? Turning to Mother Marie-
Thérèse, who spoke of spending the night beside her, she said
with her smile: 'I shan't die to-night.' She stated precisely:
'to-night', for the next day was in God's hands. It was in
entirely good faith that she had asked to take her vows, for she
really thought she was dying at the time. Then she had learnt
in some mysterious way that she had been granted a respite, but
she still did not know whether it might not expire at daybreak.
But she undoubtedly knew, and had just asserted, that she would
not die that night.

On hearing this Mother Joséphine Imbert gave a start. She
did not try to find out whether the novice had received this
assurance before the Bishop had been hurriedly summoned or
only after she had taken her vows. 'What!' she protested, 'you
knew you were not going to die to-night and you never said so!
And so you caused us to send for His Lordship at such an
awkward hour, and set everything in commotion just for you!
You're nothing but a little fool. I tell you straight that if you're
not dead to-morrow morning, I'll take away your profession veil
that has just been given you and I'll send you back to the noviceship with your simple novice's veil.'

Such were the terms in which the Superior expressed herself, according to Bishop Forcade. We may take it that the discerning Sister Marie-Bernard saw in it only a mother's reprimand to her daughter, a merely verbal threat. So she took the scolding without being in the least upset. 'Remaining quite calm and still smiling,' notes Bishop Forcade, she replied: 'As you please, dear Mother.'

The Sister Infirmarian remained alone at her bedside and allowed her to rest. Sister Marie-Bernard dozed perhaps; at any rate she seemed absorbed in deep meditation. Then about 4 a.m. she said in a playful tone—perhaps just in fun or perhaps in a veiled confidence that shed light on the strange prediction of the previous evening—'Sister Emilie, I'm feeling better. God didn't want me. I got as far as the gate but He said to me: "Be off with you! You're too early."'

On that day and the following days, Mother Marie-Thérèse sent her novices 'in small groups' to visit the convalescent. Several new arrivals saw her for the first time and were amazed to find the dying girl of yesterday so merry and full of life. Ingenuously she showed her companions her vow crucifix, her rosary, her manual and her Rule Book, all neatly arranged on her new veil. 'Oh, you thief!' exclaimed Sister Charles Ramillon with a smile. 'Thief maybe,' retorted the happy professed, 'but meanwhile they're mine and I'm keeping them. I belong to the Congregation and they won't be able to dismiss me.'

# 23

## A CHANGEABLE NOVICE MISTRESS

WE read in the chronicles of Saint-Gildard for Friday, October 26th: 'From this day onwards our little invalid improves.' There is also the evidence of Sister Lucie Cloris, who was then a novice: 'God, deeming the trial long enough, heard our prayers at last. Our good Sister began to get better, until she at last completely recovered, to the great joy of our Mothers, of the whole Community and, above all, of the noviciate.' Actually Sister Marie-Bernard was to rejoin her companions much later than they had hoped. The weather had turned severe; the convalescent alternated between health and sickness, and the doctor forbade her to resume Community life until the intensely cold weather was over. Still, when she was not obliged to keep to her bed altogether, he made no objection to her walking round the cloisters or going to the chapel gallery for a visit to the Blessed Sacrament, or being present at ceremonies, and hearing sermons. . . .

All the same there was that almost continuous irksome isolation within the walls of the infirmary. In this disappointing plight, when she thought each evening that she would find herself strong enough next day to resume life in her beloved noviceship, how did this active vibrant nature manage to surmount the depressing feeling of helplessness and escape the discouragement that dogged her? We know the answer, thanks to another novice, Sister Marcelline Lannessans, who was a patient in the infirmary from August, 1866, till the following February. She observed how her companion fought her mental depression by work, reading and prayer.

She was the enemy of idleness and displayed great activity whenever her health permitted it. Also, though unwell herself, if she was able to get up at all, she would at once set about nursing the

268

others. . . . Her reading was by preference on the Eucharist and the Passion of Our Lord; and the New Testament and the *Imitation of Christ* were her favourite books.

Through all these days which seemed so dreary she retained the freshness and zest of her piety. 'I loved to watch her praying,' continues Sister Marcelline, 'for she prayed like an angel. . . . It was above all when she received Holy Communion that I guessed the love she had for Our Lord. Her eyes were lowered, her face grew pale and was transformed; it became quite heavenly.'

Concerning her own mother, who was so often in her thoughts and whose increasing weakness she suspected, she received reassuring news. Those who wrote to her from down there, her sister Toinette, her brother Jean-Marie, her aunt Bernarde, kept the truth from her. But about December 10th an all too truthful letter arrived from Lourdes: the Hospice Sisters informed the Superior General that Louise Soubirous was dead. After languishing for some months she had agreed to take to her bed only in the last fortnight.

> Before going to Vespers on the Feast of the Immaculate Conception [related Sister Victorine], I called on Bernadette's mother, whom I knew to be extremely ill. I spoke to her about her beloved child and before leaving, as the bell for Vespers was ringing, I told her I would write to Bernadette for her. The poor dying woman gave me to understand by expressive gestures how pleased she was at this and how grateful. On coming out from Vespers I returned to the Soubirous' house; Louise was no longer of this world. [She had passed away at the age of forty-one.]

To soften the blow for so loving a heart Sister Marie-Bernard was first told that her mother was seriously ill. At once she 'asked permission to go and pray in the chapel'. When the whole truth had to be told her, 'so great was her grief and her tears,' reports one of her companions, 'that she fainted; on coming round, her strength of will reasserted itself and instead of losing heart she blessed Our Lord'. She wished to know the exact day and hour of her mother's death. She was informed that it had occurred on the 8th, between two and three o'clock in the afternoon, while the first procession in honour of Mary Immaculate was moving towards the crypt above the grotto.

Then Bernadette exclaimed: 'So much the better, for she is in Heaven! '

\*     \*     \*

Some days after Candlemas, Sister Marie-Bernard reappeared among her companions. In seven to eight months she would have to take her first annual vows and so she had resumed the novice's veil.

A saintly nun, who had been at once drawn by a supernatural attraction to the visionary of Lourdes, Mother Eléonore Cassagnes, Secretary General of the Congregation, stated that 'Sister Marie-Bernard's noviceship was not marked by anything extraordinary. A fervent and exact novice, she humbly buried herself among her companions and was perhaps the most inconspicuous of them all.' Wholly taken up with her religious training, she aimed sincerely at perfection. But perfection demands great and enduring courage, for it involves continual renunciation and therefore the sacrifice of oneself. Good little Sister Marie-Bernard! Just when she was recovering from illness, a mental trial was approaching that would cut her to the quick.

\*     \*     \*

Back among her companions she soon sensed that Mother Mistress had changed her attitude towards her, and that she no longer paid her little novice the same kindly attentions she had given her at first. . . . Why this unexpected estrangement from the visionary of Lourdes?

'Mother Marie-Thérèse Vauzou,' according to her former secretary, Mother Marie-Thérèse Bordenave, 'had a passion for shaping souls. She could find the right chisel for each, and wield it. She employed a quite particular severity towards Bernadette.' The Mistress of Novices could not be judged harshly for trying to counteract the fame of the Massabielle visions in order to keep her novice humble: such a practice is not contrary to the teaching of the spiritual writers. But severity and coldness are two different things. When a fair-minded child feels it is being punished from a motive of love, any suffering there may be is attributed to the correction, not to the mother's deliberate harshness; if on the other hand the punishment seems to the child to be tinged with ill-will, especially if the rest of the children in the family are treated with noticeable affection, it will experience much more acute distress because the mother's attitude then seems to result from lack of love. Is it possible that for some ten years or so, first as a novice then as a professed nun, Sister Marie-Bernard had to bear an affliction such as this? Yes! But did it prove a misfortune for her? No! It proved a true blessing, as the sequel was to show well enough.

The Mistress, as we are already aware, wanted complete openness of heart in her daughters. From the day the 'confidante of the Immaculate' left the infirmary, the Mother said to herself that the time had come for her to get to know this exceptional novice whose habitual reserve had surprised her without, however, as yet annoying her. It must be admitted that Sister Marie-Bernard was to respond but imperfectly to her wishes. Mother Vauzou felt herself checked on the threshold of this soul. Hence two unfortunate results: she did not understand her, and this both hurt and vexed her. Imagining that the check to her zeal was entirely the novice's fault, she branded as indifference and coarse obtuseness what was in the other mere reserve and possibly supernatural prudence.

There were some disconcerting contrasts to be found in Bernadette. She had not flinched before the Commissioner of Police, the gendarmes or the Public Prosecutor. At the Sisters' school in Lourdes she had been lively and spontaneous, and she was more or less the same during times of recreation in the noviciate at Nevers; she had kept her child-like soul. But who on this earth had ever fathomed the depths of this soul in which Heaven had been reflected? In former days at the Hospice Bernadette had not concealed her desire for the religious life; but she had not gone beyond that. In the convent she did not disclose her most intimate thoughts to anyone, not even to the sympathetic Mother Eléonore Cassagnes, who was nevertheless regarded as 'her confidante and friend': the latter was to pick up just enough confidences to detect the workings of grace in this reticent soul. But in the presence of Mother Marie-Thérèse it would seem as if Sister Marie-Bernard lost her wits and self-possession.

At this period, it is true, she would as a young novice have nothing much to reveal regarding her interior life: there was nothing to record. For the moment, no notable temptations to fight against, no mental anguish, no abandonment by God. . . . A spirituality of the very simplest, a conscience clear as a ray of sunshine. But not being a novice just like the rest (whatever Mother Marie-Thérèse might say) would not Sister Marie-Bernard have misgivings on one particular point? The Virgin of the grotto had sealed her lips on three secrets, on a mysterious prayer for herself alone, and on other matters possibly entirely personal, perhaps certain directions from Our Lady concerning her future. . . . Suppose that by allowing a Mistress of such dominating authority to penetrate the recesses of her soul, she were to find herself induced to reveal to her what she had no right to reveal to any creature. . . ?

Be that as it may, according to one of the best informed witnesses 'Mother Marie-Thérèse Vauzou, whose penetrating eye often read the hearts of her daughters, never discovered the supernatural riches of her novice's soul'. On the contrary, without refusing to recognize in her the qualities which escaped no one, she devoted herself to detecting the short-comings. And as she gauged the piety of her daughters from their confidences to her regarding their interior life, she was fated to see in the excessively reserved Sister Marie-Bernard nothing but a novice of no great worth or note. 'No raptures or ecstasies,' wrote Bishop Forcade; 'not even any pious exercises or austerities beyond what the rule prescribed.' For Mother Marie-Thérèse the brightness of Massabielle, which had at first transfigured the visionary, was fading; her own enthusiasm had collapsed, and that of her novices could no longer cause her anything but displeasure.

The question arises: had Mother Vauzou ceased to believe in Bernadette's visions? 'I have heard it said,' a priest attested, 'that she made little account of Lourdes and yet Providence summoned her there to die.' To understand such a remark one must go back several years. At the time when Bernadette was a novice it was only eight years since the events at Massabielle; the period of hesitation, discussion and denial was not yet closed. Besides, the devotion to the Blessed Virgin under the title of Our Lady of Lourdes was in no sense obligatory and Mother Marie-Thérèse followed her own inclination, which was said to be towards the mystery of Mary's Sorrows.

Assuredly she did not doubt Bernadette's truthfulness at the time when she tasted in advance the 'joy of seeing the eyes that have seen the Blessed Virgin'. Subsequently, however, there were times when certain secondary details would puzzle her. She hunted for a solution. Like M. Peyramale she would have liked certain tangible proofs. One day in thoughtful mood she said to Mother Bordenave, 'All the same the rose-bush didn't flower!' Then, as if correcting herself she added, 'The Blessed Virgin showed good taste in selecting this site.'

In September 1875, while Bernadette was still alive, Mother Vauzou attended the consecration in Lourdes of the new Bishop to succeed Bishop Forcade; afterwards she went and knelt at the grotto. Thirty-two years later, as she lay on her sick bed that was soon to be her death-bed in the Lourdes Orphanage of Mary Immaculate, she would get them to read to her as a last comfort the account of the Apparitions. On February 15th, 1907, she was to breathe her last, invoking Our Lady of Lourdes.

None the less, before coming to these acts of reparation and homage, Mother Vauzou had not only thrust the 'privileged child' of the Blessed Virgin into the shadows—which would have been enough—but had abased her. One day while she was explaining the Catechism to the novices, Sister Marie-Bernard was sitting in all simplicity on the step of her desk mending a garment. Afterwards the Mother Mistress called up Sister Bernard Dalias and asked her in a most unpleasant manner, 'Why were you looking like that at Sister Marie-Bernard?' 'I was thinking,' explained the novice, 'that you must have been very happy to have Bernadette so close to you.' 'Well,' rejoined the Mistress, 'I should have been just as happy to have any one of you beside me. Bernadette is on the common road.'

'Common road' obviously meant, on the lips of Mother Marie-Thérèse, that for Bernadette it was all over with extraordinary favours: she had sunk back to the level of ordinary mortals and would never rise from it again. Moreover the occasion on which it was said, and the tone of voice, turned it into a disparaging remark. As the shrewd Mother Bordenave points out: 'The phrase "common road" was a sort of cliché that remained fixed in Mother Marie-Thérèse's mind in spite of everything.' In default of seeing the good qualities of this twenty-three-year-old novice in their true light, she had taken to exag-

gerating the gaps. 'When sympathy is absent,' observed a
religious who was well acquainted with the facts, 'how easy it
is to magnify real faults and add imaginary ones!'

A certain clear-sighted nun pointed out one of the things—
perhaps the principal thing—that clouded the judgment of
Mother Marie-Thérèse and shut her heart against Bernadette.
The latter 'no doubt had not that artificial education that one
acquires in society, but she had what is sometimes found in
country people when they have plenty of common sense and
goodness: a formation that proceeds from within and is
undoubtedly the best of its kind. I can well understand that our
Mistress of Novices did not find in Sister Marie-Bernard that
particular kind of refinement, that "polish" which she greatly
prized; and that is perhaps one of the things—there are others,
I know—which prevented her from appreciating our Bernadette
at her true worth.'

Right from the noviceship Mother Marie-Thérèse impressed
on her publicly the difference there was in education between
herself and her mistresses and companions. On the occasion of
some festivity or other, relates Sister Paschal, 'lots were drawn
for a little statue of St Germaine Cousin and it was won by
Sister Marie-Bernard. Thereupon Mother Marie-Thérèse Vauzou
remarked in an ironical tone: "A shepherd girl could only fall
into the hands of a shepherd girl."' Another time, according to
the same witness, the public reader came to 'a passage in which
there was mention of a person of very humble station upon
whom God had conferred extraordinary favours. At that
moment the Mistress turned towards Sister Marie-Bernard and
pointed out to her that those whom God wishes to favour, He
always keeps well under.'

Months, perhaps years, after the death of Bernadette, she was
not ashamed to say quite crudely of the former shepherdess of
Bartrès: 'Oh, she was just a little peasant!' There was some
truth in that disparaging judgment. The Lourdes girl still survived in Bernadette beneath the veil: although she was the very
personification of humility and simplicity, she retained her quick-
ness of temper and that pride of race that is so difficult to define
—like the pride of her parents who, in their destitution, would
never stoop to accept a penny they had not earned. Thus, when
taken unawares by some sudden opposition, her highly sensitive

nature would react abruptly with one of those 'flashes of temper for which, however, she immediately made amends most humbly'. Hence too, as Mother Bordenave recalls, 'the occasional sharp-edged repartee which sprang from her Pyrenean temperament that is sometimes quick to answer back'.

Father Charles Payrard, who had the knack of eliciting confidences from Mother Vauzou when she was Superior Géneral, wished to learn from her, as he said, 'those replies of Sister Marie-Bernard in which she failed to find the perfectly measured tone which she considered a Saint would have maintained. She told me, but I have forgotten them,' he confessed with regret. 'But I recall that I pointed out to the Mother at the time that these answers contained nothing reprehensible and that all I saw in them was a difference in education between her and her novice. In my opinion the Mother attached too much importance to mere conventions. In my own mind I compare Bernadette to Joan of Arc, and I believe Mother Marie Thérèse Vauzou would have found Joan of Arc ill-bred.'

These spontaneous replies by which she was unreasonably upset were certainly very rare. Only one or two have been preserved. Soon after Sister Marie-Bernard returned to the noviciate the Mistress called her in for spiritual direction. 'Now,' she rapped out at her, putting her own interpretation on the 'repeated hammering' that is mentioned in the hymn (*Fabri polita malleo*), 'now we can hammer away at you!' To which the novice replied: 'I hope you'll do it gently.'

Later—but Bernadette was by then professed—a party of nuns, among whom was Sister Léontine Villaret, a teacher in the Sainte-Marie Boarding School, had come 'to pay their respects to the Mothers in the Community Hall', and Sister Marie-Bernard, although unwell, thought it her duty to go and welcome the visitors. Mother Vauzou met her in the cloister and flung a 'stinging remark at her'. 'Oh, our Mistress. . . !' exclaimed Bernadette, as if to say, explains Sister Léontine, 'She's always getting at me!'—at least, 'that is what I took it to mean. Then Mother Marie-Thérèse went on: "Ha! we've pricked that little self-love."'

'Self-love,' says that very shrewd psychologist, St Francis of Sales, 'dies only with our body.' This inflated opinion that we have of ourselves is one of the relics of original sin. Was it very noticeable in Bernadette? Her whole life proves the contrary. Mother Vauzou was undoubtedly the first and the only one who judged her a prey to this weakness in any reprehensible degree. Moreover, her judgment rested on very slender grounds. In December 1906, two months before her death, she was discussing Sister Marie-Bernard with Mother Henri Fabre, who had come to see her in Lourdes. 'Her natural side betrayed some self-love,' she said among other things.

But [Mother Henri Fabre pointed out] Mother Marie-Thérèse gave me no other proof than this account of an incident which occurred during recreation. One of the Sisters having told Sister Marie-Bernard that she had some self-love, the latter drew a circle in the sand and putting her forefinger in the centre said: 'Let the one who has no self-love put her finger there.' Never [adds Mother Bordenave], could Mother Vauzou cite any other occasion: and had there been one, she would certainly have said so.

As the day for profession drew near, the Mistress and her assistants usually met to compare their estimates of each of the novices, indicating along with their good points those faults that still required correction. Mother Vauzou entered in a private note-book the 'report' on Sister Marie-Bernard: *Caractère raide, très susceptible; modeste, pieuse, dévouée, elle a de l'ordre.* (Character stubborn, very touchy; unassuming, pious, devoted, orderly.) There was both censure and praise. On making these notes public, Mother Bordenave thought it her duty to modify what she considered the excessive severity of the first two words:

*Raide* (Stubborn). This is rather one of the characteristics of the Pyrenean temperament, especially of the people from the Upper Pyrenees.
*Très susceptible* (Very touchy). In my opinion *très sensible* (very sensitive) is what one ought to say.

But was it just a failure to understand that was at the root of this 'lack of sympathy' in Mother Marie-Thérèse's attitude? She already found it galling that Sister Marie-Bernard should be ill at ease in her own presence, but so much at home with Mother Nathalie Portat, the assistant, and with Mother Cassagnes, secretary to the Superior General. She therefore did not hold first place, as she had hoped, in the affections of the Lourdes visionary, who was only a miller's daughter, but in one respect outshone her, being one of the most renowned persons in the Catholic world. Mother Joséphine Forestier was not afraid to put forward this suggestion: 'I wonder if in view of our Mother's character, the presence of Bernadette with her great religious fame did not put her rather in the shade.' Did not Mother Vauzou give herself away when, as Superior General, she confided to her secretary, Mother Bordenave: 'I don't understand why the Blessed Virgin appeared to Bernadette. There are so many others so refined, so well-bred. . . ! Ah well!' And the sigh was full of meaning.

To unravel this riddle of misunderstanding, weighty witnesses have considered that it must be traced to some special divine permission. Let us hear one of the most discerning:

If Mother Vauzou had been able to penetrate this soul which had been so singularly refined through intimate contact with the supernatural in the Apparitions at the grotto, she would have been captivated by the intimate and constant union with God, by the love of sufferings and by that total surrender to God's good pleasure which formed the interior life of Sister Marie-Bernard. . . . It is the deep and exhaustive study I have made of the servant of God that has revealed her to me in this way. That all this escaped, even partially, a person so experienced in the guidance of souls as was Mother Marie-Thérèse, would be a mystery for me, did I not see therein the love of God moulding His little servant.

The reason why I go so thoroughly into this question is only that in conscience before God I deem it necessary to do so in order to explain to some extent the relations of Mother Marie-Thérèse with her novice, and the judgment she passes on her at the end of her year's noviceship.

In speaking like this out of her profound spiritual experience, Mother Bordenave recognized that there are trials, either physical or moral, which are intended to detach a soul from all that is not God. In the words of St Paul, the Lord 'helps to secure the good of those who love Him' (Rom. 8, 28)—that is, He arranges, as in this case, every circumstance of persons and places with a view to this higher good.

The solution then of the present problem may be found in some simple but profound words written at the time when justice on a magnificent scale was beginning to be rendered to Bernadette: 'To become a Saint our little Sister had only to let herself be fashioned first of all by the Blessed Virgin and then by her Mistress of Novices, and finally to humble herself.'

# 24

## MARTYRDOM OF HEART

B<small>Y</small> what signs did Sister Marie-Bernard detect a change of
feeling in the Mistress of Novices? There were of course
no violent outbursts or abnormal penances, but cutting
remarks, rebuffs and a punitive silence. . . . Let us first hear
Mother Marie-Thérèse making her own confession when she was
sent to the Lourdes Orphanage to end her days there in prayer
and repose. Recalling the past she acknowledged: 'Every time
I had to say anything to Bernadette I was prompted to say it
bitingly.'

It seems clear, however, that this tendency to sharpness did not
make the same impression on all the novices. For example
Sister Eugénie Calmes (well named) merely felt vaguely surprised
at it: 'I have heard it said that Sister Marie-Bernard had much
to suffer from the Mistress of Novices, but in the noviciate I
did not notice this at all. Yet I thought it odd that so little
account was made of the servant of God.' On the other hand,
shrewd Sister Anastasie Carrière made no mistake about it: 'The
Mistress of Novices treated her severely and spoke to her
sharply. . . .' 'She never had a word of encouragement for
her,' said Sister Bernard Dalias (but that is an exaggeration).
'She liked to thwart Sister Marie-Bernard more than the others,'
Sister Joseph Caldairou disclosed; 'sometimes I have heard
our Mistress say to her: "Sister Marie-Bernard, you have done
such and such a thing which you should not have done." And
we were all surprised at this reproof for we knew she did not
deserve it.'

This makes it easier to understand the outspoken admission
made by Mother Stéphanie Vareillaud, who was a companion of
Sister Marie-Bernard at Nevers before being appointed Superior
of the Orphanage at Lourdes: 'When I was a young novice and
saw the humiliations endured by Bernadette, I used to say to

myself in my scant fervour, "How lucky I am not to be Berna-dette!"'

It is not usual for a novice to find in the Mistress anything other than solicitude for the genuine welfare of souls. As Sister Dalias states: 'I think that Mother Mistress's way of acting was deliberately intended to safeguard Bernadette from any attack of self-love.' Among her former companions in the noviciate—some ten or so—who testified in her Cause, five or six use much the same terms. But one at least, Sister Valentine Gleyrose, who was at Saint-Gildard from 1866 to 1871, was 'greatly dis-tressed by the way in which Mother Marie-Thérèse treated Sister Marie-Bernard, and thought there was something unjust in it.' Whereas Sister Joseph Garnier wondered whether the Mother had not acted with this severity 'partly out of duty, and partly from her own nature.'

*     *     *

But could not the Superior General and her counsellors have restrained Mother Vauzou's zeal? To do that, it would have been necessary for the authorities first of all to sift what was 'nature' from what was 'duty' in Mother Vauzou's conduct, or else go back on the decisions which had been taken by common agreement even before Bernadette's arrival at Saint-Gildard; she was, as we know, to be placed on exactly the same level as the rest and even to be treated somewhat more strictly than the rest if that should be necessary in order to keep her humble. The Superior General and her counsellors could only leave it to the Mistress of Novices to carry out these decisions, and in fact they had evidence that Mother Vauzou was indeed keeping Bernadette conscious of her own insignificance.

What did they learn from the other novices? Very little indeed! Undoubtedly 'Sister Marie-Bernard's companions revered her, but in the belief that they were falling in with the views of superiors—so states Mother Bordenave—they kept their feelings for the most part entirely to themselves. . . .'

Had Mother Joséphine Imbert followed her natural impulses she might easily have treated the young novice like a spoilt child. To her mind the genuine visionary of Lourdes was the most beautiful soul she had among her daughters. 'She loved her nuns very much,' it has been said; 'and she particularly loved Bernadette.' Never in her heart of hearts did she subscribe to the false judgments of the Mistress of Novices. 'She was large-minded and very kind-hearted.' Yet she could not help dreading temptations to pride in a much-loved daughter. We find, in the *Community Journal* for November 14th, 1869: 'Our Reverend Mother General is anxious that (Bernadette) should remain always humble and hidden, for the good of her soul.'

All the evidence goes to show that it was out of loyalty to this agreed policy that Mother Josephine 'did not show her affection for her too much'. Indeed, 'her behaviour towards Bernadette was externally the same as that of the Mistress of Novices'. According to Bishop Forcade, 'however much it hurt Mother Imbert's own feelings, she maintained to the very end (that is, for more than ten years) this painful role she had imposed on herself; and it is in itself clear proof of the great opinion which this highly intelligent woman had of Bernadette's virtue'.

She must indeed have felt sure of her solid virtue for her to fling at Bernadette as she passed her in the cloisters: 'You are good for nothing and you'll never be anything else!'

However, it was not only a cold north wind that blew on little Sister Marie-Bernard from the upper spheres: Mother Cassagnes, who was so understanding, often gave her smiling encouragement. Sometimes she even received special favours. When, for instance, she was laid up in the infirmary with sickness, Mother Imbert departed from her self-imposed indifference and chatted familiarly with her. And one day the *Community Journal* recorded: 'Our Reverend Mother, whose health continues to improve, went for a drive to-day with Sister Marie-Bernard, who is convalescing. . . .'

The Reverend Mother General had already shown a practical interest in her in the noviciate. She was far from thinking her unintelligent; she had watched her making 'quite rapid progress in her studies', and her writing pleased her. At her request, Sister Marie-Bernard, while still following the exercises of the noviciate, assisted Sister Valentine Gleyrose in the Procurator's office for several months; the latter gave her business letters to write, but as the novice 'had no bent that way and seemed to find it tedious,' says Sister Gleyrose, 'Reverend Mother then told me to give her some other work, and I got her to arrange and check some printed sheets and papers.'

Later a more appreciable and lasting privilege, and one almost unheard of at Saint-Gildard, was conferred on her when Mother Joséphine authorized her (now professed) to visit the noviciate and take recreation with the novices.

Even Mother Marie-Thérèse, in spite of her temptation to speak to her 'bitingly', did sometimes succeed in resisting the temptation.  She gave her a post of some distinction: 'It was,' reports Sister Stanislas Tourriol, 'Sister Marie-Bernard who used to recite the public Rosary in the noviceship and "bless the hour".'  On at least one occasion she commissioned her to answer in her name the letter of a lady of high rank; and a week or two later she confided a young postulant, the future Sister Stanislas Paschal, to her care and told her to show her round the house.  Much later, Mother Vauzou summoned her to her office to see a young postulant who was in tears.  Utterly unable to comfort her, the Mother Mistress had had an idea.  'Would you be pleased to see Bernadette?'  The postulant's gloomy face lit up.  Bernadette appeared.  'Sister,' said the Mother, 'here is a child who has only just come and is already "in the dumps".  Poor little thing. . . !  Sister Marie-Bernard, embrace her.'  Bernadette threw her arms round the neck of the newcomer, and the sorrows of Mlle Louise Poujade, who was soon to be Sister Marcella, melted away in this sisterly embrace.

Mother Marie-Thérèse could 'pass in a moment from the severe to the gentle' in her attitude towards Bernadette.  It occurred in 1869 during a noviciate lesson.  They were reading about 'the marvels of Lourdes'—probably from Henri Lasserre's book, which had only just been published.  A door opened noiselessly at the back of the hall and in came the heroine of the book.  She had not taken four steps before a sharp word from the desk pinned her to the spot: 'Sister Marie-Bernard, this is not the time to come in here. . . . Kiss the ground and withdraw!'  Submissively the unwanted visitor pressed her lips to the tile floor (concerning which someone else said: 'I'm hunting for the tile I haven't kissed!'—for in those days these corporal penances were customary).  That done, Sister Marie-Bernard turned and made for the door.  Immediately came a counter-order: 'Sister Marie-Bernard, come here.'  She went up and knelt by the Mother's chair and gave the reason for her coming: it concerned an invalid Sister. Having given her decision, Mother Marie-Thérèse 'laid her hand on Bernadette's head—which was with her a gesture of love and protection. Then she added: "You may go, daughter."'

After some ten years of religious life Sister Marie-Bernard ought to have won the favour of her superiors: it had become sufficiently clear that for the visionary of Massabielle pride was no longer to be feared. However that may be, on one particular occasion Mother Vauzou happened to bring her somewhat out of the shade. In 1875, during an evening reunion at which Sister Gonzague Cointe, then a novice, was present, 'the Mistress sent for Sister Marie-Bernard to come and sit beside the Mothers, nearer the statue of the Blessed Virgin'.

Should one also read into these kindly gestures a certain expression of regret, however vague? Yet Mother Vauzou avowed to the Superior of the Senior Seminary of Nevers that, although she realized she had been sometimes hard on Bernadette, she did not believe she had been wrong, but thought she was doing her duty. Even so, did she always feel so easy in conscience? Towards the end of her period as Mother General, her thoughts returned to some touching details in Bernadette's saintly life. She had already been told of signal favours and miraculous cures due to the intercession of the servant of God, and, testifies Mother Bordenave, 'at the remembrance of her harsh treatment of Sister Marie-Bernard she felt some uneasiness'. While passing through the region of Narbonne on a visit to the southern Communities, she wished to consult 'a holy religious, Father Jean, who was regarded as a wonder-worker' and who was at that time Prior of the Cistercian monastery of Fontfroide. This mystic, accustomed to see beyond the woes and pettiness of earth, discerned the supernatural benefit that Bernadette had gained from her superiors' misunderstandings of her, and so he endeavoured above all to calm the soul that unburdened itself to him.

Nevertheless, as we have already seen, towards the end of her life, in Lourdes itself, the memory of Bernadette still tormented her. On December 5th, 1906, only a few weeks before her death, she again felt the need of exonerating herself in the eyes of Mother Henri Fabre, who had come to visit her: 'God permitted

Mother Joséphine and myself to be hard on Sister Marie-Bernard in order to keep her humble.'

\*    \*    \*

Who could now fail to understand what Mother Forestier calls the 'martyrdom of heart' endured by Sister Marie-Bernard?

In normal circumstances, once her noviceship was completed, she would have come under the immediate authority of Mother Joséphine Imbert. But this did not happen. 'At the time when Sister Marie-Bernard was a novice,' explained Mother Henri Fabre, 'the Superior General was often ill and was under the influence of Mother Vauzou, so that it is true to say that Sister Marie-Bernard was subject to Mother Marie-Thérèse during her noviceship and throughout almost the remainder of her life.' 'This Mistress of Novices,' says Mother Joséphine Forestier, 'used practically to take the place of the Superior General, at least in the Mother House, as Mother Imbert was afflicted with chest trouble and was often confined to her room.' This was to continue until the day in January 1878 when, on the death of Mother Imbert, her successor, Mother Dons, took a firm grip of the reins; and for Bernadette there was a change in the atmosphere.

But for the space of eleven years—much as she was esteemed and loved by her companions—she had been subjected to an undeserved coldness by those in authority over her. She always refused to speak of her suffering, which was a mixture of bewilderment and pain. She put up submissively with being reprimanded in public and more frequently than was her share. 'The Mistress is quite right,' she humbly confided to her compatriot, Sister Emilienne Duboé, 'for I have a great deal of pride.' But it was that deep and unrelenting coldness, rather than the passing sting of a rebuke, that was her cross.

In addition, this little invalid had to bear the constant burden of bad health, which must have had its effect on her mind and character. Bernadette was more nervous than most of her companions who, not having suffered the privations of poverty, and not being undermined by tuberculosis, were in robust health; she might easily have become ill-tempered. 'I'm seething inside, but they don't see what's going on there,' she admitted to Sister

Marthe du Rais; 'there would be no merit if one did not master oneself.'

She did master herself, not always without effort, it is true, nor without an inner struggle. One of her companions gives clear evidence of this: 'I well remember,' said Sister Dalias, 'that the Mistress of Novices was very severe with Sister Marie-Bernard. She used to reprimand her in sharp, curt terms, and Sister Marie-Bernard was seen to turn pale, but never did she make any gesture or utter any word of discontent.' And, says Sister Manhès, who lived with Bernadette in the Mother House for seven years, 'she suffered much. I have seen her weeping, but never did I hear her complain!' 'She never said a word to me about her mental suffering,' adds Mother Forestier. The kind-hearted Mother Eléonore Cassagnes, finding her once in tears in front of St Joseph's altar in the garden, could not get her to disclose the reason for her sadness.

For love of Jesus I will carry the cross hidden in my heart . . . [she wrote in her little note-book].

She made no complaint, no accusation. 'Never,' attests Mother Bordenave, 'has anyone been able to instance a single word of hers that could give pain or trouble. . . . A silence all the more heroic in that she felt things most keenly.' 'No,' affirms Sister Angèle Lompech, 'she bore no grudge against superiors who used to hurt her with their wounding criticisms. She showed them a no less filial affection and respect on that account.' Says Sister Victoire Cassou in her turn: 'She saw in them God's representatives.' 'Once when I found her very upset,' said Sister Ducout, 'she said to me: "We must always see God in our superiors. . . . I submit, come what may."' And in her private note-book she had written:

Never regard the creature, but always see God in her.

It was by reflections of this kind that she restored peace of soul to one of her companions. Sister Manent was living in a state of anguish, 'convinced that her superiors were misjudging her and putting an unfavourable interpretation on what she had done. . . . Sister Marie-Bernard said to her, among other things, "But, my dear Sister, do try and say always: move along, creatures, move along; God remains and God is sufficient for me." Sister Manent was greatly impressed by these words and recovered her peace of mind.'

Obviously Bernadette did not open up in the presence of her superiors as much as she would sometimes have wished. To Mother Vauzou's coldness there was in her a corresponding constraint, 'a most painful feeling of awkwardness'. So asserts Mother Forestier, and she was in a position to judge, having suffered a similar ordeal.

I was very fond of our Mother [she declared]. I also had much to suffer at times from her temperament, especially during the first years in my post of private secretary. Later, when I came to know her more intimately, I used humbly to make the first advance, throwing my arms round her neck, and so the coldness disappeared for the moment; but this did not always succeed.

And then Mother Forestier, recalling the memory of Sister Marie-Bernard, wondered 'if in her case her awe and reverence were not too great for her to dare to make the advances that we ourselves made who lived in close contact with her'.

A conference was about to begin one day when Sister Marie-Bernard appeared. 'Sister Marie-Bernard, go away!' shouted the well-known voice. And the novice of yesterday said in an appealing tone, 'Oh, Mother!' But the command was repeated: 'Go away!' And she had to go.

There is no doubt either that Sister Marie-Bernard could not help wondering whether the Superior General had not adopted Mother Vauzou's feelings towards her. It has been said of this Superior that 'having the head of a man she kept none the less her woman's heart'. 'When dealing with Bernadette,' observes Bishop Forcade, 'her head alone appeared . . . so much did she dread the frightful perils of pride in the privileged child of Lourdes.' This we already know, but Sister Marie-Bernard never knew that this was the sole, and indeed in itself the praiseworthy motive of her cold reserve. She only knew that the heart of this Mother, whose extreme goodness was extolled by everyone else, did not open wide to the most loving of her daughters; and so she was never able to overcome a feeling of apprehension.

I was Superior of our Boarding School in Moulins-sur-Allier from 1875 to 1880 [related Mother Henri Fabre]. During those five years I often went to the Mother House. Nothing was ever said of Sister Marie-Bernard, and I should not have known of her presence there had not the servant of God come to me one day during recreation. I don't recall all our conversation; we must have talked about Lourdes. All I remember is that she said to me, tilting the umbrella she was mending, so as to hide her face, 'Mother Joséphine! Oh, how I fear her!'

Incidents of this kind, far from belittling Sister Marie-Bernard, do but make her all the greater; they enhance the merit of her perseverance. 'Many in her position would have lost heart,' considers Sister Marcillac, whose small stature placed her always in rank beside Sister Marie-Bernard. But Mother Bordenave goes further: 'For her trust in God never to be shaken by it all, she needed a hope pushed even to the extreme of heroism.'

And what saved her was—combined with her 'heroic hope'— her supernatural optimism, the happy disposition of her child-like heart, that 'spiritual joy' so praised by St Francis of Sales, who makes it the very foundation of his spirituality. The bee extracts its sweet honey from every flower, even the bitterest; with Sister Marie-Bernard, trials though keenly felt were, so to speak, dissolved in interior peace and joy. And that is one of the mysteries of God's grace.

On this matter she always maintained the utmost reserve. But on one occasion she used a humorous and figurative word to describe her own way of viewing this 'martyrdom of heart' in order to bear it better. Sister Vincent Garros, the dear friend of her childhood, relates how, when she was a novice, she would always go to Bernadette when she was in trouble. 'I looked upon her as my mother,' is her charming expression, 'and I used to tell her all my difficulties.' And the other would answer in the patois she still loved: 'What's that? Nonsense. . . ! Don't forget the noviceship is Heaven on earth.' Sister Vincent continues: 'I happened to make some blunders and had to pay for them. Then she said to me: "Why, all that is . . . sugar!"'

*     *     *

In her evidence regarding the providential events which were so obscure in their unfolding, but which contributed to Bernadette's advance in holiness, Mother Bordenave arrives at this conclusion:

> I can affirm that had Mother Marie-Thérèse been able to penetrate this soul, she would have been so delighted with it that her affection for her novice might perhaps have been excessive, and the holiness of Sister Marie-Bernard would have lost thereby.

One day, to one of her companions who was pitying her 'for being so severely treated by the Mistress of Novices', the future Saint replied in a tone of deep feeling: 'But I owe her great gratitude for the good she has done my soul!' And this was so true that one may add without any irony that Mother Marie-Thérèse was the person who laboured most for her glorification. A consultor of the Congregation of Rites was to declare at the close of the ceremony of Beatification that nothing had done so much to establish the heroic degree of Bernadette's virtues as her difficulties with her Mother Mistress.

One last point calls for consideration. If the visionary of Massabielle had been held in honour, pampered and spoiled at Saint-Gildard and so had enjoyed a certain purely human happiness, how could that clear prediction have been fulfilled which the Apparition had made her: 'I do not promise to make you happy in this world, but in the next'?

# 25

## INFIRMARIAN AND SACRISTAN

ON that sad evening of October 25th, 1866, when Sister Marie-Bernard made her profession *in articulo mortis*, Mother Joséphine Imbert, while informing her in such an unusual fashion that if she survived till the next day she would be given back her novice's veil, had done no more than recall the custom. In fact, in Bernadette's time the question of profession *in extremis* was still regulated by a decision of the Congregation of the Council dated March 20th, 1649: a novice who is restored to health must on the completion of her year of profession renew her vows. It was agreed accordingly that Sister Marie-Bernard, now quite recovered, should be included in the first general profession. Being warned in good time she began to prepare her soul for the great day with no less earnestness than her companions.

On Sunday, September 22nd, 1867, His Lordship came to the noviciate for the canonical enquiry. It is not known whether he questioned Bernadette, but in any case the chapter of Superiors, as is evidenced by a list from which her name is absent, did not have to trouble themselves over her; she had been accepted for profession already. The chapter apparently showed itself severe with her companions: out of sixty presented, only forty-four were admitted.

The Vow ceremony was fixed for Wednesday, October 30th. It was preceded by a retreat of seven days, preached by a Jesuit, Father Pauley, from the residence in Bordeaux. Sister Marie-Bernard's private note-book has preserved the series of subjects with which he dealt. As would be expected, it is much the same as the usual plan of these pious exercises: the end of man, holy indifference, sin, St Joseph model of obedience, Jesus at Nazareth model of the interior life, the Crucifix, the Eucharist. . . . And here are our retreatant's final resolutions:

To live for God only, for God everywhere, for God always.
The way to see God in everything is by recollection, abnegation and mortification.
In all things to seek God only, God everywhere, God always.

At the moving ceremony during which Sister Marie-Bernard made 'her second profession' Bishop Forcade, who was presiding, has recorded that 'nothing extraordinary occurred'. Each recited the short formula individually, kneeling at the altar-rails before the Celebrant of the Mass, who held up in front of them the Sacred Host which he afterwards gave them in Holy Communion.

'I have a vivid memory of Sister Marie-Bernard's voice at the moment when she pronounced the vow formula,' said Sister Bernard Dalias. 'Her voice was firm and sweet without any affectation. In the gallery the choir were so moved that they held their breath in order to hear better.'

In the afternoon, according to custom, the newly professed received their first appointments. For such an important function the Community assembled in the large noviciate hall and His Lordship presided. As the Mistress of Novices called out their names they came and knelt before the prelate and received from him the paper bearing their destination, and kissed it. Then the Bishop presented them with their Crucifix, rosary and Rule Book. There was, however, nothing stiff or formal about the ceremony: it was more of a homely affair. In order to soften the shock of the appointments, which could sometimes make heroic demands on the young professed, the Bishop and the Superior General used to try and create a light-hearted atmosphere with good-natured fun and friendly teasing, whether the assignments were interesting or on the contrary demanded greater sacrifice. But the nuns who were assigned to the Mother House did not usually receive any such appointment sheet.

The Bishop and the Superiors judged that with her weak health Sister Marie-Bernard would not be able to fill a regular and fatiguing post such as one in a school or hospital, although she was attracted to this work. On the other hand would it be wise to entrust her straightway with any post at all, even a light one in some small house of the Congregation? A local Superior might feel proud of her and push her too much to the front. In that case she would be far less safeguarded from sightseers than at the Mother House; there must be no repetition among the people of Nevers of the eager attentions which had been paid to the visionary in Lourdes. That could easily be avoided: Sister Marie-Bernard would not be allowed to go away.

Here is a description of what happened, according to Bishop Forcade and some of the nuns who were present at the ceremony:

On the day of profession when the time came for distributing the assignments there was none for her [testified Sister Joseph Caldairou]. I can still see Sister Marie-Bernard kneeling there. Bishop Forcade, who was presiding, turned to the Superior General and asked: 'What are you going to do with Sister Marie-Bernard?' At this question, another nun, Sister Stanislas Tourriol, detected a smile on Mother Imbert's face as she replied: 'This child is good for nothing. She would be a burden on any house we sent her to.' There was a brief silence. The Bishop was gazing down at the hur ᵗ ᵗ ᵃ nun kneeling at his feet. Then of his own accord and by a sort ᴄ: inspiration he ordered her: 'I assign you to the post of praying.' But another thought occurred to him: in a Congregation which had St Martha for its patron there could not be for a reasonably healthy nun merely the contemplative life of St Mary Magdalene. 'So you are good for nothing?' continued the Bishop, who was obviously referring here to a post in some other convent.

'Mother General is right,' replied Sister Marie-Bernard. 'It is quite true.'

'But in that case, my poor child, what are we going to do with you, and what is the use in your entering the Congregation?'

'That is exactly what I said to you in Lourdes, and you told me it would not matter.'

('I was not expecting that reply at all . . . and frankly I did not know what to say next,' admitted the Bishop.)

A last question helped him out: 'Would you be able to make bowls of herb-tea and peel vegetables?'

'I'll try.'

'Very well,' concluded the Bishop, turning to Mother Joséphine, 'we'll keep her here for a while; then if we judge that she is capable of doing anything useful, we shall send her to another house.'

Sister Marie-Bernard accepted what she had just heard with great humility.

Her newly professed companions did not agree that she was good for nothing'; indeed they valued her skill with her fingers, but they grasped the reason for the exaggeration. 'We all realized,' said Sister Stanislas, 'that it was in order to keep her humble that they treated her in this way.' Nevertheless, the humiliating words 'good for nothing' had been spoken and Sister Marie-Bernard had heard them. 'Though she did not let it appear, she felt this humiliation very keenly, and she admitted it later. At the next recreation she redoubled her efforts to be lively and cheerful with her companions, just as though she had felt nothing.'

\*     \*     \*

In fact there was a regular appointment for Sister Marie-Bernard. Her superiors assigned her to a post in the Mother House which was a responsible one, and where her services would be most useful in this large establishment in Nevers: she was to be official assistant to the Infirmarian, Sister Marthe Forès, a gentle creature who also had bad health, but whose ardent spirit kept her going. The post suited Bernadette's taste for serving the sick, and she would be fully occupied. She was primarily responsible for the order and cleanliness of the whole infirmary. Then, although the Sister Infirmarian theoretically kept all medical attention in her own hands, she soon discovered a valuable assistant in this little Sister, a real servant of the sick, who knew so well how to cheer them up and encourage them and comfort their souls with a pious word.

In a few letters overflowing with affection which Bernadette wrote to her relations in Lourdes about this time, she gave them reassuring news about her health, but not a word about her duties at Saint-Gildard. For a view of her work in her infirmary we have to rely therefore on the evidence of others. And there is nothing to be found but unqualified praise. The 'good for nothing' of the Profession Day was described quite independently by three of her former companions as: 'lively, amiable, obliging, full of kindness, as skilful as she was attentive . . . finding the friendly and often witty word to get them to take their medicine'; but with all that, discreet and restrained in speech. 'Never any questions, looks or gestures to elicit confidences; just a single remark: "I'll pray for you."' 'The sick found it a delight to be nursed by her.'

'She nursed me with infinite tenderness, and was cheerful in spite of her own bad health,' recalled Sister Tournié. During the times when there was 'recreation' for the patients, she used to tax her wits to amuse the infirmary. 'Often,' said Sister Marcillac, 'she would sing us little songs in Pyrenean patois. She was pleased and laughed heartily on seeing that I did not understand a single word.'

As infirmarian she was not in charge of the lay servants of the Mother House, but out of the kindness of her heart she used to go up to their dormitory on the second floor when any of them happened to be ill. To avoid taking them by surprise she used to announce her arrival, before opening the door, by humming a hymn tune. 'I used to say to myself: "Here she comes," and I felt delighted,' recounted the young Jeanne Jardet. 'No other visit could equal hers. . . . She would first of all bow to a statue of Our Lady that stood above the cupboard facing the door. Then she would turn towards my bed. . . . She used to straighten my pillow, wipe away the perspiration, and take my hand with the tenderness of a real sister or mother. . . . While she was tending me she would say some little pious word to me: "We must suffer a little for the good God, my child; He suffered so much for us." She used to say to me also: "When we get to Heaven we'll be happy, but down here. . . ." And she finished the sentence with a gesture which meant: Don't rely on this life.'

Postulants or novices were often sent to the infirmary, chiefly for cleaning the wards, and thus came under the more or less direct control of Sister Marie-Bernard. She managed these young people with understanding and tact, but she also found means of helping their religious training in her own individual way. There was, for example, the story of the copper knobs that went the rounds of the noviceship several times. Sister Marie-Bernard had been in office for only a short while, as the incident occurred in 1868.

I was still a postulant [related Sister Justine in her old age], and I had been given a job in the infirmary. Well, one day when we were giving the place a thorough cleaning, I had spent the whole morning dusting, rubbing and polishing. Then the bell rang and I was getting ready to leave when Bernadette said: 'The work is

not finished. There's still this and that, but you haven't time now.
It will do some other day.' Then I foolishly said with a certain
satisfaction: 'I've rubbed the copper knobs with polishing powder.'
This referred to the knobs on the iron bedsteads. Bernadette
replied: 'Yes, they are shining brightly. You've polished them
well and thoroughly. You have taken great pains with this work
because it catches the eye.'

She delivered me this reprimand so nicely that I wasn't hurt,
but I felt the little pinprick to my vanity all the same and I
carried the lesson away with me, saying to myself: 'You understand? You have taken great pains over the knobs because they
show, but the work that doesn't show, the work that remains
hidden and which God alone sees, did you do that so carefully?'

I have always remembered those copper knobs.

In the spring of 1869 the little assistant infirmarian emerged
again for a moment from her cherished obscurity. Towards the
end of May the Superior General asked her daughters to pray to
Our Lady that all might go well on the journey she was about
to make with her Secretary, Mother Cassagnes. When she said
she was going to Lourdes, everyone felt a thrill and they all
turned spontaneously towards Sister Marie-Bernard.

Lourdes! It would soon be three years since Bernadette had
left it, and since then never a visit from any of her family! How
she would have loved to see them again, above all her poor
dear father, whose favourite she was still! Although through
the generosity of the Bishop of Tarbes he was now the owner of
the Lacadé mill, she pictured him sad and growing old by that
fireside where her mother's death had left a gap which no one
else could fill. And the grotto which the two travellers were
going to visit for the first time! What would they think of
it?

Saint-Gildard was all eagerness to know, and a letter arrived
soon for the Mother Assistant from the expansive and genial
Secretary. (Undoubtedly the cautious Superior General would
have put less feeling into it, and carefully avoided praising the
visionary with such enthusiasm.)

We are just back from the grotto and I feel I must write at once
and tell you and all our beloved Community that one's experiences
there are beyond all description. I will tell you what we saw and

heard. What we felt, I leave it to God to make you understand, should He think fit; I am unable to describe it.

Impossible to convey to you the impression that is produced on the soul by the sight of these places hallowed by the presence of Mary. These sites, so beautiful in themselves, have received, it seems, an altogether special stamp ever since the Immaculate Virgin deigned to set foot here. Our first visit was to the grotto. . . . What delightful moments I spent at the feet of that beautiful statue which marks the spot where Mary showed herself to our dear little Sister Marie-Bernard !

Bishop Laurence asks eagerly for news of Bishop Forcade and says he is hoping to see him at the Council. His Lordship never forgets our little Sister Marie-Bernard and he is very pleased that she is in the Mother House. . . .

Kindly tell our little Sister Marie-Bernard that our Mother General has seen her father and her sister (Toinette) with her little daughter, and her aunts and cousins, four of whom are with our Sisters.

I have found the visit to Lourdes all too short. It is so lovely at the grotto; we spent three hours there, and to me it seemed but a minute.

Sad news reached Bernadette in February 1870. Bishop Laurence—the ' Bishop of the Apparitions ', as he was called— had died in Rome on January 30th. He had gone there in spite of his eighty years and his great infirmities, to attend the Vatican Council. Seven months before its dogmatic definition, he had, in his last letter from the Eternal City, affirmed ' his undying belief in the Infallibility of the Pope '.

The Vatican Council was still in session when, on July 15th, the disastrous Franco-Prussian War broke out. On October 3rd a field-hospital of twenty beds was organized at the Mother House. Sister Marie-Bernard would have been glad to devote herself to the care of the wounded, but she had to remain at her post with the invalid Sisters, for she had become practically head infirmarian in place of Sister Marthe, who was growing more and more feeble. However, she reserved a large share in her sacrifices and prayers for the defenders of the fatherland.

At the same time, Bishop Forcade, who saw in her the protectress of his city, implored the help of her prayers. The visionary of Lourdes was becoming increasingly esteemed in the diocese, as can be seen from the *Community Journal* for November 7th:

> The rumour is current in several towns that Sister Marie-Bernard has had some fresh visions and that she has an important mission to fulfil with the Government. Our Mother General is receiving numberless letters on this subject and she replies that the thing is false. His Lordship also contradicts it in an article he is having published in the *Semaine Religieuse*.

For her part Bernadette declared she had no fear of the Prussians; she only feared bad Catholics. In November she wrote to her father:

> It is said that the enemy are approaching Nevers. I could do without the Prussians well enough, but I'm not afraid of them: God is everywhere, even in the midst of the Prussians. I remember when I was quite young hearing some people say after one of the Parish Priest's sermons, 'Bah, that's his job!' I also think the Prussians are only doing their job. [In the invaders she saw the ministers of justice.]

This thought of sin and its expiation again beset her when, at the end of May 1871, one of her companions told her about the burning of the Tuileries during the Commune riots. Remembering only that the imperial occupant of the Tuileries had betrayed the cause of Pius IX, whom she greatly revered, she replied: 'Don't worry. The place needed cleaning out: God is wielding the broom.'

But there were other troubles at Nevers. The *Community Journal* reflects faithfully the protracted periods of despondency and the brief moments of hope and joy during that desolate winter of 1870-1.

> *December 2nd.* They come and inform us at 10 p.m. that a victory has been won over the enemy forces in Paris. This news revives our spirits, and his Lordship orders a *Te Deum* to be sung.
>
> *December 9th.* The Prussians are reported to be at the boundaries of the department. The whole town of Nevers is in turmoil. Our wounded officers (of the field hospital), fearing capture, are fleeing southwards, but on leaving they express their gratitude for the care they have received.

At the end of November, by order of General Barrat, the Engineers began preparing gun emplacements on the terrace at Saint-Gildard. On December 13th as night fell there was a tremendous commotion at the Mother House.

> The General, accompanied by twelve troopers, arrives to inspect the position and the work done on the gun sites. His words are far from reassuring, and everything indicates that a stand will be made here and that we shall have to leave the house. . . .
> *December 16th-20th.* Our Sisters pack their trunks.
> *December 21st.* General Bourbaki arrives in Nevers with his army. The staff are billeted in the Bishop's House. We have to take eight horses in our stables.

Four days later what a melancholy Christmas they had! The chapel was closed to the public, who always liked to come to Saint-Gildard for Midnight Mass; and for the first time perhaps, the daytime Mass was not sung: the choir gallery was deserted, for the singers were with the ambulances.

When Sister Marie-Bernard had a few free moments in her infirmary that day, she scribbled a line to her sister Toinette. Their father, who had long been wanting to see his Bernadette, had taken it into his head to go to Nevers in spite of the enemy and the severely cold weather!

> My dearest sister, you tell me in your letter that Father proposes coming to see me. I myself should be very glad to see him again, but tell him not to come. If any misfortune were to befall him on the journey I should blame myself for it all my life.
> Our Reverend Mother General has promised that she will allow me to come and see all the family when the grotto chapel is blessed. I should have been delighted to see my father, but I shall be happier still to see all of you.
> My health is quite good; don't worry about me. . . .
> We have only one thing to do: pray hard to the Most Blessed Virgin that she may be kind enough to intercede with her beloved Son and obtain for us pardon and mercy. I feel confident that God's justice which is punishing us at this moment will yet be appeased by this tender Mother. . . .

For her to possess such confidence and express it so definitely one would think that the visionary had some intuition of what

was soon to follow. Further west, in the department of the
Mayenne, in the village of Pontmain and from within the dark
opening of a barn, some other children were to have a vision of
Our Lady of Hope which lasted three hours. And her mysterious message was traced out in the starlit night: 'But pray,
children. God will answer you soon.'

This event occurred on Tuesday, January 17th, 1871. On
Saturday, January 28th, the armistice was signed by the belliger-
ent forces. Two days later the news reached the Mother House
of Saint-Gildard.

\*       \*       \*

But then came fresh trials for Sister. Marie-Bernard. Her
sister Toinette, who had just given birth to a crippled boy, now
saw her own little Bernadette die in her arms. And at the
Lacadé mill François Soubirous was ill. Aunt Lucile was also
said to be growing worse. But, contrary to the doctor's forecast,
Bernadette's father was the first to die, in his sixty-fourth year,
on March 4th, the anniversary of the fifteenth Apparition. To
the very end of his life he had maintained a sort of veneration
for his little nun. Once, shortly before his death, when he
chanced to be alone in the Missionaries' parlour, he was caught
unexpectedly by Father Sempé 'kneeling before the picture of
his daughter and praying fervently'. His end had been 'that
of the just. As he lay dying he pointed with joy to the scapular
he was wearing. For several hours and even to his last breath
he never ceased praying.'

Bernadette's thoughts and bearing when she heard the heart-
rending news have been exquisitely described by one of her
infirmary assistants, Sister Madeleine Bounaix:

I went up about 7.30 to St Catherine's infirmary, where I found our
dear Sister Marie-Bernard leaning against the mantelpiece crying.
    I knelt down beside her and asked her: 'What is the matter,
Sister? Have I perhaps hurt you without meaning to?' She
answered, 'Oh, no! But a fortnight ago you had your sorrow' (I
had lost one of my brothers), 'and I comforted you; to-day it is
my turn: I have just heard of my father's death. He died on
Saturday at nine o'clock. . . . Sister,' she added, 'always have a
great devotion to the Heart of Jesus in Agony, for when you lose

your dear ones and you're far away from them, it is a comfort to think that you have prayed for them. This is what I did on Saturday evening without suspecting anything; while praying for those in agony I was praying for my poor father, who was passing into eternity.'

Twelve days later he was joined there by her devoted Aunt Lucile, aged thirty-one, who had never had any doubts about the Lady and whose blest candle Bernadette used to take to the grotto.

Under the stress of these bereavements, which followed so close on one another, Sister Marie-Bernard, who wrote so seldom, felt the need to pour out her grief in letters to her sister Toinette; to her young brother and godson, Bernard-Pierre, who was now twelve years old and who had been sent by the new Bishop of Tarbes to study with the Garaison Fathers; and lastly to her brother Jean-Marie, a young man of twenty, who was then a postulant with the Brothers of Christian Instruction of Ploërmel. Of her three letters, the one to this last brother is the most characteristic. How human and at the same time how supernatural she shows herself to be!

I unite with you to-day in embracing the crosses our Divine Master has sent us. Let us beg of Him the grace to bear them, after His example, with submission and generosity.

Our trials this year have been heavy ones, haven't they, brother dear? Three members of the family have been taken from us within a few days. God has His designs, it is true, but the shock has been very severe.

Our poor father was snatched from us so suddenly! We had the consolation of hearing that he had received the Last Sacraments. That is a great favour for which we must thank God. But let us pray hard for the repose of his soul and for our poor Aunt Lucile, whose poor children are greatly to be pitied.

I recommend you also to pray to the Blessed Virgin for our sister Marie (Toinette) who has great need of our prayers. You know that she had the misfortune to lose her little Bernadette, whom she loved so dearly. What sorrow for a mother . . . !

Good-bye, my dearest brother. Let us ask for each other from Our Lord the graces necessary to become saints. Let us be generous in the sacrifices this good Master sends us and offer them for the repose of the souls of those we have lost.

Sister Marie-Bernard was not to have the consolation of kneeling at her father's grave. She was not to be present at the blessing of the 'grotto chapel' on the Feast of the Assumption, 1871.

\*    \*    \*

In the course of that year Sister Marthe Forès grew increasingly weaker and the management of the infirmary passed gradually into the hands of Sister Marie-Bernard. She was, in fact, if
not officially, head infirmarian and 'pharmacist', for at Saint-
Gildard these two offices were combined. She realized her
responsibilities and shouldered them willingly; and her own
personality began to manifest itself more firmly. As to her
professional competence there exists an outstanding testimonial
which had a curious origin.

After the war of 1870 crowds began again to flock to Massabielle and in still greater numbers. On December 8th, 1871, a
committee of ladies published a circular inviting the Catholics
of France to a national demonstration in honour of Our Lady
of Lourdes. As a result the *Association Notre-Dame du Salut*
set about preparing for a pilgrimage that was to muster 60,000
people at the grotto of the Apparitions. It lasted from Saturday,
October 5th, to Tuesday, October 8th, 1872, and it was the first
national pilgrimage. It was called the 'Pilgrimage of Banners'
because during those memorable days 302 French banners were
carried in procession through Lourdes, and at the head, draped
in black, were the banners of Alsace and Lorraine, the two
provinces that had been wrested from France at the Treaty of
Frankfort.

The free-thinkers were exasperated and unfurled their
standard. But the Catholics proudly ignored the oracular utterance of M. Thiers, the head of the executive power of the
Republic: 'Pilgrimages no longer fit in with our way of life.'
Pilgrimages should be stopped in full career. All that was
required was to discredit the visions and the visionary; after
that no one would dare to make another attempt.

So the same old artillery was brought up. With touching
unanimity, newspapers, reviews and conferences inspired by the
Masonic Lodges launched a campaign against the hallucinated
in general and Bernadette in particular. At this juncture the

doctor of the Mother House of Saint-Gildard, Dr Robert Saint-Cyr, President of the Society of Doctors of the Nièvre, received from the President of the Society of Doctors of the Orne, Dr Damoiseau, a request for information. A Dr Voisin of the Salpêtrière in Paris had asserted at the conclusion of a course of lectures that 'the miracle of Lourdes' had been 'based on the evidence of a child who was subject to hallucinations and was now shut up in the convent of the Ursulines at Nevers'. On September 3rd, 1872, Dr Saint-Cyr replied to Dr Damoiseau:

My dear colleague, you could not have done better than apply to myself for the information you desire regarding the Lourdes girl, now Sister Marie-Bernard. As the Convent doctor I have long been attending this young Sister whose very delicate health was giving us cause for anxiety. At present her condition is improving, and from being my patient she has now become my infirmarian and performs her duties to perfection.

She is small and frail in appearance, and is twenty-seven years of age. Of a calm and gentle disposition, she nurses her patients with considerable intelligence, never omitting anything from the prescriptions which I order. Thus she exercises great authority and, as far as I am concerned, she enjoys my entire confidence.

You see, my dear colleague, that this young Sister is very far from being mentally deranged. I shall go further and affirm that her calm, simple and gentle disposition does not render her the least bit liable to tend that way. . . .'

The Catholics treated the adversaries' attacks with the scorn which they deserved. For the convenience of the crowds of pilgrims, work went ahead on improving the approach to the grotto and on restoring and widening the venerable Pont-Vieux. And Sister Marie-Bernard, unacquainted with rumours from outside and far too taken up with her duties to pay heed to them, retained her smiling serenity.

She had a keen sense of her responsibilities, and several incidents proved that she did not compromise on duty. Where others would have given up, she proved her heroism. A nun who had gone blind, Sister Lescure, was also afflicted with cancer of the breast. The disease was so repulsive that Sister Vincent Garros, then a novice helping in the infirmary, was, on her own admission, unable to bear even the sight of it: a large deep sore 'filled with maggots that fell out and were caught by Bernadette in a dish'. This horrible ulcer that no one else dared touch, she 'used to dress most tenderly'. . . . 'What sort of Sister of Charity will you make, with such little faith!' she said reprovingly to her young compatriot. When the same Sister showed herself afraid of helping her to lay out a corpse, she let fly at her: 'You coward, you'll never make a Sister of Charity.' Then when Sister Vincent felt faint merely from kissing the icy cold forehead of the deceased (as was the custom), Sister Marie-Bernard said to her: 'What's the use of a Sister of Charity who can't touch the dead?'

Certainly if Sister Marie-Bernard had been sent to nurse the poor in a hospital, it would have gratified her fondest desire, and she would have proved herself dauntless. 'She told me,' stated Sister Garros, 'that a Sister of Charity's vocation is precious because it gives one the opportunity of relieving the poor.' And she gave her this advice: 'If you are sent to a hospital, remember to see Our Lord in the person of the poor man; and the more disgusting the poor person is, the more is he to be loved.' One day when she was sending Sister Garros to take the blind Sister with the cancer for a walk, she said once again to her compatriot: 'Take care of her as if she were God Himself.'

On November 5th, 1872, Sister Marthe Forès died and Sister Marie-Bernard succeeded her officially in the post of head infirmarian. But on January 17th, 1873, she suffered an acute attack of asthma and had to be put to bed. It was the beginning of a sorrowful year.

Towards Easter (April 13th) the invalid had recovered her strength a little. On the 18th she informed her sister Toinette:

. . . Here I am once more up and about after three months in bed. It started with an attack of asthma which lasted rather a long time. Then a violent spitting of blood which prevented me from making the slightest movement for fear of bringing it on again. You can well imagine that being fastened down like this does not suit my impetuous nature.

Now my strength is returning. I attended Mass on Easter Sunday for the first time. Our Lord is good to me. I was fortunate enough to receive Him into my poor and unworthy heart three times a week all the time of my illness. The cross became light and my sufferings sweet whenever I thought I was to have a visit from Jesus and the great favour of possessing Him who comes to suffer with those who suffer, and to weep with those who weep. Where find a friend who can sympathize and at the same time soothe our pains as Jesus does? . . .

Will you, please, give my kindest regards to all my dear relations. Beg them not to forget me in their prayers, especially when you go to my beloved grotto. You'll find me there sometimes. I go there very often even without permission.

She had another relapse, with a fortnight in bed and then a precarious convalescence. On Monday, May 12th, Mother Joséphine Imbert, also convalescing, took advantage of the fine weather to visit her houses in Varennes and Fourchambault. She took Sister Marie-Bernard with her in her carriage. At the Varennes Orphanage the visionary found herself being treated as a person of importance! In front of a grove where a statue of Our Lady stood, two armchairs were placed for the Superior General and the little infirmarian. And as it was the month of Mary they sang hymns and prayed to Our Lady of Lourdes. Afterwards, Bernadette agreed to say a few words to the orphans. She contented herself with telling them that the Blessed Virgin was their mother, that she had a great love for them and that they must love her very dearly. . . . She was feeling exhausted and they noticed that she was almost fainting, so four of the senior orphans carried her off in the armchair and helped her into the carriage.

On June 3rd, Whit Tuesday, she received Extreme Unction for the third time. By October she had sufficiently recovered to make the annual Retreat which opened on the evening of the 20th. Her notes betray an interior struggle. After making her confession to Father Douce she noted down the conversation she had just had with him:

You must carry the cross hidden in your heart, after the example of Mary.

. . . I will go to the parlour cheerfully even though I'm all sadness within. . . . O Mother! It is in your heart that I come and lay the anguish of my own heart.

Do not be afraid to carry the cross, even the naked cross. . . .

For love of Jesus I must conquer myself or die.

She had reappeared in the infirmary . . . as infirmarian, with the pious, devoted and kindly Sister Ambroise Revoux as her deputy. But on November 5th, 1873, the latter was sent to the hospital at Brive. Winter was already in evidence; would it spare Sister Marie-Bernard? After six years Dr Saint-Cyr came to realize that the close atmosphere of an infirmary was not suitable for her bronchial weakness, and the convent counsellors thought it wise to hand over the post of infirmarian to one of Sister Marie-Bernard's occasional assistants, a young professed nun, Sister Gabrielle de Vigouroux. ' I know,' says Mother Cassagnes, ' that it cost Bernadette a great deal to leave the infirmary, where she was very much loved and where her patients missed her greatly.'

* * *

The office assigned her at the beginning of 1874 was better suited to her strength. During her noviceship she had for a while been assistant sacristan. She became so again. There is scarcely any need for us to be told by one of her companions that ' she loved this work ' and that ' she took delight in decorating Our Lady's altar and in finding herself close to Our Lord '. As she performed her duties about the altar she was so filled with the thought of God's presence there that she lived almost the life of a contemplative. The work was to her no mere matter of routine or habit. In this office of sacristan ' where one runs the risk of becoming too familiar with God and sacred things,' observes Sister du Rais, ' she was conspicuous for her recollection and her piety, showing always great reverence and great regard for holy things.'

As her duties in the sacristy left her some leisure, she employed it either in ' seeing to the flowers for the decoration of the altar ' —which gave her great pleasure—or in reading spiritual works and lives of the saints, especially the life of St Bernard, or in collecting notes on spiritual matters. In fine weather she took her embroidery work into a corner of the cloister where she was sheltered from the wind and the sun. There ' she spent long hours in solitude and silence ', and it was then that she made a magnificent alb for Bishop Forcade, who had been promoted Archbishop of Aix-en-Provence.

Frequently her beloved companion, Sister Vincent Garros, helped her with her work. ' One day,' the latter relates, ' I wanted to handle a purificator. Bernadette stopped me and said:

The armchair in which Bernadette gave up her soul to God on April 16, 1879, after months of intense suffering of body and soul. Shortly before she died, she prayed beseechingly, "Holy Mary, Mother of God, pray for me . . . poor sinner . . . poor sinner . . . ."

Bernadette in death. As soon as Bernadette was dead, her face became young and peaceful again, with a look of purity and blessedness. A double crown of white roses was placed on her head and her rosary was entwined around her clasped hands, with her crucifix and the formula of her perpetual vows between her fingers. Bernadette's body remained supple until the funeral, which had to be delayed until three days later because of the crowds who came in veneration. The coffin was even carried still open to the place of burial, to enable everyone to see the face of her who had seen the Blessed Virgin Mary.

304-2

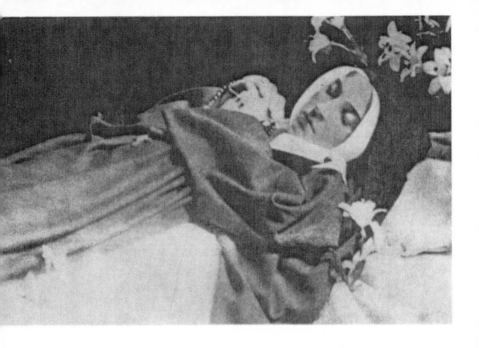

When Bernadette's body was exhumed on September 23, 1909, 30 years after her death, as part of the ecclesiastical investigation leading up to beatification and canonization, it was found to be incorrupt. The body had preserved its whiteness, and there was no odor or trace of corruption, though the body was parched. But when the sisters washed the body again before reclothing it, the skin became darkened, so it was decided to have the face and hands covered with wax. These photographs were taken at a subsequent (the last) exhumation, on April 18, 1925.

304-3

*Above and following 3 pages:* St. Bernadette's beautiful incorrupt body, which rests in a crystal reliquary in the chapel of her convent, St. Gildard, in Nevers, awaiting the final Resurrection at the end of the world.

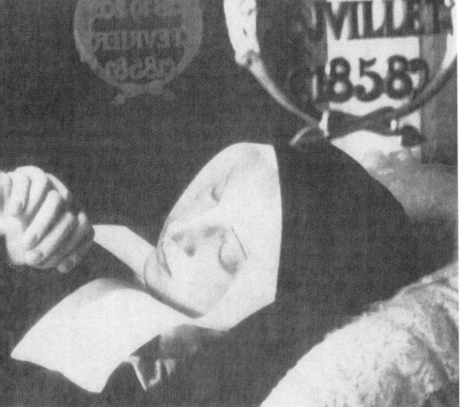

von Matt

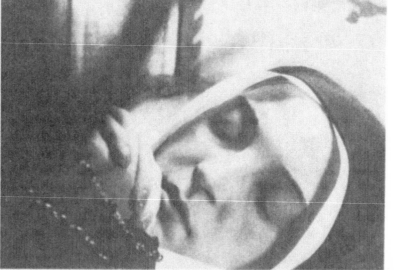

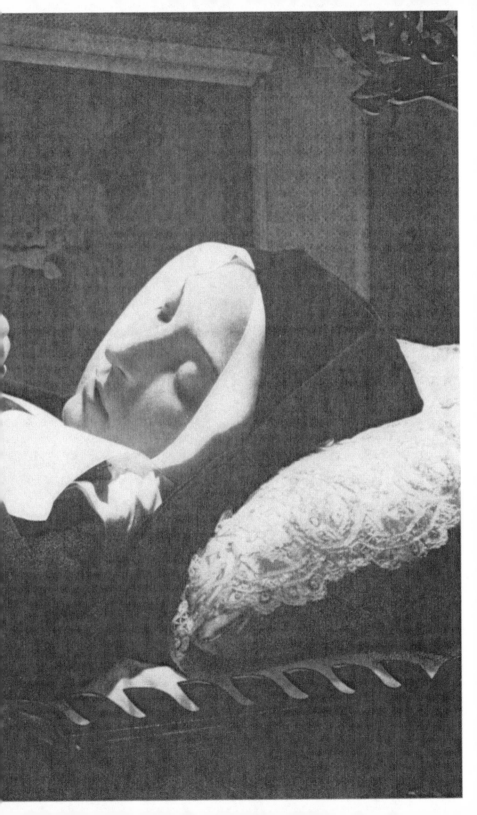

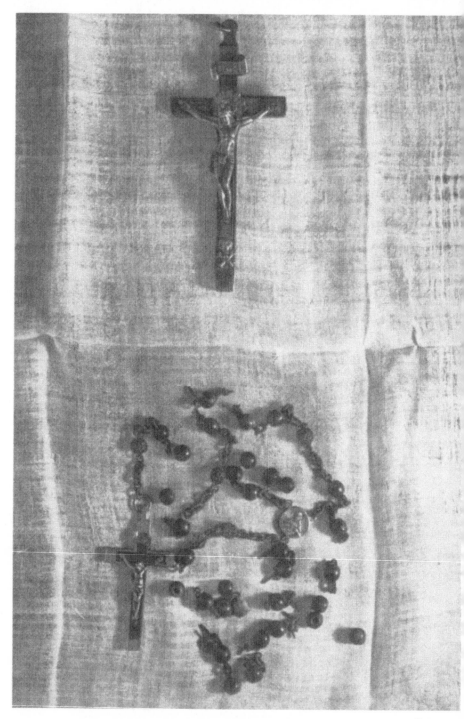

*Above:* The rosary beads and the crucifix which rested on St. Bernadette's breast for the entire 46 years her body was buried.

*Right:* Pope Pius XI, the pope who beatified and canonized Bernadette.

*Above:* The final step leading up to canonization: The consistorial advocate formally petitions His Holiness Pope Pius XI for the canonization of Blessed Bernadette Soubirous.

*Right:* The canonization of St. Bernadette in St. Peter's Basilica on December 8, 1933, Feast of the Immaculate Conception. Pope Pius XI made the formal decree:

"To the honor of the Most Holy and Indivisible Trinity, for the exaltation of the Catholic Faith and for the spread of the Christian Religion, by the authority of Our Lord Jesus Christ, of the Blessed Apostles Peter and Paul and by Our own, after mature deliberation and having often implored the Divine assistance, on the advice of Our venerable brethren the Cardinals of the Holy Roman Church, the Patriarchs, Archbishops and Bishops, We define and declare the Blessed Marie-Bernarde Soubirous a Saint, and We enroll her in the catalogue of Saints, ordaining that her memory shall be piously celebrated in the Universal Church on April 16th of each year, the day of her birth in Heaven. In the name of the Father and of the Son and of the Holy Ghost."

304-10

*Dura*

*Left:* The triple churches at Lourdes. In the center of this picture, at ground level, is the domed Rosary Basilica. Above the Rosary Basilica is the crypt (which was the first of the three churches to be built), and towering above these is the Basilica of the Immaculate Conception. Not visible here is the underground Basilica of St. Pius X.

*Below:* Candlelight procession at Lourdes; the Blessed Virgin told Bernadette that she wanted people to come there in procession. The castle of Lourdes is visible off to the right.

*Previous 2 pages:* View of the Lourdes Basilica. Beneath the great Basilica the statue and candles in the grotto can be faintly seen. When facing the grotto, one is looking south toward the Pyrenees and Spain.

*Durand*

*Viron*

The grotto of Massabielle at Lourdes. Note the statue of the Blessed Virgin Mary, the famous display of candles, and the crutches of those who have been cured.

*Above:* The water from the miraculous spring of Lourdes is available to pilgrims through these water taps.

*Below:* Pilgrims—especially the sick—also bathe in the water from the spring; shown here is one of the bathing compartments, or piscines. The actual piscine is in the center, and on either side is a place for the volunteer attendants to stand. Though the water becomes heavily contaminated with germs, no one has ever contracted any disease from it. The bath volunteers often drink of the water at the end of the day, as a sacrifice for sinners and the sick—but none of them, either, has ever thereby contracted a disease.

304-18

For over a century, pilgrims have drunk Lourdes water for the health of their bodies and souls.

*Above:* The blessing of the sick with the Blessed Sacrament, here being conducted by the Bishop of Tarbes (the diocese in which Lourdes is located). Many of the cures at Lourdes have taken place at this blessing. *Right:* Holy Communion of the sick at Lourdes.

304-20

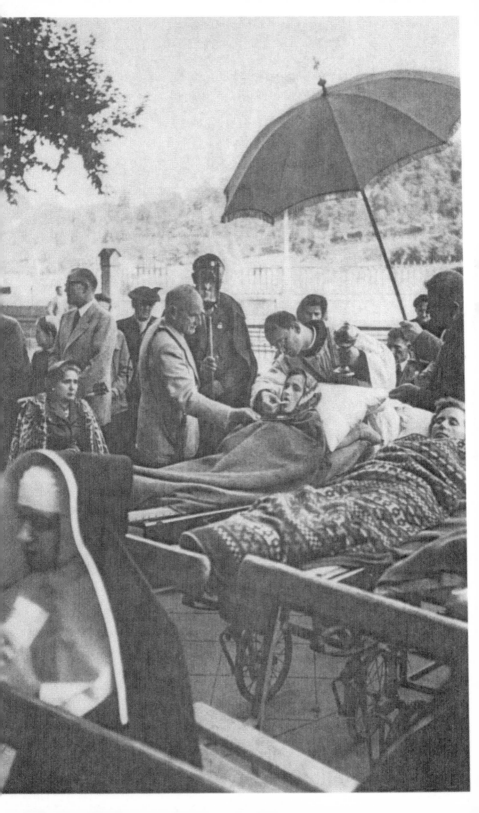

*Above:* Holy Communion in the grotto.

*Right:* The marble statue of Our Lady which adorns the grotto at Lourdes. The famous sculptor of the statue, Joseph Fabisch, received his direction from Bernadette, yet both he and Bernadette were disappointed with the results. Nevertheless, it is through this holy image that Our Lady of Lourdes has received the veneration of millions. Beneath Our Lady's feet, in the *patois* of Lourdes, are her words: "I am the Immaculate Conception."

*Next page:* No seeker leaves Lourdes empty-handed. To those whom Our Lady does not cure, she gives the strength and consolation to accept and bear their crosses. Many have acknowledged that this was indeed an even greater gift than the one they had sought.

"You've not got that far yet!" And I watched her take this purificator with great reverence and put it back into the burse. You would have thought she was praying while handling these objects, so great was the reverence with which she treated them.'

At times also she treated them with a tender affection. On Christmas Eve, 1874, 'when the crib was ready, Sister Marie-Bernard took the Infant Jesus to lay Him down in it. She was heard saying: "You must have been very cold, my poor little Jesus, in the stable at Bethlehem. Those people were heartless not to give you hospitality, but I am glad to prepare your crib for you."' Like the Mass candles, she seemed to be consumed in the service of the altar. Several times she fell fainting from fatigue in the choir. On coming round she found strength enough for a smile and a word. '*Mon Dieu!*' she would say, 'how scandalized you must be, Sisters, by my lack of courage!'

October 1875 was to see the end of her active life: she had become incapable of holding any post. Mother Joséphine Imbert's words had come true; from a superficial human point of view Bernadette was now 'good for nothing'. Yet, as we shall see, a new mission was opening for her at Saint-Gildard—one that might be called her great personal mission.

Henceforth, while still showing herself as pleasant and affable as ever to all her Sisters, she followed perseveringly that fundamental counsel of the founder, Dom de Laveyne: 'Love silence . . . and practise the advice of St Gregory never to break silence except with words that are worth more than silence.'

# 26

## NATURAL CHARACTER

W E must now take a closer look at Sister Marie-Bernard buried in her apparent uselessness. After all that has been said there still remains something further to be added in order to give a clearer and more profound picture of her engaging personality. It will also help to explain why the Church sets before the eyes of all Christendom this little nun of Nevers as a masterpiece of grace, *a Saint*.

A Saint is a human being who 'fulfils all the demands of the law' (Rom. 13, 10). How? By loving God with all his heart, with all his strength, and his neighbour as himself. Such is the sanctity which the Church crowns with a halo. Extraordinary signs, intuitions, visions, prophecies, miracles do not constitute it by themselves. Sanctity is love—supernatural charity, the life and core of all the other virtues. A Superior General of Saint-Gildard affirmed of Bernadette: 'I think I ought to say that the Lourdes Apparitions would not alone justify her reputation for sanctity.'

Yet one must not look for absolute perfection, for a constant and uniformly high level of virtue, either in Bernadette or in any other one of the children of men who has been raised to the honours of the altar. The fact is that grace is grafted on to nature, and a human soul, being no more impeccable than it is impassible, can attain only human perfection and not that of an angel. As Bishop Lelong of Nevers declared, 'Sister Marie-Bernard had remained a daughter of Eve even after she had become so especially the daughter of Mary. Like every other creature she had to pay her tribute to human frailty. God had left her with her imperfections and her weaknesses, as he had formerly done with St Paul, that they might preserve her from any temptation to pride.'

The eminent virtue of Sister Marie-Bernard, veiled by humility and thirsting for obscurity, was to pass completely unnoticed before the eyes of those who were too prejudiced or too blind to see. But sanctity is not assessed according to the amount of affection or opposition that it evokes; it is measured by its degree of love. That is why we see her exalted above all her companions.

Before the solemn verdict of the Church was pronounced, there were some discordant voices, and it is only fair to give them a hearing. Yet it should be noted that certain objections were only apparent, and were transformed in the course of time into definite approbation. Such was the case with the redoubtable Mother Marie-Thérèse Vauzou. One of the Garaison missionaries, Father Burosse, who had just been appointed chaplain to the Orphanage of the Sisters of Nevers in Lourdes, gives this account of a conversation which he had with her:

> The first time that I was introduced to Reverend Mother Vauzou I turned the conversation on to Bernadette. Straightway she said to me: 'Ah, Father, don't imagine that Bernadette was so extraordinary as all that.'
> 'Was Bernadette pious?' I added.
> 'Oh, very pious.'
> 'Was she obedient?'
> 'Oh, yes.'
> 'But was she humble?'
> 'Yes, very humble. She never of her own accord spoke about the Apparitions.'
> 'In that case, Mother, what more do you want? She was an excellent nun.'

As Sister Lucie Cloris testified, Mother Vauzou seems to have 'altered her way of thinking' in the later months of her life. Among some notes 'that are, so to say, her last will and testament' there occur these words which were inscribed later on her mortuary card: 'Let us not forget how much Mary loves our Congregation, since She gave us her privileged child.'

In any case, whatever may have been the final opinion of Mother Marie-Thérèse regarding her former novice, many of the nuns at Saint-Gildard besides her did not at first appreciate Sister Marie-Bernard at her true value. For that they required maturity of age and a more accurate understanding of the events.

A nun from the Bourbonnais, who had become a postulant in 1875 in the freshness of her sixteen years, stated frankly to Canon

Guynot after more than fifty years of religious life:

> Well, I'll tell you honestly that I was not enthusiastic over Berna-
> dette. When I consider that it is that little dark girl who is being
> elevated to such heights to-day . . . !
>   It is very true that I was not able at that time to discern in her
> all the holiness that is being extolled to-day. I was too young.
> But since then, after much reflection and with the knowledge I
> have acquired of life and the human heart, I can perceive more
> clearly what escaped me in large measure at the time.
>   I must admit that I still feel a sort of shock when I see her now
> so great after having known her so small and so insignificant. But
> I realize that it is right, and that this greatness was truly hidden
> within her littleness.

But her own companions admired her virtues. 'I always
regarded Sister Marie-Bernard as a little saint. I used to want
to keep as close to her as possible; I used to feel better from
contact with her: her religious modesty, her obedience put me to
shame.' And Sister Garnier added: 'I regard Sister Marie-
Bernard as a saint in whom God had left some imperfections
only to keep her more humble.' 'My feeling towards Sister
Marie-Bernard was one of veneration,' said Sister Caldairou. And
the humble Mother Elisabeth Blanc: 'It was impossible to imitate her. I tried several times, and did my level best, but I never
managed it.' Lastly—for we must make a choice among these
bouquets—Sister Chautard testified: 'I never saw her do anything, or heard her say anything, but what was right and good.
And so I love her, I pray to her, and I look on her as a saint.'

But what exactly did Bernadette think about herself? She
expressed her view on many occasions, and more particularly
on one day in September 1874 or 1875, during the general Retreat.
Mother Philomène Roques describes the incident:

> There were several of us in the infirmary, and as the Saint was
> leaving us in the evening she said: 'Pray for me, children, I'm
> going off to confession.' We had such a high opinion of her
> virtue that we all answered together: 'You! You have no sins!'
>   These words upset her, and she replied: 'Oh, don't tell me
> that!' Then, raising her arms and joining her hands, she said:
> 'I have such a lot of sins!' This was said with a humble expres-
> sion which one felt was genuine and sincere. She added: 'But
> who is without sin?'

'A lot of sins!' She would have found it hard to say what they were. She could, in fact, have classed under this ugly word nothing but involuntary imperfections. Only once did she reveal herself clearly on this subject; this was an admission that she let slip and which is explained by the circumstances. It was towards the end of October 1876. M. Febvre, who had succeeded Father Douce in the chaplaincy at Saint-Gildard, had just been preaching on sin. Sister Marie-Bernard was on her way back to the infirmary on the arm of the infirmarian, Sister Casimir Callery. A fortnight previously, Sister Casimir had played the part of a seraph in a comedy which had been staged to celebrate Mother Vauzou's feast. 'O *Seraph*,' Bernadette suddenly exclaimed, 'how happy I am!'

'Why, what's the matter?' asked the other in astonishment.

'Didn't you hear the sermon?'

'Oh, yes.'

'Well, the Chaplain said that if you don't intend to commit a sin, there is no sin at all.'

'Yes, I heard that. What about it?'

'Well, I've never wished to commit a sin, so I've never committed any.'

'She was beaming with joy,' relates Sister Casimir, 'and seemed to be in a rapture of gratitude. I could not help saying to her: "You are very lucky. That is more than I can say."'

In spite of this, Sister Marie-Bernard was free from all presumption. One day an assistant mistress of novices said of her, without perhaps realizing how sound a theologian she was: 'But because she has seen the Blessed Virgin she is not confirmed in grace.' The humble visionary was well aware of that herself. 'Why are you crying?' asked a companion who found her all in tears. 'I have received so many graces,' she replied, 'that I'm afraid of not responding to them.' This was an admission she had already made at the Lourdes Hospice when Father Vigne remarked to her: 'Since the Lady has promised to make you happy in the next world, you have nothing more to worry about and you can rely peacefully on this promise.' 'Oh, Father,' she replied, 'not so fast! I shall be happy, yes; but be careful! Only if I do my duty and keep on the straight road.'

One day, however, at the end of her retreat in 1873, she wrote in an impulse of complete confidence: 'I must become a great Saint. My Jesus wants it.'

＊　　＊　　＊

To attain as full a knowledge of her as possible, let us first of all consider the human side of St Bernadette. Here there cannot be any real surprises, for we have already seen her in her childhood days, gentle and sedate, yet impulsive; one moment effusive, then reserved, almost impenetrable, with her heart tightly closed on its secrets; merry in the midst of her school friends, then downcast by the trials of her family or the opposition to her message. . . . Shall we find her very much different as a nun?

But first let us take another look at her at the age of thirty, as she was described in detail by various contemporaries:

> She was small and dainty, with small hands. . . . She was charming without a doubt, and even pretty. . . . She seemed to me quite young. I can still see her dark and lively eyes with their slightly mischievous look. . . . You were immediately struck by the brilliance of her eyes; once you had seen them, you could never forget them . . . but you were attracted above all by their depth, which was truly extraordinary. You had the impression that their gaze hardly rested on this earth but was mysteriously fixed on something afar off, on something enthralling that kept escaping her, and this gave her eyes and her pretty smile a touch of melancholy that still more enhanced her charm. Her smile was restrained, but you were not conscious of any effort at repression; and the same was true of everything else about her. . . . Even though she lacked education and fine manners—I would almost venture to say, the breeding of high society—she was not by any means the vulgar little peasant girl one might suppose.

This did not prevent her remaining to the very end a Pyrenean. When she was only a girl of sixteen a Lourdes priest was told by some visitors that 'she returned rather sharp answers to people who sought to make her contradict herself; yet her liveliness of voice and expression never turned to harshness or bitterness. . . . This turn of mind is fairly characteristic of the people of that region.'

Seven or eight years later, during the period of formation in the noviceship, her temperament was fundamentally the same, though its abrupt manifestations were less frequent and less marked. 'On watching her more closely,' observes Mother Henri Fabre, 'one could detect in Sister Marie-Bernard, when a novice, a touch of hastiness, a too-ready repartee, which, however, was never offensive, and some passing fits of bad humour or impatience.'

After profession, the slight flashes of temper died away. Even though, as was noted by the kind-hearted Mother Eléonore Cassagnes, she sometimes had her 'moods', the word as used by Mother Eléonore signified nothing more than 'a little vehemence in a remark or an explanation'. Similarly, when she attributes 'caprices' to her, she merely means 'little rebellious airs which in no way impaired her respect or submission'.

Again she was reproached with being 'very tenacious of her own opinions'. She herself admitted it readily, but judging from her own statements it may be conjectured that her obstinacy had nothing to do with subversive views: 'I have been headstrong all my life,' she confessed good-humouredly. 'Even at the grotto I had to be told twice by the Blessed Virgin to drink the muddy water. But she punished me well by making me ask her three times for her name.'

So, then, Sister Marie-Bernard 'was not without her faults', and she made no attempt to 'disguise these imperfections inherent in human nature'.

Mention is also made of some harmless jokes of hers, some merry sallies of innocent mischief; but this is not a case of 'imperfections', but rather of genuine acts of sisterly charity. Sister Marie-Bernard's 'little fits of roguishness', and certain remarks that were 'seasoned with the garlic of the south' raised the spirits and gladdened the hearts of those around her.

When Julie Garros arrived at Saint-Gildard as a postulant she had the great comfort of rejoining her old classmate of Lourdes. And she was a little imp, this young Garros girl! Five years younger than Bernadette, she had had to be placed next to the latter in order to have a little sense put into her. 'It appears,' she admits, 'that the mistress was unable to cope with me, I was so unruly.' One day in mischievous mood she had even set fire to her well-behaved neighbour's distaff. Now as Sister Marie-

Bernard put her arms round her and welcomed her to the convent, she said: 'So here you are, you scamp! You've given in at last!' And Julie recovered her smile.

There was another touching incident. A trunk had arrived the day before (together with a sweet young girl of sixteen) and had been deposited in the linen-room. When the girl came up to the linen-room on the following day, the sight of her trunk reminded her of Mamma and her family and home and birthplace. . . . And she cried and cried, her elbows on a table and her head in her hands. Then someone came quietly up to her and said in a soft playful voice: 'Oh, mademoiselle! What a solid vocation! It's going to grow well, this one . . . for I see you are watering it thoroughly. That's right, dear. Water it!' As the postulant was later to say when she had become Mother Julienne Capmartin, 'These simple words had more effect on me than a sermon. I could not help laughing. I was laughing and crying at the same time. But the tears stopped almost immediately and did not return, whilst the smile remained. . . . I even laughed so much afterwards that our Mistress told me several times: "You'll have to do some Purgatory later on, my dear; you're not serious enough."'

During recreation Sister Chantal Guinet, who had become deeply attached to Bernadette, saw her take out . . . a snuffbox (for she had started to take snuff again on the doctor's orders). 'Sister Marie-Bernard,' said Sister Chantal teasingly, 'you won't be canonized.' 'Why?' 'Because you take snuff. St Vincent de Paul very nearly missed it on account of his snuffbox.' 'But you, Sister Chantal, you don't take snuff, so you will no doubt be canonized?'

'At the Mother House,' said Sister Vincent Garros, 'she never to my knowledge failed in charity.' And who would not agree with this opinion, even on seeing Sister Marie-Bernard at recreation exploiting her talent for mimicry, which, to judge by results, must have been above the ordinary. But on this subject we must hear Mother Elizabeth Meyrignac, who was Superior of the convent in Tonbridge, Kent, England:

She used to join us (the novices) at recreation and make herself at home with her charming simplicity and tell us amusing stories that made us laugh uproariously—as one does laugh at that age.

What happy times I owe to her! What a fund of good humour she brought us . . . !

The stories usually concerned little incidents in the infirmary in which Dr Robert Saint-Cyr sometimes figured. That excellent man had some little whims and mannerisms which we all knew, and Bernadette used to entertain us with imitations of him which made us laugh so much that tears came into our eyes. Her mimicry was brilliant, full of delicate touches of wit and sometimes of sly roguishness. But I must say that there was never anything unkind. It was good genial fun that used to leave us under the charm of her saintliness. . . .

However, Mother Elizabeth did not wish to leave the reader with a picture of Bernadette as a mere entertainer, so she hastened to add:

When recreation was ended, the dear Sister got up, bowed to us graciously and immediately resumed her grave demeanour, to bring home to us that we young novices had also to return to the silence that was our rule.

Such an instantaneous return to silence at the first sound of the bell, after a bout of merriment, demonstrates that in spite of her youthful appearance and girlish frolics Sister Marie-Bernard had a strong will and prompt control of her feelings. A sudden emotion, it is true, might overtake her by surprise, but she could curb it. One day during recreation she was strolling with Sister Dalias in the meadow (which has now disappeared) where there were some tall poplar trees. 'Oh, those poplars,' she sighed, 'every time I see them I feel a quiver. They take me back to Lourdes.' Then the conversation was immediately turned on to some other topic.

Assuredly she had all the tender feelings of a woman. Affectionate, compassionate, 'religiously loyal in friendship . . . with an exquisite gratefulness when one had done her some favour', 'she was deeply affected by the smallest attentions paid to her'. She loved flowers: Mother Julienne Capmartin always remembered her bending over a flower-bed alongside the greenhouses at Saint-Gildard and 'tenderly handling a simple daisy as though she wished to bestow a friendly caress on this tiny creature of God'.

But one must not deduce from this poetic gesture that she was a dreamer or a sentimentalist.  Indeed, though 'she was feminine in her prodigious power of feeling, suffering and loving', she was manly in her sureness and maturity of judgment. The 'perfect common sense which was her outstanding characteristic' is to be found not only in the homely incidents of everyday life, but especially in her letters, in her autograph accounts of the Apparitions and in her Retreat notes. . . . In these she displays scarcely any imagination, nor does she linger over explanations or details.  With her practical mind she goes straight to the point, whether it is a question of satisfying a legitimate curiosity, of uplifting a wavering or afflicted soul, or of putting someone else back on the road again.  With her well-balanced mind she had a liking for order and moderation.  She can be recognized by this mark, and at times by a strong but controlled depth of feeling.

# 27

## MYSTICAL PURIFICATION

THERE is no state of life in which one cannot love God with all one's heart, and there are therefore in this world a thousand paths to sanctity. Nevertheless there remains but one method, the one taught by St Paul to the early Christians in Corinth: 'It is by the grace of God I am what I am; and His grace hath not been void in me, but I have laboured more abundantly than all they: yet not I, but the grace of God with me' (1 Cor. 15, 10). A humble but proud assertion, on which St Augustine makes this comment: 'Neither the grace of God alone, nor himself alone, but the grace of God together with him.'

Like St Paul, Bernadette was conscious of God's lavishness. We have recorded her tearful avowal: 'I have received so many graces!' That is, so many gratuitous blessings that she trembled at the thought of not responding to them adequately: the choice of so insignificant an individual as herself for visions and ineffable secrets; those inspirations and that supernatural strength which enabled her, despite her weakness and ignorance, to deliver 'to the priests' and then to the world the various messages of the Immaculate Virgin; and lastly her religious vocation, together with her precious spiritual dowry. No, she would not forget nor be ungrateful. Confident that her adorable Benefactor would provide her with the means, she would repay Almighty God by becoming—the sole ambition permitted to her—a Saint.

No doubt so sublime an aspiration had taken time to mature. But then came the decisive hour: the Retreat in September, 1874, which concluded with a kind of 'election' after the manner of the *Exercises* of St Ignatius. We read in her private notebook:

Abandonment as regards the past, and trust for the future. . . .
'I am the Way, the Truth, and the Life. But to follow Me it is

necessary to renounce oneself, take up one's cross and carry it to the very end.'

My Divine Master, my choice is made . . . I have examined the broad road. I have weighed the value of the perishable riches of earth, and measured the duration of its fleeting pleasures. . . . Thanks to Thy divine light I have seen through them all, and averting my lips from the poisoned cup I have cried out with the Wise Man: 'Vanity of vanities, all is vanity on earth save loving God and serving Him alone.'

Then I raised my eyes and all I saw now was Jesus alone. . . . My Jesus, be Thou alone henceforth my life, my all. I will follow Thee wherever Thou goest. . . . Obedience, even blind obedience; poverty in evangelical privation, mortification even to crucifixion, humility even to annihilation. . . .

That such intense words as these were inspired by the preacher's exhortations is probable enough; but even so they express the straining of her whole soul towards heroism. Among her Retreat notes she had written: 'No middle course; crush nature in order to save my soul.' What did she mean by 'nature'? For her it included every imperfection, even though involuntary, which she wished to correct in herself.

During this period of prayer in 1874, she had made with the guidance of her confessor a thorough review of her soul. While leaving her in peace as to all the rest, what particular tendency did Father Douce single out for correction? Sister Marie-Bernard indicates this clearly: after eight years of religious life it was still 'touchiness'. Would she be able to cure herself completely of this?

But would it be more accurate to say that this derogatory word 'touchiness' had been suggested to her, and even thrust upon her, by Mother Vauzou, who must certainly have used it sometimes in her presence to indicate what was in the case of Sister Marie-Bernard merely an acute sensitiveness? We may recall Mother Bordenave's remark that Sister Marie-Bernard's sensitiveness had grown very acute and manifested itself in a word or gesture at the most painful moment of some physical or mental suffering. But one must not lose sight of the fact that at this period of her life Sister Marie-Bernard, though not completely bedridden, was never free from pain. One should also bear in mind that Mother Vauzou, who acted as Superior

General from time to time, had in no way relaxed in her coldness towards her; and, as will presently be seen, this was not
Sister Marie-Bernard's only interior trial.

However that may be, the confessor considered that 'touchiness' should be the regular subject for her particular examination of conscience, as is shown by a special little note-book,
which, however, was scarcely used from September to December.
During the course of the year 1874, she had already copied out a
subject for particular examination, 'evenness of temper'. The
passage opens with a prayer:

> In troubles and afflictions from without as well as from within, grant
> me the grace, my God, to pluck out the evil root of 'touchiness'.

It was the 'generous love of Our Lord', as she said later, that
was to cut at this root. But why did she have such difficulty
in submitting to the discipline of the small *examen* note-
book? She had every intention of remaining faithful to the
particular examination of conscience as a practice laid down by
rule. But she experienced an almost insuperable difficulty in
dwelling constantly on an imperfection. Her spiritual life was
not complicated. Concentrating on the 'generous love of Our
Lord', she preferred henceforward to examine herself each day
on the care, fervour and courage she had put into this love.

She never lost heart along this road, 'gaining patience', as
St Francis de Sales says, 'from the thought that she possessed
the nature of a human being and not that of an angel . . . and
drawing profit not only from her tribulations, but also from her
imperfections' so as 'to establish and ground herself on a
courageous humility'. On the least show of temper she would
immediately, whether during recreation or in the infirmary,
'ask pardon, sometimes on her knees and with her arms outstretched in the form of a cross, for these impulses of nature'.
Thus Sister Marie-Bernard made this treacherous nature serve
her progress in grace.

\*     \*     \*

Even before this transforming Retreat of 1874 a mysterious
purification had begun in her soul. This was a hidden agony

quite different from her usual trials, one of those springs of
anguish such as well up only in souls predestined by God to
sanctity. Could the visionary of Massabielle, over whom the
most perfect of creatures never ceased to watch, be deprived
of this extraordinary grace?

A soul that God wished specially to sanctify might possibly
fall even from the heights, if with a sort of spiritual gluttony it
were to seek gratification and consolations in the virtues it prac-
tises, and even in its self-imposed sacrifices. That is the human
way, and God resolved that this human element should die. To
effect this He was going to plunge the soul into the mystical
purgatory which St John of the Cross calls the 'night of the
soul'. In this the soul sounds the depths of its own nothingness
and, finding itself so poor and so worthless, deems itself deserv-
ing of abandonment. Previously she had found comfort in the
advice of a confessor or in the pages of a book; now in the darkness these gave her but a semblance of consolation. What could
she do but resign herself blindly to the will of her Father in
Heaven? It was to this point that God planned to lead her.
Beyond that there was no longer any barrier between Him and
her.

It was only by stages that Bernadette reached this peak. We
have not yet come to the time when one of her former companions, who lived with her towards the end of her life, gave an
unreservedly enthusiastic appreciation of her. 'Tell me,' Canon
Guynot asked this venerable nun, 'how should I picture Bernadette to myself at Saint-Gildard? I want to see her just as you
saw her and as you see her still.' After some reflection the nun
replied: 'You are asking me a difficult question. You want me
to describe perfection itself, for that is what Bernadette was:
perfection become a Sister of Nevers.'

The sanctifying ordeal began to weigh heavy on her soul
during the course of 1872, to judge from her correspondence.
Usually cheerful in her letters, she now slipped in some vague
allusions to a secret suffering. In one of her notes to Mother
Alexandrine Roques, Superior of the Lourdes Hospice, dated
April 3rd, 1872, after some good-natured joking a great sadness
comes over her at the thought of sinners, and then she reverts to
her own misery: 'Forget my body; it is all right; but pray hard
for my soul.' Similarly in other letters written about this time

she tells her correspondents not to worry over her health, but to beg in their prayers for her the 'love of Our Lord', giving us a glimpse of the cause of her anguish, namely, the 'insufficiency of her love'.

On March 30th, 1875, she wrote to the friend of her childhood, Jeanne Védère, who had become a Cistercian nun in 1867:

> My dearest cousin, ask Our Lord to be so kind as to give me a tiny spark of His love. If only you knew how much I need it! I entreat you, promise me to say every day a little prayer that I may become a holy and fervent nun—even just a little aspiration. I can count on your charity, can't I?

For most of her Sisters in the convent there was no indication of the deep suffering she was undergoing. It was indeed, as she wrote in her private note-book, 'a cross concealed in her heart'. Externally she remained calm and serene. Sister Vidal wrote after a visit to the Mother House:

> I wish I had the time to talk to you about this angelic Sister (Marie-Bernard). If you only knew how kind she is! What impresses me is her sweet simplicity and serenity, and also her gaiety which in times of recreation turns into real roguishness. You can see that she enjoys the sweetest happiness. How lovable the saints are, and how good it will be up there in Heaven in such good company!

Among her closest associates, however, there were some who had their suspicions. About the time when Sister Vidal was writing such optimistic lines, Bernadette made this admission to Sister Vincent Garros in between two attacks of asthma: 'It's very painful not to be able to breathe, but it's far more distressing to be tortured by interior sufferings. It's terrible!'

At times it would seem that a veil was cast over her fondest memories of Massabielle. Although she had received from the Queen of Heaven an assurance of eternal bliss, the thought of the Judgment made her tremble. 'I don't understand your fears,' replied Sister Marthe du Rais, to whom she had confided this, 'you are sure of your salvation.' 'Not so sure as all that!' retorted Bernadette, without further explanation.

In 1872 or 1873 she had jotted down on a loose sheet of paper
a kind of poem, seemingly her own, in which she expressed the
yearnings of her heart:

> Have pity on your little servant,
> who despite all would like to become one of your greatest lovers.
> In following you alone
> I will make my happiness consist;
> in living with you alone, alone and forgotten,
> that so I may be able to love you all the more.

To love Our Lord as much as a Catherine of Siena, a Teresa
of Avila, a Margaret Mary—this seemed to be her ardent desire.
But in the course of her ordeal she felt herself far away from her
Beloved, and she could only bemoan her scanty love.  It was
truly for her the 'dark night of the soul' through which nevertheless there broke one gleam of comfort: the conviction that
she was suffering as a victim for sinners and that thus her
Massabielle mission was being continued. Abbé Febvre gathered
'a most distinct impression that Sister Marie-Bernard was given
the mission of living in the Mother House the lessons that came
from the lips of Mary Immaculate in Lourdes: to do penance,
to pray, to mortify herself and to suffer for sinners'.

In the privacy of the confessional Father Douce, Abbé Febvre
and other priests heard her sorrowful confidences on this subject;
they carried the secret with them to the grave.  But her private
note-book has preserved unmistakable echoes of it.  In these
simple pages, it is true, Sister Marie-Bernard has not described
her interior torment in detail; and probably she has drawn
sometimes on her own reading, or perhaps her directors, who
were sympathetic witnesses of her struggle, communicated to her
the writings of souls who were tried like herself.  These borrow-
ings are distinguishable in spelling and style from Sister Marie-
Bernard's own composition.  Let us take a glance at the precious
notes.

Sorely tried by sadness and discouragement, Bernadette sought
help from Our Lord in His Agony.

> O my most sweet Jesus, the longings of my heart mount up to
> you! . . .
>     O Jesus, desolate and also the refuge of the desolate, your love

teaches me that it is from your dereliction that I must draw all the strength I need to endure mine. . . .

I do not beg you, my God, not to afflict me, but that you abandon me not in my affliction. I beseech you to teach me to seek you as my sole comfort, to sustain my faith, fortify my hope and purify my love. Grant me the grace to recognize there your hand and to wish for no other comforter but you. . . .

And you Saints in Heaven who have passed through this ordeal, have compassion on those who are enduring it, and obtain for me the grace to be faithful unto death.

In the presence of Sister Marthe du Rais, the discreet and sympathetic infirmarian, she happened to show some signs of faltering: 'I have seen her sometimes crushed; she would say to me: "I'm disheartened."' No doubt it was during one of these cruel phases that she copied out in her note-book a 'poor beggar's prayer to Jesus':

O Jesus, give me, I entreat you,
the bread of strength to break my will and blend it with yours;
the bread of interior mortification,
the bread of detachment from creatures,
the bread of patience to endure the pangs my heart suffers.
O Jesus, you want me crucified, *fiat*!

She had just written:

The just man is a victim and his life a continual sacrifice. Out of love for Jesus I will do violence to myself in the very smallest matters. . . .

O most compassionate Heart of my Jesus, accept each of my tears, each cry of pain from me as a supplication for all those who suffer, for all those who weep, for all those who forget you.

My Jesus, I am in pain, and I love you. . . . I suffer, and my groans go up unceasingly to you, my Comforter. Into your most adorable Heart I shed my tears, to It I confide my sighs and my anguish; to Its bitter sorrows I confide my bitter sorrows. Sanctify them, my Jesus, by this holy union.

In these hours of distress she summoned to her aid again her beloved Virgin of Lourdes. To her she addressed her entreaties, pouring into them all the agitation of her downcast heart.

O Mary, O Mother of Sorrows! At the foot of the Cross, you received the title of our Mother. I am the child of your sorrows, the child of Calvary.

O Mary, my tender Mother, behold your child who can go no further. Have pity on me. Make me be with you in Heaven one day!

You who have seen and felt the utter desolation of your dear Son, assist me in the hour of mine. In your heart I come to lay the anguish of my heart and to draw strength and courage.

Let me stay like you at the foot of the Cross, if so be the pleasure of your Divine Son! Let me begin here below, my soul united to yours, to glorify Our Lord by this perpetual homage of perfect submission.

'I am suffering . . .' she admits to herself. And yet her face wore a serene smile far more often than a sorrowful expression. How could such peace and genuine joy exist in a soul so deeply harrowed by grace? St Teresa seeks to explain it. She writes that the pains that result from this 'harrowing', in what she calls 'the perfect soul', 'affect only its senses and its powers'. But it still remains a mystery, and those saintly souls who suffer and at the same time are happy, are indeed a puzzle.

Normally, according to spiritual writers, the purifying night of the soul ought to lead into the 'transforming union, a calm and lasting union (with God) which seems to be the final stage of the mystical union, the immediate preparation for the beatific vision.' Then comes complete childlike surrender of the soul to the Divine Will. Without becoming impeccable it acts solely from love. We shall see Bernadette attain this summit. But fresh rays, hitherto unknown to her soul, were surely piercing her 'dark night' at the time when she committed these glowing lines to one of the last pages in her note-book:

Jesus asks for detachment from every possession, every human honour, every creature: humility. But the lovableness of Jesus, the love of Jesus renders this detachment less difficult and less cruel to nature.

Nothing is mine, I no longer have anything but Jesus. No place, nothing, no person, no thought, no feelings, no honours, no suffering can turn me away from Jesus. He is for me honour, delight, heart and soul. He whom I love is fatherland, Heaven already! My treasure! My love! Jesus, and Jesus crucified alone makes my happiness . . . !

Intimate union with Jesus, heart to heart with Jesus, like St John in purity and in love.

To make such a self-comparison with complete frankness and in such language, Sister Marie-Bernard must have reached an heroic degree of charity and the other virtues. And surely it was heroic that, during the last years of her life and in arduous circumstances, she displayed, with the help of God's grace, an energy beyond her natural strength, and not in any transitory fashion but whenever the opportunity arose.

# 28

## HUMILITY, PURITY, OBEDIENCE

AMONG the nuns at Saint-Gildard we have already singled
out the friendly figure of Sister Vincent Garros. She was
the one among Bernadette's companions who lived longest
with her and, no doubt, as a compatriot—in accordance with
the saying that 'no man is a prophet in his own country'—she
was not likely to judge her too easily. Speaking under oath, she
left this incomparable testimony: 'Sister Marie-Bernard was
for all the Sisters a model of all the virtues.' On the lips of this
witness it meant that purity and humility, kindness, gentleness
and patience, sincerity and obedience to superiors—natural
virtues which even in good people are too frequently very imperfect—were transformed by Bernadette, through grace from on
high, into supernatural virtues impregnated with the love of
God, and that she became their living embodiment.

Without doubt the 'most pure Virgin' had chosen well.

What inclined Bishop Laurence to believe in Bernadette, even
at his first interview with her, was 'the simplicity, the candour,
the modesty of this child'. Seventeen years later Bishop Lelong
of Nevers, not being so bound by discretion, was able to express
his thoughts fully in the presence of Sister Marie-Bernard's dead
body. He began his panegyric by extolling the purity which
shone in her 'like a flawless diamond' and 'which was so perfectly reflected in her calm deep gaze'. And such a grave
theologian as the Very Reverend Father Raffin paid her this
tribute of admiration:

> What immediately impressed you on seeing her was an air
> of candour, innocence, modesty and reserve that completely
> enveloped her and radiated from her through her eyes, her atti-
> tude and her bearing. It was the common opinion that she had
> kept her baptismal innocence, had remained entirely free of any
> fault contrary to the evangelical virtue of chastity, and had

retained in all its loveliness, freshness and fragrance the lily of virginity.

Birds of a feather flock together, and one might guess that Sister Marie-Bernard would have a special love for little children; and they in turn were especially attracted to her. At Easter time in Nevers the head-mistresses of the infant schools used to ask the Superior General to bring them Bernadette as a special favour. Sitting in her invalid chair the visionary of Lourdes used to decorate Easter eggs for their little boys and girls, and it was her great delight to come and distribute them.

One noticed [remarked Father Raffin on this occasion] the more than usual eagerness of the children to meet her, the great joy they took in gathering around her and gazing on her, and how reluctant they were to leave her.

It seemed as though there emanated from Sister Marie-Bernard a sincere simplicity, innocence and purity that captivated these little children, themselves also pure, simple and sincere.

\* \* \*

By virtue as well as by inclination Sister Marie-Bernard was a humble soul, and so her heart was well guarded. She was in virtue as in vocation a most worthy daughter of the founder who inserted in his *Directoire* this golden maxim: 'A novice who is not resolved to remain all her life in the lowest rank, is not making a good start in her religious life.' Bernadette—as so many incidents and words of hers have already shown us—had always looked on herself as the very least and lowest of all. 'All her life she had an aversion to putting herself forward,' said Mother Bordenave. 'Only now do I realize how wonderful her humility was,' a venerable nun admitted forty years after the death of the Saint. 'I was taught that humility is the "silence of the Ego". With Bernadette it was exactly that. For her there was no "I" . . . no thought for herself. . . . I was edified by that, of course, but I did not see, as I do now, that it was the effect of very high virtue.' 'I believe,' suggests Sister Marcillac, unable to find any human explanation for this marvel of self-effacement, 'that she was inspired with this humility by the Blessed Virgin herself at the time of the Apparitions.'

The Superior of the Cahors Orphanage, on a visit to the Mother House, asked her one day whether she had not experienced some feeling of complacency in consequence of such exceptional favours. Sister Marie-Bernard gave her almost word for word the well-known reply of the Curé d'Ars (though she was probably not aware of it): 'What do you take me for? Don't I know that the Blessed Virgin chose me because I was the most ignorant? If she had found anyone else more ignorant than me, she would have chosen her.'

What indeed always amazed her was that the Blessed Virgin had fixed her choice on herself, a poor and sickly child. She would have been willing to disappear entirely in the light of Massabielle. 'She never gave the appearance,' a bishop remarked, 'of suspecting that she was in any way extraordinary.' And so she maintained a profound silence regarding everything that might have made her conspicuous. In 1874 she entered this resolution in her Retreat note-book:

> Chief grace to ask for: to live more and more hidden, after the example of Jesus and Mary.

One day two postulants who had arrived from Lourdes were showing her some photographs of the grotto, secretly hoping, no doubt, to hear her speak of the Apparitions. Gazing on these pictures that spoke volumes to her heart, she merely remarked quite impersonally: 'Oh, how the poplars have grown!' Then she went away.

Nor did she fall into the trap on a certain Sunday in 1876 when again a photograph of the grotto was shown her by Sister Molinéry, who watched her face closely to see the effect.

'What do you do with a broom?' asked Bernadette abruptly.

'Well, that's a fine question! You use it for sweeping.'

'And afterwards?'

'You put it back in its place behind the door.'

'And that's my history. The Blessed Virgin used me and then put me back in my place. I'm glad of it, and there I stay.'

Certain new arrivals among the postulants recognized her at

the first meeting. On the other hand one of them, unobservant, no doubt, and shy, took a month to identify her, such was Sister Marie-Bernard's skill in passing unnoticed among the rest. The future Sister Bernard Dalias, however, did not take so long. As she related, 'she felt, like everyone else, a keen desire to make the acquaintance of Our Lady's confidante'. But she had imagined a Bernadette 'with something solemn about her, a serious look, sedate movements, dignified speech and a stature appropriate to great deeds'. For three days she sought among the various groups for the Bernadette of her fancy. . . . Meanwhile, a 'thin and very youthful' nun particularly attracted her interest. But no, it could not be that one! At length Mlle Dalias found the courage to go and ask Mother Berganot, who was standing at that moment in the noviciate cloister with this charming little Sister. 'Mother, it's very strange, but I have been here three days now and I have not been able yet to discover Bernadette. I'm quite annoyed about it.'

'But here's Bernadette.'

'I was so flabbergasted,' continued Sister Dalias, 'that before I had time to stop it, out shot the unhappy word: "What, that!"'

With her sweetest smile, Sister Marie-Bernard took her young companion's hand, saying merrily: 'Yes, mademoiselle, only that.' With a compliment of this sort the newcomer had won her heart: the contemptuous syllable 'that' summed up so well what Bernadette thought of herself!

'She had asked the favour of being excused from going to the parlour. She only went there under obedience, and her reluctance was even stronger when it was a case of meeting important people.' As she confided one day to Sister Caldairou on her way to the parlour, 'If you only knew what it costs me, especially when they are bishops!' She never had the presumption to imagine that Princes of the Church would come to the Mother House for the sole purpose of seeing her.

However, the Bishop of Nevers was always on the alert. 'Noticing one day,' he relates, 'that a very eminent prelate had fallen as it were into ecstasy before her, I was afraid she would notice it too, and I said to her abruptly and in a curt tone: "What are you waiting for? You've been seen. That's enough; you're not wanted any longer." She retired at once without saying a word, without showing any annoyance; she even smiled at me.'

She used to write about once a year to the chief members of her family. 'She wrote little, out of humility,' observed Canon Perreau, 'and begged that her letters should not be made public.' When her brother Jean-Marie asked her in the name of all the family why she appeared to forget them, she replied (October 7th, 1878):

This is the reason why I write to you so seldom: I was told that my letters were being passed on everywhere. I was vexed at that, and if it happens again I shall not write any more to anyone.

\*    \*    \*

So, profoundly detached from all self-love, she was able to practise great obedience. Not only 'did she display no discontent' when an order was irksome to her, but 'she leapt to obey the least command'. Such is the evidence of Mother Forestier, who adds, as the authorized spokesman for Saint-Gildard: 'We all admired her love for our holy Rules.' She complied with them in the smallest details. One of her companions, who was trying to get a souvenir of her, gave her a picture and a pencil and asked her to write a few words or her name on the picture. 'Oh, I haven't permission,' she said. . . . 'But wait a moment. . . .' Then she took the picture and made a cross on it with her finger-nail.

By her vow of obedience she was obliged to consent to the hardest sacrifice of all: to keep silent about her visions—she who was Our Lady's messenger! Mother Bordenave declared:

To my mind her obedience stands out most clearly in the way she submitted to the order never to speak about the events in Lourdes. But her mind must have been full of them, and her companions would certainly have been eager to hear her speak of the Apparitions; yet she always kept silence on this matter.

It is true that in order not to arouse her regrets—a certain superior would have said her self-love—they avoided speaking about Lourdes in her presence. One day, after she had been professed, a book was being read in the noviciate on the events of Massabielle. The door opened and there stood Sister Marie-Bernard. 'Imagine our feelings,' says Sister Capmartin. 'We were being told of the wonders of Lourdes, and suddenly there before our eyes stood the very instrument of Providence, the chosen witness, the one who had first narrated these glorious events. . . . Dear little thing! Did she have any idea that we were all thinking of her at that moment, that the book was speaking about her or rather that it was she herself who was speaking to us through the book?' Instinctively, or 'on a sign from our Mistress' the reader stopped. Sister Marie-Bernard, who had come to ask a permission for one of the sick, never wondered why everyone went silent as soon as she entered.

Although her companions had been forbidden to ask her about the actual visions, certain questions did not fall entirely under the ban. 'Whereabouts were you when Our Lady appeared to you?' one of them enquired, showing her a photograph of the grotto. With the tip of her forefinger Sister Marie-Bernard pointed to the spot where she used to kneel. 'It must be a very sweet memory for you, Sister.' With a grave and almost sad expression, she replied: 'Oh, yes! But I had no right to that favour.'

'I go there every day in spirit,' she confided, 'and make my little pilgrimage.' But in fact she ended by making a sacrifice even of the desire to return. 'My mission at Lourdes is finished; what would I go there for?' she said to Mother Lassale. She had now 'one only ambition: to see the Blessed Virgin glorified and loved.' When Bishop de Ladoue was setting out on a pilgrimage to Lourdes he asked her if she also would like to go there, but she replied: 'I have made the sacrifice of Lourdes. I shall see Our Lady in Heaven; that will be far finer.'

# 29

## CHARITY, TRUTH AND DETACHMENT

WE have already heard Bernadette in a time of trial confiding to Sister Ducout: 'We must always see God in our superiors; I submit, come what may.' That meant, no matter how hard it might be. It was therefore in a spirit of faith that she accepted the sacrifices, at times excruciating, that were demanded by her vow. An obedience that was merely external or self-interested, 'serving to the eye', as St Paul says (Eph. 6, 6), was completely foreign to her. 'Submissive both externally and inwardly, she always respected and reverenced her superiors in whom, I repeat, she saw God constantly.'

Likewise it was with a charity grounded on faith that she loved all her companions, without looking for any return, but with the most perfect disinterestedness. For the love of God she forgave uncivil treatment and undue humiliations. 'She never harboured the slightest resentment. If she was reminded that someone had been against her or caused her trouble, she would say: "I've forgotten it."'

She enjoyed the pleasures of friendship, for even in a religious community there are legitimate preferences. Sister Vincent Garros recalled with deep feeling: 'She was a sincere friend to me. Her love for me was supernatural, or she would not have put up with me as she did.' Perhaps her dearest companion was the thoughtful Sister du Rais who lived long months with her in the infirmary. 'Sister Marie-Bernard,' she disclosed, 'was an excellent friend, with a faithful memory for those she loved. She did not squander her friendship, but once she had given it, she never took it back. I myself was a recipient of this friendship; she maintained it until her death, and I hope beyond. She sometimes rebuked me severely, but I knew it was for my good.'

Sister Marie-Bernard loved in the right way. She possessed

what Lacordaire described as 'the great secret of loving God in loving other things besides'. Instinctively therefore she was the enemy of those so-called 'particular' friendships that do harm to charity in a Community. Even if these sentimental weaknesses remain hidden, they occupy the mind to excess, they weaken piety and obstruct the love of God. When they are blatant they divide hearts and can end by creating cliques. Against this insidious danger Mother Vauzou, as we have seen, did not fail to caution her novices. Sister Marie-Bernard adhered scrupulously to her lessons, and as occasion offered, she saw to it that others profited by them also. This resolution is to be found in her Retreat notes:

Never any particular friendship. Love all my Sisters solely to please God.
Keep a watch over the feelings of my heart. Listen to Jesus who will often say to me: 'My daughter, give Me thy heart. I want it whole and undivided.'

'Strong, unselfish love does not consist in feelings,' she wrote in her private note-book. Nevertheless neither her compassion nor her sympathy was devoid of the human touch. When the news arrived that exceptional floods had devastated the banks of the Garonne, the Gave de Pau and the Adour, it made her tremble with pity for the unfortunate people in the low-lying areas. She wrote to her sister Toinette on 4th July, 1875:

It appears that the Gave has overflowed. I am most anxious to know whether the water has done much damage to the grotto and the mills. . . .
I am very afraid for our relatives at Momères. I am anxious about our cousin Jeanne, who is quite near Toulouse, where the floods have caused havoc. It appears that a number of people have been carried away and drowned in the flood. Nothing like it has ever been seen before.

But Sister Marie-Bernard was far more depressed by the moral ruin, and she saw in it the explanation of these material disasters.

God is chastening us, but still like a father. The streets of Paris were bathed in the blood of large numbers of people, but that did not suffice to touch hearts hardened in evil, and the streets of the south had also to be bathed in blood and have their victims.

My God, how blind man is, if he does not open his heart to the light of faith after such terrible calamities! Were we not tempted to ask who could have provoked this terrible chastisement? Let us listen carefully and we shall hear a voice saying to us deep down in our hearts: it is sin, yes, sin, that is the greatest disaster; it is sin that draws down chastisements on us all. . . . Such are the happiness and the advantages procured for us by the work of sin. O my God, forgive us once more and show us mercy.

Bernadette did not consider her family incapable of grasping such stern lessons. Canon Perreau of Nevers—to whom she commended her brother Bernard-Pierre, asking him 'to watch over his religious education'—stresses the fact that 'she loved her relations with a pure supernatural love. . . . In her prayers she did not ask God to give them good health and material comfort so much as progress in goodness and the practice of their religious duties. She asked them as a favour and a personal service to remain good, upright Catholics; and this she did in all her letters.' When the same priest was setting out for Lourdes, in June, 1876, on the eve of the Crowning of Our Lady, he asked Bernadette if she had any messages for her brothers and sisters and brother-in-law; she gave him some, adding with peculiar emphasis: 'But they must not become rich . . . ! Tell them specially not to get rich!'

Certain rumours from Lourdes had caused her intense sorrow. Some nuns from the Hospice, on a visit to the Mother House, had informed her that several of her relations were neglecting their religious duties and that Toinette, who had most influence in the family, was shirking her duty of admonishing them. What worried Bernadette even more was the future of Jean-Marie and Bernard-Pierre. Jean-Marie was twenty-five and no longer bore the fine name of Brother Marie-Bernard, which he had taken in memory of his elder sister. He had always been negligent in writing to her, as though her tender love—an unappreciated treasure—was a burden to him. Called up for military service, he abandoned the idea of a religious life, and on his return to Lourdes he took up work as a miller. Bernard-Pierre, who was seventeen, had not returned to the Garaison Fathers on the reopening of school in October. Perhaps it was merely that he felt undecided about his vocation, or perhaps he was definitely giving it up. He was a brilliant pupil, and his sister dreaded that he might go on to Holy Orders for purely human considerations.

On November 3rd she made up her mind to speak firmly. In a letter addressed to her most regular correspondent, her young cousin, Lucile-Conradette Pène, whose parents kept an inn, she enclosed two other letters, one for her sister Toinette, the other for her brother Jean-Marie.

I shudder with fear for you all [she wrote to Lucile-Conradette, directing her sermon over the head of the girl to the whole of her family]. I shudder when I consider that Our Lord told us to seek first of all things the Kingdom of God and His justice. . . .

I entreat you, keep Sundays holy. Working on Sunday will not make you rich; on the contrary you will bring down misfortunes on yourselves and your children. For pity's sake do not do that. You should set an example not only to the people of the town but still more so to strangers who come to Lourdes.

Please give my kind regards to my dear uncle and aunts, as well as to my dear godmother. I exhort my cousins to be always faithful to their religious duties. . . .

Then Toinette, in a letter addressed to her personally, received a lecture:

My dear sister, I am surprised that you do not send me news of yourself more often, now that Pierre is at home. What is he doing? Please let me know if he is thinking of returning to Garaison. It is essential to know what he intends to do, for he is at an age when he should be learning a trade, supposing of course that he has no religious vocation. I do not want him to spend his time running here and there. . . .

I hope, dear friend, that you and Joseph are not careless about your religious duties. I exhort you at least to do your level best to serve God well. Do not forget that Our Lord told us to seek the Kingdom of God and then all the other things will be given us. . . .

With regard to Pierre, the poor little fellow who had grown up far away from her—he was only seven when Bernadette had left for Nevers—she would have liked to be more close at hand for him, so she pursued her obligations on the spiritual side as elder sister and godmother:

My dear brother, I have heard that you worked hard at the grotto during the holidays. I have been told that you may not perhaps return to Garaison this year. If you really think that God does not call you to religious life, I urge you to make up your mind to learn a trade. It is a question, my dear, of your future. As far as I am concerned I should not be happy for you to continue working as you have done so far at the grotto. Later on you would find yourself without a situation; whereas if you learn a trade and are keen on the work you will always be sure of making a living and you will be able to make your way in the world.

I urge you, my dear brother, to reflect well before God. Not for the whole world would I want you to become a priest just in order to secure a position for yourself. No, I would rather you became a rag-picker.

I hope, dear brother, you will understand that it is the keen interest I take in your soul that prompts me to speak like this. Once again, do think things out carefully and above all ask Our Lord and the Blessed Virgin to make known to you their holy will.

I beg you to be always faithful to your religious duties and obedient to (your uncle) Joseph and (your aunt) Marie. Give me some news of yourself as soon as possible.

Good-bye, dear godson; I end by embracing you most affectionately.

Your very devoted sister and godmother,
SISTER MARIE-BERNARD SOUBIROUS.

These three letters, so outspoken and direct, would themselves suffice to show that Bernadette did not know the art of disguising her thoughts.

'She worshipped truth,' affirmed Sister Bounaix; 'her straight and sincere soul could not endure shiftiness.' 'She could not tolerate falsehood,' said Sister Cassou; 'she was straight and open in her ways.' Bishop Laurence had long before proclaimed in his Decree of January 18th, 1862, 'Bernadette's sincerity is indisputable. And let us add, it is undisputed.'

\*　　\*　　\*

One might have expected to see Sister Marie-Bernard engaging in unusual austerities, for she had a lasting memory of the call three times repeated by the Lady of the Apparitions: 'Penance, penance, penance!' Sensibly and submissively she complied with her confessor's directions: in view of her feeble health there were to be no corporal penances beyond those permitted by the rule: abstinence on the days prescribed, the constraints of obedience, the discomforts of common life; then the practices of daily self-denial: custody of the eyes, silence of the tongue; finally, resigned endurance of infirmities and sickness. . . . Those 'mortifications that are not served up with the sauce of our own desire,' as St Francis de Sales says so prettily, 'are the best and most excellent, and also those that are met with in the streets—or in the gardens or cloisters—without our thinking about them or looking for them; and such as we meet with daily, however trifling'.

In the course of the Retreat of 1874 given at Saint-Gildard by Father Condalon, S.J., Sister Marie-Bernard accumulated notes on mortification:

> Serious attention to all our duties necessarily involves the exercise of incessant mortification. . . .
>
> The mortification God asks of us is the exact observance of our Rule, of the practices, customs and instructions given by superiors. A Sister who is faithful in all this is practising a high degree of mortification and with no risk of vanity. In my opinion [here the preacher is speaking] she would be able to enter Heaven without passing through the flames of Purgatory.
>
> There are many daily mortifications which a recollected and attentive soul does not let slip: that of rising during winter at the fixed hour and with no delay, without turning over and over in bed, is most pleasing to God. . . . Again, if anyone comes in, don't look or ask who it is. As for the sense of taste there is an infinity of mortifications one can do, without anyone noticing them. A nun should never make known her likes or dislikes for this or that food. . . .

Before the close of the Retreat of 1875 Sister Marie-Bernard went again to Father Douce, who had already heard her confession. She desired his advice about a life of greater penance. 'Your mortification,' said the Marist, 'should be that of the sense of taste. Never complain about food. . . .'

The sick are inclined to give way to little self-indulgences: Sister Marie-Bernard, on the contrary, used illness to mortify herself. 'If she was offered anything unpleasant to the taste,' reported Sister Viguerie, 'she would take it willingly and seize this opportunity of making a sacrifice.' How many mornings she woke up—supposing that she had managed to sleep—with a disgust for any sort of food! 'When I brought her breakfast,' relates Sister Marcillac, then second infirmarian, 'she would say with a smile: "That's my penance you're bringing me!" But she used to take it all the same.'

Far from advertising her ailments, she tried rather to conceal them out of virtue. Her practice of mortification consisted in hidden sacrifices incessantly renewed. This perseverance was in itself heroism, nor did God ask more of her.

\*   \*   \*

In Sister Marie-Bernard the spirit of poverty was on a par with her spirit of penance. We read in her Retreat notes of 1873:

> Poverty should not be merely irksome, but crucifying. Jesus chose the meanest things on earth for His use. . . .
> What was once mine belongs to me no longer. I have given all to Jesus.

Thus she was, as Father Raffin said, 'a model of religious poverty. By the care she took of everything that was provided for her use, by the minute precautions she employed to preserve her clothes, to keep them in good order and to repair them so as to make them last as long as possible; by the scrupulousness she showed in asking all due permissions in what concerned the vow of poverty, and by her carefulness not to lose a single moment of time, even when she was a patient in the infirmary, she showed clearly how anxious she was to live and die really poor, so as to profit by the promises made by Our Lord to the poor in spirit. The virtue of poverty practised by the servant of God to this degree of perfection certainly deserves to be called heroic.'

'Wonderfully neat and tidy,' says Mother Forestier, 'she took the greatest care of the things provided for her use. She did not set her heart on them. . . . It was on old exercise-books and odd sheets of paper, which she afterwards put together in the form of note-books, that she used to take notes for her spiritual life.' 'If she were offered some little souvenirs,' adds Sister Marcillac, 'she would accept them kindly and get rid of them at once. She complained sometimes that the great charity of the Sisters led them to be too kind in their attentions to her. 'The poor don't get such treatment,' she would say.

# 30

## PRAYER AND SPECIAL DEVOTIONS

ALTHOUGH Sister Marie-Bernard wore exactly the same dress as all the other nuns at Saint-Gildard, a sharp eye would have been able to pick her out among her companions, even without seeing her face, by the mere arrangement of her veil and by her general appearance: the humble nun, who during the week was dressed only in old darned clothes, never failed for all that to look, as was said of her, 'as if she had just come out of a bandbox'. Likewise in matters of piety, although she did 'what all the others did', she put into her devotions a sort of supernatural richness such as no one else did. She did not make the sign of the cross more frequently than her companions, but she made it with impressive dignity.

'I loved to watch her at prayer,' confided Sister Lannessans, 'for she prayed like an angel.' 'I can still see her on her knees, motionless, head erect, her hands on the bench, her eyes on the ground or on the Tabernacle. One felt that the presence of God pervaded her through and through. We novices, when we were leaving the chapel after Mass, used to slow down as we drew near her in order to have a better view of her in her converse with Our Lord.' So said an old nun reviving her past. But no witness has related that Bernadette herself ever turned her head or slackened her pace to watch some companion at prayer. Even when walking in file along the cloisters on her way to the chapel, 'she had,' reported Mother Forestier, 'an attitude of piety and recollectedness that I did not notice to the same degree in the other nuns.'

She was 'most regular in taking part in Community prayer whenever her health allowed.' She always went there not merely because it was the rule, but above all because it was her rendezvous with God. In the Lourdes Hospice, at least during her months as a postulant, the Sisters had invited her to join with

them in the early morning practice of prayer. On arrival at
Saint-Gildard she was acquainted with the method in use in the
Congregation, as also in many other religious Orders: the reading in public of various points on which each would make her
own meditation. Bernadette did not ask herself if there were
other ways of 'saying prayers'. The traditional method, which
corresponds to the 'ordinary paths', was certainly a help to her
for several years; she found comfort and sweetness in it. We
have seen her drawing up for herself in the course of 1871 a
whole collection of subjects for meditation according to this
method. But at the end of five or six years what a change had
taken place in her interior life! She was worried and distressed
about it, for she did not understand that the spiritual dryness
from which she suffered was a trial from Providence, a normal
occurrence in a life directed towards perfection. Her heart was
no longer moved by her reading; her Communions were in-
fluenced also: she went up to receive Holy Communion full of
a great longing, but then she did not know how to express in
words her deep love for Our Lord. She wrote in her note-book
this melancholy reflection: 'The secret of meditation is in
preparation. I do it so badly!'

What remedy was there for this but to apply herself once
again to the work of meditation? Did not the Mistress of
Novices, the chaplain, and her confessor, hint that there was presumption and danger in not following the customary method?
So Sister Marie-Bernard, in 1874, after seven years of religious
life, began heroically to make for herself a second collection of
meditations drawn, like the previous one, from the *Méditations
et Entretiens Spirituels* of Father Le Maistre, S.J. And it was
about this time that she recorded in her small note-book these
words which reveal her distress:

But I am so tired out in the morning! Remember the temptations of Father Avila, hesitating one day on account of his
fatigue to continue on his way to say Mass. Our Lord appeared
to him and pointed to His Heart, reminding him that exhaustion
did not prevent Him from going on to the summit of Calvary.
Courage! I too must learn to force myself. Even if I am tired,
even if exhausted, at the end I can find rest on the Heart of Jesus.

Was it physical exhaustion or mental prostration? Doubtless
it was both together, for there was in Bernadette's case a close

connection between this weariness that only a manly courage could surmount and the purgatory of the 'dark night of the soul' in which she was plunged. But the aridity of the soul that tortured her was the prelude to sublime contemplation whose existence she did not even suspect. She thought she was falling back in her spiritual life and was distressed about it, whereas without her knowing it she was rising towards union with God along the road of total deprivation. She was being weaned away from graces which she could feel and take pleasure in, and God was drawing nearer to her to fill the void which He Himself had created.

St Margaret Mary's soul passed through this ordeal. She also used to listen to the points being read out for meditation and used to compel herself to reflect on them. But, she confesses, 'nothing stayed in my mind; everything vanished, and I could not grasp or remember anything except what my Divine Master taught me . . .' And then, as her contemporaries stated, she used to remain before Our Lord 'as helpless as though her heart were held fast, in the presence of her God, with no other emotion or desire except to love Him. . . .'

Such were the heights to which Sister Marie-Bernard had risen without any human teacher, without any book written by the hand of man. On her sick-bed, in the chapel gallery to which the infirmarian carried her in her arms, she practised this 'prayer of simple regard' composed chiefly of silent love. Moreover, apart from the hours devoted to prayer, she lived, as it were, continuously in the presence of God, at her work and at rest, in joy and in suffering. 'She prayed almost continually,' remarked the observant Sister du Rais. And Sister Marie-Bernard copied into her note-book the words: 'Every moment that I live I shall spend in loving.'

Spontaneous remarks betray how familiar she was with the holiest, loftiest thoughts. At the sight of a flower she exclaimed: 'How powerful and good God is!' In the days when she was able to walk along by the vines in the garden, she confided to those near her: 'I'm very fond of grapes; they remind me of Our Lord's blood.' But in the orchard she said: 'I don't care for apples because they remind me of original sin.' She often uttered ejaculatory prayers even aloud, putting all her heart into them. 'My Jesus, mercy . . . ! My God, I am all yours . . . !

I love you. . . . Convert sinners . . . ! ' 'God alone, God alone! '
she hinted gently to a visitor in the infirmary who would have
liked to prolong the conversation when she was so eager to be
alone and to converse with her sole Beloved.

'Oh how an ignorant and simple soul, who knows only how
to love God without loving self, surpasses all the learned! '
exclaimed Bossuet to an audience of teaching nuns.   'The
Spirit intimates all truth to it without detailed study; for by an
intimate, profound enlightenment, an enlightenment of truth,
experience and feeling, it makes it realize that it itself is nothing
and that God is everything.'   There was much of this in Sister
Marie-Bernard's prayer, and there was even more than this.
Together with the secrets from the Lady and the prayer which
she was taught at Massabielle, she carried away from Lourdes,
as someone wrote, 'that magnificent spiritual store, the honour
and burden of which she could not share with anyone.'

The main subjects of her contemplation and devotion were
the sufferings of Our Lord, the Eucharist and the Blessed Virgin.
She knew the four Gospel accounts of the Passion almost by
heart.   She had made them her most regular study, reading
them 'preferably without commentaries, just as they are in the
holy Gospel.   She used to say it impressed her more.'   Abbé
Febvre had noticed this strong attraction of hers.   One day when
Sister Vincent Garros, a mere beginner in prayer, was complaining to her of 'not being able to meditate', she passed on to her
this advice from the chaplain: 'Take yourself off to the Garden
of Olives or the foot of the Cross, and stay there.   Our Lord will
speak to you; and you listen to Him.'   To tell the truth, Sister
Vincent, less advanced in spiritual ways, admitted frankly afterwards: 'I went there, but Our Lord said nothing to me.'

When she made the Way of the Cross, she did each Station
slowly, making a contemplation of it.   She made the Stations
every day, either in the chapel where it was edifying to see her
in spite of her weakness kneeling on the flagstones, or in bed
when she was kept there through illness.   In her note-book she
made her own the words of a saintly soul that seemed to express
her own love of the Crucified and the Cross:

O Jesus, keep me under the standard of your Cross. . . .
Let the crucifix be not merely before my eyes and on my breast,
but in my heart, alive within me!   Let me be crucified alive like

Him, transformed into Him by the union of the Eucharist, by meditation on His life, on the inmost feelings of His Heart, drawing souls not to myself but to Him, from this high Cross to which His love fastens me alive for ever!

'The Holy Eucharist was the breath of her soul.' How beautiful and eloquent is this testimony from Sister Dalias! She drew from it 'the strength to endure in peace of soul her indescribable sufferings,' as Mother Cassagnes said. She saw in it the fount of all purification and of every virtue. Sister Robert confessed to her one day: 'How hard it is to correct one's faults!' Sister Marie-Bernard, opening her eyes wide, replied spiritedly: 'How can one receive the Bread of the Strong and not be more courageous?' Canon Perreau, who often gave Bernadette Holy Communion, was able to judge how deep was her faith and her love. Her eyes as she gazed on the Sacred Host 'profoundly moved' the priest, especially when he saw her approaching 'with heaving breast'. He had often to wait 'until the emotion had subsided a little'.

She looked upon 'this moment of Holy Communion as a most precious time; she always found it too short.' Sister Vincent Garros asked her: 'How do you manage to remain so long at your thanksgiving?' She answered: 'I think to myself that the Blessed Virgin is giving me the Infant Jesus, I welcome Him, I speak to Him and He speaks to me.' To encourage her young compatriot to greater recollection, for she was subject to sudden distractions and uneasy at not feeling any sense of God's presence in her thanksgiving, Sister Marie-Bernard said nicely: 'You must give God a good reception. We have every interest in welcoming Him for then He has to pay us for His lodging.'

Her cousin and compatriot, Sister Cassou, after being moved about from one convent to another, had come to spend Christmas in the Mother House, and the transfer made her sad. Bernadette hit on a very simple way of cheering her up. 'For Midnight Mass,' she suggested, 'come next to me; there's room.' 'I was so delighted at this,' reported Sister Cassou. 'It gave me the opportunity of seeing for myself how devout she was. . . . Nothing could distract her.' Once she had received Holy Communion 'she became so deeply absorbed that everybody left the chapel without her seeming to notice it. I stayed beside her, for I had no desire to go and join in the meal with my companions. I watched her for a long time without her noticing. Her face was radiant and heavenly, just as it was during the ecstasy at Massabielle. When the Sister came to close the doors she rattled the bolts vigorously. Then Bernadette came out of her ecstasy, as it were. She left the chapel and I followed her. She leaned towards me and said gently: "You haven't had anything to eat?" "Nor have you," I replied. Then she retired without saying a word, and we parted company.'

It was not yet customary for Holy Communion to be brought to the infirmary every morning, but when Mother Imbert was confined to her bed, Sister Marie-Bernard benefited by a privileged arrangement: she received Holy Communion three times a week like her Superior General. Otherwise she had to make a spiritual Communion.

Whenever it was possible for her she used to visit the Blessed Sacrament 'like the rest of us, at the times fixed by rule,' says Sister Carrière, 'but always with a something extra that stimulated us to devotion'. When more weak than usual, she used to go on her own to the chapel gallery or ask to be carried there, and so she was to be found before the altar several times a day. There she came to seek strength, as Mother Cassagnes noted, 'to bear with peace of soul her indescribable sufferings'.

*　　*　　*

Her devotion to the Blessed Virgin was bound to be 'particularly tender, particularly childlike'. Mary, her living ideal, 'was in her heart very close to Our Lord', as Sister du Rais, her neighbour in the infirmary witnessed. You should have heard her say the Hail Mary! What devotion there was in her voice, especially when she pronounced the words 'pauvres pêcheurs'! When someone boldly asked her if the image of the Apparition was not fading gradually from her memory, she exclaimed disapprovingly: 'Forget her! No, never!' And with a forceful gesture she put her right hand to her forehead, saying: 'It's there!' One of her companions suggested: 'You should paint a picture of the Blessed Virgin for us, for you know what she is like.' 'I can't, I don't know how,' she had to answer. 'For me there is no need, I have it in my heart.'

Devotion to Our Lady 'filled her whole life'. What need had she to 'meditate' on the Blessed Virgin? She 'saw Mary again in everything and everywhere, with her heart and her memory'. Never for a religious soul could the 'prayer of simple regard' have been easier. 'Whenever she was praying to the Blessed Virgin,' said Sister Gonzague Champy, 'it seemed as though she still saw her. . . . If one asked her to obtain some favour, she used to say straightway that she would speak to Our Lady about it.'

One day, on the Feast of the Assumption, Mother Fabre chanced to be kneeling in the chapel a short distance away from Sister Marie-Bernard in such a position as to be able to observe her closely. 'At the words in the hymn: *Je l'aperçois, ah! c'est ma Mère!* I saw her give a start and almost leap for joy.'

Naturally in her own private prayers Bernadette used to prefer to address the Blessed Virgin by the title of Our Lady of Lourdes, which by that time was widely known. She reproached herself sometimes for not having sufficiently realized her good fortune during the days when the Blessed Virgin used to appear to her. 'Ah, if it were now!' she would sigh.

Even though she showed no enthusiastic appreciation of the statues of Our Lady of Lourdes, she liked them all the same because of Her whose pale image they were. Happening to be alone one day in the infirmary, she was dusting the mantelpiece on which stood one of those blue and white statues, and Sister Claire Bordes was watching her through the half-open door. Bernadette took the small statue in her hands, 'kissed its feet and put it back in its place. Then she stayed motionless before it, with her hands joined on the edge of the mantelpiece and keeping her eyes raised towards the statue. She remained like this for about five minutes'.

As for her Rosary, she must have said her beads for all the rest of her life just as she did at Lourdes. 'The Rosary was her favourite prayer,' said a Superior General. Often in the infirmary Sister Champy said the Hail Marys alternately with her. On such occasions, the Sister recalls, 'Bernadette's dark, deep-set, sparkling eyes became heavenly. She was seeing Our Lady in spirit, and looked as though she were in ecstasy.' 'At night when you retire to rest,' she recommended to a companion, 'take your beads and go off to sleep while saying them; do the same as little children who fall asleep saying: "Mamma, Mamma. . . ." '

No less childlike was her devotion to St Joseph. When she was infirmarian she promised to pray for one of her patients, saying in her own original way: 'You're in pain? Wait a moment, I'll go and see my father.' 'Your father?' 'Oh, yes! Surely you know that St Joseph is my father now?'

During the purifying ordeal, the 'dark night of the soul', when she used to fear for her eternal salvation and began 'to have a great dread of death', she put her trust in him who is 'the patron of a happy death'. 'She kept devoutly with me,' said Sister du Rais, 'the month dedicated to St Joseph. We had placed by her bed a tiny statue of the Saint, which she used to decorate with flowers and in front of which burned two small candles. We used to recite the Litany, adding all the prayers to St Joseph that she knew. Sometimes I would say to her: "Is that the lot? Haven't you any more?" She would answer: "No, that's the lot." She told me also that she had obtained many favours through St Joseph, and that we should keep well in with him.'

She treated her Guardian Angel like a brother—as can be seen in the homely advice she gave to Sister Vincent, still a novice. 'When you pass by the chapel and haven't time to stop, tell your Guardian Angel to take your messages to Our Lord in the Tabernacle. He will take them and then have time to catch up with you.' 'I've kept up this practice ever since,' declared Sister Vincent Garros over thirty years later. Certainly Bernadette herself did likewise.

In her invocations, to the names of Mary and Joseph she frequently joined that of St Bernard, her other baptismal patron. 'I certainly ought to try and imitate him,' she owned; 'he had such a great love of Our Lady.'

There was an affinity of soul between Bernadette and St Francis of Assisi, and so the little Lourdes girl had an affectionate devotion to the Poverello. What attracted her above all was 'his great love of suffering and of Jesus crucified'. As the Constitutions of Saint-Gildard did not allow one to join the Third Order of St Francis, she had herself affiliated to the Franciscan Confraternity of the Cord. This she received in the infirmary on December 8th, 1878, from the hands of a Capuchin who had come to Nevers to preach a Retreat.

In the course of her religious life she read a large number of Saints' lives. With her refined understanding of spiritual matters, she was astonished that most of these biographies were from start to finish nothing but panegyrics. She would have liked the historians to bring out more clearly the imperfections of these great friends of God. 'I think,' she used to say, 'that they ought to point out the faults the Saints had, and indicate the means they employed to correct them. That would be helpful to us. We would learn how to set about it. But all that is mentioned is their revelations or the wonders they performed. That cannot serve our advancement.'

She failed to add that even so these imperfect authors are to be commended for praising the pre-eminent qualities of the Saints, and that she found in them examples to imitate. The Church in its infallible decisions was one day to adopt the well-founded verdict of a Superior General of Saint-Gildard: 'It is my own opinion that during her life Sister Marie-Bernard put into practice the virtues that constitute sanctity.'

# 31

## THE EXCEPTIONAL GIFTS OF GOD

OFTEN, 'with a view to the common good' (1 Cor. 12, 7), God grants to his favourites, such as the Saints, extra-ordinary gifts, gratuitous gifts, called by St Paul *charis-mata*, among which he ranks the gift of miracles and the gift of prophecy. Did Sister Marie-Bernard receive and manifest these exceptional favours in her lifetime? It would certainly seem so according to numerous testimonies.

The favours she obtained for others through her prayers were not miracles in the ordinary meaning of the word; more especially as she herself, in order no doubt to be more surely heard, besought them from God through the intercession of Our Lady of Lourdes. Moreover, these prayers, especially when they took the form of a novena, were always offered up by Sister Marie-Bernard conjointly with some appointed companion (for every ingenuity was used to safeguard her from temptations to pride). In this way the successful outcome of these joint novenas could not be attributed exclusively to either of the partners.

But when writing to express thanks for an improvement or a cure, outsiders, who had no suspicion of the pious ruse, men-tioned, of course, only Bernadette. Mother Vauzou, who was responsible for going through the correspondence, always con-cealed these flattering items of news. 'She never said a word about these cures,' testified Mother Bordenave, her secretary. Nevertheless, she added, 'it is an accredited opinion among the community that Sister Marie-Bernard, during her lifetime, obtained some cures through her prayers'.

Some of these seem to have occurred merely by contact with her and even at the time when she was still a boarder at the Hospice in Lourdes. In June 1862—Bernadette was then eighteen —a lady and gentleman, who were on their way from Cauterets with their young invalid daughter, stopped at Lourdes and asked

the Superior of the Hospice if she would kindly send for Bernadette, for they were convinced that if she touched their daughter
she would be cured.  Bernadette came and the Superior told her
to straighten the child's pillow. . . . She did so and the girl
immediately felt better.  And it is known that she went on foot
next day to the grotto.

This first case was recorded in the Process of Beatification on
the testimony of Mother Bordenave.  It must have been reported
to her by nuns of the Hospice, or by Sister Vincent Garros, who
testified also to having witnessed the following cure.  A woman,
who was a stranger to the town, had brought her child, a boy
of just over a year old, to Lourdes.  'The face and head' of the
poor little child 'were covered with sores'.  On the fourth day
of a novena to Our Lady of Lourdes the lady called at the
Hospice with her infant.  The child was crying, and it was
handed over to Bernadette who 'carried it through the cloisters,
and when she returned she gave it back to its mother completely
cured.  Every trace of the sores had disappeared.'

The Mother House witnessed another prodigy.  'A lady,'
testified Sister Bordes, 'had brought a small child who could not
walk.  She wanted Bernadette to touch him, hoping that he
would then be able to walk.'  The Superior General, Mother
Imbert, called Sister Marie-Bernard and told her: "Take this
child out into the garden while I am with this lady."  Bernadette, continued Sister Dalias, 'had a great love for children.  She
took him in her arms, then finding him too heavy, put him on
the ground.  The little fellow ran off gaily to his mother.'

\*        \*        \*

'In the Community,' affirmed Mother Bordenave again,
'Sister Marie-Bernard showed on several occasions that she could
foresee the future.'  Some wonderful instances of this have been
recorded.

Regarding the date of her own death she seems clearly to have
had some supernatural intuitions.  One day in 1870, when she
was temporarily confined to bed in the infirmary, one of the
Sisters was sent by the Novice Mistress to ask how she was.
'Tell her not to worry,' she replied, 'I shan't die to-day nor for
a long while yet.'

In August or September 1878, one of the nuns arranged for extra nurses at her bedside. 'Don't put yourself to so much trouble,' said Sister Marie-Bernard. 'They imagine I am going to die, but I'll last for another six months and more.'

One day in 1873 a group of novices had gone up to see her in the infirmary, where she was in bed with an attack of asthma. One of them, tall and robust, asked her bluntly, 'Sister Marie-Bernard, are you afraid of dying?' '*Mon Dieu*, no!' 'But your choking fits are so violent you may easily die in one.' Bernadette, who could see further, replied: 'Oh, no! You'll die before me.' A few months after this caution the novice was sent to another house in the south and died there as the result of a chill.

Bernadette seems likewise to have predicted the future of Mgr Peyramale and of Bishop de Ladoue. Of the former she is claimed to have foretold: 'He will have difficulty in building his church. He will not finish it, but he will have his tomb in it.' And of Bishop de Ladoue Sister Vincent Garros recorded that one day when they were returning from welcoming him to Nevers as their new bishop, she asked Bernadette: 'Well, what do you think of our new bishop?' 'He's small and reserved, and he won't stay long,' Bernadette replied. In the event, Mgr Peyramale was buried in the crypt of his church, which was far from complete, and Bishop de Ladoue died after only four years as bishop.

In May 1870, Sister Angèle Lompech had been a postulant for two months when a letter arrived from home informing her that her mother, who had just given birth to her ninth child, was at death's door. Sister Marie-Bernard, seeing her sobbing her heart out in front of Mother Mistress's office, went straight up to her. Sister Angèle continues the story: 'I think she was enlightened by Our Lady, for she came up to me because she had something to say to me, something that came from on high. "You're crying! What's the matter?" she asked me. "I've just learned that Mamma is very ill. She is perhaps dead by now." Then Bernadette looked at me with a smile and eyes that I shall never forget. "No," she said, "don't cry. The Blessed Virgin will cure your Mamma. I'm going to pray hard for her." And she left me. I was stunned; but I felt reassured and I stopped crying. A second letter was not long in coming, and this time it was a cheerful one. The crisis was past and the invalid out of danger. I learned later that the change for the better had come about at the very time when Bernadette had said to me: "Don't cry . . ." My dear Mamma lived for thirty-seven years more.'

In 1878, there arrived from the village of Gouttières in Puy-de-Dôme, a young girl named Anna Basset. She had only just been admitted as a postulant when she had to retire to the infirmary and was given a bed facing Sister Marie-Bernard's. She did not seem likely to get better, and the cautious Dr Robert Saint-Cyr judged that this pious girl should be sent back to her native hills. What a disappointment it was for her! She at once confided this to her 'little neighbour'. 'Don't cry,' said Sister Marie-Bernard after a moment's reflection. 'God wants you to be a nun; 'you will become one in another Congregation.' Then as if to take a rise out of the doctor she concluded: 'You have still many years to live.' According to reliable witnesses she is supposed to have stated definitely: 'You will die on a Sunday in a poor little convent.' Anna Basset went and recovered her health in her own village in Auvergne and then sent a request for re-admission to Saint-Gildard. It was in vain: Dr Robert was adamant. Anna then asked to join the nuns of St Joseph of Cluny and was accepted. She became Sister Berthilie and was posted to Edern in Finistère. There she departed this life full of good works and merits, one Sunday in 1926 at the age of seventy-one, after forty-eight years of religious profession.

One day, in May 1872, there was an unusual flutter in the Superior's parlour. A postulant of twenty-nine burst in, wearing evening dress. She introduced herself as Jeanne-Isabelle du Rais, daughter of a Beauvais magistrate, and she had run away from home of her own accord. . . . She had seized the opportunity of a family party to slip away and gain a freedom that had been obstinately refused, namely, to join those Sisters of Nevers who nursed the sick in the public hospital in her native town. She arrived accompanied by her maid and asked humbly for some little corner in the noviceship. The embarrassment of the superiors may be imagined! More especially since the father was following close on the heels of the fugitive—as was only to be expected—'determined to take her back by force if necessary. He laid siege to Saint-Gildard and to Bishop's House with all the arts of his profession and with such vigour that poor Isabelle considered herself lost'. Who should come and restore her confidence but Sister Marie-Bernard! 'God wants you here,' she asserted. 'He will keep you here in spite of all opposition.' In fact 'the paternal wrath gradually abated. . . . And this proved the beginning of a solid friendship between the former shepherdess of Bartrès and the dazzling young lady of Beauvais. Forty years later Mother Marthe du Rais, Superior of the 'Providence' in Montmartre and a Dame of the Legion of Honour, came to give testimony to the sanctity of Sister Marie Bernard before the ecclesiastical tribunal.

# 32

## THE FINAL TASK

HAD we gone into the infirmary where Sister Marie-Bernard lay bed-ridden, and asked one of her companions who was also confined within those four walls through age or sickness, 'What is her job here? Does she do anything?' she would undoubtedly have answered, 'No, nothing any more. Like the rest of us she no longer has any job.' But suppose we had asked Sister Marie-Bernard herself. . . .

One day a Superior (the documents do not reveal her name) having gone up to see her, asked her point-blank: 'What are you doing there in bed, you lazy little thing?' 'Why, my dear Mother, I'm doing my job.' 'And what's your job?' 'Being ill.'

It was a masterly reply that deserves to be recorded in the annals of sanctity. Underlying what seems at first sight just an exchange of banter was the exact definition of what has since been styled the apostolate of the sick. 'Her work,' as Canon Perreau was to explain in a wise comment, 'was to be a victim.' She used to say: 'I must be a victim.' She knew that it was Our Lord's precise call to her. Had the three Massabielle secrets some connection with this mysterious vocation to suffering? The Saint-Gildard chaplain, Abbé Febvre, was inclined to think so. 'My uncle had a clear conviction,' declared Abbé Picq at the Process, 'that Sister Marie-Bernard had a mission to live at the Mother House the lessons she received in Lourdes from the lips of Mary Immaculate: to pray, to do penance, to mortify herself and to suffer for sinners.'

Hence the hidden 'martyrdom' of a tender childlike heart confronted with inexplicable coldness, hence the agonizing ordeal of purification, the 'unending suffering' of a poor little body in which no part was without its pain, the wearying idleness in an infirmary when 'she would have loved to be on the move, actively employed and speeding through the house as formerly she had sped across the hills'. Sister Marie-Bernard offered up to God in heroic oblation this mass of physical and mental sufferings for the expiation of sin and for the conversion of sinners.

How many other sick and crippled would be raised to unsuspected heights by her example! One has only to see and hear those who come to Lourdes to beg a cure but, failing to obtain it, have received there a greater blessing: that of learning to suffer well.

The *Community Journal* records that Sister Marie-Bernard was relieved of her post of assistant-sacristan and resumed her place as a patient in the infirmary in the month of October, 1875. There followed this pessimistic entry on Thursday, November 18th:

> Sister Marie-Bernard begins spitting blood. Her condition gives cause for anxiety.

Until the month of May, 1876, she was never able to hear Mass, for she could not be moved. This was one of the biggest sacrifices of her life. On June 25th she was delighted to inform her brother Pierre that she now had the consolation of hearing Mass on Sundays. But how feeble she still was! The same day, being in the mood for writing, she sent a few lines to Sister Victoire, who was nursing in Lourdes:

> I am still in my 'white chapel'. I've been able, however, during the last three weeks to attend Holy Mass on Sundays, but have to go back to bed on my return.
> I have completely lost the use of my legs, and have to submit to the humiliation of being carried. But our Sisters do this so willingly that really the sacrifice is not so great. I am always afraid they may injure themselves, and when I tell them so they start laughing and even poke fun at me.

A month later Abbé Perreau asked her if she would have liked to be present at the Crowning of Our Lady in Lourdes, but she replied, pointing to her invalid's bed: 'My place is here.' No, she was not to return to Lourdes. But a taste of the grace and gladness of Lourdes was about to come her way. The *Com-*

*munity Journal* had this happy announcement for September 15th:

> M. l'Abbé Pomian comes to Nevers on business concerning the Lourdes Orphanage.

What a comforting surprise for Sister Marie-Bernard, who was passing through a period of weakness verging on prostration! M. Pomian, her first confessor, her first confidant after the first Apparition, the one who had prepared her for her First Communion and Confirmation, who had encouraged and guided her aspirations to the religious life . . . How many memories full of sweetness and delight! Still chaplain at the Lourdes Hospice, he came to Saint-Gildard to discuss with the Superiors the erection of a large orphanage on a site close to the grotto. This establishment was intended for poor girls and Bernadette had already wanted it in the days when she was still a boarder with the Sisters in Lourdes. The few moments which M. Pomian was able to spend at her bedside brought her real delight and restored her spirits.

Some days after this memorable visit she received a present that filled her with a supernatural joy. Ever since she had become confined to her 'white chapel' (an expression which she took a fancy to), she had often dreamed of this present, the only one she was permitted to set her heart on in her role of 'victim'. On September 21st she wrote to the donor, Mother Cresseil, Superior of the boarding-school at Cahors:

> I do not know how to express my great gratitude to you for the beautiful crucifix you have so kindly sent me. I cannot describe the happiness I felt on seeing it. I had long been wanting a large crucifix to place beside my bed. And so on seeing it, I exclaimed to myself, as I clasped and kissed it, that my dear Mother Sophie must surely have been inspired. I have permission to keep it. I'm happier on my bed with my crucifix than a queen on her throne. . . .

Strong spiritual comfort thus mingled with exhausting pain, the memory of which Bernadette has recorded in this private note:

> The Christian life has not only its struggles and trials; it has also its consolations. Even though we must go from Tabor to Calvary,

from Calvary we return to Tabor with Jesus. Herein lies the foretaste of Heaven.

At Christmas of this year, 1876, Mgr Peyramale (he had been made a Protonotary Apostolic in March 1874) did not receive such reassuring news from his saintly parishioner:

I have now been over a year in my 'white chapel'. On Sundays I summon up what little strength I have and go to Mass on somebody's arm. I shall be lucky if I last out this winter . . . !

Sister Marie-Bernard had written this letter to her Curé—prelate though he was—with a carefree pen. It had been a different matter nine days earlier when she wrote to the most august personage in the world. She herself would never have dreamed of writing to Pope Pius IX, but she had been obliged to obey.

Bishop de Ladoue, on the eve of his departure for his first visit *ad limina*, thought that the Pope would be sure to question him about the Lourdes visionary who was now in his diocese. A few lines from Bernadette would no doubt give pleasure to the Holy Father. On Saturday, December 16th, the Bishop of Nevers called at Saint-Gildard and asked to be taken to the infirmary. What an event for our humble invalid . . . ! And His Lordship wanted her to compose her message to His Holiness without assistance from anyone! Frightened at first, she then regained confidence, and by the next day she had set to work. 'I held the writing-pad so as to enable her to write,' says the infirmarian, Sister de Vigouroux. And here is the text of the letter which she wrote by herself and with some fumbling and difficulty, but which, of course, had to be examined by the superiors for revision.

Most Holy Father, I should never have dared to take up my pen to write to Your Holiness—a poor little Sister like me—if our worthy Bishop had not encouraged me by telling me that the sure way to receive a blessing from the Holy Father was to write to You and that he would have the kindness to take charge of my letter. I am torn between fear and confidence. Never could a poor, ignorant little invalid Sister like me dare to write to the Most Holy Father. Never!
But why be so afraid? He is my Father, since He represents

God on earth, the thrice holy God whom I dare to receive so often into my poor heart. It is because I am weak that I dare to receive almighty God. The same motive encourages me, Most Holy Father, to come and cast myself at your feet and beg Your Apostolic Blessing which will, I am sure, give a new strength to so feeble a soul as mine.

What could I do, Most Holy Father, to show You my deep gratitude? For a long time now I have been one of Your Holiness's zouaves,[1] though an unworthy one. My weapons are prayer and sacrifice, which I will hold on to till my last breath. Then only will the weapon of sacrifice fall from my hand; but that of prayer will accompany me to Heaven, where it will be more powerful than in this land of exile.

I pray every day to the Sacred Heart of Jesus and the Immaculate Heart of Mary to keep You among us for a long time to come, since You make them so well known and loved. Every time I pray for Your intentions it seems to me that the Blessed Virgin must often look down from Heaven upon You, Most Holy Father, because You proclaimed her 'Immaculate'; and four years later this good Mother came on earth to say: 'I am the Immaculate. . . .' I did not know what that meant; I had never heard that word. But since then, whenever I ponder the matter, I say to myself: How good the Blessed Virgin is! One would think she came to confirm the words of Our Holy Father.

Sister Marie-Bernard's first draft ended there. Submitted to the Mothers Counsellor, the effort was no doubt judged to be not sufficiently in the style of a letter to the Sovereign Pontiff. Sister Marie-Bernard therefore set about a second draft. This time she endeavoured to draw up a solemn version, longer but too highly polished, more refined but with less flavour, and she ended as follows:

It is this that makes me believe that she must protect You quite specially. I hope that this good Mother will have pity on her children and that she will deign once again to put her foot on the head of the accursed serpent.

At length, the text being approved, Sister Marie-Bernard had

---

[1] This name, derived from the *Zouaves pontificaux* who had done heroic service in the papal cause, was given to an association of young people of school age, pledged to the support of the Holy See by sacrifice and prayer. Its founder was Father Léonard Cros, S.J., who had visited Bernadette at the Lourdes Hospice.

to write out a final copy. She put all her talent and all her heart into it. It was a magnificent page of penmanship that Bishop de Ladoue conveyed to the august recipient.

In acknowledgment of her letter Pius IX presented her with a silver crucifix. 'She made me kiss it reverently,' reported Sister Cassou, and she appeared 'bewildered that the Holy Father should have shown her this attention'.

In a letter to her family in June, 1876, Sister Marie-Bernard spoke of her 'habitual state of suffering'. Between the spring and autumn of 1877 she enjoyed periods of relative tranquillity. But a profound and filial sorrow assailed her on the otherwise joyful feast of Mary's Birthday, Saturday, September 8th. A telegram from Lourdes arrived at Saint-Gildard: 'Mgr Peyramale seriously ill.' He died that very day at 11.15 a.m. On the following day the news of his death reached the Mother House in a further message. Assisted in his last hours by his beloved curate, M. Pomian, and Father Sempé, Superior of the Grotto missionaries, the Curé of Lourdes died of the stone, aged sixty-six, still in full vigour. In the Community Hall to which Sister Marie-Bernard had laboriously made her way down, Mother Vauzou asked prayers for the soul of Mgr Peyramale, now returned to God. Although they had informed Bernadette of the first telegram during the morning, the shock was too much for her. She was sitting beside Sister Cassou, who had helped her to come down, and as she was choking with sobs she tugged hastily at her cousin's sleeve and the two of them went out into the cloister. Then Bernadette of Lourdes gave free rein to her tears. She had forgotten her Curé's scoldings of twenty years before. All she thought of now was his great-heartedness, his devotion to the poor Soubirous, his zeal for the cause of Our Lady. He himself had had nothing but affection for his little parishioner; the year previously he had entrusted this message to Abbé Perreau: 'Tell Bernadette she is still as always my child and I give her my blessing.' On that 8th September, 1877, she sobbed as she clung to the arm of Sister Cassou, who was also weeping for her Curé: 'Monseigneur Peyramale and Father Sempé are the two persons I've loved most on earth. They have done the work I was unable to do.'

Dating from this death it was noticed that the thought of her own end came more frequently to Sister Marie-Bernard's mind. When on October 27th Sister Callery, newly professed and posted to another house, was bidding her an affectionate 'au revoir', Sister Marie-Bernard intimated that it was rather 'good-bye'. 'Seraph,' she said, 'when you hear I'm dead, pray hard for me, because they'll say: "Oh, that pious little thing doesn't need any." And they'll leave me to frizzle in Purgatory.'

As Sister Marie-Bernard had not yet been ten years professed, she was still under annual vows. She was due to renew them for the last time on the usual date, November 21st of this year, 1877, on the Feast of the Presentation of Mary. As she happened to be the eldest of the renovants she was the first one to come forward to the statue of the Blessed Virgin, which was surrounded by candles and flowers, and pronounce the vow formula. An incident occurred which, alas, was not entirely unforeseen. Bernadette suddenly stopped speaking. . . . But the attack of asthma subsided and she quietly finished her consecration.

\*     \*     \*

On January 27th, Mother Imbert, who for the last six years had scarcely ever left her room, received the Last Sacraments. Next day the new Bishop of Nevers, Bishop Lelong, successor to Bishop de Ladoue prematurely deceased, came to Saint-Gildard to preside over the election of a Superior General. The votes were unanimous in favour of Mother Adélaïde Dons. She was at the time sixty-six, and had been for twelve years Superior of the Lourdes Hospice.

'A sturdy native of the Cévennes from Castres, with broad masculine features', as she has been described, Mother Adélaïde was kindness itself. Mother Joséphine Imbert, although in reality very kind-hearted, had feigned a cold reserve, with the purpose, no doubt, of keeping Sister Marie-Bernard humble. This stern policy, declared Mother Dons, had no longer any justification: she knew Bernadette extremely well and she had secretly marvelled at her flawless humility. What purpose could be served by testing her further? For the short time left her to live and suffer, Sister Marie-Bernard was to enjoy a more affectionate and motherly treatment.

The spring of 1878 was exceptionally mild at Nevers. Somewhat less oppressed by her asthma, Bernadette was able from time to time to appear again at recreation. Mother Cassagnes or other venerable veterans led her from group to group. She was eager to make the acquaintance of the new postulants. 'We were all eyes for her,' one of them declared.

There was quite a marked improvement during the holidays. Her swollen knee, the cause of such acute suffering, had its better moments too, and Sister Marie-Bernard was able to exchange her crutches for a stick. Then came a most welcome visitor: her cousin, Victoire Cassou, who had a short while before been posted to another house, made a call at Saint-Gildard. She was on her way back from Lourdes, where she had seen her family. What a host of things they had to tell each other: a whole afternoon would not be too long! Mother Adélaïde Dons, anticipating the wishes of the two Lourdaises, granted them all necessary permissions. But to spend all those hours gossiping in the garden might shock the novices and postulants, so the ingenious Bernadette hit on a quick solution. Going clopity-clop she led Sister Victoire along to the coach-house where the Community carriage was kept. The two cousins climbed up into it and there at their ease they discussed 'the grotto, their relations, Father Sempé and lots of other things'. At one moment Sister Victoire remarked: 'You have been fortunate, Sister Marie-Bernard, to stay at the Mother House.' 'Oh,' she replied, 'what would they have done with me? I'm good for nothing.' —'Here at least you are praying for those who don't pray.'— 'That's all I have to do. Prayer is my only weapon. I can only pray and suffer.' Thus right to the end Sister Marie-Bernard remained 'humble of heart'.

*　　*　　*

At this time she was preparing to take her perpetual vows. It was eleven years since she had first pronounced her annual vows. Now for ever, publicly and officially, she was going to consecrate herself to the Lord. The ceremony was fixed for Sunday, September 22nd, the Feast of the Seven Sorrows of Our Lady.

'I saw her in 1878 during the Retreat preceding her vows,' records Sister Ganier. 'I was most edified to see how strictly she followed the exercises, though very much fatigued and finding it difficult to kneel.' Did Father Rabussier, S.J., speak at too great length? During one instruction she seemed near to fainting. Sister Ganier, who was sitting beside her, leaned over to her. 'I can't go on,' said Bernadette as if half unconscious. 'I shan't come back again. . . . I'll stay in the infirmary.' But she plucked up courage again and continued the Retreat to the end.

'Given his devotion to the Blessed Virgin,' it has been said of Father Rabussier, 'he could not but be interested in this soul so dear to Mary. But out of respect for Bernadette's predilection for humility and a hidden life, he never spoke to her about the Apparitions at Lourdes.' The saintly priest has left this recollection of his stay at Nevers:

> I received some precious graces on the Feast of the Purity of the Blessed Virgin. . . . I said Mass that day in an alb embroidered by our good little Sister Marie-Bernard who followed the whole of my Retreat. What I like most in her is her great simplicity and her abhorrence of all show. She is not afraid of me because I do not speak to her about anything extraordinary, and I give her useful advice. I saw the spotless innocence of her soul; she is being led along the path of sickness and suffering.

One of Sister Marie-Bernard's remarks would suffice to describe her immense happiness when together with sixty-one of her companions she pronounced her 'major vows': 'I felt I was in Heaven,' she confided to Sister du Rais. 'Had I died, I was sure of my future, for the vows are a second Baptism.'

The first signs of autumn in 1878 were merely the drawing in of the evenings. The Superior General judged that although Sister Marie-Bernard was suffering more since the taking of her perpetual vows, she ought not to miss the sunshine and fresh air, and she often made it her pleasure to take her into the garden.

# 33

## DEATH

On Sunday, December 8th, Sister Marie-Bernard had the
pleasure of going down for the last time to the chapel to
celebrate with the Mothers and Sisters the Feast of the
Immaculate Conception, which always appealed so tenderly to
her heart. Three days later she became permanently bedridden.

She had been suffering since 1867 or 1868 from a tumour on
the right knee. During the winter of 1877 a deep abscess had
aggravated the trouble. The tumour was now assuming huge
proportions and there was continuous pain in this area. At the
same time decay of the bones was spreading relentlessly through
all her enfeebled frame. Ten years of anaemia on the banks of
the Lapaca, months in the damp darkness of the 'dungeon' in
the Rue des Petits-Fossés—all her poverty-stricken past was now
taking its revenge.

> Her sufferings were so acute [wrote Mother Bordenave] that the
> nuns exerted all their kindest efforts to try and ease her pain. The
> invalid's face became cadaverous; she seemed almost dead. She
> spent nights without sleep, and if, when overcome by exhaustion,
> she managed to doze for a few moments, acute pains soon woke
> her up again to rack her almost without respite.

On several occasions she had very nearly expired in the arms
of her infirmarian. When the crisis was over she would say:
'Have no fear, it's not my last day yet.' Or else: 'I've a long
time to go yet.' But from now on, she made no more remarks
of this kind.

She might have hoped to be allowed to suffer in peace, but no!
The rumour had spread that Bernadette was very ill in her
convent at Nevers. There were still some points in her wonderful story that needed to be cleared up. There was no time to

lose! On December 13th the *Community Journal* recorded this new development:

> The Reverend Father Sempé has been sent by the Bishop of Tarbes, with the authorization of the Holy Father, to question Sister Marie-Bernard concerning the Apparitions. M. Dubarbier, Vicar General [of Nevers] and our Reverend Mother General were present.

In his rather grandiloquent style Father Sempé has left an account of this memorable meeting:

> On December 12th and 13th, 1878, God asked Bernadette to proclaim again in a last solemn testimony the marvels revealed to her by the Immaculate Virgin at the Grotto. Sister Marie-Bernard manifested at this moment a very great joy that was not usual with her on such occasions. She replied readily to several long series of questions; she repeated with charm and in her sweet Pyrenean tongue the words that fell from Mary's lips. More than twenty-one years after the events, and in the presence of death and eternity, the nun reaffirmed what she had said when a child. She was the ever faithful echo of the Mother of the Divine Word.

After Father Sempé's departure, someone else from Lourdes paid Bernadette a surprise visit on December 18th. For the first time in twelve years she saw one of her family again. 'Oh, Jean-Marie!' she exclaimed, when she was told of the visitor. There, waiting for her in the Superior General's parlour was the eldest of her brothers. Having left him a youth of fifteen, she was going to find him now a grown-up man of twenty-seven. With him was the generous pilgrim from the north who was paying for his journey. Bernadette was brought down to the parlour in an armchair. 'This meeting was full of emotion for both of them,' wrote Mother Dons. It is a pity that we have not more details of this last meeting of brother and sister!

Weak and suffering though she was, Sister Marie-Bernard had not finished with enquiries and cross-examinations. Father Sempé had put to her orally a 'double series of questions' drawn up beforehand by Father Léonard Cros, S.J. The latter had been entrusted by Bishop Jourdan of Tarbes and Father Peydessus of Garaison with the task of completing the work of the Commission instituted by Bishop Laurence in 1859, by discovering and collecting as many documents as possible concerning the

Lourdes events. Tenacious and passionately devoted to a work
like this, he despatched to Saint-Gildard one set of questions
after another: Bernadette was expected to give him information
on the tiniest details. But she was no longer in a fit state to
make such an effort of memory on demand. For instance, as
the Superior General said:

> When she was questioned about the arrangement of the veil, the
> folds, etc., Sister Marie-Bernard made a very expressive gesture
> saying: 'How can I possibly remember all that? If they want to
> know this, they must get *Her* to come again!'

Later, Father Sempé and Father Cros regretted having harassed her in this way just at the time when she was nearing her
end. 'Perhaps,' Father Cros confessed, 'we would not have had
the heart to question her so much had we been more fully aware
of Bernadette's sufferings.'

*       *       *

She was thirty-five on January 7th, 1879.

She was growing weaker and weaker, taking scarcely any
nourishment. It would soon be necessary to sit up with her
every night. Usually, on account of the enormous tumour, her
right leg remained outside the bed resting on a chair. The
decay of the bones, 'a particularly painful disease like a most
acute toothache, as it has been described, wrung from her'
incessantly, in spite of herself, 'a dull half-stifled moan. . . . No
cries. No articulate word. No impatient movement; but always
the same groaning, spasmodic and gasping, like the groans of a
victim offering herself in willing sacrifice without being able to
repress her cry under the knife that is slaughtering her; the
groaning of a will that remains steadfast and heroic in a failing
body. . . .' These words were said of Sister Marie-Bernard by
one of her companions who nursed her the whole of one night
in February 1879, and who, powerless to ease her martyrdom,
was unable to take a moment's rest herself.

Yet when people asked her how she was, she tried to put them
off: 'The same to-day as yesterday, and yesterday the same as
to-day,' was her answer to Sister Apolline Vernet, the assistant

infirmarian. She was anxious not to give any trouble to anyone. She insisted on their placing at her bedside only such nuns as had strong nerves and could get off to sleep. If she herself fell asleep for a few minutes, her sleep was disturbed by nightmares. One night she was given Sister Philomène Roques as her nurse. As soon as the latter came in, she urged her: 'My dear Sister, stretch yourself out comfortably in the armchair and go to sleep. If I need you, I'll call you.' The young nun soon fell asleep, and Bernadette's moans must have subsided, for she, in her turn, dozed off. Then, wrenched suddenly out of her light sleep, she asked in a changed voice: 'Who has been sent to sit up with me?' Sister Philomène woke with a start and rushed to her. A heavy sweat was standing out in beads on the invalid's temples. Sister Marie-Bernard 'uttered a few groans as if under the influence of a painful dream. . . . Then in broken words: "I was down there . . . at Massabielle. . . . There was a small boy . . . who was throwing stones into the stream. . . ."' Probably she had just been witnessing in her dream one of those sacrilegious 'devilries' which, twenty years earlier, had haunted the surroundings of the grotto.

Mostly Bernadette's thoughts were fixed beyond this earth. 'During her long nights,' reported Canon Perreau, 'she used to say the Rosary.' At other times she placed herself as it were in adoration before the Tabernacle. On her curtains had been fastened the picture of a monstrance. 'I am happy in my sleepless hours,' she confided to Mother Audidier, 'uniting myself with Our Lord. One glance at this picture gives me the longing and the strength to immolate myself, when I am feeling my loneliness and my pains.' But 'her great happiness,' asserts Canon Perreau, 'was to join in spirit in the holy sacrifices which, at that very moment, were being celebrated in this or that part of the world.' She used to note the country where priests were going up to the altar at that moment; and for this she used another well-known pious picture: a clock-face on which could be read the hours of Mass in every part of the globe. She loved also to gaze at a simple print, likewise fastened to the bed curtains, representing the Elevation of the Host. Bowing down behind the celebrant was a darling little altar-boy, and Bernadette would sometimes call out to him: 'Now then, ring the bell!'

She would have liked to make herself useful still.  Every Lent until now, she had prepared Easter eggs for the Nevers orphans. One day in this Lent of 1879, despite her exhaustion, she set herself again to the task.  One of her companions caught her by surprise, 'a small penknife in one hand, and in the other a fine Easter egg all rosy pink'.  She was drawing a heart on it by scraping off the colouring so that it showed the white of the shell.  Still finding strength to joke and smile she said: 'People no longer have any heart, so I'm putting some on the eggs.'

She might have got relief by changing her position a little in bed.  She refrained from doing this as far as possible, from a motive of charity so as not to disturb other invalids who were asleep near her, and also for a secret reason which she confided to Sister Garros: 'When you are in bed you should remain still and think of yourself as Our Lord on the Cross.'

Even so she was restless, a prey to intolerable pains.  'Don't take any notice of my contortions,' she used to say with a sigh; 'it's nothing.'  In fact, 'she reckoned she had endured nothing compared with Our Lord's sufferings'.  Following His example she was paying the penalty for guilty souls.  In the midst of excruciating pains or before swallowing medicines that were repulsive to her—and that was frequently, observes her infirmarian—she used to say: 'This is for the big sinner.'  'And where is he, this big sinner?'  'Oh, the Blessed Virgin knows him well!'

She had now only three pious pictures, and these she obtained leave to give to some companions.  She kept only her crucifix. 'Now,' she said, 'all I need is the One there!'  And, grasping it, she would add with humble resignation, 'I am like Him.'

\*       \*       \*

The disease had run through her whole system.  Sores were opening all over her body and growing continually larger.  By the end of February she was taking scarcely any nourishment at all; she eventually became 'so thin that her flesh was all but reduced to nothing'.  She was in this condition when, on Tuesday, March 18th, she received a visit from her sister, Toinette, and her brother-in-law, Joseph Sabathé.  She was very ill when they called and she spoke to them chiefly by gestures and looks. She was still just able to raise her head slightly.

Next day, Saint-Gildard celebrated the solemn feast of St Joseph. She caught the echo of it in the distant singing of her companions and the pealing of the bells. 'What grace did you beg of him?' asked Abbé Febvre. She answered energetically: 'The grace of a happy death.'

As the doctor thought her end was near, Mother Dons mentioned the Last Sacraments to her. She agreed at once. This was the fourth time in her life that she received them. It was Wednesday, March 28th, the Feast of the Compassion of the Blessed Virgin. The motherly Superior General presided over the simple preparations. Mother Vauzou was not with her at this pathetic moment. After being herself confined to bed in January, she had left Saint-Gildard on March 20th to continue her convalescence at St. Anne's Retreat, Neuilly-sur-Seine.

Let us listen to the recollections of Abbé Febvre. 'At half-past two in the afternoon I gave her Viaticum and then anointed her. After the few words which I addressed to her before giving her Holy Communion, she began to speak to the large number of Sisters there and in a strong clear voice which surprised us, considering her weak condition, she expressed herself more or less as follows: "My dear Mother, I ask your forgiveness for all the trouble I have caused you by my infidelities in religious life, and I ask forgiveness also from my companions for the bad example I have set them. . . !" And she added in a still more emphatic tone: "And above all for my pride."' This final confession of the most humble Bernadette moved Mother Cassagnes to tears as she stood on the threshold of the infirmary listening to every word.

Resigned to dying that very day if it pleased God, Sister Marie-Bernard 'received the Last Sacraments with great fervour'. But her martyrdom was going to go on for almost another three weeks.

'She was, as it were, homesick for Heaven. "Heaven, heaven. . . !" she kept murmuring. "They say there are some saints who did not go straight there because they had not longed for it enough. It won't be so in my case!"'

'You will soon be tasting the joys of Paradise,' suggested M. Febvre. 'You'll be gazing on the beauty and glory of Our

Lord which the Blessed Virgin gave you some idea of.' 'Oh, how that does me good!' she acknowledged. And another day the chaplain, finding her very dejected, reminded her of the great promise made to her by Our Lady of Lourdes: eternal happiness after a passing trial. 'Be brave, Sister,' he added; 'remember Mary's promises. There's Heaven at the end.' 'Yes,' she gasped, 'but the end is a long time coming! But the memory of it comforts me and turns my heart to hope.'

During Holy Week he spoke to her of our Risen Lord, trans-figured and glorious after so painful a Passion. 'My passion,' she said very definitely, 'will go on after Easter.'

There is one thing [the chaplain recorded] that we noticed in the last stages of her illness: her eyes, which were usually bright and clear, assumed a very special expression which was particularly striking whenever she uttered ejaculatory prayers and fixed her gaze on the crucifix, or looked up to Heaven when she heard mention of the joys of Paradise.

On Easter Monday Sister Léontine Villaret came to 'bring her *Alleluia*' as was the custom among the nuns on these Easter days. 'I'm being ground like a grain of wheat,' sighed the gentle patient, more and more oppressed by suffering. The same day during midday recreation some other nuns went up to the infirmary. Among them was that Sister Bernard Dalias who, twelve years before, had exclaimed: 'That!' when she first met Bernadette, and had immediately received such a grateful handshake. Now Bernadette was dying and they were coming to bid her farewell. As Sister Bernard Dalias observes: 'It was a visit of devotion as much as of charity.' They had been obliged to remove the large white curtains around the bed in order to allow the invalid to breathe more freely. With her face turned towards the wall she appeared to be sleeping. For fear of waking her the visitors remained at a distance. 'I could not bring myself to observe the same discretion as my companions,' relates Sister Dalias. 'I moved up to the foot of the bed . . . and there, leaning against the metal bar, I gazed in silence at this saintly friend. . . . I think she realized that there was some-one present. . . . I saw her turn her head slightly, open her eyes and fix them on me. . . . She stretched out her little burning hand to me and I hastened to grasp it affectionately. Then, in a stifled voice, she managed to say "Good-bye, *Bernard*. . . ! This time it's all over. . . ! " ' Sister Dalias, whom she had called familiarly 'Bernard', bent down to kiss her hand. Abruptly she withdrew it and hid it under the bedclothes; then she 'resumed her former position in silence, for her last hours of silent recollection'.

•    •    •

Easter Monday night was her Gethsemani. For some time she had shown no sign of fear for her salvation, but that night it was evident from her agitation and her gasping cries that she was enduring no ordinary temptation, but an assault by the enemy from without. She was heard shouting several times: 'Get out, Satan. . . !   Get out, Satan. . . ! ' Next day she confided to the chaplain that 'the devil had tried to hurl himself on her, but she had invoked the name of Jesus and had regained confidence'.

The *Community Journal* relates that on the morning of Easter Tuesday, April 15th, she still had strength to receive Holy Communion. 'But she is much worse,' it continued. 'She is most edifying, full of resignation in the midst of her great sufferings.' Some of the previous night's agitation was still affecting her. Before noon she asked again for the chaplain, and she mentioned Confession. M. Febvre, believing her end was quite near, gave her the Plenary Indulgence for the hour of death. 'My child,' he said, before blessing her, 'make a fervent renewal of the sacrifice of your life.' 'What sacrifice?' she asked, with a liveliness that surprised him. 'It's no sacrifice to leave a poor wretched life where one finds so many difficulties in trying to belong to God.' The priest stayed by her for a considerable time. She was seized with dreadful choking fits, during which she would invoke the Heart of Jesus, Mary Immaculate, St Joseph. . . . 'Oh,' she said, on one occasion when she was a little easier, 'how right the author of the *Imitation* is to teach us that we must not wait until the last moment to serve God. . . . You're fit for so very little then.'

That whole afternoon was continuous torture. At her request her large crucifix had been placed where she could see it clearly.

And as evening came on an extraordinary thing occurred. Mother Nathalie Portat, the second Assistant (whose affection for Bernadette went back to the earliest days and who had more frequent access to her after Mother Dons became Superior General) happened to be praying in the chapel. Kneeling before Our Lady's altar she was recommending to her the child of her predilection. Suddenly she thought she heard a voice within her bidding her go back to the infirmary. As soon as she reached the threshold she heard an agonizing appeal: 'Sister . . . Sister. . . ! ' 'What's the matter, Sister Marie-Bernard? ' I'm afraid! ' A cold sweat stood out on the dying nun's fore- head. Her soul was passing through that final phase of the purifying ordeal from which she had emerged sanctified. ' I'm afraid,' she began again. . . . 'I've received so many graces . . . and I've made so little use of them! '

Poor dear child! Mother Nathalie bent over the pallid brow. 'Dear little Sister,' she murmured tenderly, 'all the merits of the Heart of Jesus are ours. Offer them to God in payment of your debts and in thanksgiving for all His benefits.' The venerable nun added a few more words in a low voice. 'Oh, thank you . . . ! ' said Bernadette; and she 'seemed as if relieved of a heavy burden'.

Her last night on earth has been described by her nurse with moving simplicity:

I went up to the infirmary after night prayers about nine o'clock. I approached the dear invalid and wished her good night. She answered me sweetly but feebly. I found her so exhausted that I thought it wise not to lie down like those who had preceded me. I sat by the bedside so as to be ready to help her.

From time to time her sufferings forced from her a slight moan that made me start in my chair. She asked me several times to help her to turn over so that she might be able to find a little relief, for her poor body was all raw and she could be said to be lying on her sores.

Then we tried to come to some agreement for carrying out this manœuvre which was difficult. I took hold of the foot of her bad leg and made every effort to follow closely the movement of her body so that she could turn all in one piece without having to move the joints of her leg. I noticed that during this intermin- able night she did not let slip a single word of impatience or discontent. . . .

And now it was Wednesday of Easter Week. (It had been Wednesday of Easter Week when Massabielle had witnessed the 'miracle of the candle' twenty-one years ago.) What Bernadette endured the whole morning of this April 16th is inconceivable. Mother Cassagnes, who went to her bedside several times, has left the very brief note: 'The sufferings of the pious victim redoubled in intensity.' Shortly after eleven o'clock she appeared to be suffocating. She was laid in an armchair with her feet on a support in front of the fireplace where a large fire was blazing. Her eyes travelled from the crucifix hanging on the wall to the statue of Our Lady which stood on the mantelpiece. She was then left to herself.

'Between half-past twelve and one o'clock Mother Joséphine Forestier went up to her. Bernadette was trying unsuccessfully to put a basin to her lips. Her hands were trembling. "I thought it my duty," said the Mother, "to warn the infirmarian and the Community."'

While someone went to fetch the chaplain, several nuns made their way to the infirmary on the heels of Mother Cassagnes. The latter, who deserved to be called Bernadette's 'Guardian Angel', knelt down close to her. 'Dear Sister,' she said to her, 'you are now on the cross.' Like one actually crucified, the dying saint stretched out her arms, and with her eyes on the crucifix exclaimed, 'My Jesus! . . . Oh, how I love him!' Mother Cassagnes thought she was doing right in adding: 'I'll ask our Immaculate Mother to give you consolation.' 'No, no consolations, but strength and patience. . . . All this is good for Heaven.' Then, as if the word Heaven revived imperishable memories: 'I saw Her,' she went on, as she gazed at the statue of Our Lady; 'I saw Her! How lovely She was and how I long to go and see Her again!'

She was fully conscious. The thought occurred to her that she might benefit by a further Plenary Indulgence, and she asked for the indult of Pius IX that granted her this privilege. She was told that she had no need to hold the paper in her hand in order to gain the indulgence. Then M. Febvre arrived and, according to his own account, 'found the invalid sitting in an armchair, breathing with great difficulty and suffering most cruel pains'. He got her to pronounce the name of Jesus, which was the only condition required by the Pope's indult.

Almost at once, with her eyes fixed on a point on the wall, she uttered an exclamation of surprise: 'Oh! . . . Oh! . . . Oh!' And, her right hand clutching the armchair, she tried to raise herself. But her eyes fell.

As she was no longer able to hold her crucifix, they fastened it on her breast. She pressed her hands to it while repeating acts of Faith and Love which were suggested to her by her companions. The priest was due to go and hear confessions, and, although he did not judge death to be imminent, he recommended the Sisters to recite the Prayers for the Dying.

Shortly before three o'clock the bell rang for a Community duty and the nuns, with the exception of the two nurses, left the infirmary in obedience to the rule. At that very moment Mother Nathalie Portat, on coming out of the confessional in the chapel, felt an urge to return to the infirmary. (It was believed later that on her previous visit she had promised Sister Marie-Bernard, who was still trembling after the visit of the Evil One, that she would come back and assist her in her final struggle, and that the dying Bernadette had thanked her in advance.) In fact, as soon as Mother Nathalie reached the threshold she saw that the poor little soul was 'a prey to the torment of an indescribable interior suffering'. While the nurses were sprinkling her with Holy Water 'she was slowly kissing one by one the wounds of Christ'. Catching sight of Mother Nathalie she sighed: 'Forgive me. . . . Pray for me, pray for me!'

A terrible struggle [wrote the Assistant] seemed to be raging again in this innocent and privileged soul, to whom no doubt God wished to give some marks of resemblance to our Divine Saviour expiring on the Cross.

She began to groan in an agonizing voice: 'My God, my God!' It was her *Eli, Eli, lamma sabacthani* in these moments of dereliction on her Calvary. Once more she stretched out her arms like her crucified God; then she said: 'I thirst.' When one of the Sisters approached to give her a drink she found strength to make one last gesture, her majestic sign of the cross. Then she moistened her lips.

Bent over her, powerless to help her, Mother Nathalie watched her in silence. With her head inclined to the right, Bernadette was leaning on the arm of the infirmarian. Suddenly, the Assistant remembered her promise, and besought the aid of the Blessed Virgin by reciting the Hail Mary. She pronounced it very slowly. . . . At the words of the angel's salutation, 'Holy Mary', the dying nun joined in with her. So startled was Mother Nathalie that she let her continue by herself. Humble and trusting to the end, Bernadette said twice over, with great fervour, 'Holy Mary, Mother of God!' Then she went on: 'Pray for me . . . poor sinner . . . poor sinner. . . .'

Almost immediately, the saint expired. It was a quarter-past three. She was still clasping the crucifix. Two large tears were rolling down her cheeks. The infirmarian closed her eyes.

Bernadette Soubirous, in religion Sister Marie-Bernard, had died at the age of thirty-five years, three months and nine days; of which she had spent twelve years, three months and eighteen days at Saint-Gildard.

Years before, when she had been a patient in the Lourdes' Hospice, a visitor had asked her: 'Why don't you ask Our Lady to cure you completely?' 'It's no use,' she replied. 'Our Lady told me I shall die young.'

If this prospect of an early death had helped her to detach herself from transitory things, a further prediction made by the Lady had turned her trials here below into a constant motive for hope. As the first half of the prediction, 'I do not promise to make you happy in this world . . .' was so evidently fulfilled, Bernadette could have no doubt of seeing the second half realized: 'but in the next'.

Thus she had written with a firm hand in her private note-book: 'I will do everything for Heaven. . . . There I shall find my Mother in all the splendour of her glory.'

# 34

## 'HE HATH EXALTED THE HUMBLE'

'As soon as she was dead,' stated Sister Bernard Dalias, 'Bernadette's face became young and peaceful again, with a look of purity and blessedness.' The infirmarians clothed her in her religious habit. 'We had no difficulty in doing so,' observed Sister de Vigouroux, 'for her body was supple even though she had been dead for two hours.' Moreover, it remained like that until the funeral. All the nuns in the Mother House came in turn on that evening of Wednesday, April 16th, to pray around the bed on which she was laid out.

About eleven o'clock on the following day the body was brought down to the chapel. There it lay in state in a temporary coffin surrounded with white draperies and lilies. There was a crown of white roses over her black veil and her beads were entwined around her clasped hands, with her crucifix and the formula of her Perpetual Vows between her fingers. Bernadette appeared to be sleeping.

'I was in a position to vouch for the speed with which the news of her death spread through the whole town and the sensation it caused among the people,' said Father Raffin. In Nevers, and well beyond Nevers, there was but one cry in religious houses and Catholic homes: 'She's gone to see the Blessed Virgin again in Heaven!' In spite of continuous rain large crowds set out for Saint-Gildard. 'It seemed,' remarked Mother Forestier, 'as if all this multitude wanted to make up for not having been able to approach Bernadette during her life.' Among the number, observed a lady of the town, 'were many indifferent Catholics and even unbelievers', yet there was no commotion or disorder. And far from feeling any apprehension, people were 'drawn towards her. Even little children found it a joy to look at her'. 'It isn't just talk,' said a homely woman on coming out of the chapel, 'it's not merely the face of a Christian, it's a real saint's face.'

For the whole of the two days that the body remained lying in state, the main doors of the chapel were kept 'open as on Holy Thursday', when every one is allowed to go in and pray before the Altar of Repose.  Four Sisters were kept busy the whole time touching the corpse with the pious objects handed to them.  After those two days, it is said, there was not a single medal, cross or rosary left in the shops of Nevers. . . . Working men and women were seen handing up their tools or their scissors and thimbles to be touched against Bernadette's hands. Several of the garrison officers laid the hilt of their swords on them and remained a long time afterwards in prayer, withdrawing to the back of the chapel so as not to hinder the crowd from approaching.

The funeral was at first fixed for Friday, April 18th, but it had to be deferred a day because, notwithstanding the efficient arrangements, there were still too many people who had not yet been able to get into the chapel.  Early on a lovely morning (Saturday the 19th) the public began to invade the courtyards of the Mother House and the adjoining streets.  At the railway station in Nevers the number of travellers alighting from the trains astonished everyone.  'What's happening?' they asked. 'It's the funeral of the little saint of Lourdes,' was the reply.

At ten o'clock the Requiem Mass began, celebrated by Canon Greuzard, Administrator of the Cathedral.  The two Perreau brothers directed the music.  Bishop Lelong, who had interrupted his round of Confirmation visits to assist at the funeral, was presiding, supported by his Vicars General.  The members of the Cathedral Chapter occupied the choir stalls and had in their midst Father Sempé, Superior of the Grotto Chaplains, and Abbé Pomian, Bernadette's former confessor.  None of her relations had been able to come.  Together with the professors and students from the Senior Seminary, eighty priests and religious filled the side-chapels.  The nuns of the Congregation, with representatives from the Sisters of the Holy Family, the Sisters of Hope and the Little Sisters of the Poor, occupied the whole of the large nave.  In the transept were eminent people of the town and representatives of the leading families.  In the first row of laity knelt the author of the book, *Notre-Dame de Lourdes*, M. Henri Lasserre.

Before giving the Absolution, Bishop Lelong, vested in pontificals, delivered an extempore panegyric whose words still stir the emotions. He extolled the 'work of God' in the humble virginal life of Bernadette and in the marvels of Lourdes, which were the consequence of her faithful witness.

'By a unique exception,' stated Mother Forestier, 'Sister Marie-Bernard was not buried in the town cemetery where even Superiors General were usually buried.' Mother Dons, led by a presentiment, insisted on keeping her within the convent walls, 'on account of the great favours she had received and also on account of the holiness of her life'. Accordingly she had a vault constructed in the secluded oratory which had been erected twenty years before in the midst of the vines, and dedicated to St Joseph.

In order to enable everyone to see the sweet face of 'her who had seen the Blessed Virgin', the coffin was carried still open to the place of burial. One might have truly thought that Bernadette was only drowsing: her beautiful eyes had opened slightly, and her hands and nails were life-like in colour.

At that moment 'an immense crowd filled the courtyards, the terrace and the garden as far as St Joseph's chapel'. It was more of a triumph than a scene of mourning. In accordance with a touching custom at Saint-Gildard, the Absolution was followed by the *Salve Regina*. Thus by the grave of her privileged child the final act of homage was paid in fitting recognition to the merciful and compassionate Queen of Heaven.

When, about two o'clock, it was necessary to start sealing the coffin—a casket of lead encased in oak—'the throng of people was so great that the Police Commissioner had to be summoned to keep back the crowd'. The only ones present in the chapel were Father Sempé, MM. Pomian, Febvre and Lasserre, the Superior General, the Assistants, a few Sisters, the Commissioner and two constables, in addition to the undertakers. While the latter were attending to their mournful task, the bystanders recited alternately the five decades of the Rosary. On the invitation of the chaplain, Father Sempé announced each of the mysteries—the Glorious Mysteries—and commented briefly on them in relation to the present occasion.

On Ascension Day, May 22nd, 1879, Sister Marie-Bernard was finally buried in the chapel of St Joseph. From that day onwards the Mothers General, with the full approval of the Bishops of Nevers, never refused anyone permission to go and pray there. Year by year the number of visitors was to go on increasing. They came from every rank of society and from every point in Christendom. Even if the nuns did nothing to stop these crowds, they did nothing, either, to encourage them. Moreover they resolutely kept away from the tomb anything that might look like a public cult. At most they had to agree to giving certain persons who asked for them souvenir pictures bearing a small portion of Bernadette's linen or clothing.

Soon letters began to reach Saint-Gildard from all quarters reporting remarkable favours, astounding cures and conversions attributed to the intercession of the 'little Saint'. Many correspondents expressed their desire that the Blessed Virgin's confidante should be raised to the honours of the altar. The 'voice of the people' was in fact going to become the 'voice of God'.

*     *     *

Thirty years went by, and it was no longer the order of the day to keep Bernadette in the depths of obscurity. The witnesses of her life were never-ending in their praises of her; and Mother Vauzou was no longer there to hold her down. After succeeding Mother Dons in January, 1881, Mother Vauzou was re-elected Superior General five times, and was at the helm eighteen years in all, having the great happiness of seeing her Congregation finally approved by the Holy See. Having struggled step by step with indomitable courage against the persecution laws, she was obliged, in May 1899, to resign her high office, worn out by her labours. At first she retired to St Anne's Retreat at Neuilly, then, in August 1901, by a singular act of Providence, she set out for . . . the land of Bernadette. Her last home was to be the Orphanage of Mary Immaculate, from which there is a splendid view of the grotto and the basilicas.

There she was, condemned to long periods of confinement in her room. 'Tell the good God that he has certainly put me under detention,' she said to her Sisters with a faint smile, 'but I bear Him no grudge for it.' Nevertheless, she was not yet entirely reconciled. 'Sometimes, when she saw the demonstrations of the crowds at the grotto, it set her nerves on edge, and she would abruptly close the shutters of her room.' She was 'tormented by mental anguish', but little by little the charm of Lourdes had its effect on her soul. 'One of her last consolations,' as her obituary notice disclosed, 'was to feel her love increasing for Bernadette's heavenly Lady.' After celebrating in the homely surroundings of the Orphanage the diamond jubilee of her religious profession, on June 11th, 1906, she died in her eighty-second year on February 15th, 1907, 'after imploring Our Lady of Lourdes to protect her in her agony'.

Some months earlier Mother Forestier had paid her a visit on her way back from the Eternal City. 'I told her,' reported the Superior General, 'that they had spoken to me in Rome about the possibility of having Bernadette's cause introduced. She answered: 'Wait till I am dead.' Sister Paschal indeed affirmed: 'From what I have heard say, Mother Marie-Thérèse Vauzou is supposed to have stated that she would have turned devil's advocate in the Cause of Canonization . . . Which I take to mean that she would have put a spoke in the wheel!'

Would she have dared to do so, considering how greatly her former novice's reputation for sanctity had increased? Be that as it may, she was recalled to God at the very moment when the initial proceedings were being taken, but—astonishing as it may seem—it was to her who had died but the day before that Mother Forestier prayed to procure the Holy See's consent to petitions which she would have rejected had she been still alive.

On the 16th or 17th of February, 1907, in the presence of her mortal remains in Lourdes [discloses the Superior General], I made the following prayer: 'Mother, things do not always look the same in Heaven as they do on earth. Now that you are, I trust, illuminated by the pure light above, be so good as to take Bernadette's cause in hand. I leave the initiative in this matter to you. I shall not take any steps myself. I shall wait for a sign from Heaven.'

I confided this to my two travelling companions, Mother Fabre, Assistant, and Mother Bordenave, Secretary General, and we prayed about it.

On March 5th I received a letter from Bishop Gauthey of Nevers, written from Rome, in which I believed was the sign I requested. He did not know of my prayer, and he wrote: 'Cardinal Vivès has strongly urged me to prepare Bernadette's cause. He says that evidence must be collected without delay from all those who knew her. Extraordinary deeds are not required; it is the practice of virtue that must be brought out clearly. I believe it is our duty, and I looked upon the words of this saintly Cardinal as an invitation from Providence.'

It is permissible to think with Mother Forestier that there was more than mere coincidence here, and that the late Mother Vauzou, having rid herself of her earthly misconceptions, was hastening to make amends for them before God.

So now we see contact established between Rome and Nevers. The Holy See wished to be enlightened on the primary question: should the Cause of Sister Marie-Bernard be taken up? On August 20th, 1908, in the chapel of Saint-Gildard, in the presence of more than two hundred nuns assembled for the annual Retreat, was formally constituted, under the efficient presidency of Bishop Gauthey, the ecclesiastical court which was to conduct the first enquiry, known as the Informative Process, concerning the life, virtues, reputation for sanctity and miracles of the servant of God. Before closing this initial session at which Bernadette's cause had just been opened, the Bishop of Nevers pointed out the propitious circumstances: it was the Feast of St Bernard; it was the jubilee year of the Apparitions. . . .

One hundred and thirty-two sessions were to follow, in the course of which appeared the survivors of the Soubirous family, a number of clergy, nuns and layfolk who had known Bernadette well. The Ecclesiastical Commission displayed prodigious activity, for by October 23rd, 1909, the Congregation of Rites was in possession of all the documents of the Enquiry.

At Nevers, on the previous September 22nd, before finally closing the Informative Process, Bishop Gauthey had ordered proceedings to be taken, in due canonical form, for the exhumation of the body of Sister Marie-Bernard. In St Joseph's chapel there was profound emotion when the 'confidante of the Immaculate', after being buried for thirty years and five months, was again brought into the light of day.

There was no trace of corruption. The flesh was parched but

intact, and it had preserved its whiteness. Her head, which was covered in the cap and veil, and her hands, which were crossed over her heart, holding the tarnished crucifix and the rosary corroded with rust, were slightly inclined towards the left. Her eyes, deeply sunk in their sockets, were found to be completely closed. Her lips were partially open, as in a smile. . . . The touching attitude of the little dead body, as Bishop Gauthey remarked, recalled that of the young virgins of the first centuries discovered in the catacombs.

On August 13th, 1913, Pope Pius X signed the decree for the introduction of the Cause. By that very fact Bernadette received the title of Venerable. Then was to follow under the authority of Cardinal Vico the 'Apostolic Process' concerning her reputation for sanctity, her virtues and miracles. Delayed by the war, this did not open until September 17th, 1917, and was presided over by Bishop Chatelus, successor to Bishop Gauthey, who had now become Archbishop of Besançon. Two hundred and three sessions were required. At length, on February 11th, 1920, the resulting documents were lodged with the Congregation of Rites.

On November 18th, 1923, in the Ducal Hall, before the whole French colony in Rome, Pope Pius XI published the 'Decree on the heroic nature of the virtues of the Venerable Sister Marie-Bernard Soubirous'. In his reply to the discourse of Bishop Chatelus, the Pope insisted on expressing his own thoughts about Bernadette's sanctity:

> There is no doubt that we are here in the presence of sanctity in the precise and exact meaning of the word. . . .
> In fact, when one considers Bernadette's life such as it appears at every stage of the Processes, which have been lengthy, careful, considered and strict, as they should always be, we are pleased to say, for the greater glory of God, this life can be summed up in three words: Bernadette was faithful to her mission, she was humble in glory, she was valiant under trial.

Meanwhile the Congregation of Rites was examining the authenticity of the miracles put forward for the Beatification. From some ten of them it had selected two cases of cures which had been meticulously checked by the doctors.

A youth of seventeen, Henri Boisselet, attacked in November,

1913, by tubercular peritonitis, had received the Last Sacraments. A novena to Bernadette was begun, for him and with him, and was due to end on December 8th. On that very day he was instantaneously and completely cured. Passed as fit for military service during the 1914-1918 war, he was drafted to the front, where he was later taken prisoner. After thirty-two months of captivity in Germany, he returned home still in sound health.

Sister Marie-Mélanie Meyer, of the Sisters of Providence of Ribeauvillé, was infirmarian in the Sacred Heart Convent in Moulins. In 1910, when she was thirty years of age, acute pains and frequent vomiting revealed a gastric ulcer. Soon she became incapable of taking any nourishment, was reduced to extreme weakness and near to death. She vowed a pilgrimage to Bernadette's tomb. On the journey from Moulins to Nevers she suffered intense pain. Once in the little chapel of St Joseph she summoned up strength to prostrate herself on the tombstone and then to remain there in prayer, now on her knees, now seated, for an hour. Suddenly her pains disappeared. Seized with violent hunger she took a meal without any difficulty. She felt her strength returning already, and the return journey to Moulins was accomplished without fatigue or suffering. The next day Sister Marie-Mélanie returned to normal life and resumed her post.

The doctors' certificates and the witnesses' statements were examined by the Congregation of Rites in three sessions. On May 1st, 1925, the Holy Father was present at the solemn reading of the Decree in which he acknowledged the genuineness and validity of the two miracles for the Cause. From that moment the Beatification of Bernadette was assured. On June 2nd, in the Consistorial Hall, His Holiness declared by the Apostolic Decree that she could in all security be proclaimed Blessed. On hearing this good news, how many in Christendom must have reflected that, through the voice of her august Head, the Catholic Church had just officially acknowledged the fulfilment of Our Lady's promise: 'I will make you happy in the next world.'

*    *    *

On the morning of Sunday, June 14th, during the Octave of Corpus Christi, St Peter's in Rome was a thrilling blaze of light and rejoicing. Beneath its gilded vaults and dome stood the Superior General, the Reverend Mother Bordenave, with a large number of her nuns, and an immense gathering of people. After Cardinal Merry del Val, Archpriest of the Vatican Basilica and former Secretary of State to Pius X, had had the Brief of Beatification read, applause broke out everywhere. Then the soaring chant of the *Te Deum* began, the bells of St Peter's rang out, and the veil fell from 'Bernini's Glory': in this unique setting the visionary of Lourdes was portrayed borne aloft by angels towards the outstretched arms of the Immaculate Virgin.

Henceforward, Bernadette, honoured as Blessed, would have her own liturgical feast and her own office, wherever Rome allowed it. Her relics could be publicly displayed and venerated. The earthly representative of God, who 'exalts the humble', reserved to himself, so to speak, the inauguration of this public cult in honour of the little Soubirous girl. On the evening of the Beatification, His Holiness was carried in the gestatorial chair into St Peter's, while fifty thousand voices acclaimed him. Kneeling in the centre of the choir, Pius XI lifted his eyes to 'Bernini's Glory' and then meditated devoutly. While he was still deep in prayer, someone started to walk towards him: it was the youngest of Bernadette's brothers, Pierre Soubirous, coming to present to the Head of the Church a relic, in a sumptuous monstrance, of his godmother, now 'Blessed'.

The following August 3rd, amid splendours worthy of a queen, the mortal remains of Bernadette were laid in the place befitting them, in the choir of the main chapel of Saint-Gildard, enclosed in a casket of gilded bronze and crystal whose chasing and enamels summarized her life and symbolized her soul.

Once this stately reliquary was put on view, it became clear that the little Soubirous girl, this humble star, had not been altogether eclipsed in the radiance of the 'Woman clothed with the sun'. More and more people began to come and pray to her: individual pilgrims, parish groups and diocesan pilgrimages.

Lourdes also was far from neglecting its purest glory. Her statues multiplied in the town and in the Grotto domain; her poor 'dungeon' became an oratory. On August 21st, 1927, Bishop Schœpfer solemnly blessed a magnificent altar in her honour beneath one of the arches of the Rosary Esplanade. Even the hills of Bartrès, where the enchanting memory of her still lived, were becoming a place of pilgrimage. God was soon to show by fresh wonders that it was His good pleasure that she also should be prayed to. And that would be the completion of her Cause.

*     *     *

Two instantaneous cures, certified subsequently as complete and permanent, were submitted to the Congregation of Rites. Scarcely forty days after the Beatification, an illustrious native of Nevers, His Grace Archbishop Lemaître of Carthage, left Paris for Saint-Gildard, where he was to attend the solemn translation of the Reliquary on August 3rd. The missionary Archbishop 'had been suffering for over ten years from a grave amœbic infection which had attacked him in the tropical countries where he had been working zealously as Vicar Apostolic. Several different treatments had been tried, but in vain; the disease was so far advanced as to leave, in the opinion of the doctors, no hope of a cure, or at any rate no hope of an instantaneous cure.' During the journey 'he had a severe attack of the same illness'. However, he found sufficient strength to attend the ceremony of translation, 'and was completely cured there and then'. The prelate resumed his arduous ministry in Carthage and was able 'to display therein the same extraordinary activity as before'.

The second miraculous cure attributed to the intercession of Blessed Bernadette occurred two and a half years later, not at Nevers but in Lourdes. Sister Marie de Saint-Fidèle, a Good Shepherd nun, after having endured many other illnesses, was afflicted with a tumour on the knee and with dorso-lumbar Potts' disease. The disease had 'progressed so far that the doctor declared a cure impossible by natural means except perhaps after a long period of time. . . . As the condition of the invalid was growing worse, a novena of prayers was made to Blessed Bernadette. On the fifth day of this novena, namely February 6th, 1928, at 6.0 p.m., Sister Marie felt herself suddenly cured. Next morning she left her bed. . . . After a lapse of three years, medical specialists who subjected her to a thorough examination found no trace of the disease from which she had been suffering.'

On Wednesday, May 31st, 1933, the Decree of Approbation of the Miracles was read in the Vatican Palace in the presence of the Holy Father. On Sunday, July 2nd, on the Feast of Our Lady's Visitation, the Decree *De Tuto* was published. It was the final act in a Process which had begun twenty-five years before.

Then, on Friday, December 8th, 1933—the Feast of the Immaculate Conception—the Catholic Church lavished its splendours on little Bernadette. The great Basilica of St Peter in Rome threw open its doors, and there, radiantly happy and proud, were her family by birth and her family by grace. The widow of her brother, Jean-Marie; her nephews Pierre, François and Bernard, and other members of the Soubirous family, made their way to the Tribune of the Postulation with the Very Reverend Mother Crapard, Superior General of the Sisters of Charity of Nevers, and a hundred and sixty of her nuns. Ten thousand pilgrims had come from France, and about forty thousand people filled the naves when, towards 8.15 a.m., Pope Pius XI appeared, carried aloft in the gestatorial chair.

He was preceded by a long procession in which walked eighteen Cardinals, eighty-five Patriarchs, Primates, Archbishops and Bishops. Among them, and immediately recognizable by his tall stature and his missionary's beard, was Archbishop Lemaître, Primate of Africa, whose portrait also could be seen on one of the two banners hanging from the loggias of the cupola. And among the prelates could be seen Bishop Flynn of Nevers, and Bishop Gerlier of Tarbes and Lourdes.

The silver trumpets sounded. Then, to the singing of the liturgical hymns were added the swelling voices of the multitude cheering the Pontiff as he came forward giving his blessing, and cheering the banner of the Saint-to-be. After the triple petition of the Consistorial Advocate and the chanting of the Litany of the Saints and the *Veni Creator*, the whole assembly rose and there was an impressive silence. Seated on the Chair of the Apostle and with the mitre on his head, Pope Pius XI, Bishop and Teacher of the Universal Church, pronounced the formula of Canonization, in his warm resonant voice that vibrated with a certain tenderness as he reached the final words: 'To the honour of the Most Holy and Indivisible Trinity, for the exaltation of the Catholic Faith and for the spread of the Christian Religion, by the authority of Our Lord Jesus Christ, of the Blessed Apostles Peter and Paul and by Our own, after mature deliberation and having often implored the Divine assistance, on the advice of Our venerable brethren the Cardinals of the Holy Roman Church, the Patriarchs, Archbishops and Bishops, We define and declare the Blessed Marie-Bernard Soubirous a Saint, and We enrol her in the catalogue of Saints, ordaining that her memory shall be piously celebrated in the Universal Church on April 16th of each year, the day of her birth in Heaven. In the name of the Father and of the Son and of the Holy Ghost.'

The hymn of triumph burst forth: *Te Deum laudamus.* At the same moment the great bell of St Peter's rang out, and with it every bell in the Eternal City.

When, about one o'clock in the afternoon, after his Solemn High Mass, the Pope, wearing the tiara, the mark of his royalty, returned once more through the Basilica in his chair, the noise of the ovations drowned the fanfares of the silver trumpets. . . . Then spontaneously the massive crowd began to sing the *Ave Maria*, just as at Massabielle.

In his homily after the Gospel of his Mass, Pius XI had stressed the humility of this 'ignorant girl, a simple miller's daughter, who possessed no other wealth than the candour of her exquisite soul'; an authentic Saint, nevertheless, whose message, after the revelations of the Queen of Heaven and her exhortations to penance, procured for the world the magnificent spectacle of Lourdes, its three sanctuaries, its pilgrimages, its graces of conversion, of calls to perfection, and of miraculous cures. . . .

On this day of her supreme glorification, God was exalting His little servant.

Truly—and this is the great lesson of St Bernadette's life— *God exalts none but the humble.*

# NOTES

# BERNADETTE'S ECSTASIES[1]

We have put forward the view that there were two distinct phases in Bernadette's ecstasy on Sunday, February 14th, 1858. An explanation is necessary, and it will help to clarify many points in the subsequent visions.

Ecstasy may take possession of a soul suddenly or merely by degrees; it may stop at a stage when there is not complete suspension of the senses, either internal or external.

Here is its usual method of progression. The soul being absorbed by the vision presented to it, the external senses are, as the mystics say, thereby suspended, resulting in bodily insensibility and a slowing down of physical vitality. As St Teresa points out: 'The soul seems to leave the organs animated by it' (*Autobiography*, XX). Thus there is a lowering of body temperature, producing paleness and 'transparency' of the face. Usually the body remains fixed in the attitude in which the rapture seized it; it remains standing or seated, hands open or closed, and the eyes fixed on the object under contemplation.

The total suspension of the senses, or of all the 'powers', as St Teresa puts it, 'never lasts long; it is considerable when it lasts as long as half an hour', save in quite exceptional cases in the lives of some saints. The rapture is not necessarily continuous: it may leave the soul and then return and recapture it.

Thus ecstasy is not governed by absolute laws and does not always occur in the same way. Its intensity, fullness and detail depend on God's good pleasure. In the course of the same ecstasy, St Teresa of Avila was seen to pass from 'an agony of suffering' to intoxicating delight; while St Francis of Assisi felt nothing but joy from start to finish. The same St Francis, while in ecstasy, travelled on foot or on a donkey; absorbed in adoration and praise, he did not notice the villages through which he passed, nor the roads along which he journeyed. St Catherine of Siena, at a time when 'her eyes do not see, her ears do not hear, her smell perceives no odour, her taste no savour, her touch no feeling', dictates to secretaries the revelations published later under the title of *The Dialogues*.

The ecstasy of the Christian mystic has nothing in common with

[1] Cf. p. 51 ff.

387

the 'ecstasy', if the term may be tolerated here, of the Yogi, the Hindu ascetic who by numbing his personality loses himself in *nirvâna* or final 'extinction', the last stage of the *sâmsara* or transmigration.

Likewise the ecstasies of our mystics—wherein the higher life of the soul is enriched, enlightenment is received, encouragement is given to the undertaking of charitable enterprises and the will is braced to carry them out—such ecstasies differ essentially from the phenomena of hypnosis, which is an artificial sleep in which the 'patient' acts as an automaton, or from catalepsy, which is the result of some nervous disease, or from hysteria, which turns the victim into a creature of impulse, with no will, no resistance, no initiative.

With this information in mind, the reader is in a position to appreciate Bernadette's varied behaviour during the Apparitions.


## THE MIRACULOUS SPRING[1]

What exactly was this 'miracle of the Spring'? As early as 1858 the question was being asked whether or not the spring had existed before the Apparitions. On November 17th of that year, as no boring had yet been carried out, the 'Sub-Commission of Enquiry' appointed by Bishop Laurence in Lourdes was content to examine witnesses—'some old men who had always frequented this spot'. According to the report of the investigators, 'their evidence is not entirely unanimous as to the complete absence of any spring previous to the events at the Grotto; but all agree in asserting that if there was any water there before, it was scarcely noticeable, and that there is an enormous difference between the previous state and the present one, although no work has been done on it. This amounted to saying that a small amount of stagnant water on the bank within the grotto (the Sub-Commission merely recorded the evident fact without determining its cause) was found transformed into a copious spring.

In 1862 the gravel bank was levelled without touching the debris deposited in the past by the ancient moraine of Argelès, and the spring was led through pipes to the Grotto entrance on the left where the 'Fontaine du Parvis', as it was called, was erected. (This is now preserved as a souvenir.) No study was made at this time of the spring itself.

[1] Cf. p. 106.

In April, 1879, a famous hydrogeologist, Abbé Richard, thought the origin of the 'miraculous fountain' could be described and stated thus:

1. In Lourdes there was not a miracle of *creation* of a spring, as there was in the desert when God ordered Moses to strike the rock and cause water to gush forth.
2. Nor was there at Lourdes a transformation of an intermittent spring into a permanent one, as at La Salette.
3. There was at Lourdes simply a miracle of discovery of an already existing spring through its being expressly pointed out to Bernadette by the Blessed Virgin.

Without being able to show from which precise point the water had come up—since he had not been able to examine the geological formation of the Grotto—M. Richard had judged correctly.

In 1948 a chance occasion led to a deep excavation which revealed the solution of the problem. Thanks to this excavation, they came upon the 'spout' of the water gushing from the actual rock of Massabielle. Until then, the spring had supplied 85 litres per minute, 5,100 per hour, 122,400 per day. But it was showing signs of fatigue; its discharge was growing gradually less. The pipeline was becoming blocked; so Bishop Théas of Tarbes and Lourdes took steps to remedy this.

During the night of August 12-13, 1948, thanks to the motor-pump from the town, which freed the conduit temporarily from foreign matter, sufficient water was assured for the pilgrimage season. But this was only a temporary measure. 'It was necessary to consider a methodical catchment of the Massabielle spring; for this had never been done and it was now imperative.' In future the limestone deposit that came from the rock and obstructed the pipes must be stopped.

'An extensive excavation three yards across was therefore carried out', according to Canon Mailhet's report, countersigned by M. Cachin, Mining Engineer, and M. Cazenave, Public Works Engineer. 'At a depth of about six feet, in a fissure of the limestone, we discovered the very bed of the spring. The water came gushing out of the rock under a pressure that points to an abundant supply. Its water is wonderfully clear. . . .

'A splendid result had just been obtained: we had reached the hitherto unknown geological bed of the Massabielle spring. We were now catching it at its very exit from the fissure in the rock which gave it outlet, before it could have any contact with the surrounding moraine through which it had until then been rising to a height of six feet.

'In fact the spring of Massabielle was unknown; no one had ever seen it. The people had not been using its water in the state in which it came out of the rock, but only after it had passed through a layer of adventitious material from which inevitably it picked up foreign elements. . . .

'The work was carried out speedily, and was finished in less than two months. The spring of Massabielle was caught and conducted with reverent care straight from its rocky bed. It is now preserved from any dangerous contamination, and it rises absolutely pure, straight to its conduit which has also been renewed. The pilgrims will henceforward have water from the very rock of the Grotto, the virgin water given by the Immaculate Virgin's Spring.'

# BIBLIOGRAPHY

Mgr Trochu's original text is copiously annotated with references to his sources, for he is a most scrupulous and careful historian. But as most of his sources are manuscript or are otherwise unavailable outside France, it seems pointless to reproduce all his references in this translation. Instead, a list of his sources is given below, while the reader who is eager to go into the subject more thoroughly is urged to consult the author's original text in French.

1. Autograph Letters of Bernadette.
2. Letters and personal notes of Bishop Laurence, Mgr Fouran (Vicar General), Canon Fourcade, Mgr Peyramale, Bernadette's family, and nuns of the Congregation of the Sisters of Charity of Nevers.
3. Municipal registers and minutes of the meetings of the Municipal Council of Lourdes.
4. Official documents on the 'Lourdes Affair', now preserved in the national archives in Paris. These include letters, reports, orders and notes of the various police, legal and government officials, ranging from the Minister of the Interior, the Minister of Justice and the Minister of Education in Paris, down to the local village constable. A wealth of conscientious paper work.
5. The two reports, dated 17th November, 1858 and 7th December, 1860, of the Episcopal Commission set up by Bishop Laurence.
6. The Ecclesiastical Processes drawn up for the beatification and canonization of Bernadette.
7. The Community Journal and the Noviciate Journal of the convent of Saint-Gildard in Nevers.
8. Various memoirs on the events at Massabielle written by the Abbés Pène, Labayle, Fontan, Glère, Dézirat; by Brother Léobard and the schoolmasters, Clarens and Jean Barbet; by Drs Lacrampe, Peyrus and Balencie; by the police lieutenant Bourriot and Sergeant d'Angla; by Jeanne-Marie Védère, Mlle Estrade and others.

PRINTED SOURCES

1. Contemporary newspapers such as the *Lavedan* which incidentally, after a change of name in 1866, became finally in 1898 the *Journal of the Lourdes Grotto*.
2. *Annales de Notre-Dame de Lourdes*, and the *Revue Bernadette*.


BOOKS AND BROCHURES

These are so numerous that only a small selection of the more useful and significant ones can be given.

1. *L'Apparition à la grotte de Lourdes* (1862), by Canon Fourcade, who was Secretary of Bishop Laurence's Commission of Enquiry.
2. *Notre-Dame de Lourdes* (1869), by Henri Lasserre, a barrister and writer who had recovered his eyesight at the grotto. He was commissioned by Bishop Laurence and given free access to the archives, but his work is somewhat marred by exaggerations, especially in his outright condemnation of the police and civil authorities.
3. *Petite Histoire de Notre-Dame de Lourdes*, which appeared as a series of articles in the *Annales de Notre-Dame de Lourdes* (1868-9), written by two of the Lourdes chaplains, Fathers Duboé and Sempé; but it was not published in book form until 1931. It is a more reliable and balanced work than Henri Lasserre's.
4. *La Grotte de Lourdes* (1874), by Dr Dozous, who was present at the Apparitions and often attended the Soubirous as their family doctor. He gives a careful description of Bernadette with special regard to her mental health, and a personal investigation of twenty-seven of the miraculous cures.
5. *Notice sur la vie de Sœur Marie-Bernard* (1879), by Archbishop Forcade, dealing chiefly with her vocation and life as a nun, as he knew her in Nevers.
6. *Les Apparitions de Notre-Dame de Lourdes. Souvenirs intimes d'un témoin* (1899), by Jean-Baptiste Estrade, who had known Bernadette intimately and had been present at many of the Apparitions, and so was able to add many significant details and corrections.
7. The private notes of Jean Barbet, published in 1909 by his nephew. He had been headmaster of the senior primary school in Lourdes and knew Bernadette and her family.
8. *Histoire de Notre-Dame de Lourdes* (1925), by Father Léonard Cros, S.J., edited by Father Cavallera. Father Cros had been a conscientious and indefatigable investigator (as Bernadette knew

to her sorrow) and these three volumes are only a digest of his researches.

9. *La Confidente de l'Immaculée, Bernadette Soubirous* (1912), by Mother Marie-Thérèse Bordenave, Secretary to the Superior General, Mother Forestier. A woman of penetrating intellect and keen sensitiveness, she dealt chiefly with the period of Bernadette's life as a nun.

10. *Sainte Bernadette, Souvenirs inédits* (1936), by Canon Guynot, a devoted and tireless investigator.

11. *En Marge de l'Histoire de Lourdes.* The recollections, published posthumously, of Bernadette's cousin, Jeanne Védère.

12. *Histoire exacte des Apparitions de Notre-Dame de Lourdes à Bernadette* and *Histoire exacte de la vie intérieure et religieuse de sainte Bernadette.* These two volumes, published in 1935 and 1936, by the Reverend Father Petitot, O.P., while not perhaps faultlessly exact, are nevertheless the work of a conscientious scholar who was also a psychologist and mystical theologian of great experience.

# INDEX

Abadie, Jeanne ('Baloum'), 39; at First Apparition, 40 ff.; rebuked by Bernadette for swearing, 42, 210; at Second Apparition, 51

Ader, Abbé, 27; opinion of Bernadette, 28, 32

Albario, Joséphine, pretended visionary, 175 ff.

Apostolate of the sick: Bernadette's definition and example of, 352

Apparitions: First, 11 Feb., 42-5; Second, 14 Feb., 50-3; Third, 18 Feb., 57-9; Fourth, 19 Feb., 63-4; Fifth, 20 Feb., 66; Sixth, 21 Feb., 69-70; Seventh, 23 Feb., 96-7; Eighth, 24 Feb., 102-3; Ninth, 25 Feb., 105-7; Tenth, 27 Feb., 112-13; Eleventh, 28 Feb., 119-20; Twelfth, 1 March, 125-7; Thirteenth, 2 March, 128; Fourteenth, 3 March, 134; Fifteenth, 4 March, 140-2; Sixteenth, 25 March, 155-7; Seventeenth, 7 April, 171-2; Eighteenth, 16 July, 197

Aravant, Jean-Louis, Abbé, 27, 32

Balencie, Dr, Hospice doctor: heads commission to examine Bernadette, 164-7; his confession, 165; attends Bernadette, 229; astonished at her cure, 230

Barbet, Jean, 6, 11; schoolmaster at Bartrès, 28

Bartrès: Bernadette nursed by Marie Lagües at, 8; often returned there, 10

Basset, Anna, Bernadette foretells vocation of, 350

Bernadette Soubirous, St: birth and baptism, 3-4; infancy at Boly mill, 8-9; poverty of family, 11, 22, 40; contracts asthma, 10, and cholera, 12; with Aunt Bernarde, 14; in the 'dungeon', 17-20; the 'little mother', 12; ignorance, 22, 24, 29, 33; shepherdess at Bartrès, 30 ff.; longing for instruction and First Holy Communion, 22, 25, 29, 32, 34; at Hospice school, 36; First Apparition, 42-5; forbidden to return to grotto, 47; disbelieved by nuns, 48,

55, 62; and by priests, 49, 67; Second Apparition, 50-3; her beauty in ecstasy, 52, 96; Third Apparition, 57-9; promises to return daily for fortnight, 59; receives promise of happiness from Our Lady, 59; Fourth Apparition, 63-4; Fifth Apparition, 66; Sixth Apparition, 69-70; examined by Public Prosecutor, 74-7; examined by Jacomet, 79-87; under police surveillance, 87; parents renew ban on grotto, 89; suspected and frowned upon by nuns, 89; followed to grotto by two policemen, 90; Vision fails to appear, 91; abiding trust in Vision, 93; Seventh Apparition, 96-7; called cataleptic and hallucinated, 100; Eighth Apparition, 102-3; Ninth Apparition, 105-7; derided by crowd, 109; heartbroken at second failure of Vision, 111; Tenth Apparition, 112-13; badly received by Curé, 116-18; Eleventh Apparition, 119-20; before Examining Magistrate Rives, 122; Twelfth Apparition, 125-7; Thirteenth Apparition, 128; badly received by Curé, 128; distress at third failure of Vision, 134; Fourteenth Apparition, 134; third visit to Curé, 135; Fifteenth Apparition, 140-2; visited by crowds at home, 144; home watched by police, 145; fourth visit to Curé—he demands the Lady's name, 145; Sixteenth Apparition, 155-7; fifth visit to Curé, 158; threatened with internment in mental hospital, 163; doctors' report, 166; Seventeenth Apparition, 171-2; unaffected by false visionaries, 181; examined by Public Prosecutor, 184; at Cauterets, 186; First Holy Communion, 189; internment decided upon by Prefect, 191; at Tarbes Seminary, 194; Eighteenth Apparition, 197; interviewed by Veuillot, 200; becomes Child of Mary, 204; back to school in earnest, 205; interviewed by Ecclesiastical Commission, 206; and by group of priests, 211; godmother

## THE AUTHOR

Monsignor Francis Trochu is internationally noted as a masterly historian of great religious figures. St. Jean-Marie Vianney, the Curé of Ars; St. Francis de Sales; and various founders of religious orders are the subjects of his definitive biographies. Monsignor Trochu follows the strict historical method with meticulous scholarship, basing himself mainly on primary sources, unpublished documents and records. Many of his books have been honored by the Académie Française.

# NOTES

CPSIA information can be obtained
at www.ICGtesting.com
Printed in the USA
LVOW08s0926301016
510895LV00001B/214/P